# AMERICAN
# FAMILY
# COOKING

# AMERICAN FAMILY COOKING

*The Best of Regional Recipes*

Consulting Editor:
JUDI OLSTEIN

NEW YORK

ISBN 0-671-07198-X

Typeset by Publishers Phototype International Inc.
Color separations by Hong Kong Scannercraft Company Ltd.
Printed by Lee Fung-Asco Printers Ltd.
Printed in Hong Kong

This book was designed and produced by
FOOTNOTE PRODUCTIONS LTD.,
32 Kingly Court, London W1

Editorial Director: Sheila Rosenzweig
Art Director: Ken Diamond/Art Patrol, NYC
Production Artist: Joel Miskin

1 2 3 4 5 6 7 8 9 0

ACKNOWLEDGMENTS
I would like to thank the many people around the country who
generously contributed recipes and offered valuable aid and
advice. In particular, I want to express my gratitude to my
editor, Sheila Rosenzweig, for her unstinting concern and
bouyant enthusiasm; Ruth Baum for her expertise and broad
knowledge of American regional cooking; Angela Phelan for
her advice on techniques and ingredients; Ken Diamond and
Joel Miskin for their excellent design work; and Derek
Hastings—that treasure trove of culinary knowledge—for
reading and correcting the entire manuscript. —Judi Olstein

ISBN: 0-671-07198-X

# Contents

Introduction   xii

## The East  1
Menus   3
Soups and Appetizers   5
Salads   13
Dairy Dishes   17
Meat and Poultry   21
Fish and Seafood   34
Vegetables   45
Noodles, Grains, and Beans   51
Breads   54
Desserts   60
Accents   72

## The South   77
Menus   79
Soups and Appetizers   81
Salads   89
Dairy Dishes   93
Meat and Poultry   98
Fish and Seafood   116
Vegetables   125
Grains and Beans   131
Breads   136
Desserts   142
Accents   149

# The Heartland    169

Menus    171
Soups and Appetizers    173
Salads    179
Dairy Dishes    183
Meat and Poultry    187
Fish and Seafood    202
Vegetables    209
Noodles, Grains, and Beans    215
Breads    218
Desserts    226
Accents    238

# The West    243

Menus    245
Soups and Appetizers    247
Salads    253
Dairy Dishes    259
Meat and Poultry    264
Fish and Seafood    275
Vegetables    284
Noodles, Grains, and Beans    292
Breads    297
Desserts    306
Accents    315

Home Jarring Information    319
Recipe Index    321

# Introduction

If America is a multicultural melting pot, then its cuisine is made up of dozens of simmering stews. Over two hundred years we have created not a homogenized national cuisine but rather many distinct and exciting cooking styles, evolving through local produce, shifting populations, ethnic differences and the love of good eating.

From the day the Pilgrims landed, the question "What's for dinner?" has rung across this land. And in answering it, the cooks—both amateur and professional—have brought forth a remarkable diversity of approach to the same ingredients and, equally, different ingredients to the same approach. Luckily, we are blessed with some of the best raw materials, both native and imported, that can be obtained anywhere on the face of the globe. From the very native bean and tomato to the sweet potato, Maine lobster and Gulf shrimp, America has provided specialties to the rest of the world. We have taken the best and used it in our own unique ways . . . not always with discretion, but always with gusto.

Additionally, America has had the opportunity to take advantage of a bounty virtually unknown elsewhere. From the earliest accounts of Colonial days, we know that vast flocks of feathered game literally darkened the skies, that Boston Harbor was crowded with lobsters, that even well into the nineteenth century, oysters were as plentiful as the ubiquitous french-fried potato is today. That largesse has been replaced by mechanized farming and changing tastes, but the heaping vegetable stalls and bursting silos still attest to our extraordinary good fortune and fertile lands.

No one "American" cuisine exists. We are, after all, a nation of immigrants. Yet each new wave of immigration brought an authentic foreign cuisine with it, and within a generation transformed that cuisine into something different. Veal parmagiana—breaded veal topped with mozzarella cheese and tomato sauce—is as unknown in Italy, especially in Parma, as a rare tenderloin steak slathered with barbecue sauce is in Peking. Bouillabaisse turned into the crawfish and filé-laden gumbo of Cajun cooking. Elizabeth David, the great English food writer, once said that "a country's national food is authentic only in that country." True enough!

But when transformed by circumstance, geography, available ingredients and *imagination,* that national food can—as it did in America—become an integral part of a *new* national food. One of the joys of traveling around the country is to search out local specialties at village inns or local eateries: oyster stew in Maine, pheasant in buttermilk in Minnesota, pompano en papillote in New Orleans, Dungeness crab in Oregon. Each and every state, and many distinct areas within that state, has managed, over the years, to develop its own specialties. Even within one small geographical area, two towns may have very different ways of preparing the same dish.

Despite the explosion of new restaurants around the country offering Tex-Mex, Creole, New England and California cooking, the best is still to be found in private homes . . . family cooking. After all, what makes good cooking is care and watchfulness and precision, all easier to achieve at home than in the high-pressure confines of a commercial kitchen. Thus the title of this volume.

The recipes herein are meant to be representative of the kind of cooking we grew up with, wherever we grew up! They have been collected and edited with a constant eye to the home cook, so you won't find directions calling for a duck press or fermented Thai fish sauce. But you will be encouraged to use the very freshest ingredients you can find, to watch your cooking times to preserve that freshness, and to experiment with the unfamiliar. I have taken the space to include specific regional menus, something to brighten the holiday table or to surprise your family and guests.

A good cook is really an entertainer; he or she must bring pleasure to an audience. I hope this book will garner *you* applause!

Judi Olstein

# THE EAST

From the apples and clams of New England to the home-cured hams
and cornfields of Tidewater Virginia, the East Coast is blessed with a
variety of comestibles that has given rise to a multitude of culinary en-
claves. When the Pilgrim fathers (and mothers) landed at Plymouth
Rock, they were faced with a winter the severity of which they were totally unprepared—bodily or culturally. Were it not for the aid of the local Indians, there is little doubt that the settlement of America would
have been far different than it was.

Between the corn, cranberries, wild game and local shellfish, the
early settlers of Massachusetts were able to forestall the starvation that
decimated the Jamestown, Virginia colonizers. In fact, soon they flour-
ished. But, with few exceptions, they were subject to the same culinary
prejudices that all national groups suffer. What they craved were apples,
a Sunday joint and an endless supply of ale. Given time, that is exactly
what they were able to produce; and it is a fact that the cooking of
America, not just the Northeast, is based, with a few notable exceptions,
on the stodge of seventeenth-century middle-class English sustenance.

But time and circumstances do play a part in the eating habits of
any group. By the time of the Revolution, the inhabitants of the original
thirteen colonies had not only accepted the native bounty, but had developed new ways of preparing it.

Institutions that have become part of the East's culinary traditions
developed: the clambake with its layers of clams, lobsters, corn and potatoes steamed in a seaweed-lined pit of hot rocks; crab boils; baked beans
. . . the real thing, slow-baked with molasses and salt pork, not the trav-
esty sold in cans; the salmon, new potatoes and first tender pe :s served
on the Fourth of July in New England; springtime shad and shad roe in
the middle Atlantic states; the succulent home-cured hams of tidewater
Virginia; the spicy relishes and dried apple dishes of the Pennsylvania

Dutch; even the once-aristocratic dishes of 19th-century New York such as chicken à lá king (named after one Foxhall Keene but corrupted through both common usage *and* preparation).

The cider and rum that poured down every gullet in Colonial America have been replaced by soft drinks, beer and, increasingly, wine. But the pursuit of culinary pleasures has never deserted the rich and populous East. It was here that the first restaurants were established, foremost among them Delmonico's in New York, for over a century the best eatery in these United States. And it is in the East, most especially in New York, where one can indulge in different cuisines for weeks on end, never repeating. Finally it is in the East where foreign influences have played the largest parts in creating new, wholly American dishes.

# Suggested Menus

### THANKSGIVING DINNER
for 8
New England Clam Chowder
Roasted Turkey with Sausage and Sage Dressing
Orange and Cranberry Relish or Cranberry Chutney
Eastern-Style Sweet Potato Casserole
Succotash
Braised Turnips
Watercress Salad with Mushrooms
Cranberry-Nut Loaf
Early American Apple Pie or Pumpkin Pie
Apple Cider or Sparkling Water
Wines: Chenin Blanc, Beaujolais, Vouvray, or Chablis

### FAMILY SEAFOOD DINNER
for 4 to 6
Fruit of the Sea Chowder
Boiled Lobsters
Creamy Cole Slaw or Tangy Cabbage Salad
Eastern Shore Corn Fritters or
Parker House Rolls
Snickerdoodles and Cranberry Snow
Beer, Iced Tea, or Sparkling Water
Wines: Frascati, Muscadet, or Liebfraumilch

### EARLY SUMMER
### INFORMAL BUFFET DINNER
for 6 to 8
Apple Slices with Bacon
Dutch Oven-Barbecued Chicken
Hot Potato Salad
New England Scalloped Tomatoes
Tossed Green Salad with Vinaigrette Dressing
Delaware Spoon Bread
Nut Brownies or Toll House Cookies
Beer, Iced Tea, or Sparkling Water

### AUTUMN DINNER PARTY
for 6 to 8
Baked Oysters or Dutch Wine Soup
Roast Leg of Lamb
Acorn Squash with Rum Butter Glaze
Long Island Rice Casserole
Dutch Cucumber Salad
Wellesley Fudge Cake
Wines: Beaujolais, Valpolicella, Pinot Noir

## MIDWEEK LUNCHEON

(choose one menu or use both)

for 4

MENU 1:

New England Cheese and Chives Soufflé
Dutch Dandelion and Lettuce Salad
Vermont Cheddar Biscuits
Gingersnaps
Coffee, Tea, or Sparkling Water

MENU 2:

Pennsylvania Dutch Cream Corn Soup
Clam Omelet
Dutch Dandelion
Acorn Squash Muffins
Cape Cod Oatmeal Cookies or Joe Froggers
Coffee, Tea, or Sparkling Water

## HEARTY WINTER DINNER

for 4 to 6

Senate Bean Soup or
Cream of Tomato Soup
Mushroom-Olive Salad
Braised Short Ribs
Potato and Turnip Bake
New England Fiddleheads
Popovers
Vermont Maple Syrup Cake or Shoofly Pie
Wines: Cabernet Sauvignon, Burgundy,
or Valpolicella

## SUNDAY BREAKFAST

(choose one menu or use both)

for 4

MENU 1:

Orange or Grapefruit Juice
New England Griddlecakes or
Old-Fashioned Rhode Island Johnnycakes
Pure Maple Syrup
Fried Bacon or Sausage
Coffee or Tea

MENU 2:

Orange or Grapefruit Juice
Maple Omelet
Toasted Honey Bread with
Strawberry Rhubarb Jam
or Spicy Plum Jam
Coffee or Tea

# ❧ ——·Soups and Appetizers·—— ❧

## YANKEE VEGETABLE SOUP

serves 6

1 tablespoon butter or lard
½ pound lean beef, cubed
½ pound veal, cubed
1 large onion, chopped
1 green pepper, chopped
1 cup sliced potato
1 cup diced carrot
½ turnip, pared and chopped
4 cups water
⅓ cup chopped celery
¼ teaspoon dried thyme
1 bay leaf
¼ teaspoon pepper
2 cups fresh corn cut from the cob
1 cup chopped tomatoes

Heat the butter in a large saucepan. Add the beef, veal, onion, and green pepper and sauté until onion is golden brown.

Add the potato, carrot, and turnip and cook 3 minutes longer. Add the water and the celery, thyme, bay leaf, and salt and pepper. Cover and simmer for 4 hours.

Add the corn and cook 1 hour. Remove the bay leaf and the meat. Stir in the tomatoes and simmer 5 minutes longer. Season to taste and serve.

## PENNSYLVANIA PEPPER POT SOUP WITH DUMPLINGS

serves 4

5 pounds beef or veal bones
½ pound tripe, cut into small pieces
6 cups water
1 bay leaf
1 teaspoon salt or to taste
1 teaspoon pepper or to taste
3 medium onions, chopped
2 medium potatoes, diced
2 carrots, chopped
½ cup celery, chopped
½ green pepper, chopped
2 tablespoons lard or butter
    dumpling batter (see the bread chapter of the Heartland section)

Place bones and tripe in a large pot with the water, bay leaf, salt, pepper, and one-third of the chopped onions. Bring to a boil and simmer, covered, for 2 hours.

In a skillet sauté the remaining onion, potatoes, carrots, celery, and green pepper in the lard or butter for 5 minutes.

Remove the bones from the soup mixture. Add the sautéed vegetables. Cover pot and simmer for 30 minutes longer.

Drop the dumpling batter by heaping tablespoons into the soup. Cover and cook for 15 minutes longer.

## CHICKEN-CORN SOUP WITH RIVELS

serves 6

1 4-pound chicken
1 large onion, chopped
4 quarts water
  salt and pepper to taste
10 ears of fresh corn or 2 10-ounce packages
  of frozen corn
½ cup chopped celery with leaves

*Rivels:*

1 cup flour
⅛ teaspoon salt
1 egg
¼ cup milk or a little more

Cut the chicken into eighths and place in a large pot. Add the onions, water, and salt and pepper to taste. Bring to a boil, then cover and simmer until chicken is done, about 40 minutes.

Remove the chicken from the pot and cool. Cut the chicken into bite-sized pieces. Discard skin and bones.

Cut the kernels from the ears of corn. Return the chicken to the pot, add the corn and celery, and simmer for 30 minutes.

While the soup is simmering, prepare the *rivels* (tiny dumplings). Mix the flour, salt, egg, and sufficient milk to make a crumb-like mixture. Mix with fingertips until the crumbs are the size of small marbles. Drop the *rivels* into the soup. Cook 15 minutes longer. Season to taste.

This soup is a favorite in Lancaster County, Pennsylvania, where it is often served on summer picnics.

## PENNSYLVANIA DUTCH CREAM CORN SOUP

serves 4

4 cups fresh corn cut from the cob or 1 cup
  Shaker dried corn
2 stalks celery, chopped with leaves
2 cups water (approximately)
2 cups milk
2 teaspoons salt
1 teaspoon pepper
2 tablespoons butter
1 tablespoon corn starch dissolved in
  a little cold water
3 hard-boiled eggs, chopped
1 teaspoon parsley

Place the corn and celery in a pot, add sufficient water to cover, and boil for 20 minutes. Add the salt, pepper, butter, and cornstarch.

Boil for 5 minutes longer and then add the milk, parsley, and eggs. Serve hot.

Shaker dried corn has less starch and a more intense flavor than either fresh or packaged corn. It can be purchased from John F. Cope Co., P.O. Box 56, Rheems, Pennsylvania 17570.

# DUTCH WINE SOUP

serves 4 to 6

¾ cup rice
4 cups water
2 pounds tart apples
¼ teaspoon salt
1 cup white wine
½ lemon
1 cup sugar

Boil the rice in 2 cups of water for 5 minutes. Pour off the rice water and add 4 cups water. Boil for 1 hour.

Peel and core the apples, cut them into eighths, and add them to the rice.

Slice the lemon and add it to the soup. Add the sugar and the wine. Boil for 20 minutes. Serve hot or cold.

# DUTCH NAVY BEAN SOUP

serves 6

*2 pounds navy beans (about 5 cups)*
*1 pork shank or bacon end*
*3 leeks, chopped*
*2 tablespoons flour*
*2 tablespoons butter*
*3 medium potatoes*
*2 whole cloves*
*salt and pepper to taste*

Place the pork or bacon in a large pot and add the navy beans, leeks, cloves, and salt and pepper. Add water to cover.

Heat the butter in a small pan until it foams. Add the flour and mix until it browns. Add two tablespoons of the bean stock to this mixture and stir to blend.

Add the flour mixture to the pot. Simmer until the beans are tender, approximately two hours.

Boil the potatoes separately, dice, and add to soup just before serving.

# BLOCK ISLAND CODFISH CHOWDER

serves 6

*3 pounds fresh codfish*
*3 onions, finely chopped*
*1 carrot*
*3 sprigs parsley*
*1 bay leaf*
*1 whole clove*
*1½ teaspoons salt*
*2 pounds potatoes*
*2 tablespoons butter*
*salt and pepper to taste*
*2 cups milk*
*1 tablespoon chopped parsley*
*½ cup shredded lettuce*

Trim the skin and bones from the codfish and place the trimmings in a large pot. Add water to cover and add one-third of the onions, the carrot, parsley sprigs, bay leaf, salt, and clove. Bring to a boil and cook for 15 minutes.

Dice the codfish fillets and the potatoes into small pieces about ½-inch square.

Melt the butter in a deep saucepan and sauté the remaining onions until lightly browned. Strain the fish broth over the onions. Add the diced codfish and potatoes. Cook just below the boiling point for about 30 minutes, or until the potatoes are soft.

Add salt and pepper to taste, the milk, chopped parlsey, and lettuce. Heat thoroughly and serve at once.

## PHILADELPHIA SNAPPER SOUP

serves 4

    1  snapper turtle
    8  cups beef or chicken broth
    ½  pound chicken fat or lard
    4  pounds veal knuckle
    1  cup flour
    1  carrot, chopped
    3  medium onions, chopped
    ½  teaspoon dried marjoram
    2  bay leaves
    3  stalks celery, chopped
    6  tomatoes, chopped
    1  hard-boiled egg, chopped
    2  cups sherry
    3  slices lemon
       salt and pepper to taste
       dash Tabasco sauce

Place the veal knuckles, carrot, onions, celery, and chicken fat or lard in a baking pan. Add the marjoram, salt and pepper, and bay leaves and place the pan in an oven set at 375°.

When the veal knuckles are browned, sprinkle the flour over the ingredients in the baking pan and return it to the oven until ingredients brown again.

Transfer the mixture to a large pot; add the broth and tomatoes, cover, and simmer for 3½ to 4 hours.

Dice the turtle meat, place it in a saucepan, and simmer for 5 minutes with 1 cup sherry and the lemon slices, salt, and Tabasco. Remove the lemon slices and turtle meat and strain the liquid into the soup pot. Add the turtle meat to the pot along with the egg and remaining sherry.

Prepared frozen turtle meat is available in well-stocked gourmet shops.

## DUTCH APPLE SOUP

serves 6

    2  pounds apples
    2  quarts water
    ½  cup sugar
    1  stick cinnamon
       juice of ½ lemon
       small piece lemon rind
    ¼  cup currants or raisins
    1  cup white wine

Do not peel the apples; core them and cut into eighths. Place the apples, water, sugar, cinnamon stick, lemon juice and lemon rind in a large pot and boil until apples are soft.

Mix the flour with a little water and add it to the apple mixture while it boils.

Strain the apples through a sieve and return to the pot. Add the currants and white wine and cook for 3 minutes more. Serve hot or cold.

## SENATE BEAN SOUP

serves 6

    2  cups dried pea beans
    3  quarts cold water
    1  ham bone with meat
    3  potatoes, peeled, cooked, and mashed
    3  onions, finely chopped
    2  cloves garlic, crushed
    1  small head celery, chopped
    ¼  cup finely chopped parsley

Cook the pea beans, covered, in boiling salted water until tender. Drain well.

Place the pea beans, water, and ham bone in a large pot. Simmer, covered, for 2 hours, skimming occasionally.

Add the potatoes, onions, garlic, celery, and parsley. Simmer, covered, for 1 hour.

Remove the ham bone and return any meat on the bone to the soup. Serve hot.

# NEW ENGLAND CLAM CHOWDER

serves 6 to 8

1 quart hard-shelled clams
½ pound salt pork, diced
3 onions, finely chopped
2 cups boiling water
3 potatoes, finely diced
½ teaspoon pepper
3 cups milk
2 cups heavy cream

Scrub the clams and open them, reserving the juice. Chop the clams and save the juice.

Sauté the salt pork in large pot until half-cooked; pour off most of the fat. Add the onions and sauté until brown. Add the boiling water, potatoes, pepper, and clam juice. Cover and cook over medium heat for 20 minutes.

Add the clams, milk, and cream, stirring gently. Cook over low heat for 15 minutes, being careful not to let the soup boil. Season to taste.

# FRUIT OF THE SEA CHOWDER

serves 4

12 oysters
12 clams, steamed and shelled (reserve the liquid)
1 quart mussels, steamed and shelled
6 shrimp, boiled and shelled
1 stalk celery, chopped
1 medium onion, finely chopped
2 leeks, finely chopped
¼ pound butter
2 cups milk
3 medium potatoes, diced
1 cup light cream
3 egg yolks

Cook the oysters in their liquid just until their edges curl; drain and reserve the liquid. Prepare the other shellfish as directed above and set aside.

In a medium saucepan, sauté the celery, onions, and leeks gently in the butter. Add ½ cup oysters, ½ cup clam liquid, milk, and potatoes to the saucepan. Cook for 20 minutes, then press ingredients through a sieve and return them to the saucepan.

Place the eggs yolks in a bowl and beat them. Heat the cream and pour it over the egg yolks, beating constantly. Add this mixture to the ingredients in the saucepan.

Place the prepared shellfish in a soup tureen and pour the liquid over it.

## MANHATTAN CLAM CHOWDER

serves 6 generously

1 quart hard-shell clams
¼ pound bacon, chopped
4 medium onions, chopped
2 cups diced tomatoes
2 quarts water
¾ cup chopped celery
4 tablespoons chopped parsley
1 bay leaf
½ teaspoon dried thyme
3 small potatoes, diced
1 teaspoon pepper

Scrub the clams and open them, reserving the juice. Chop the clams and save the juice.

Place the bacon in a large pot and cook until browned. Remove the bacon pieces.

Add the onions to the bacon fat and sauté for 10 minutes. Add the tomatoes, water, celery, potatoes, parsley, bay leaf, and thyme. Cover and simmer for 2 hours.

Add the clams and pepper to the stock. Bring to a boil and simmer for 15 minutes. Season to taste.

## RHODE ISLAND CABBAGE SOUP

serves 4

1 small head green cabbage
3 cups milk
1 cup light cream
3 tablespoons butter
salt and pepper to taste

Chop the cabbage finely and place in a large pot. Cover with boiling water and cook for 7 minutes in an uncovered pot. Drain and reserve one cup of the liquid.

To the cabbage add the milk, reserved cabbage liquid, and cream. Simmer for 3 minutes. Season to taste.

Serve in a large bowl and top with the butter.

## NEW HAMPSHIRE CREAM OF TOMATO SOUP

serves 6

3 large tomatoes, peeled, seeded, and chopped
4 cups chicken stock
1 bay leaf
2 cups heavy cream
salt and pepper to taste

In a large pot, combine the chicken stock, bay leaf, and chopped tomatoes. Cover and simmer for 20 minutes.

Meanwhile, heat the cream in a saucepan.

Add the warm cream to the pot and cook, stirring until ingredients are well blended. Do not let the mixture boil. Season to taste.

# LONG ISLAND STUFFED CLAMS

serves 4 to 6

24 *medium cherrystone or little neck clams*
 4 *large mushrooms, chopped*
 5 *tablespoons butter*
   *salt and pepper to taste*
½ *cup freshly grated Parmesan cheese*
 3 *sprigs parsley*
 2 *lemons, halved*

Open the clams and shell them. Wash the shells thoroughly and set aside.

Chop the clams and mix them with the mushrooms, 3 tablespoons butter, salt and pepper.

Fill the clam shells with the mixture, sprinkle with cheese, and dot with the remaining butter.

Place the filled shells in a baking pan and bake at 350° for 15 minutes. Serve garnished with parsley sprigs and lemon halves.

# VERMONT CHEESE PUFFS

serves 6

  1 *cup sifted flour*
  1 *teaspoon baking powder*
 ½ *teaspoon salt*
 ½ *teaspoon dry mustard*
  2 *eggs, separated*
 ½ *cup milk*
  1 *cup grated Vermont cheddar cheese*
1½ *cups vegetable oil*

Sift flour, baking powder, salt, and dry mustard together into a bowl and set aside.

Put the milk into a small bowl. Beat the egg yolks and add them to the milk. Stir this mixture into the dry ingredients and combine thoroughly. Add the grated cheese to the mixture.

Beat the egg whites in a separate bowl and fold them into the batter.

Heat the oil in a skillet until it is very hot (365°–370°). Drop the batter by teaspoons into the oil and fry until golden brown. Remove and drain on paper towels.

# DUTCH CHEESE SPREAD

serves 4 to 6

  1 *cup cottage cheese*
 ½ *cup milk*
 ½ *cup cream*
  1 *teaspoon salt*
 ½ *teaspoon pepper*
 ¼ *cup watercress, chopped*

Put the cottage cheese in a bowl. Slowly pour in the milk and cream, mixing with the back of a spoon. Blend to the consistency of a medium-soft paste while adding the salt, pepper and watercress. Serve with bread.

In former times, the Pennsylvania Dutch served this on bread topped with old-fashioned New Orleans molasses.

## ROBBIN'S ISLAND BAKED OYSTERS

serves 4 to 6

24  large oysters
 2  tablespoons butter
    salt and pepper to taste
 2  teaspoons chopped chives

Scrub the oysters well. Place them, unopened, in a deep baking pan and bake at 375° for 2 to 3 minutes until they open.

Remove the upper half of the shell. Place a bit of butter, salt and pepper, and some chopped chives on each oyster and return the pan to the oven for 3 minutes more. Serve piping hot.

## DEEP-FRIED CODFISH BALLS

serves 6 to 8

  1  pound salt codfish
  2  cups mashed potatoes
 ¾  teaspoon pepper
 ½  teaspoon grated nutmeg
  4  eggs, beaten
1½  cups vegetable oil

Soak the codfish in cold water for 4 hours, changing the water after 2 hours.

Drain the fish, place it in a pot, cover with fresh water and bring to the boil. Drain and flake the fish. Combine it with the mashed potatoes, pepper, and nutmeg. Add the eggs and mix thoroughly.

Heat the oil in a heavy skillet until it is very hot (375°). Drop the fish mixture by teaspoons into the oil and fry until golden brown.

## PECONIC PICKLED MUSSELS

serves 10 to 12

 3  quarts mussels
 2 or 3 onions, thinly sliced
 3 or 4 cloves garlic, crushed
    mixed pickling spices
    salt and pepper to taste
    cider vinegar or white wine vinegar

Wash, scrub, and debeard mussels thoroughly. Steam them open in a large pot with 1 cup water.

Lift out the mussels and shells, reserving the broth.

In a large crock or glass jar arrange layers of shelled mussels, onion slices, garlic, pickling spices, salt, and pepper. Add strained mussel broth to one-third the depth of the mussels, then add vinegar to cover.

Let the container stand, uncovered, for at least 3 days before serving. Stir once or twice.

## APPLE SLICES AND BACON

serves 6

  1  pound sliced bacon
  6  large tart apples
 ½  cup all-purpose flour
 ½  cup sugar
  1  teaspoon grated nutmeg

In a large skillet fry the bacon until crisp. Remove the bacon and drain on paper towels. Drain all but ¼ cup fat from the skillet.

Core the apples but do not peel them.
Cut them into round slices.

Combine the flour, sugar, and nutmeg in
a bowl. Coat the apple slices with the
flour mixture and fry them in the bacon
fat until golden brown, turning
frequently. Apples are done when they are
easily pierced with a fork. Serve with the
bacon slices.

## Salads

### MAINE WATERCRESS SALAD WITH MUSHROOMS

serves 4

- 3 or 4 bunches fresh watercress
- ½ pound mushrooms
- ⅓ cup olive oil
- 2 tablespoons tarragon vinegar
- ½ teaspoon salt
- pepper to taste

Wash and trim the watercress. Wipe the
mushrooms clean and slice thinly.

In a large bowl, mix together the vinegar,
salt, and pepper. Slowly whisk in the oil.
Add the watercress and mushrooms. Toss
before serving.

### DUTCH CUCUMBER SALAD

serves 4

- 1 teaspoon salt
- 1 medium onion
- 2 cucumbers
- 2 tablespoons tarragon vinegar
- 1 pint sour cream
- ½ teaspoon pepper

Slice the cucumbers and onion thinly.
Sprinkle with salt and let stand for a
½ hour.

Place the cucumbers and onion in a
cheesecloth and squeeze out the liquid.
Put the cucumbers and onion in a shallow
bowl, add the vinegar, and mix. Pour the
sour cream over the mixture and sprinkle
with pepper.

## TANGY DUTCH CABBAGE SALAD

serves 4 to 6

    3 cups finely shredded cabbage
    3 tablespoons sugar
    ½ teaspoon salt
    ¼ teaspoon pepper
    1 cup sour cream
    ¼ cup vinegar

In a large bowl combine the cabbage, sugar, salt, and pepper. Chill thoroughly.

When sufficiently chilled, add the sour cream and vinegar to the cabbage mixture. Toss lightly.

## DUTCH DANDELION SALAD

serves 4

    1 pound young dandelion greens or arugala
    5 slices bacon
    2 eggs
    ½ cup light cream
    2 tablespoons butter
    4 tablespoons vinegar
    1 tablespoon sugar
    1 teaspoon salt
    ½ teaspoon paprika
    ½ teaspoon pepper

Wash and trim the dandelion. Place the leaves in a salad bowl and let stand in a warm place.

Dice and fry the bacon. Drop the bacon fat and pieces on top of the dandelions.

Place the butter and light cream in a saucepan and melt butter over low heat.

In a separate bowl, beat the eggs. Add the pepper, salt, vinegar and sugar. Add this mixture to the cream and butter mixture. Stir until mixture is very hot and thickens to the consistency of a custard. Pour over dandelions and stir well.

## DUTCH DANDELION AND LETTUCE SALAD

serves 4 to 6

    1 pound young dandelion greens or arugala
    1 head lettuce
    4 onions, thinly sliced
    2 tomatoes, diced
    2 teaspoons salt
    3 tablespoons olive oil
    ½ green pepper
    2 hard-boiled eggs, chopped
    ¼ pound Swiss cheese
    ¼ teaspoon cayenne pepper
    ½ teaspoon pepper
    4 tablespoons vinegar

Wash and trim the dandelion. Coarsely chop the dandelion, lettuce, and green pepper.

Grate the cheese. Mix with the dandelion, lettuce, and green pepper in a bowl. Add cayenne, salt, and pepper and mix again. Add the oil and vinegar and mix.

Add the tomatoes, onions, and eggs to the bowl. Toss lightly.

# WALDORF SALAD

serves 6

> 3 large apples
> 2 tablespoons lemon juice
> 3 medium celery stalks, diced
> 1 cup coarsely chopped walnuts
> 1 cup mayonnaise
> ½ cup heavy cream
> 2 heads Boston lettuce, washed and chilled.

Peel and core the apples and cut them into small pieces. There should be about 4 cups.

In a large bowl, combine the apples and lemon juice. Stir the apples to coat them thoroughly with the lemon juice. Add the celery and walnuts and mix well.

In a separate bowl combine the mayonnaise and heavy cream and mix until smooth. Pour over apple mixture and toss.

To serve, place the Boston lettuce leaves on serving plates and spoon the salad evenly among them.

This salad is the invention of Oscar Tschirsky, known simply as Oscar of the Waldorf. He was the mâitre d'hôtel of that famous New York hotel from 1893 to 1943. The original recipe did not call for walnuts, although they are considered indispensable now.

# CREAMY COLE SLAW

serves 6 to 8

> 1 medium head cabbage, finely shredded
> ½ cup heavy cream, whipped
> ¼ to ½ cup sugar
> ½ cup vinegar
> ½ teaspoon salt
> ½ teaspoon pepper

Place the shredded cabbage in a large bowl.

Beat the sugar into the whipped cream. Taste to test sweetness. Beat in the vinegar.

Pour this mixture over the shredded cabbage. Season with salt and pepper. Refrigerate until ready to serve.

# HOT POTATO SALAD

serves 6

> 10 new potatoes
> 1 onion
> 2 slices bacon
> 2 tablespoons vinegar
> ½ teaspoon salt

Boil the new potatoes in their skins until tender. Slice them thinly. Slice the onion thinly. Place the potatoes and onion in a serving bowl.

Dice the bacon and fry the pieces until crisp. Add the vinegar and salt to the skillet. Pour this mixture over the potatoes and onion. Mix well and serve hot.

# MARINATED VEGETABLE SALAD

serves 6 to 8

1 small head cauliflower, broken into flowerets
3 small white onions, quartered
1 pound small whole mushrooms
2 green peppers, thinly julienned
2 carrots, thinly julienned
1 cup cherry tomatoes

Marinade:
1 cup olive oil
1½ cups red wine vinegar
¼ cup sugar
1 teaspoon pepper
2 teaspoons salt
1 clove garlic, crushed

Wash all the vegetables and prepare as directed above. Place all vegetables except cherry tomatoes in a large bowl and set aside.

In a saucepan, combine the olive oil, vinegar, sugar, salt, pepper, and garlic. Bring the mixture to a boil. Remove from heat and let cool slightly.

Pour the marinade over the vegetables. When the mixture is cool, add the cherry tomatoes.

Refrigerate for a day, stirring often, before serving.

# ENDIVE SALAD

serves 4 to 6

6 medium potatoes
2 or 3 heads endive
1 small stalk celery

Sour cream dressing:
1 cup white wine vinegar
  salt and pepper to taste
1 tablespoon sugar or to taste
1 tablespoon butter
1 egg, beaten
¼ cup sour cream

Parboil the potatoes and dice when cool. Dice the endive and the celery.

Combine the vinegar, salt and pepper, sugar, butter, egg, and sour cream in a saucepan. Bring to a boil and stir until mixture thickens.

Add the potatoes, endive, and celery and heat thoroughly. Stir gently and do not allow ingredients to boil.

# MUSHROOM-OLIVE SALAD

serves 4

3 cups mushrooms, sliced
4 tablespoons chopped scallions
2 teaspoons chopped fresh basil or 1 teaspoon dried basil
4 tablespoons fresh lemon juice
¼ teaspoon salt
¼ teaspoon pepper
6 pitted black olives, sliced

Combine all the ingredients and mix well. Serve on lettuce leaves.

# ❧ ── Dairy Dishes ── ❦

## PROVIDENCE SEAFOOD-EGG BAKE

serves 4

6 hard-boiled eggs, chopped
2 tablespoons butter
½ teaspoon dried chervil
1 teaspoon Dijon-style mustard
1 teaspoon salt
½ teaspoon pepper
½ cup cooked shrimp, chopped
1 cup heavy cream
½ cup freshly grated Parmesan cheese
    butter

Preheat the oven to 400°.

Divide the eggs and shrimp among 4 small, buttered ovenproof dishes.

Mix the chervil, mustard, salt, and pepper with the cream and spoon evenly over the egg-shrimp mixture. Sprinkle with grated cheese, dot with butter, and bake until cheese melts and turns golden brown.

## MAPLE OMELET

serves 4 to 6

6 eggs, separated
6 tablespoons pure maple syrup
1 teaspoon vanilla
¼ teaspoon salt
4 to 6 teaspoons butter
¾ cup finely sliced almonds

Preheat the oven to 350°.

In a medium-sized mixing bowl, beat the egg yolks until thick and lemon-colored. Beat in the maple syrup, vanilla, and salt.

Beat the egg whites until stiff but not dry. Fold into the yolk mixture.

Melt the butter in a heavy 10- or 12-inch skillet. Cover the bottom of the skillet with the sliced almonds, then add the egg mixture. Reduce the heat to medium-low and cook until the egg mixture is a light brown color underneath, approximately 10 minutes.

Remove the skillet from the heat and place it in the oven for 8 to 10 minutes. Fold the omelet onto a platter and serve with maple syrup.

## POACHED EGGS IN CREAM

serves 4

½ cup light cream
6 eggs
    salt and pepper to taste
    toast

Pour the cream into a 10- or 12-inch skillet. Heat the cream until it begins to bubble.

Break the eggs carefully into the cream and season with salt and pepper. Cook slowly over low heat until the eggs are firm and set. Serve on toast.

# CLAM OMELET

serves 4

6 *eggs, separated*
6 *tablespoons butter*
1 *cup milk*
½ *teaspoon salt*
¼ *teaspoon pepper*
1 *cup chopped clams*
2 *tablespoons melted butter*

Melt the 6 tablespoons butter in an omelet pan over low heat.

Meanwhile, beat the egg yolks in a bowl until blended. Add the milk, stir well, and add the salt, pepper, and clams. Stir and add the 2 tablespoons melted butter.

In a separate bowl, beat the egg whites until stiff but not dry. Fold into the egg yolk mixture.

Pour the egg mixture into the omelet pan (the butter should all be melted by now). With a spatula, lift the omelet as it sets so that the butter reaches every part. When omelet is golden brown, fold it and serve very hot.

# WATER ISLAND SCRAMBLED OYSTERS

serves 4 to 6

36 *oysters*
 *salt and pepper to taste*
7 *eggs, beaten*
4 *tablespoons light cream*
½ *cup unseasoned croutons*
1 *tablespoon butter*
 *parsley sprigs*

Shell and chop the oysters. Season them with salt and pepper.

Beat the eggs in a mixing bowl. Stir in the cream and add the croutons. Mix until croutons are coated with egg mixture.

Melt the butter in a skillet over moderate heat. Add the egg mixture. When the eggs begin to get firm, stir in the oysters and scramble. Serve garnished with parsley.

# RHODE ISLAND SHRIMP AND CORN SOUFFLE

serves 4 to 6

6 *ears fresh corn*
3 *eggs, separated*
2 *teaspoons sugar*
1 *tablespoon melted butter*
½ *teaspoon salt*
1½ *pounds shrimp, cooked, peeled, and deveined*

Preheat the oven to 300°.

Cut the corn from the cob.

Beat the egg yolks in a mixing bowl until blended. Stir in the corn, sugar, melted butter, salt, and shrimp.

In a separate bowl beat the egg whites until stiff but not dry. Fold into the yolk mixture.

Turn the egg mixture into a buttered 1½-quart soufflé dish, cover, and set dish in a pan of hot water. Bake for 1 hour or until firm. Remove the cover for the last 15 minutes to let the top of the soufflé brown. Serve *immediately*.

# DUTCH EGG PFANNKUCHEN

serves 4

> 6 eggs, separated
> 3 tablespoons milk
> 2 teaspoons chopped parsley
> 3 tablespoons butter
> 1 teaspoon salt
> ½ teaspoon pepper

Beat the egg yolks in a mixing bowl until blended. Stir in the milk, parsley, salt and pepper.

In a separate bowl beat the egg whites until stiff but not dry. Fold into the yolk mixture.

Melt the butter in a skillet, pour in the egg mixture, and cook over moderate heat until golden brown. Garnish with additional parsley. Serve rolled and hot.

# NEW ENGLAND CHEESE AND CHIVES SOUFFLE

serves 4

> 4 tablespoons butter
> 4 tablespoons flour
> 1 cup milk, scalded
> ½ teaspoon salt
> ¼ teaspoon pepper
> 1 cup grated Vermont cheddar cheese
> 4 egg yolks, beaten until light
> 4 egg whites, beaten until stiff
> 2 teaspoons chopped chives

Preheat the oven to 375°.

Melt the butter in a saucepan, stir in the flour, and add the milk gradually. Stir until mixture is thick and smooth.

Stir in the salt, pepper, and grated cheese. Mix until smooth and remove saucepan from heat.

When the mixture is cool, stir in the egg yolks.

Add two teaspoons of the egg whites, then fold in the remainder.

Turn the mixture into an unbuttered 1½-quart soufflé dish and place the dish in a pan of hot water. Place in oven and bake 25 minutes or until firm. Serve *immediately.*

# BAKED BREAD-AND-CHEESE

serves 4

> 6 thin slices buttered white bread, preferably home-made
> 2 tablespoons butter
> 1 cup grated Vermont cheddar cheese
> 1 cup milk
> ⅛ teaspoon cayenne pepper
> ½ teaspoon salt
> 1 onion, chopped

Preheat the oven to 375°.

Remove the crusts from the bread and cut it into 2-inch cubes.

Place a layer of the bread cubes in a buttered baking dish. Cover with grated cheese. Repeat until bread cubes are used up, reserving ¼ cup of the cheese.

Heat the milk with the pepper, salt, and onion. Strain the milk over the bread and cheese. Sprinkle with the remaining cheese. Bake for 25 minutes. Serve hot from the baking dish.

# GREEN MOUNTAINS ONIONS AND EGGS

serves 4

4 medium-sized bunches of green onions or scallions
2 to 3 tablespoons bacon fat or butter
1 tablespoon water
6 eggs
1 teaspoon salt
½ teaspoon pepper

Wash and trim the green onions or scallions. Do not trim away the green tops. Chop coarsely.

In a skillet, heat the bacon fat or butter. Add the water and green onions and cook until tender.

Break eggs into a bowl, season with salt and pepper, and whisk until blended. Pour eggs over onions and scramble.

# CORN OMELET

serves 4 to 6

½ cup fresh corn cut from the cob
8 eggs
2 teaspoons salt
2 tablespoons milk
½ teaspoon paprika
2 tablespoons butter
½ teaspoon pepper

Melt the butter in a skillet. Add the corn, salt, and pepper and simmer.

Beat the eggs with the milk in a mixing bowl. Pour mixture into the skillet and scramble. Serve the omelet sprinkled with paprika.

# SPRINGHOUSE WATERCRESS OMELET

serves 4 to 6

8 eggs, separated
½ cup chopped watercress
2 tablespoons butter
½ teaspoon salt
½ teaspoon pepper

Wash and trim the watercress and chop it coarsely.

Beat the egg yolks in a mixing bowl until blended.

In a separate bowl beat the egg whites until stiff but not dry. Add the salt and pepper. Gently stir whites into egg yolks.

Melt the butter in a skillet. Add the egg mixture and cook for 5 minutes or until underside is lightly browned. Fold in the watercress and serve.

# NEW BEDFORD SAILOR'S OMELET

serves 4 to 5

6 eggs, separated
¼ teaspoon salt
⅛ teaspoon pepper
1 teaspoon anchovy paste
1 tablespoon butter

Preheat the oven to 350°.

Beat the egg yolks in a bowl until light and lemon-colored. Add the salt, pepper, and anchovy paste.

Beat the egg whites until stiff but not dry. Fold into the yolk mixture.

Melt the butter in a heavy skillet and pour in the egg mixture. Cook until the bottom of the omelet is brown, then remove from heat and place skillet in the oven.

Bake until brown. Serve at once.

# · Meat and Poultry ·

# NEW BEDFORD POT ROAST

serves 6 to 8

5 pounds rump roast
2 cups red wine
2 large onions, chopped
1 clove garlic, chopped
1 teaspoon salt
¼ teaspoon pepper
4 tablespoons olive oil
1 onion, thinly sliced
3 tomatoes, thickly sliced
6 medium potatoes, peeled and cut into eighths

In a bowl make a marinade by combining the wine, onions, garlic, salt, and pepper.

Place the meat in a large bowl and pour the marinade over it. Refrigerate the meat for 8 to 10 hours, turning frequently.

Heat the oil in a large, heavy pot. Remove the meat from the marinade (but reserve the marinade), pat dry, and brown well in the hot oil.

Add the sliced onion to the pot. Add the marinade and cover. Cook over low heat for 3 hours or until meat is tender.

Add the tomatoes and potatoes and cook for another 30 minutes.

The many Portuguese fishermen who came to Massachusetts contributed Mediterranean zest to New England cooking.

# NEW ENGLAND POT ROAST

serves 6 to 8

4 pounds chuck or rump roast
1 cup apple cider
1 cup cider vinegar
4 cups water
8 whole cloves
2 bay leaves
1 tablespoon salt
1 tablespoon sugar
3 tablespoons flour
1/4 cup butter

Combine the apple cider, vinegar, water, cloves, bay leaves, salt, and sugar in a bowl to make a marinade.

Place the meat in a large bowl and pour the marinade over it. Refrigerate for 8 to 10 hours, turning frequently.

When ready to begin cooking, remove the meat from the bowl (but reserve the marinade) and pat dry. Coat the meat with the flour.

In a large, heavy pot melt the butter. Add the meat and brown on all sides. Add 1/2 cup marinade. Cover tightly and simmer 2 1/2 hours or until tender.

Turn the meat once about halfway through the cooking period. If necessary, add some additional marinade.

# YANKEE POT ROAST

serves 6

3 pounds bottom round, chuck, or rump roast
2 tablespoons flour
1/2 teaspoon grated nutmeg
3 tablespoons bacon drippings, lard, or butter
2 cups fresh cranberries
1 cup apple cider
2 tablespoons brown sugar
1 stick cinnamon
6 whole cloves
1 teaspoon salt

In a small bowl combine the flour and nutmeg. Rub the mixture into the meat.

In a large, heavy pot melt the bacon drippings and add the meat, browning it on all sides.

In a saucepan combine the cranberries, apple cider, and sugar. Bring to a boil. Simmer over low heat until the cranberries are tender, about 8 minutes. Pour this mixture over the meat.

Place the cinnamon stick and cloves in a cheesecloth bag. Place bag in pot with meat. Sprinkle meat with salt.

Cover and simmer 2 to 2 1/4 hours or until meat is tender. To serve, remove the spice bag and place meat on a serving platter with the sauce.

The ingredients and style of cooking in this recipe are exactly the same as in Colonial times.

# NEW ENGLAND BOILED DINNER

serves 6 to 8

5 to 6 pounds corned beef brisket
½ pound salt pork
8 carrots
8 parsnips
8 small white turnips, peeled
1 medium onion
8 medium potatoes
1 medium head green cabbage, cored and quartered

Place the corned beef in a large pot and add cold water to cover. Simmer, covered, for 2 hours. Add the salt pork and continue simmering for another 2 hours.

Skim the pot carefully and add the carrots, parsnips, turnips and onions. Cover and cook for 30 minutes.

Add the potatoes and cabbage. Cover and continue cooking until potatoes are tender.

Place the meat in the center of a large platter. Surround with the vegetables.

# NEW ENGLAND SALT PORK DINNER WITH MILK GRAVY

serves 4

2 pounds salt pork
  water for soaking
4 tablespoons flour
2 tablespoons lard
Milk gravy:
¼ cup fat from salt pork
3 tablespoons flour
  milk divided into: 2 tablespoons, 2 tablespoons, and 2 cups

Select salt pork with streaks of lean in it. Cut the pork into ½-inch slices. Soak the slices in warm water for 4 hours, changing the water 3 or 4 times.

Pat the pork slices dry. Coat each slice with flour.

In a skillet greased with the lard, cook the pork slowly, turning occasionally until the slices are a rich crusty brown.

To make the milk gravy, remove the slices from the skillet. Remove the skillet from the heat and drain off all but ¼ cup fat. Into this stir 3 tablespoons flour. Blend thoroughly and add 2 tablespoons milk. Stir until smooth; add 2 more tablespoons milk. Mix well.

Gradually stir in 2 cups of milk. Cook over low heat, stirring constantly, until mixture thickens. Serve the salt pork with the gravy.

# SCRAPPLE

serves 8

1½ pounds pork shoulder
¼ pound pork liver
4 cups water
1 cup yellow corn meal
1 cup water
1 teaspoon salt
¼ cup onions, finely chopped
¼ teaspoon dried thyme
1 teaspoon dried marjoram
½ teaspoon pepper
4 tablespoons flour
4 tablespoons lard or vegetable oil

In a saucepan combine the pork shoulder and liver with 4 cups water. Cook over moderate heat for 1 hour.

*(continued on next page)*

Drain the meat, reserving the broth. Discard all bones and chop the meat finely.

In a saucepan, combine the corn meal, salt, 1 cup water, and 2 cups of the reserved broth. Cook the mixture over moderate heat, stirring constantly until it thickens.

Add the meat, onions, and spices to the corn meal mixture. Cover the pot and simmer for about 1 hour. Place the mixture into a 9 × 5 × 3-inch loaf pan and chill until firm. Cut into slices about ½-inch thick. Coat the slices with flour and fry in lard over moderate heat until crisp on both sides. Serve at once.

Scrapple, a quintessential Pennsylvania Dutch dish, is also called *ponhaws*.

## ROAST FRESH SHOULDER OF PORK WITH APPLE STUFFING

serves 4

  1  4- to 5-pound shoulder of pork, with bone removed
Apple stuffing:
  ¼ cup salt pork, diced
  ½ cup celery, chopped
  ½ cup onion, chopped
  ¼ cup parsley, chopped
  5 apples, diced
  ⅓ cup sugar
  2 cups unseasoned bread crumbs

If you cannot do it easily yourself, have your butcher remove the bone from the pork. Reserve the bone.

Preheat the oven to 350°.

To make the apple stuffing, fry the salt pork in a large skillet until crisp. Remove from skillet

Sauté the celery, onion, and parsley in the fat for 5 minutes. Remove vegetables from skillet.

Place the apples in the skillet. Sprinkle with sugar. Cook, covered, until tender. Remove the cover and continue to cook until juice evaporates. Add the other ingredients and mix well.

Spread the apple stuffing on the meat, roll the meat like a jelly roll, and tie with string.

Place roast on a rack in a baking dish. Add reserved bones to dish. Place in the oven and bake, uncovered, for 3 hours or 45 minutes to the pound. Turn roast every half-hour.

## NEW ENGLAND HAM AND APPLE PIE

serves 4

  2 pounds cooked ham, diced
  5 tart apples, cored and sliced
  ¼ cup light brown sugar
  ⅛ teaspoon salt
  ½ teaspoon cinnamon
  2 tablespoons butter
  2 tablespoons lemon juice
  ¼ cup apple cider
  1 unbaked 9-inch pastry

Preheat the oven to 375°.

Combine the sugar, salt, and cinnamon in a small bowl; mix well.

Butter a deep baking dish. Place alternate layers of ham and apples in the dish, sprinkling each layer with the sugar mixture and dotting each with butter. Be sure to end with a layer of apples.

Combine the lemon juice and apple cider in a small bowl. Pour over the top layer of apples. Cover the baking dish and bake in oven for 20 minutes.

At the end of 20 minutes, remove the dish from the oven and uncover it. Fit the pastry over the top of the dish. Crimp around the edge and flute. Cut a few slits in the center. Return the dish to the oven for 25 minutes longer, or until pastry is golden.

## PENNSYLVANIA BAKED HAM WITH SPICED ORANGES

serves 4

3 to 4 pounds smoked ham
2 cups water
½ cup brown sugar
1 tablespoon flour
¼ cup whole cloves (for ham)
4 whole oranges
2 cups water
2 cups sugar
¼ cup whole cloves (for oranges)

Preheat the ham in a baking pan with 2 cups water. Bake until tender, allowing 20 minutes per pound.

Carve off the rind and stud the ham with ¼ cup cloves. In a small bowl make a paste of the brown sugar and flour and rub the ham with it. Bake for 25 minutes longer.

To make the spiced oranges, stud the whole, unpeeled oranges with ¼ cup cloves (about 7 cloves per orange). Combine 2 cups water and the sugar in a medium saucepan and boil the oranges until their skins are very tender.

To serve, place the ham in the center of a platter. Cut the oranges in half and arrange them around the ham. Pour some of the syrup over them.

## BRAISED PORK WITH LEEKS

serves 6

6 loin pork chops
1 tablespoon salt
½ teaspoon pepper
¼ cup olive oil
1 cup leeks, finely chopped (use the white part only)
2 teaspoons garlic, chopped
2 cups water
2 tablespoons dry vermouth (or white vinegar)

Season the pork chops on both sides with the salt and pepper.

In a heavy skillet, heat the oil. When it is hot, add the pork chops and sauté, turning occasionally, for about 15 minutes or until chops are evenly browned.

Stir in the leeks and garlic, add the water, and bring to a boil over high heat. Reduce the heat, cover the skillet, and simmer for 30 minutes, turning the chops twice.

Remove the pork chops from skillet and place on a serving platter. Stir the vermouth into the remaining liquid, cook for 2 minutes, and pour over the chops.

## UPSTATE BRAISED PORK CHOPS WITH SAUERKRAUT

serves 4

1 tablespoon lard or butter
4 pork chops
2 cups sauerkraut, drained and rinsed
¼ cup onion, chopped
4 tart apples, peeled, cored, and sliced
4 tablespoons brown sugar
1 teaspoon caraway seeds

Melt the lard in a large skillet. Add the pork chops and slowly brown on both sides. Remove the chops from the skillet and drain off fat.

Combine the sauerkraut, onion, apples, sugar, and caraway seeds in a bowl. Pour this mixture into the skillet and place the pork chops on top of it. Cover and simmer about 45 minutes or until tender.

## BRAISED SHORT RIBS

serves 4

¼ pound bacon, diced
8 lean, meaty short ribs
¼ cup flour
1 large onion, thinly sliced
1 large clove garlic, crushed
2 carrots, sliced
¼ cup celery, chopped
1 leek (white part only)
½ cup red wine
½ cup beef broth
   salt and pepper to taste

Preheat the oven to 350°.

In a heavy, ovenproof pot sauté the bacon until golden.

Dust the ribs with flour, add them to the pot, and brown on all sides. Remove ribs and set aside in a warm place.

Add the onion, carrots, celery, and leek to the pot. Sauté, stirring, for 3 or 4 minutes. Add garlic and sauté for another minute.

Pour off excess fat from the pot. Return ribs to pot and add red wine, broth, salt, and pepper. Stir and cover.

Place pot in oven and bake for about 2 hours or until ribs are tender. When done, remove the bones from the ribs. Place the meat on a hot platter and keep warm. Strain the sauce, pour it over the meat, and serve. If desired, reduce the sauce to a thicker consistency.

## RED FLANNEL HASH

serves 4

1½ cups cooked, chopped corned beef
½ cups cooked, chopped beets
3 cups cooked, chopped potatoes
1 small onion, finely chopped
   salt and pepper to taste
1 teaspoon Worcestershire sauce
   light cream as needed
¼ cup bacon drippings

In a large bowl combine the corned beef, beets, potatoes, onion, salt, pepper, and Worcestershire sauce with enough cream to bind ingredients together.

Melt the bacon drippings in a skillet and spread the meat mixture evenly in the bottom. Cook over low heat. Loosen around the edges and shake skillet occasionally to prevent bottom from scorching. When crust forms on the bottom, flip the hash over and brown on the other side. Remove from skillet and serve on a platter.

# BOILED LEG OF LAMB WITH CAPER SAUCE

serves 6 to 8

   1 *leg of lamb, about 5 to 6 pounds*
   2 *cloves garlic, cut into thin slivers*
   1 *teaspoon dried rosemary, crumbled*
   3 *quarts water*
   1 *tablespoon salt*
   1 *teaspoon pepper*
   1 *teaspoon dried thyme*
   1 *onion*
     *salt and pepper to taste*
Caper sauce:
   3 *tablespoons butter*
   3 *tablespoons flour*
1½ *cups lamb broth*
     *salt and pepper*
   1 *tablespoon lemon juice*
 ½ *cup capers*

Trim the leg of lamb of excess fat. Rub it with the salt and pepper. If desired, make 10 shallow incisions in the fat side of the lamb and insert the garlic slivers and rosemary.

Place the leg into a large, heavy pot containing 3 quarts of boiling water, 1 tablespoon salt, 1 teaspoon pepper, thyme, and rosemary. Bring the water back to a boil and simmer, partially covered, until the lamb is tender and pink. Allow 12 to 15 minutes per pound once the water has resumed boiling.

When lamb is done, transfer it to a platter and let it rest before carving. Prepare the caper sauce in the meantime.

In a deep saucepan, melt the butter, then stir in the flour and cook for about 3 minutes over low heat. Add the lamb broth and stir over heat until mixture is thickened. Season to taste. Add the lemon juice and capers and simmer for 2 minutes.

# ROAST LEG OF LAMB

serves 6 to 8

   1 *leg of lamb, about 5 to 6 pounds*
   2 *teaspoons salt*
 ¼ *teaspoon pepper*
     *fresh mint leaves*
   6 *cloves garlic, crushed*

Preheat the oven to 325°.

Trim the leg of lamb of excess fat. Place it, skin side down, on a rack in a shallow roasting pan. Season with salt and pepper and rub with crushed cloves of garlic.

Roast the lamb uncovered for approximately 3 hours, allowing 25 to 35 minutes per pound.

Serve on a warm platter garnished with mint leaves.

# NEW ENGLAND LAMB STEW

serves 4 to 6

*½ cup bacon drippings or butter*
*2 pounds stewing lamb, cut into 2-inch cubes*
*2 large onions, chopped*
*2 tablespoons flour*
*1 clove garlic, chopped*
*6 small white onions*
*1 bunch baby carrots, trimmed and left whole*
*1 tomato, chopped*
*½ cup lima beans*
*2 bay leaves*
*salt and pepper to taste*

In a large, deep saucepan melt the bacon dripping. Add the meat and onions, sprinkle with flour, and brown well.

Add the garlic, white onions, carrots, tomato, lima beans, and bay leaves to the saucepan. Add enough water to cover.

Simmer, covered, until meat is tender. Season to taste when meat is almost cooked.

# PENNSYLVANIA LAMB AND APPLES

serves 4

*4 medium apples, peeled, cored, and halved*
*juice of 1 lemon*
*1 cup sugar*
*½ cup water*
*2 pounds breast of lamb*
*¼ cup honey*
*¼ cup lemon juice*
*½ teaspoon salt*

Preheat the oven to 325°.

Place apples in bowl and add enough cold water to cover. Stir in the juice of 1 lemon. Be certain the apples are covered.

In a saucepan combine the sugar and ½ cup water. Simmer until the sugar is dissolved, then boil for 5 minutes. Drain the apple halves and simmer in the sugar syrup until glazed.

Place the lamb on a rack in a baking dish. Bake for 1 hour. Drain off fat and bake for 45 minutes longer. Arrange the apples around the lamb, reserving the syrup.

Combine the reserved syrup, honey, lemon juice, and salt in a bowl; pour over the lamb and apples. Roast 20 minutes longer.

# ROAST TURKEY WITH SAUSAGE AND SAGE DRESSING

serves 12 to 15

*1 14-pound turkey*
*1½ large loaves stale country bread, cubed*
*milk as needed*
*1 teaspoon salt*
*1 teaspoon pepper*
*3 teaspoons dried thyme*
*6 large sprigs parsley, chopped*
*2 large onions, finely chopped*
*3 stalks celery, finely chopped*
*4 tablespoons butter*
*18 pitted black olives, chopped*
*3 teaspoons dried sage*
*1¾ pounds fresh country sausage*

To make the dressing, place the bread cubes in a large mixing bowl and soak them in enough milk to moisten them.

In a medium skillet sauté the onions and celery together in butter until soft but not brown. Add to bowl with bread cubes.

In the same skillet, slightly brown the sausage, then break it into pieces with a fork. Add to the bread-cube mixture, Add the salt, pepper, thyme, parsley, sage, and olives. Blend well. Stuff the cavity of the turkey, sew the cavity shut, and truss the bird.

Immediately after stuffing, place the bird in a large roasting pan and cover it with several layers of cheesecloth soaked in butter. Bake the bird in a 325° oven for 5 hours or until the leg joint can be moved up and down with ease. Baste frequently through the cheesecloth during the roasting period with butter and natural juices from the bottom of the pan. Some applejack added to the basting juices gives a delightful flavor. Remove the cheesecloth during the last half-hour of roasting to allow the bird to brown.

## LONG ISLAND BRAISED DUCKLING

serves 4

  1 *large duckling*
1½ *tablespoons salt*
  1 *teaspoon pepper*
  1 *teaspoon coriander*
 ½ *cup white wine*

Quarter the duckling, rinse, and pat dry. Mix the salt, pepper, and coriander together and sprinkle over duckling pieces.

Sauté the duck, breast side down, in an ungreased heavy skillet over medium heat until browned. Cover the skillet and cook for 1¼ hours. Turn the pieces every 20 minutes. Do not pour off any of the fat during this time.

When duck is done, pour off the fat and remove pieces from skillet. Pour the wine into the pan and stir and scrape to blend all the browned particles into a pan gravy.

For an extra crisp skin on the duckling, place the cooked pieces under a medium-hot broiler for 2 minutes.

## QUAIL STUFFED WITH GRAPES

serves 4

  4 *quails*
  1 *lemon, cut in half*
  1 *teaspoon salt*
  1 *teaspoon pepper*
  4 *teaspoons butter*
1¼ *cups red grapes*
  4 *tablespoons butter*
 ½ *cup white wine*

Squeeze the lemon halves over the quails, then season with salt and pepper.

Stuff the cavity of each bird with ¼ cup grapes and 1 teaspoon butter. Let the birds dry for 15 to 20 minutes.

Heat 4 tablespoons butter in a heavy skillet. Add the quails and brown, turning often. Add the white wine and cover. Simmer for 15 to 20 minutes.

Add the remaining grapes and simmer 5 minutes longer. Spoon juices over birds before serving.

# QUAIL WITH MUSHROOM AND ONIONS

serves 6

6 *quails*

4 to 6 *tablespoons butter*

½ to 1 *pound mushrooms, sliced*

1 *medium onion, chopped*

2 *stalks celery, chopped*

½ *cup heavy cream*

½ *cup chicken broth*

⅓ *cup sherry*

Preheat the oven to 375°.

In a skillet, sauté the quails in butter until they are brown. Remove the birds from skillet and place in a casserole dish. Add the onions, mushrooms, and celery to the skillet and sauté until lightly browned. Add additional butter if needed. Spoon the mixture into the casserole with the birds.

Combine the heavy cream, chicken broth, and sherry in a bowl; pour over the birds. Cover the casserole and place in oven for 30 minutes.

# ROAST GOOSE

serves 4

1 *4- to 5-pound goose*

  *goose giblets and neck*

3 *stalks celery, cut into thirds*

½ *teaspoon dried rosemary*

½ *teaspoon pepper*

½ *teaspoon salt*

2 *cups water*

⅓ *cup white wine*

2 *cloves garlic, chopped*

1 *medium onion, chopped*

4 *tablespoons flour*

1 *cup sour cream*

  *salt, pepper, and paprika to taste*

Two hours before roasting goose (about 5 hours before you plan to serve the goose), combine the giblets, neck, celery, rosemary, salt, and pepper with the water and wine in a saucepan. Simmer the mixture until the giblets are tender. Set aside.

Preheat the oven to 325°. Rinse the goose and pat dry. Season the goose by gently rubbing it with salt, pepper, paprika, and chopped garlic.

Prick the goose all over with a fork and tie its legs together. Place on a rack in a shallow roasting pan. Roast uncovered for 1 hour. Remove from oven.

In a saucepan sauté the onion in 3 tablespoons of fat taken from the roasting pan. To this add 2 tablespoons flour and 1 cup of the hot giblet broth. Stir well. Combine the remaining flour with the sour cream and stir into the gravy. Pour mixture over goose. Cover and roast 1½ hours longer.

# GOOSE STUFFED WITH APPLES

serves 6

> 1  7- to 8-pound goose
> 1  tablespoon salt
> ½  onion, sliced
> 1½  pounds apples, peeled, cored, and quartered
> 1½  cups water
> 6  peppercorns
> 2  tablespoons flour
> ½  cup currants

Preheat the oven to 325°.

Rinse the goose and pat dry. Rub bird with salt inside and out.

In a small bowl mix the apples with the currants and stuff the goose with mixture. Sew the cavity closed.

Place the goose in covered roasting pan with the water, sliced onion, and peppercorns. Roast for 1 hour.

Remove the cover and continue cooking, basting with the drippings every 10 to 15 minutes. If the water boils down, add more by spoonfuls as needed to keep the fat from getting too brown.

The goose will need to roast for 2 to 3 hours longer before it is well done and crisp. Sprinkle a tablespoon of cold water over the skin to make it crisper.

To make a gravy for the goose, combine the flour with the pan drippings in a saucepan. Heat, stirring often, until gravy thickens.

# DUTCH OVEN BARBECUED CHICKEN

serves 4

> 1  2- to 3-pound broiling chicken
> ⅓  cup cider vinegar
> 1  teaspoon Worcestershire sauce
> 3  teaspoons onion, very finely chopped
> ½  teaspoon salt
> ½  teaspoon pepper
> ½  teaspoon paprika
> 1  clove garlic, chopped
> 1  tablespoon tomato paste
> ½  cup melted butter

Set the oven temperature to broil.

Split the chicken halfway down the back. Heat the broiling pan and rack and grease lightly.

Lay the chicken on the rack and put it under the broiler as close as possible to the heat. Remove the chicken as soon as it is seared on both sides (approximately 3 minutes a side).

In a small bowl combine the ingredients listed above to make the barbecue sauce.

Baste the chicken with the sauce and place it back under the broiler, this time a moderate distance from the heat. Baste at least 3 times as chicken cooks; it will be done in 35 to 40 minutes.

# CHICKEN POT PIE

serves 4 to 6

1 4-pound chicken, cut into serving pieces
1 stalk celery
1 carrot
1 onion
1 tablespoon salt

Dough:

2 cups flour
½ teaspoon salt
2 eggs
2 to 3 tablespoons water
4 medium potatoes, peeled and sliced
6 sprigs parsley, chopped

In a large pot place the chicken pieces, celery, carrot, onion, salt, and enough cold water to cover. Bring the mixture to a boil. Reduce heat, cover tightly, and simmer for 40 minutes or until chicken is almost tender when tested with a fork. Remove the vegetables and discard them. Leave the chicken in the pot with its broth while you make the dough.

Blend the flour and salt together into a bowl. In the center of this make a small well and drop the eggs in one at a time. Combine thoroughly with the fingers to make a stiff dough. Add 2 to 3 tablespoons water as needed.

Roll the dough out very thin on a lightly floured board and cut into 1-inch square pieces with a pastry wheel or sharp knife.

Bring the chicken and broth back to a boil. Drop the potato slices and pastry squares into the boiling broth, cover, and cook over moderate heat for 20 minutes. Sprinkle in the chopped parsley and serve.

# DUTCH BAKED CHICKEN

serves 6

3 small chickens, split
½ cup flour
2 eggs, beaten
2½ cups unseasoned bread crumbs
3 pounds lard
1 lemon, sliced

Preheat the oven to 375°.

Rinse the chickens and pat dry. Rub them with salt. Dip the chicken first in the flour, then in the beaten eggs, and then in the bread crumbs.

Heat the lard in a large, heavy, ovenproof pot. When it is hot, carefully place the chicken halves, one at a time so that the lard is not cooled too much and the coating is not loosened, into the pot. Place the pot in the oven and bake until chicken is golden brown, approximately 20 to 25 minutes.

When coating on chicken is hard, reduce heat to 325° and bake until well done, about another 20 to 25 minutes. Remove chicken from pot and drain on paper towels. Sprinkle lightly with salt and place on a serving platter. Garnish with lemon slices.

# PERFECT BROILED CHICKEN

serves 4

1 2½-pound broiling chicken
juice of 1 lemon
salt and pepper to taste
2 tablespoons butter

Split the chicken in half. Rinse and pat dry. Brush with lemon juice and sprinkle with salt and pepper. Place butter in the chest cavity.

Broil, split side up, 3 inches from heat for 15 to 20 minutes. Turn and broil on other side until done, about another 10 minutes.

# MARYLAND FRIED CHICKEN

serves 4

1  3- to 3½-pound frying chicken,
   cut into serving pieces
6  slices bacon
   vegetable oil for frying
¾  cup flour
1  teaspoon salt
¼  teaspoon pepper
2  tablespoons flour
1  cup milk
1  cup heavy cream

In a large skillet, fry the bacon until browned. Remove the bacon and drain on paper towels. Reserve.

Add sufficient vegetable oil to the bacon drippings to make a layer 1 inch deep in the skillet.

Place ¾ cup flour, the salt, and the pepper in a large plastic or paper bag. Shake well to blend. Place the chicken pieces in the bag and shake to coat the chicken with the flour mixture.

Heat the fat in the skillet. When it is bubbling hot, add the chicken pieces and fry, turning occasionally, until they are nicely browned on all sides.

Cover skillet, reduce heat, and cook over low heat for 25 minutes or until tender when tested with a fork. Remove the chicken and set aside, keeping it warm.

Drain all but 4 tablespoons of fat from the skillet. Stir in two tablespoons of flour and cook for about 3 minutes. Add the milk and cream. Continue cooking, stirring occasionally, until gravy is thick and smooth. Add salt and pepper to taste. Pour gravy over the hot chicken and garnish with the bacon strips.

# DUTCH LIVER OYSTERS

serves 4

1  pound fresh calf's liver
   water
2  teaspoons salt
2  eggs, beaten
½  cup bread crumbs
   vegetable oil for frying
1  lemon, cut in wedges

Place the liver in salted water to cover and boil for 30 minutes.

Cut the liver into pieces about the size of an oyster (about 1-inch square). Dip the pieces in the bread crumbs, then the beaten eggs, and then in the bread crumbs again. Deep fry in oil at 375° until well browned.

Remove pieces from oil and drain on paper towels. Serve with lemon wedges.

# Fish and Seafood

## LOBSTER NEWBURG

serves 4

    4 cups cold boiled lobster meat
    ½ pound butter
    ¼ cup dry sherry
    3 tablespoons flour
    1 cup heavy cream
    ½ teaspoon salt
    ⅛ teaspoon cayenne pepper

Cut the lobster meat into chunks. Melt ¼ pound butter in a skillet and sauté the lobster meat in it for 1 minute. Pour the sherry over the meat. Remove skillet from heat and set aside.

Place the remaining ¼ pound butter, flour, and cream in the top of a double boiler. The bottom half of the double boiler should contain hot but not boiling water. Stir the ingredients constantly until the sauce thickens and is smooth. Add the salt and cayenne and stir to blend. Add the lobster meat to the cream sauce and continue to cook for 10 to 15 minutes.

Remove from heat and cool. Chill in refrigerator for 24 hours and reheat before serving.

A steady patron of Delmonico's in New York City was a certain Mr. Wenburg, who invented this dish. But one day, Mr. Wenburg quarreled with Mr. Delmonico, who promptly changed the name of the dish to Newburg.

## BROILED LOBSTER

serves 4

    4 1- to 2-pound live lobsters
    ⅛ cup melted butter
      paprika
      bread crumbs
Sauce for basting:
    ½ pound butter
    1 clove garlic, crushed
    ½ teaspoon parsley, chopped

Split the live lobsters from head to tail and crack the claws. Place the lobsters on their backs in a broiling pan. Brush them with ⅛ cup melted butter. Be sure to brush the claws as well to keep them from drying out. Sprinkle paprika and bread crumbs over the exposed meat.

Place the pan under the broiler for about 10 minutes, being careful to avoid under- or overbroiling. Turn lobsters over and broil for about 8 minutes. As the lobster broils, baste it frequently with the sauce. Serve hot.

To make the basting sauce, melt ½ pound butter in a small saucepan. Stir in the garlic and parsley.

## BOILED LOBSTER

serves 4

    4 1- to 2-pound live lobsters
    4 quarts boiling water
    4 tablespoons salt
    6 whole peppercorns
    ¼ pound melted butter

Place the water in a large pot with the salt and peppercorns. Bring to a boil.

Wash the lobsters under cold running water. When the water is boiling rapidly, plunge the lobsters head-first into the water. Cover and bring the water back to a boil. Reduce heat and simmer 15 minutes for 1-pound lobsters or 20 minutes for 2-pound lobsters.

Remove the lobsters from the water and place in the sink until they are cool enough to handle. Serve whole with melted butter for dipping. If you wish to cut the lobster for easier handling, place it on its back and cut it in half from head to tail. Remove the stomach and intestinal vein.

## NEW YORK SAUTEED SCALLOPS

serves 4

1 *pint whole bay scallops*
¼ *cup flour*
½ *teaspoon salt*
½ *teaspoon pepper*
6 *tablespoons butter*
½ *cup white wine or dry vermouth*
2 *tablespoons chives, chopped*

Place the scallops on paper towels to dry.

In a small bowl, combine the flour, salt, and pepper. Add the scallops to the bowl and toss to coat on all sides. Shake off excess flour.

Heat the butter in a large skillet. Add the scallops. Sauté over medium heat, stirring frequently, for 4 to 5 minutes. Do not overcook. Remove the scallops to a heated serving platter.

Add the wine to the skillet. Bring to a boil, stirring and scraping to blend in the brown bits left in the pan. Pour the pan gravy over the scallops and sprinkle with chives.

## BOSTON FRIED SCALLOPS

serves 4

1 *pint whole bay scallops*
1 *egg*
¼ *cup milk*
2 *tablespoons flour*
½ *cup bread crumbs*
¼ *cup flour*
1 *cup olive oil*

Place the scallops on paper towels to dry. Dredge the scallops in flour.

In a small bowl, beat the egg and milk together. Dip the floured scallops into the mixture.

In another bowl, combine ¼ cup flour and the bread crumbs. Roll the scallops in the mixture.

Heat the olive oil to 375° in a deep skillet. Drop the scallops, a few at a time, into the oil. Fry until browned, about 4 minutes. Skim the oil and reheat as necessary.

Drain scallops on paper towels. Serve very hot.

# BLOCK ISLAND SCALLOP STEW

serves 4

2 pounds scallops
½ cup dry vermouth or white wine
1 clove garlic, chopped
5 tablespoons olive oil
2 cups Spanish red onions, thinly sliced
2 cups plum tomatoes, peeled and chopped
3 tablespoons butter
  salt and pepper to taste
2 tablespoons parsley, chopped

Place the scallops with their liquid in a small bowl. Add the vermouth and garlic and let stand for 30 minutes.

In a large skillet heat the olive oil. Sauté the onions until they are translucent and lightly golden. Add the tomatoes, cover, and cook until tomatoes soften.

Add the butter and scallops with marinade. Season with salt and pepper to taste. Simmer, uncovered, until scallops are opaque. Sprinkle with parsley and simmer 1 minute more. Serve hot.

# OYSTER FRY

serves 4

3 to 4 dozen oysters
1 cup fine bread crumbs
½ teaspoon salt
¼ teaspoon pepper
2 eggs
½ teaspoon Tabasco sauce
1 cup olive oil

Dry the oysters thoroughly on paper towels.

Combine the bread crumbs with the salt and pepper. Dip the oysters in the mixture.

In a small bowl beat the eggs and Tabasco sauce together. Dip the oysters in this mixture, then roll them in the bread crumbs again.

In a deep skillet, heat the olive oil to 375°. Fry the oysters until they are golden brown. Drain on paper towels.

# SCALLOPED OYSTERS

serves 6

1 quart oysters with liquid
1 cup corn flake crumbs
1 cup bread crumbs
½ teaspoon salt
¼ teaspoon pepper
2 tablespoons sherry
2 tablespoons light cream
½ cup butter, melted
1 clove garlic, crushed

Preheat the oven to 400°.

In a mixing bowl combine the corn flake crumbs and the bread crumbs. Add the salt and pepper. Stir in the sherry, cream, butter, and garlic.

Butter a shallow baking dish and place a layer of the crumb mixture on the bottom. Place a layer of oysters over this. Continue to fill dish with alternate layers of crumb mixture and oysters. Be sure not to have more than two layers of oysters. Pour the oyster liquid over the top. Top with crumbs and dot with butter. Bake for 30 minutes.

# BATTER SHRIMP

serves 4

  1 *pound shrimp, uncooked and shelled*
  3 *tablespoons olive oil*
  ¼ *teaspoon salt*
  ¼ *teaspoon pepper*
  2 *tablespoons lemon juice*
  1 *cup olive oil*
    *small skewers or long toothpicks*

Batter:
  1 *cup flour*
  1 *egg, beaten*
  ¾ *cup warm water*
  ¼ *teaspoon salt*

In a small bowl beat together 1½ tablespoons olive oil with ¼ teaspoon salt, pepper, and lemon juice. Place the shrimp in a bowl and pour this mixture over. Let stand for 30 minutes.

To make the batter, mix the flour and ¼ teaspoon salt in a bowl. In a separate bowl, combine the beaten egg, 1½ tablespoons olive oil, and water. Add gradually to flour, beating until smooth.

Skewer the shrimp and dip them into the batter. In a deep skillet, heat the olive oil to 375°. Fry the shrimp until they are golden brown. Drain on paper towels.

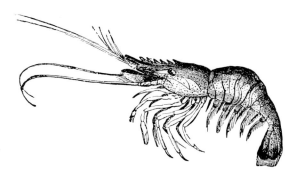

# FIRE ISLAND BROILED SOFT-SHELL CRABS

serves 6

 12 *live soft-shell crabs*
  ½ *pound butter*
  9 *tablespoons lemon juice*
  ⅛ *teaspoon cayenne pepper*
    *salt and pepper to taste*
  ½ *cup flour*

Sauce:
 1½ *tablespoons butter*
  1 *teaspoon flour*
  1 *cup fish stock or water*
    *salt and pepper to taste*
  2 *egg yolks, beaten*
  ¼ *cup cream*
  1 *tablespoon lemon juice*

Wash the crabs in cold water and dry well.

In a small saucepan melt the butter. Add the lemon juice and cayenne.

Sprinkle the crabs with salt and pepper. Dip them in the butter sauce and then dredge in the flour, shaking off the excess.

Lay the crabs on a broiler rack and place 4 inches from flame for 8 minutes, turning frequently.

To make the sauce, melt the butter in the top of a double boiler over hot but not boiling water. Blend in the flour; stir in fish stock or water. Simmer for 10 minutes and season with salt and pepper. Remove from heat. Add the egg yolks and the cream. Return to heat and cook, stirring constantly, for 3 minutes. Add the lemon juice and serve sauce immediately, poured over the crabs.

# FRIED SOFT-SHELL CRABS

serves 6

12  soft-shell crabs
 2  eggs, beaten
½  cup flour
½  teaspoon salt
¼  teaspoon pepper
½  cup butter

Wash the crabs in cold water and dry thoroughly.

In a small bowl, beat the eggs. In another bowl, combine the flour, salt, and pepper. Dip the crabs in the eggs and then dredge them in the flour mixture. Shake off the excess flour.

Heat the butter in a skillet over a low flame. Place in the skillet as many crabs as will lie flat at one time. Fry crabs until they are browned and crisp on the edges. Turn and fry until other side is browned. Serve very hot with butter.

# MARYLAND CRAB CAKES

serves 4 to 6

 3  tablespoons butter
¾  cup onion, finely chopped
 1  cup soft bread crumbs
 1  pound crabmeat, flaked and cleaned
 3  eggs, beaten
¾  teaspoon salt
 1  teaspoon dry mustard
 1  teaspoon Worcestershire sauce
 1  to 2 tablespoons light cream
½  cup flour
    olive oil for frying

In a large skillet melt the butter and add the onions. Cook until onions are soft but not brown, about 3 minutes. Remove skillet from heat and stir in bread crumbs and then crabmeat.

In a large bowl mix together the eggs, salt, mustard, and Worcestershire sauce. To this add the crab mixture and enough cream to hold the mixture together.

Shape the mixture into 12 cakes. Dredge the cakes in the flour.

Heat a ¼-inch layer of the olive oil in a large skillet. When hot add the crab cakes. Fry until golden brown, about 3 minutes a side. Serve with lemon wedges.

# SUNKEN MEADOW FRIED MUSSELS

serves 4

48  medium-sized mussels
 2  eggs, beaten
½  cup bread crumbs
 1  cup olive oil
    watercress and lemon slices for garnish

Scrub, rinse, and debeard the mussels.

Steam the mussels in a large pot until they open. Shell the mussels and reserve some of their liquid. Chill.

Dry the mussels thoroughly on paper towels. In a small bowl beat the eggs with 2 tablespoons of the cold mussel liquid. Dip the mussels in the egg mixture and roll in the bread crumbs.

In a deep skillet heat the olive oil to 375°. Fry the mussels until golden brown. Drain on paper towels. Serve hot, garnished with watercress and lemon slices.

# STUFFED STRIPED BASS WITH RAISIN SAUCE

serves 4 to 6

1  4- to 5-pound striped bass
2  cups bread crumbs
    hot water
2  tablespoons butter
1  tablespoon onion, chopped
1  tablespoon parsley, chopped
1  tablespoon capers
1  teaspoon salt
½  teaspoon pepper
1  egg, beaten

Raisin sauce:

2  tablespoons butter
2  tablespoons flour
1  teaspoon salt
¼  teaspoon pepper
1  tablespoon brown sugar
1½ cups water
¼  cup chopped raisins
¼  cup ground almonds
2  tablespoons grated horseradish
¼  cup fine bread crumbs
    juice of 1 lemon

Preheat the oven to 400°.

Clean, wash, and dry the fish.

In a mixing bowl moisten the bread crumbs with hot water. Remove crumbs from bowl and press dry in a clean towel. Return crumbs to bowl and add butter, onion, parsley, capers, salt, pepper, and egg. Stuff the fish with this mixture and sew cavity closed. Bake fish for 40 to 50 minutes, or 10 minutes a pound.

To make the raisin sauce, melt the butter in a saucepan and blend in the flour, salt, pepper, brown sugar, and water. Stir mixture until it begins to boil, then add the raisins, ground almonds, and horseradish. Heat thoroughly. Just before serving, add the bread crumbs and lemon juice. Arrange fish on serving platter and pour sauce over it.

# MONTAUK POINT BROILED BLUEFISH WITH SPICY SAUCE

serves 4

1½ to 2 pounds bluefish fillets
    salt and pepper to taste
2  tablespoons olive oil
2  tablespoons butter, melted

Sauce:

6  red pimentos, finely chopped
4  teaspoons tarragon vinegar
6  shallots, finely chopped
4  egg yolks, beaten
¾  cup butter, melted
½  teaspoon dried tarragon
½  teaspoon parsley, chopped

Season the fillets with salt and pepper.

Mix the olive oil and butter in a bowl and dip the fillets in the mixture. Place the fillets in a broiling pan and broil for 8 to 10 minutes for the first side and 5 to 8 minutes for the second side.

To make the spicy sauce, combine the pimentos, vinegar, and shallots in a saucepan and cook together until almost all the liquid is gone. Stir in the egg yolks.

*(continued on next page)*

Transfer the mixture to the top of a double boiler and cook, stirring constantly, over hot water until the mixture thickens. Add the melted butter little by little until the mixture is as thick as mayonnaise. Add tarragon and parsley. Serve on the side at once with fish.

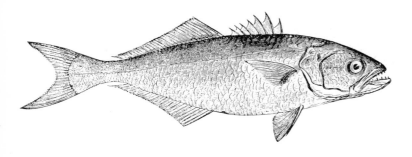

## BAKED BLUEFISH

serves 4 to 6

1 4- to 5-pound whole bluefish
  salt and pepper to taste
4 tablespoons mayonnaise
2 lemons, sliced
4 scallions, chopped (including green part)

Preheat the oven to 400°.

Clean, wash and dry the fish. Rub it with salt and pepper inside and out. Coat the fish with the mayonnaise inside and out.

Place the fish in a baking dish that has been lined with aluminum foil. Arrange the lemon slices on top of the fish and sprinkle the fish with the chopped scallions.

Bake fish for 40 to 50 minutes, or 10 minutes per pound.

## BROILED WEAKFISH

serves 4 to 6

6 weakfish fillets
2 tablespoons tarragon vinegar
2 tablespoons olive oil
¼ teaspoon pepper
½ teaspoon salt
1 lemon, quartered

Drawn butter sauce:
  3 tablespoons flour
  3 tablespoons butter, melted
  ¼ teaspoon salt
  ¼ teaspoon pepper
1½ cups hot water
  3 tablespoons butter, cut into small pieces
  1 teaspoon lemon juice

Wash and dry the fillets. Rub with the vinegar.

In a small bowl combine the oil, salt, and pepper. Roll the fillets in the oil mixture.

Place fillets in a greased broiler pan and broil slowly, turning frequently and basting with the olive oil.

To make the drawn butter sauce, combine the butter, melted butter, salt, and pepper in a medium saucepan. Slowly stir in the hot water and boil for 5 minutes. Lower the heat and add the pieces of cut-up butter alternately with the lemon juice. Stir well and serve hot over fish. Garnish with lemon quarters.

Weakfish is another name for sea trout.

# SOUTH YARMOUTH SWORDFISH

serves 4 to 6

    2 pounds swordfish steaks
    3 tablespoons olive oil
    ¼ teaspoon paprika
    ½ teaspoon salt
    12 teaspoons corn meal
    4 teaspoons flour

Wipe but do not wash the fish. Pour olive oil into a shallow baking dish and blend in paprika and salt.

Place the swordfish steaks in the dish one at a time and turn to coat both sides with the oil mixture. Place the fish in a shallow dish and sprinkle with a mixture of the corn meal and flour.

Return the fish to the baking dish and bake in a 350° oven for 5 minutes. Remove the pan from the oven and place it under the broiler until the coating is golden brown, about 15 to 20 minutes. Do not turn fish as it broils.

# SWORDFISH AND APPLES

serves 4

    1½ pounds swordfish steaks
    2 tablespoons butter
    4 tablespoons light brown sugar
    2 apples, peeled, cored, and finely chopped
    ½ teaspoon grated nutmeg

In a large skillet, melt the butter. When it is completely melted, add the brown sugar and mix well. Add the chopped apples and nutmeg. Stir and cook for 1 minute.

Move about one-quarter of the apple mixture to the side of the skillet. Place the fish in the skillet on top of the apple mixture. Place the reserved apple mixture on top of the fish.

Cover the skillet and simmer for 6 minutes or more, depending on the thickness of the swordfish steaks. When the fish flakes easily, it is done.

# CIDER FLOUNDER

serves 4

    6 flounder fillets
      salt and pepper to taste
    3 tablespoons shallots, chopped
    2 to 3 cups apple cider
    3 tablespoons butter
    2 tablespoons flour
    1 teaspoon chopped parsley

Preheat the oven to 375°.

Wash and dry the flounder fillets. Sprinkle with salt and pepper.

Place the fillets in a buttered baking dish and sprinkle with shallots. Add just enough cider to cover and bake for 20 minutes. Remove flounder to a hot serving platter.

Pour the liquid in the baking pan into a saucepan. Add the butter, heat, and blend in the flour. Stir until sauce begins to thicken, then cook 5 minutes longer, stirring occasionally. Add the parsley and pour sauce over the fish.

# BROILED BLOWFISH

serves 4 to 6

6 *blowfish tails*
  *melted butter*
Maitre d'hotel sauce:
  2 *teaspoons parsley, chopped*
  5 *tablespoons butter, softened*
  1 *tablespoon lemon juice*
    *salt and pepper to taste*

Clean and wash the blowfish tails. Carefully remove the small fillets.

Place the fillets in a broiling pan and brush with melted butter. Broil until done, about 15 to 20 minutes.

To make the maitre d'hotel sauce, cream the parsley with the softened butter in a small bowl. Add the salt, pepper, and lemon juice. Blend thoroughly.

Serve fish with maitre d'hotel sauce spread on it. This sauce is excellent for any broiled fish.

# CRANBERRY-STUFFED MACKEREL

serves 4

2 *mackerel, totalling 3 pounds*
½ *pound cranberries*
4 *tablespoons bread crumbs*
4 *tablespoons butter*
1 *teaspoon anchovy paste*
  *salt and pepper to taste*
⅛ *teaspoon cayenne pepper*

Preheat the oven to 350°.

Clean and wash the mackerel. Split them down the spine and remove bones.

Chop the cranberries coarsely. In a mixing bowl, combine the cranberries, bread crumbs, butter, anchovy paste, salt, pepper, and cayenne.

Stuff each mackerel with the cranberry mixture. Wrap the fish in aluminum foil and place in a buttered baking dish. Bake for 30 minutes. Carefully remove foil and serve.

If gooseberries are available, substitute them for the cranberries.

# CRAB-STUFFED HADDOCK

serves 4

1 *3-pound haddock*
1½ *cups crabmeat, flaked*
¼ *cup celery, finely chopped*
½ *cup tart apple, finely chopped*
1 *tablespoon green pepper, chopped*
1 *cup bread crumbs*
1 *egg, beaten*
2 *tablespoons butter, melted*
1 *lime, sliced*

Preheat the oven to 400°.

Clean, wash, and dry the haddock.

In a mixing bowl, combine the crabmeat, celery, apple, pepper, bread crumbs, and egg. Stuff the haddock with the mixture. Close the cavity with skewers and twine.

Place the fish in a buttered baking dish. Bake 35 minutes. Garnish with lime slices and parsley sprigs.

# PLANKED CONNECTICUT SHAD

serves 4 to 6

> 3 to 4 pounds shad
> melted butter
> salt and pepper to taste
> ¼ cup butter
> 1 tablespoon lemon juice

Clean and split the shad. Place fish skin-side down on an oiled and preheated plank. Brush fish with melted butter and sprinkle with salt and pepper.

Broil fish for 15 to 20 minutes, or until tender. Place fish on a serving platter.

In a mixing bowl, cream the butter until softened. Add the lemon juice slowly, creaming until it is entirely blended. Spread mixture over cooked fish and serve at once.

If a plank is not available, use a broiler-proof platter.

# MANHATTAN-STYLE MUSTARD SHAD ROE

serves 4

> 2 large shad roe
> 4 tablespoons butter
> Mustard sauce:
> 2 teaspoons butter
> 1 teaspoon dry mustard
> 6 tablespoons heavy cream
> ½ teaspoon lemon juice
> salt and pepper to taste

Parboil the roe for 2 to 3 minutes. Remove roe from water and place in a broiling pan. Dot roe with 4 tablespoons butter. Broil each side for 5 minutes or until brown. Remove from broiler.

To make the mustard sauce, blend the mustard and butter together in a small saucepan. Add the cream and simmer for 10 minutes. Stir in the lemon juice, salt, and pepper. Pour sauce over roe.

# BROILED SALMON STEAKS WITH LEMON BUTTER

serves 4

> 4 salmon steaks
> 1 teaspoon salt
> ½ teaspoon pepper
> ¼ cup butter, melted
> ¼ teaspoon grated lemon rind
> ¼ lemon juice
> 1 lemon, sliced

Preheat the broiler.

Sprinkle the salmon steaks on both sides with the salt and pepper. Place steaks in a broiling pan lined with aluminum foil.

In a small bowl, mix together the melted butter, lemon rind, and lemon juice. Brush the fish lightly with the mixture.

Broil fish 2 inches from flame for 5 to 6 minutes or until slightly browned. Brush the fish again with the lemon mixture, turn carefully, and brush the other side. Broil 5 to 6 minutes longer or until fish flakes easily. Brush with the remaining lemon mixture and serve garnished with lemon slices.

## COD BROILED IN LEMON BUTTER

serves 4

2 pounds codfish fillets
6 tablespoons butter, melted
1 teaspoon salt
½ teaspoon pepper
2 tablespoons soft fresh bread crumbs

Preheat the broiler to its highest temperature.

In a baking dish mix the melted butter, lemon juice, salt, and pepper. Dip the cod fillets in the mixture until they are coated on both sides. Arrange the fillets in one layer in the dish.

Broil the fish 3 to 4 inches from the flame for 5 minutes. Baste the fillets with the pan liquids. Sprinkle the bread crumbs over the fillets and broil for 5 minutes longer or until the fish flakes easily.

Serve fish at once with some of the pan liquids poured over it.

## TILE FISH SIMMERED IN WINE

serves 4

3 pounds tile fish steaks
1 cup white wine or dry vermouth
   salt and pepper to taste
4 tablespoons butter
2 tablespoons olive oil
2 tablespoons French mustard
2 tablespoons lemon juice
4 tablespoons light cream

Wash and dry the tile fish steaks. Sprinkle with salt and pepper on both sides.

Melt butter in a large skillet and blend in olive oil. Place steaks in skillet and lightly brown on both sides. Add the wine and simmer, covered, for 5 to 8 minutes.

To make the sauce, mix together in a saucepan the mustard, lemon juice, and cream. Heat thoroughly and pour over fish.

## CHILLED POACHED SALMON STEAKS

serves 6

6 salmon steaks
4 cups water
5 whole black peppercorns
1 tablespoon lemon juice
1 tablespoon lime juice
1 cup cucumber, finely grated
½ cup sour cream
¼ cup mayonnaise
1 tablespoon minced parsley
1 tablespoon onion, finely chopped
2 teaspoons vinegar
   salt and pepper to taste

In a large pot place the salt, peppercorns, lemon juice, and lime juice and bring to a boil. Add 3 salmon steaks and simmer for 10 minutes. Remove and repeat with the remaining steaks. Chill.

To make the sauce, in a mixing bowl combine the cucumber, sour cream, mayonnaise, parsley, onion, vinegar, salt, and pepper. Mix well and chill.

This is a traditional Fourth of July dish in New England.

# BAKED HALIBUT

serves 4

3 pounds halibut fillets
12 tablespoons butter
4 tablespoons lemon
1 teaspoon salt
½ teaspoon pepper
6 scallions, chopped (including green parts)
5 tablespoons parsley, chopped

Preheat the oven to 350°.

Wash and dry the fillets.

Melt the butter in a saucepan over low heat. Stir in the lemon juice, salt, pepper, scallions, and parsley. Pour half this sauce into a shallow baking dish. Place the fillets in the dish and pour the remaining sauce on top. Bake 15 to 20 minutes or until fish flakes easily.

# ACORN SQUASH WITH RUM BUTTER GLAZE

serves 6 to 8

4 large acorn squash
½ cup butter
⅔ cup water
½ cup light rum
1 cup dark brown sugar, firmly packed
    rind of 1 large orange, grated

Preheat the oven to 350°.

Trim the ends from the squash. Cut each squash into 4 rings. Remove the seeds.

Place the rings side-by-side in 2 buttered shallow baking pans. Add ⅓ cup water to each pan. Cover with foil and place in the oven for 40 to 45 minutes or until almost tender. Remove foil.

Melt the butter in a saucepan. Add the rum, brown sugar, and orange rind and stir well. Pour one-quarter of the mixture into each pan. Lift rings to allow liquid to run underneath. Bake uncovered for another 10 minutes. Turn the rings and pour the remaining butter and rum mixture over them.

Bake another 10 minutes. Serve rings on platter with pan juices poured over them.

# STUFFED ACORN SQUASH

serves 5 to 6

3 acorn squash
1 cup unsweetened applesauce
⅓ cup light brown sugar
1 tablespoon lemon juice
⅓ cup mixed dark and golden seedless raisins
¼ cup walnuts, coarsely chopped
2 tablespoons butter
   hot water

Preheat the oven to 400°.

Cut the squash in half lengthwise. Remove the seeds and stringy pulp.

In a mixing bowl combine the applesauce, brown sugar, lemon juice, raisins, and walnuts. Spoon mixture into squash halves. Place squash in a baking dish and add enough hot water to cover the bottom of the dish. Dot with butter.

Cover and bake for 25 minutes. Remove cover and bake 30 minutes longer or until squash is tender.

# HUBBARD SQUASH PIE

serves 5 to 6

2 cups cooked mashed Hubbard squash
¾ cup light brown sugar, firmly packed
¾ teaspoon cinnamon
½ teaspoon grated nutmeg
¼ teaspoon ground ginger
½ teaspoon salt
3 tablespoons melted butter
1 tablespoon molasses
2 eggs, beaten
2 cups milk, scalded
   pastry for 1 9-inch pie crust

Preheat the oven to 450°.

In a large mixing bowl combine the squash, sugar, cinnamon, nutmeg, ginger, salt, melted butter, molasses, eggs, and milk. Blend thoroughly. Turn mixture into a 9-inch pie pan lined with pastry.

Bake for 20 minutes. Reduce heat to 350° and bake for 35 minutes longer or until filling is firm to the touch.

# EASTERN SHORE CORN FRITTERS

serves 4

2 eggs, separated
2 cups fresh corn kernels, cut from the cob
2 tablespoons sugar
½ teaspoon salt
1 slice stale bread, crumbled
   butter

In a mixing bowl combine the egg yolks, corn kernels, sugar, salt, and bread crumbs.

In another bowl, beat the egg whites until they are stiff but not dry. Carefully fold the corn mixture into the egg whites.

Heat a griddle or skillet. Add enough butter to fry the fritters. When the butter has melted, add the fritters. Form the fritters by molding a tablespoon of the batter gently in your hands. Fry one side at a time until golden brown. Add additional butter as needed. Serve immediately.

## NEW ENGLAND FIDDLEHEADS

serves 4

*1 pound fiddleheads*
*2 cups water*
*1 tablespoon lemon juice*
*2 tablespoons butter*
*½ teaspoon salt*

Remove fuzz from fiddleheads and wash.

In a large skillet, bring the water to a boil. Drop in the fiddleheads and simmer, uncovered, until tender, about 30 minutes.

Drain the water, leaving the fiddleheads in the skillet. Add the lemon juice, butter, and salt. Shake skillet to distribute the butter and salt. Serve warm.

Fiddlehead ferns grow wild in New England in the very early spring. Frozen fiddleheads are often found in well-stocked supermarkets.

## DUTCH POTATO CROQUETTES

serves 4

*1½ cups cold mashed potatoes*
*1 tablespoon butter*
*1 teaspoon parsley, chopped*
*2 tablespoons light cream*
*¼ teaspoon salt*
*½ teaspoon onion, chopped*
*⅛ teaspoon cayenne pepper*
*1 egg, separated*
*olive oil or butter*
*bread crumbs*

Combine the potatoes and butter in a mixing bowl. Mix into a paste. Add the parsley, salt, cayenne, cream, onion, and egg yolk.

Shape the mixture into small patties or croquettes. Dip the patties into the beaten egg white, then roll in bread crumbs to coat.

Heat the oil or butter in a skillet. Fry the patties until golden brown on both sides. Add additional oil as needed. Serve hot.

## DUTCH BAKED CORN

serves 4

*4 ears fresh corn or 1 17-ounce can of corn*
*1 tablespoon butter*
*2 tablespoons flour*
*1 cup milk*
*2 eggs, separated*
*2 teaspoons sugar*
*1 teaspoon salt*
*1 teaspoon pepper*
*1 teaspoon paprika*

Preheat the oven to 350°.

In a saucepan melt the butter. Mix in the flour and pour in the milk gradually. Bring to a boil. Add the corn, the sugar, salt, pepper, paprika, and egg yolks. Mix well.

In a separate bowl beat the egg whites until they are stiff but not dry. Fold the egg whites into the corn mixture.

Place the mixture in a buttered casserole dish and bake for 30 minutes. Serve hot.

# GREEN PEAS AND NEW POTATOES

serves 4

¼ pound salt pork or bacon
2 small onions, chopped
8 small new potatoes
2 cups cooked fresh peas
1 cup heavy cream

In a small skillet fry the pork or bacon slices until crisp. Remove meat from skillet and add onions. Cook until lightly browned.

Scrub but do not peel the potatoes. Place them in a saucepan, add pork and onions and just enough water to cover. Cook, covered, for 20 minutes.

Remove the pork slices. Add the peas to the potatoes and onions. Pour cream over the vegetables and simmer until well blended.

# BRAISED TURNIPS

serves 6

1½ pounds turnips, peeled and cut into matchsticks
½ cup sweet butter
⅓ cup beef broth
1 tablespoon lemon juice
3 tablespoons parsley, chopped
salt and pepper to taste

Sauté the turnips in the butter in a large skillet, stirring occasionally, for 3 minutes. Stir in the beef broth and lemon juice. Braise the turnips, covered, over low heat for 8 minutes, or until they are tender. Stir in the parsley and salt and pepper to taste.

# NEW ENGLAND HASHED BROWN POTATOES

serves 4

2 cups cold baked potatoes, skinned and chopped
1 small onion, chopped
¼ teaspoon salt
¼ teaspoon pepper
⅓ cup salt pork fat, butter, or bacon fat

Combine the potatoes, onion, salt, and pepper in a mixing bowl.

Heat the fat in a skillet. When it is very hot, add the potato mixture. Cook 3 minutes, stirring constantly.

Reduce heat and cook until potatoes are brown and crisp on the bottom. Fold like an omelet and serve.

# FRIED MUSHROOMS

serves 4 to 6

1 pound fresh small mushrooms
1 egg, beaten
bread crumbs
salt to taste
olive oil

Wash and dry the mushrooms.

Dip the mushrooms in the beaten egg and then in the bread crumbs.

Place the oil in a deep skillet and heat it to 375°. Fry mushrooms until brown. Drain on paper towels. Season with salt.

# NEW ENGLAND SCALLOPED TOMATOES

serves 4 to 6

½ *cup butter*
1 *medium onion, chopped*
2 *cups fresh or canned tomatoes, chopped*
1 *teaspoon salt*
1 *tablespoon sugar*
½ *teaspoon pepper*
2 *cups bread crumbs*

Preheat the oven to 375°.

In a skillet melt 2 tablespoons butter. Add the onion and cook until translucent but not brown.

In a mixing bowl combine the onions, tomatoes, salt, sugar, and pepper.

Butter a baking dish. Place a layer of the tomato mixture in the dish, followed by a layer of bread crumbs. Repeat, alternating layers, and ending with a layer of crumbs. Dot with remaining butter. Bake for 30 to 40 minutes.

# PAN-FRIED TOMATOES

serves 4

3 *large firm tomatoes*
¼ *cup flour*
¼ *cup butter*
*salt and pepper to taste*

Cut the tomatoes into ½-inch slices. Do not peel.

Place the flour in a small bowl and dip the tomato slices into it.

Melt the butter in a skillet and add the tomatoes. Sauté until brown on both sides. Sprinkle with salt and pepper and serve.

# GLAZED PARSNIPS

serves 6

2 *pounds parsnips*
½ *cup butter*
*salt to taste*
½ *cup maple syrup*

Wash the parsnips. Place them in a saucepan and cover with water. Boil until parsnips are tender when tested with a fork.

Remove parsnips from water. When cool, peel, halve, and remove cores.

Melt the butter in a skillet. Add the parsnips and sprinkle lightly with salt. Add the maple syrup. Cook, turning once, until the parsnips are slightly browned and glazed.

# EASTERN-STYLE SWEET POTATO CASSEROLE

serves 6

6 *parboiled sweet potatoes, peeled and halved*
2 *cups apples, peeled, cored, and thinly sliced*
½ *cup Vermont maple syrup*
½ *teaspoon salt*
1 *tablespoon lemon juice*
3 *tablespoons butter*

Preheat the oven to 350°.

*(continued on next page)*

In a buttered, 1-quart baking dish, arrange layers of the sweet potato and apple.

In a bowl, combine the maple syrup, salt, and lemon juice. Pour over the sweet potato mixture in the baking dish. Dot with butter and bake for 45 minutes.

# HARVARD BEETS

serves 6

12 small fresh beets
½ cup sugar
2 teaspoons cornstarch
½ cup wine vinegar
2 tablespoons butter

Cut the tops from the beets, leaving 1 inch of stem. Wash the beets and place them in a saucepan with enough cold water to cover. Bring to the boil. When water begins to boil, cover the saucepan and reduce the heat. Simmer until beets are tender. Test often with a fork.

When beets are done, remove from water. Peel the beets (the skins should slip off easily). Cut them into slices or julienne strips and place in a large saucepan.

Combine the sugar, cornstarch, and vinegar in a small saucepan. Bring to a boil and simmer for 4 to 5 minutes. Pour over the beets and heat through very slowly. Shake the saucepan several times during this time. Just before serving the beets, add the butter and let it melt into the sauce.

# SUCCOTASH

serves 4

3 tablespoons butter
2 cups cooked lima beans
2 cups corn, fresh, canned, or frozen
½ cup water
1 teaspoon salt
1 teaspoon sugar
½ teaspoon pepper
¼ cup light cream

Melt the butter in a saucepan. Add the lima beans and the corn. (If using fresh corn, cook it first.) Toss lightly until coated with butter.

Add the water, salt, sugar, and pepper. Cover and cook over low heat until water is absorbed.

Stir in the cream. Cook over low heat until thoroughly heated. Serve hot.

The Narragansett Indians taught the Pilgrims how to make succotash. The dish was served at the first Thanksgiving dinner.

## GLAZED ONIONS

serves 4 to 5

10  medium onions
10  teaspoons honey
 4  tablespoons butter
½  teaspoon salt
¼  teaspoon pepper

Preheat the oven to 450°.

Cut the onions in half horizontally.
Butter each onion and arrange
in a buttered baking dish, cut-side
up. Add the salt and pepper.

Pour 1 teaspoon honey over each onion.
Dot with butter.

Bake uncovered for 45 minutes.

## CONNECTICUT SPINACH

serves 4

 2  pounds fresh spinach
¼  teaspoon fresh or ½ teaspoon dried rosemary
 1  scallion, chopped (including green part)
 2  tablespoons butter
    salt and pepper to taste

Wash the spinach carefully to remove all
grit. Remove the tough stems.

Chop the spinach coarsely and place it in
a large saucepan with the rosemary,
scallion, butter, salt, and pepper. Cook,
covered, for about 5 minutes or until
spinach is limp but still bright green. Do
not add any water to the saucepan; the
spinach will cook in its own juices.

# ⇒⟶ Noodles, Grains, and Beans ⟵⇐

## MACARONI AND CHEESE BAKE

serves 4 to 6

½  pound macaroni
 8  to 10 tablespoons butter
    salt and pepper to taste
1½  cups shredded sharp Cheddar cheese
1½  cups hot milk
    buttered bread crumbs

Preheat the oven to 350°.

In a large pot filled with boiling salted
water, cook the macaroni until just
tender. Drain thoroughly.

Butter a 2-quart baking dish and arrange
in it alternate layers of the macaroni,
butter, and shredded cheese. Pour hot
milk over the casserole. Top with cheese
and sprinkle with the bread crumbs.

Bake for 30 to 35 minutes or until the
cheese is melted and the macaroni is
heated through.

# KIDNEY BEAN BAKE

serves 4 to 6

    1  pound dried red kidney beans
  1½  quarts water
    ½  pound salt pork or bacon
    1  cup Vermont maple syrup
    ½  cup tomato sauce or ketchup
    1  teaspoon salt
    ½  teaspoon dry mustard
    ¼  teaspoon pepper
    1  small onion, chopped
       boiling water

Place the beans in a saucepan, add water, and sprinkle with salt. Bring to a boil, reduce heat, and simmer 5 to 10 minutes. Drain and rinse beans with cold water.

Put half the beans in a bean pot, heavy casserole, or iron pot. Slice the salt pork and add to beans. Then add remaining beans.

In a small bowl mix the maple syrup, tomato sauce, salt, dry mustard, pepper, and onion. Pour mixture over the beans. Add enough boiling water to cover the beans. Cover the bean pot.

Bake at 300° for 4 hours or until beans are tender. Add water during this time if necessary. To brown the top, remove the cover for the last half hour.

# BOSTON BAKED BEANS

serves 5 to 8

    4  cups pea beans
    1  medium onion
    ½  pound salt pork
    ½  cup dark brown sugar, firmly packed
    ⅓  cup molasses
    1  tablespoon salt
    1  teaspoon dry mustard

Soak the beans overnight in 12 cups of cold water. Drain and place in a saucepan. Cover with fresh water and slowly bring to a boil. Simmer until beans are tender, about 1 hour or longer. Test for doneness by scooping up a few beans in a spoon and blowing on them. If the skins blow off, the beans are done.

Drain the beans and place 1 cup in a bean pot, heavy casserole, or iron pot. Add the onion and cover with the remaining beans. Score the salt pork to the rind and push it down among the beans until it just shows through the top.

Combine the brown sugar, molasses, salt, and dry mustard and mix with the beans. Add enough hot water to fill the pot. The pork should protrude a little above the water line so that it can brown nicely.

Bake in a 300° oven for at least 8 hours. The juice should bubble at the top of the pot all day. Add more water if necessary during baking. Check beans every hour or so. Serve in the pot.

Baked beans are a traditional Saturday night Boston meal.

# LONG ISLAND RICE CASSEROLE

serves 4 to 6

    3 cups cooked rice
    1 cup spinach, chopped
    2 eggs, beaten
    1 cup milk
    1 teaspoon Worcestershire sauce
 1¼ teaspoons salt
    2 teaspoons onions, chopped
    ¼ cup butter
    ½ cup grated sharp Cheddar cheese

Preheat the oven to 325°.

In a large mixing bowl combine the rice and spinach. Add the eggs, milk, Worcestershire sauce, salt, and onion. Combine gently.

Place mixture in a buttered 2-quart baking dish. Dot with butter and sprinkle with cheese. Bake 30 to 40 minutes or until heated through.

# RICE WITH MUSSELS

serves 4 to 6

  48 mussels
    2 tablespoons butter
    2 tablespoons beef marrow
    2 onions, chopped
    1 cup uncooked rice
    ½ cup white wine
    ½ teaspoon saffron
       salt and pepper to taste
    ½ cup freshly grated Parmesan cheese
    4 tablespoons butter, melted

Wash and debeard the mussels. Place in a large pot with water and steam until mussels open. Remove the mussels from their shells and reserve liquid.

Melt the butter and beef marrow in a deep skillet. Add the onions and brown. Add the rice and 1 cup reserved mussel liquid. Stir well and cook for 15 minutes.

Add the remaining mussel liquid, adding enough water to make 2 cups. Then add the wine, saffron, salt, and pepper. Mix well and simmer for 20 minutes, stirring occasionally.

Add the mussels, mix well, and simmer for 10 minutes longer. When ready to serve, sprinkle with the cheese and butter.

# Breads

## PARKER HOUSE ROLLS

yields 24 rolls

½ cup scalded milk
½ cup boiling water
1 teaspoon salt
1 tablespoon butter
1 teaspoon sugar
1 package active dry yeast dissolved in ¼ cup lukewarm water
3 cups flour
½ cup melted butter

Preheat the oven to 400°.

Place the milk, water, salt, butter, and sugar in a mixing bowl and mix well. Add the yeast. Add the flour and mix until dough is stiff enough to knead. Cover and let dough rise until double in bulk, about 20 minutes.

Shape the dough into 24 balls and place on buttered cookie sheets or in muffin pans. Cover with a clean cloth and let rise in a warm place for 15 to 20 minutes or until doubled in bulk.

Before placing in the oven, flour the handle of a wooden spoon and press it against the balls until they are almost cut in half.

Brush one half of each ball with melted butter. Fold over the other half and press halves together. Let rise once more for 15 to 20 minutes.

Bake in oven for 15 minutes. Brush tops with butter after baking. Serve warm.

## CRANBERRY-NUT LOAF

yields 1 loaf

3 cups flour
4 teaspoons baking powder
¼ cup sugar
1 teaspoon salt
½ cup chopped walnuts
1 egg
1 cup milk
2 tablespoons melted butter
1 cup cranberries
¼ cup sugar
1 teaspoon almond or vanilla extract

Preheat the oven to 350°.

In a large bowl, mix the flour with the baking powder, ¼ cup sugar, and salt. Add walnuts and mix lightly.

In a small mixing bowl beat the egg, add the milk and butter, and mix well.

Chop the cranberries finely and mix with ¼ cup sugar. Add the cranberries and the almond extract to the egg mixture.

Stir the flour mixture into the egg-cranberry mixture. Mix until well-blended. Pour batter into a buttered 9 × 5 × 3-inch loaf pan. Bake for 1 hour or until bread tests done with a cake tester. When done, remove from oven and place pan on cooling rack. Cool in pan for 10 minutes; turn loaf out and continue to cool on rack.

# NEW ENGLAND GRIDDLECAKES

yields approximately 18 cakes

2 cups flour
4 teaspoons baking powder
½ teaspoon salt
2 tablespoons sugar
2 eggs
1¾ cups milk
2 tablespoons butter

In a large mixing bowl combine flour, baking powder, salt, and sugar.

Beat the eggs in another large bowl and add the milk. Melt the butter in a saucepan and add it to the egg-milk mixture. Blend in the dry ingredients. Stir gently only until ingredients are well mixed. Do not overbeat.

Heat an ungreased griddle over medium-high heat. Drop the batter from a large spoon onto the griddle. Cook about 1 minute on each side. The cakes will bubble on top and be dry around the edges; they are ready to be turned at this point.

Remove cakes from griddle when done and continue cooking until batter is gone. Serve hot with butter and pure maple syrup.

# POPOVERS

yields 12 popovers

1 cup flour
½ teaspoon salt
2 to 3 eggs, beaten (use 3 eggs if they are small)
1 cup milk
1 tablespoon melted butter

Preheat the oven to 450°.

Combine all the ingredients in a large mixing bowl. Beat with a spoon or mix in a blender until batter is completely smooth.

Fill each cup in a well-buttered preheated muffin pan one-third full. Place in the oven for 15 minutes. Reduce heat to 350° and continue baking for 20 to 25 minutes. Serve hot with butter.

Popovers pop when the steam that forms inside them expands as they cook. If your popovers don't pop, it is probably because the oven isn't hot enough or the batter doesn't have enough eggs in it.

# CORN MUFFINS

yields 12 muffins

2 cups yellow corn meal
1 teaspoon salt
2 cups rapidly boiling water
1 cup cold milk
2 eggs, beaten
4 teaspoons baking powder
2 tablespoons melted butter

Preheat the oven to 375°.

Combine the corn meal and salt in a mixing bowl.

Pour the *boiling* water over the corn meal. Stir immediately. It is crucial that the water be boiling when it is poured.

Add the milk immediately. Add the eggs and stir well. Mix in the baking powder and butter. Stir well.

Pour batter into greased muffin pans. Bake for 20 to 25 minutes or until golden brown.

# FRUIT BREAD (HUTZEL BROD)

yields 4 to 5 small loaves

2 eggs
3 cups dried pears
2 cups pear juice
1 pound dark seedless raisins, plumped
½ teaspoon salt
3 cups flour
1 cup dark brown sugar, firmly packed
1 package dry active yeast
⅓ teaspoon baking soda
½ cup butter
¼ cup lard
2 teaspoons cinnamon

Stew the dried pears gently for 30 minutes. hour in a medium saucepan. Drain the juice from the pears into a large bowl. Dissolve the yeast in ¼ cup warm water and add it to the juice. Set the pears aside.

Combine the flour and salt in a bowl. Add to the yeast-juice mixture. Cover and let stand overnight.

In the morning add to this mixture the baking soda dissolved in 1 tablespoon warm water. Mix the lard, butter, eggs, and sugar in a large bowl. Dice the pears, sift flour over them, and add to bowl. Add the raisins and cinnamon. Add additional flour as needed and knead.

Set the dough aside in a greased bowl. Cover and let rise for 1 hour or until nearly doubled in bulk.

When bread has risen, punch it down and knead for 1 minute. Shape the dough into 4 to 5 small loaves. Brush the tops with melted butter.

Place the loaves on a greased cookie sheet and bake in a 350° oven for 1¼ hours. Remove from oven when done and cool completely before serving.

# DUTCH CORN PANCAKES (WELSHKORN PFANNKUCHEN)

serves 4

2 cups milk
8 tablespoons corn meal
½ teaspoon salt
2 tablespoons butter
4 tablespoons flour
4 teaspoons baking flour
oil for frying

Scald the milk in a saucepan. Stir in the corn meal and the butter. Allow mixture to cool.

When cool, stir in the flour, adding enough cold milk to make a medium-thin batter. Add the baking powder.

Heat a griddle and grease it with the oil. Fry the pancakes until golden brown on both sides. Serve hot with butter.

# LANCASTER CORN MEAL MUSH

yields 2 to 3 molded loaves

3 cups corn meal
3 cups cold water
12 cups boiling water
salt to taste
oil or butter for frying

Mix the corn meal with the water in a very large pot. Heat the mixture and then add the boiling water. Stir constantly to break up lumps. Add salt to taste.

Boil the mixture for 35 minutes over moderate heat. When done pour into 2 or 3 greased loaf pans. Place pans in refrigerator. When corn meal is cold, cut it into thin slices. Fry the slices and serve with bacon.

## OLD-FASHIONED RHODE ISLAND JOHNNYCAKES

serves 6

1 teaspoon salt
1 tablespoon butter
1 cup yellow corn meal
1 cup boiling water
¼ cup milk
2 tablespoons bacon drippings or butter

Preheat the oven to 475°.

Place the corn meal in a mixing bowl. Add the salt and butter to the corn meal.

Pour the *boiling* water over the corn meal. Stir immediately. It is crucial that the water be boiling when it is poured. Add milk and stir until well mixed.

Melt the bacon drippings in an 8- or 9-inch round cake pan. Grease the sides of the pan and pour in the batter. Place the pan over heat until the batter begins to bubble around the edges.

Place the pan in the oven. Bake for about 30 minutes. After the first 10 minutes, dot the top with butter if desired.

## BOSTON BROWN BREAD

yields 3 loaves

1 cup rye flour
1 cup corn meal
1 cup whole wheat or graham flour
¾ teaspoon baking soda
1 teaspoon salt
¾ cup dark molasses
2 cups buttermilk
1 cup dark seedless raisins

Into a large bowl sift the rye flour, corn meal, whole wheat flour, baking soda, and salt. Add the molasses, buttermilk, and raisins. Stir well.

Divide the batter into 3 equal parts. Place each part into a buttered 1-pound coffee can, filling the can about three-quarters of the way full (large juice cans also work well). Cover the top of each can with buttered wax paper and then aluminum foil. Puff the foil and allow approximately 1 inch of space so that the bread has room to rise. Tie the foil and wax paper in place with string.

Place the cans on a rack set in a very large pot. Fill the pot with enough boiling water to reach three-quarters of the way up the cans. Return water to a boil, cover pot, reduce heat, and steam for 2½ hours. Check the pot occasionally and add water if needed to keep the water at the original level.

When bread is done, carefully remove cans and cool just enough to remove the bread. Serve the bread hot with butter.

The Pilgrims used to say, "Brown bread and Gospel is good fare."

## NEW ENGLAND HONEY BREAD

yields 2 loaves

1¼ cups milk
 2 teaspoons salt
 4 tablespoons butter
¼ cup honey
¼ cup sugar
 2 packages active dry yeast
½ cup lukewarm water
¼ teaspoon sugar
 1 large egg
 5 cups flour

In a large saucepan combine the milk, salt, butter, honey, and ¼ cup sugar. Cook over a low flame until the butter is completely melted.

Dissolve the yeast in the water with ¼ teaspoon sugar. Add to the heated milk mixture. Add the egg and flour. Combine thoroughly.

Knead the dough for 10 minutes. Place the dough in a large greased bowl. Cover with a clean cloth or a piece of plastic wrap. Place the bowl in the oven (do not light the oven) with a bowl of hot water underneath. Let the dough rise until doubled in bulk, approximately 1 hour.

Remove the dough from the oven and divide in half. Knead each half for 1 minute. Place the halves in greased 9 × 5 × 3-inch loaf pans. Place the pans in the oven with a bowl of hot water underneath until the dough rises above the edge of the pans. This should take about 1 hour.

Bake at 350° for 30 minutes or until bread is lightly browned, firm to the touch, and sounds hollow when tapped. Cool thoroughly before slicing.

## ANADAMA BREAD

yields 1 loaf

½ cup corn meal
 3 tablespoons butter
¼ cup dark molasses
 2 teaspoons salt
¾ cup boiling water
 1 package active dry yeast
¼ cup warm water
 1 egg, beaten
 3 cups flour

In a large bowl combine the corn meal, butter, molasses, salt, and boiling water. Mix well and allow to stand at room temperature until it is lukewarm.

Dissolve the yeast in a few tablespoons of lukewarm water. Stir it into the corn meal mixture. Stir in the egg and 1½ cups of flour. Beat well. Stir in the remaining 1½ cups flour and mix until the dough forms a soft ball. Use your hands to mix the dough if it is easier.

Place the dough in a greased 9 × 5 × 3-inch loaf pan. Cover with a clean cloth and set in a warm place until dough doubles in bulk, approximately 1 to 1½ hours. Sprinkle the top with a little corn meal and salt. Bake in a 350° oven for 50 to 55 minutes. Cool completely before slicing.

# INDIAN BREAD

*yields 1 loaf*

*½ cup flour*
*1½ cups corn meal*
*½ teaspoon salt*
*4 tablespoons sugar*
*2 eggs, beaten*
*1 cup sour cream*
*1 teaspoon baking soda*
*1½ cups milk*

Preheat the oven to 400°.

Combine the flour, corn meal, salt, and sugar in a large bowl. Add the eggs and sour cream and beat well until smooth.

Dissolve the baking soda in the milk in a small bowl. Add to the flour mixture and mix well.

Pour the mixture into a buttered 12-inch loaf pan. Bake for 25 minutes or until a cake tester comes out clean and the bread is lightly browned.

# OLD-FASHIONED RAISIN BREAD

*yields 1 loaf*

*1 cup dark seedless raisins*
*1 teaspoon baking soda*
*1 cup boiling water*
*1½ cups flour*
*½ cup sugar*
*½ teaspoon salt*
*1 egg*
*½ teaspoon vanilla extract*
*1 tablespoon vegetable oil*

Preheat the oven to 350°.

Combine the raisins and baking soda in a mixing bowl. Add the water, cover, and set aside until cool, about 1 hour.

In a medium mixing bowl stir together the flour, sugar, and salt. Add the raisins with their liquid, the egg, vanilla, and oil. Stir until well mixed.

Pour into a greased and floured 9 × 5 × 3-inch loaf pan and bake for 35 to 45 minutes, or until bread is lightly browned and firm to the touch.

# DELAWARE SPOON BREAD

*serves 4*

*1 tablespoon butter*
*1½ cups milk*
*½ cup yellow corn meal*
*2 eggs*
*2 teaspoons baking powder*
*1 teaspoon salt*

Preheat the oven to 350°.

Melt the butter in a 1-quart casserole in the oven.

In a saucepan, scald 1 cup milk. Mix in the corn meal. When mixture thickens, remove from heat and cool slightly.

Beat in ½ cup milk, eggs, baking powder, and salt. Pour the melted butter into the saucepan. Pour the entire mixture back into the casserole and bake for 1 hour or until golden.

# Desserts

## VERMONT MAPLE SYRUP CAKE

serves 8

⅓ cup butter
½ cup sugar
¾ cup pure Vermont maple syrup
2¼ cups flour
1 tablespoon baking powder
½ teaspoon salt
⅓ cup milk
3 egg whites
1 teaspoon vanilla extract

Preheat the oven to 350°.

In a mixing bowl cream the butter and sugar until light and fluffy. Add the maple syrup and mix well.

Combine the flour, baking powder, and salt. Add this to the butter mixture alternately with the milk.

In a separate bowl beat the egg whites until they are still but not dry. Fold into the batter. Add vanilla and mix.

Pour into a greased 9 × 5 × 3-inch loaf pan and bake for 35 minutes or until a cake tester inserted in the center comes out clean. Remove cake to a cooling rack. Cool in the pan for 15 minutes, then turn out onto rack and continue cooling.

When cake is cool, frost with Maple Nut Frosting.

## MAPLE NUT FROSTING

1 cup sugar
1 cup pure Vermont maple syrup
⅓ cup water
¼ teaspoon cream of tartar
1 egg white
½ cup chopped nuts

Place the sugar, maple syrup, water, and cream of tartar in a saucepan. Cook, stirring constantly, until mixture spins a thread when dropped from spoon.

Beat the egg white in a mixing bowl until it is stiff but not dry. Pour the sugar mixture slowly over the egg white, beating constantly. Continue to beat mixture until it is of spreading consistency.

Fold in nuts and spread frosting on cake.

## WELLESLEY FUDGE CAKE

serves 8 to 10

4 squares unsweetened chocolate
½ cup hot water
½ cup sugar
2 cups flour
1 teaspoon baking soda
1 teaspoon salt
½ cup butter
1¼ cups sugar
3 eggs
1 teaspoon vanilla extract
⅔ cup milk

Preheat the oven to 350°.

Combine the chocolate and water in the top of a double boiler. Cook over hot, not boiling, water until chocolate is melted. Add ½ cup sugar and cook for 2 minutes longer. Set aside.

Onto a large piece of wax paper sift the flour, baking soda, and salt. Sift together twice more and set aside.

Cream the butter in a mixing bowl. Add 1¼ cups sugar. Cream together until light and fluffy. Add the eggs, 1 at a time, beating well after each addition. Add the vanilla. Add the flour alternately with the milk, beating well after each addition. Begin and end with the flour. Add the chocolate mixture and blend well.

Pour the batter into 2 greased and floured 9-inch square pans. Bake for 25 to 30 minutes or until cake tester inserted into the center comes out clean. Cool pans on rack for 10 minutes. Turn out and continue to cool. When cool, frost with Fudge Frosting (see below).

Named for the famed New England women's college, this cake was served in village tearooms on Wellesley Square.

# FUDGE FROSTING

  4 squares unsweetened chocolate
1½ cups milk
  4 cups sugar
 ⅛ teaspoon salt
  4 teaspoons light corn syrup
 ¼ cup butter
  2 teaspoons vanilla extract

Place the chocolate and milk in a heavy saucepan. Cook over low heat, stirring constantly, until well blended.

Add the sugar, salt, and corn syrup. Stir until the sugar is dissolved. Boil the mixture over very low heat, stirring occasionally, until small amounts dropped into cold water form soft balls. This will be when the mixture is approximately 234° to 240° on a candy thermometer.

Remove the saucepan from heat. Add the butter and vanilla and mix well. Cool to lukewarm and then beat until creamy.

To frost the Wellesley Fudge Cake, place one layer top-side down on a cake plate. Spread with approximately one-third of the frosting. Place the second layer on top, right-side up, and frost the sides with approximately one-third the frosting. Then frost the top of the cake with the remaining frosting. Smooth frosting and swirl with a knife. Let frosting set before cutting cake.

# CAPE COD OATMEAL COOKIES

yields 36 cookies

  1 egg, beaten
 ½ cup sugar
 ¼ cup melted butter
 ¼ cup melted lard
  2 teaspoons molasses
  2 teaspoons milk
  1 cup rolled oats (not instant oatmeal)
 ¼ cup raisins
 ¼ cup chopped nuts
 ¾ cup flour
 ½ teaspoon cinnamon
 ¼ teaspoon baking soda
 ¼ teaspoon salt

(continued on next page)

Preheat the oven to 325°.

In a large mixing bowl combine the egg, sugar, melted buter, melted lard, molasses, and milk. Mix well.

In another bowl combine the oats, flour, cinnamon, baking soda and salt. Stir in the raisins and the nuts. Add to first mixture and combine until well blended.

Drop by heaping teaspoons about 2 inches apart onto greased baking sheets. Bake for 10 to 12 minutes or until browned. Cool cookies on racks.

# SNICKERDOODLES

yields 36 cookies

2 eggs
2 cups water
½ cup butter, softened
1 teaspoon vanilla extract
4 cups flour
4 teaspoons baking powder
1 teaspoon salt
1 cup milk
1 cup raisins, chopped
1 tablespoon sugar
1 teaspoon cinnamon

Preheat the oven to 350°.

Beat the eggs in a mixing bowl, gradually adding the sugar. Stir in the butter and add vanilla.

Combine the flour, baking powder, and salt. Add flour to egg mixture alternately with milk. Beat well after each addition. Stir in the raisins.

Drop by teaspoons about 1 inch apart onto greased cookie sheets. Combine 1 tablespoon sugar and the cinnamon. Sprinkle generously over the cookies. Bake for 20 minutes or until cookies are golden. Cool on racks.

# JOE FROGGERS

yields 48 to 60 cookies

1 cup butter
2 cups sugar
1 tablespoon salt
¾ cup water
¼ cup dark rum
2 teaspoons baking soda
2 cups dark molasses
7 cups flour
1 tablespoon ground ginger
1 teaspoon grated nutmeg
½ teaspoon ground cloves

Preheat the oven to 375°.

Cream the butter and sugar together in a mixing bowl until light and fluffy.

In a small bowl dissolve the salt in the water and mix in the rum. In another small bowl, add the baking soda to the molasses.

Combine the flour, ginger, cloves, and nutmeg. Add alternately with liquid ingredients to creamed butter and sugar. Stir well between additions. The dough will be sticky. Chill overnight in refrigerator.

Flour a work surface and rolling pin. Roll the dough out to ½-inch thickness. Cut into circles or shapes with a large cookie cutter. Place cookies 2 inches apart on greased cookie sheets. Bake for 10 to 12 minutes or until golden. Cool on racks.

# HERMITS

yields 72 cookies

½ cup sugar
⅓ cup butter
1 egg
3 cups flour
½ teaspoon salt
1 teaspoon cinnamon
½ teaspoon grated nutmeg
½ cup dark molasses
½ cup buttermilk
1 cup raisins

Preheat the oven to 350°.

In a mixing bowl cream together the sugar and butter until light and fluffy. Beat in the egg.

Combine the flour, salt, cinnamon, and nutmeg. Mix the molasses with the buttermilk. Add the molasses mixture alternately with the flour to the creamed sugar and butter. Stir in the raisins.

Drop by teaspoons approximately 1 inch apart onto a greased cookie sheet. Bake for 8 to 10 minutes, or until lightly browned. Cool on a rack.

# GINGERSNAPS

yields 60 cookies

4 cups flour
½ cup sugar
½ teaspoon salt
1 teaspoon ground ginger
½ cup butter
½ cup lard
1 teaspoon baking soda
1 tablespoon hot water
1 cup molasses

Preheat the oven to 350°.

Combine the sugar, salt, and ginger in a large mixing bowl. Cut in the butter and lard with a pastry blender, two knives, or your fingers. Blend until particles are like coarse crumbs.

Dissolve the baking soda in the water. Make a well in the center of the flour mixture and pour in the hot water and molasses. Mix well.

Form dough into a ball and wrap in aluminum foil. Chill thoroughly in refrigerator. Cut dough into slices ½ inch thick.

Place slices 2 inches apart on a greased cookie sheet. Bake for 5 to 7 minutes. Cool on a rack.

# NUT BROWNIES

yields 16 to 20 brownies

4 squares unsweetened baking chocolate
1 cup butter, cut into pieces
2 cups sugar
4 eggs
1½ cups flour
¼ teaspoon salt
1½ teaspoons vanilla extract
1½ cups coarsely chopped walnuts or pecans

Preheat the oven to 375°.

In the top of a double boiler over hot but not boiling water, melt the chocolate. Add the butter gradually, stirring well after each addition. Add the sugar and stir until completely melted. Remove from heat.

Drop in the eggs, 1 at a time, beating after each addition. Beat in the flour, salt, and vanilla extract. Add the nuts and stir.

Turn batter into a buttered and floured 9 × 9 × 2-inch square baking pan. Bake for 40 minutes or until brownies begin to shrink away from sides of pan. Do not overbake. Cool in pan, then cut into squares.

# MAINE DOUGHNUTS

yields 6 to 8 doughnuts

1 scant cup milk
⅓ cup sugar
1 egg, beaten
4 tablespoons butter
½ teaspoon baking powder
1 to 1½ cups flour
   lard for frying

In a large bowl combine the milk, sugar, egg, butter, baking powder, and flour. Mix together well, knead gently, and add more flour if necessary. Knead about 8 times and then roll dough out onto a lightly floured surface. Cut dough with a doughnut cutter.

Heat the lard to 370° in a deep skillet. Fry the doughnuts until brown and light. Drain on paper towels; sprinkle with sugar if desired.

Why do doughnuts have holes? One day half the crew of a New England fishing boat fell overboard after eating doughnuts and sank like stones. The captain was so annoyed that he punched holes in the doughnuts with a belaying pin; after that, he never lost a man.

# TOLL HOUSE COOKIES

yields 48 cookies

½ cup butter
½ cup sugar
¼ cup light brown sugar, firmly packed
1 egg, beaten
1 teaspoon vanilla extract
1 cup flour
½ teaspoon baking soda
½ cup chopped walnuts or pecans
6 ounces semisweet chocolate bits

Preheat the oven to 375°.

In a large mixing bowl cream the butter until soft. Gradually beat in the sugar and brown sugar, beating well after each addition. Beat in the egg and vanilla extract.

Add the flour and baking soda to the mixture. Stir until smooth. Stir in the nuts and chocolate bits, making sure they are evenly distributed throughout the batter.

Drop by scant teaspoons 2 inches apart onto lightly greased cookie sheets. Bake for 8 to 10 minutes or until edges are beginning to brown. Transfer to racks and cool.

The famous Toll House Inn in Massachusetts was established by Ruth Wakefield. This is her personal recipe.

# PHILADELPHIA CINNAMON BUNS

yields 12 buns

*4 cups flour*
*5 teaspoon baking powder*
*1½ teaspoons salt*
*¾ cup butter*
*½ cup light cream*
*2 eggs*
*1 cup brown sugar*
*1 teaspoon cinnamon*
*½ cup walnuts, finely chopped*
*½ cup raisins*
*2 tablespoons cream*

Preheat the oven to 400°.

In a large bowl combine the flour, baking powder, and salt. Cut the butter into this mixture, using a pastry blender or two knives, until the flour forms coarse crumbs.

In a separate bowl beat the eggs and add the cream. Add this to the flour mixture and mix well.

Roll out the dough onto a floured surface. Form it into a square ½ inch thick and approximately 12 × 12 inches square.

In a separate bowl mix together the brown sugar, cinnamon, chopped nuts, and raisins. Spread this evenly over the dough. Roll up like a jelly roll and pinch closed. Cut the roll with a sharp knife into 12 1-inch slices. Lay the slices on a buttered cookie sheet, brush with cream, and bake for 20 minutes or until brown.

# COLONIAL SPICE-AND-VINEGAR PIE

serves 8

*4 egg yolks*
*2 egg whites*
*1 cup sugar*
*¼ cup flour*
*½ teaspoon grated nutmeg*
*½ teaspoon cinnamon*
*½ teaspoon ground cloves*
*¼ teaspoon salt*
*1 cup sour cream*
*3 tablespoons melted butter*
*3 tablespoons cider vinegar*
*1 cup chopped walnuts or pecans*
*1 cup raisins*
*1 pastry for 9-inch pie*

Bake the pie crust in a preheated 450° oven for 10 minutes. Remove from oven and set aside. Turn oven down to 400°.

In a small bowl, beat the egg yolks.

In a separate bowl, beat the egg whites until they are stiff but not dry. Fold the sugar into the whites and mix with the yolks.

Combine the flour with nutmeg, cinnamon, cloves, and salt in a large bowl. Add alternately with the sour cream to the egg mixture. Add the butter and vinegar. Fold in the nuts and raisins and stir to distribute them evenly.

Pour the batter into the pie crust. Bake for 5 minutes at 400°. Reduce heat to 350° and bake until filling begins to get firm, about 15 minutes. Remove from oven. Cool and top with whipped cream.

# APPLE FRITTERS

serves 6

*½ cup flour*
*½ cup sugar*
*⅛ teaspoon salt*
*2 teaspoons baking powder*
*2 eggs*
*½ cup milk*
*½ cup light cream*
*2 cups tart apples, peeled, cored, and finely chopped*
*oil for frying*
*confectioner's sugar*

In a mixing bowl combine the flour, sugar, salt, and baking powder. Beat in the eggs, milk, and light cream. Continue beating until batter is smooth. Stir in chopped apples.

Heat the oil in a deep skillet until it is hot, about 370° to 375° on a deep-fat thermometer. Drop the batter by teaspoons into the oil and fry until lightly golden brown. Drain on paper towels and sprinkle with confectioner's sugar. Serve with maple syrup or honey.

# INDIAN PUDDING

serves 6 to 8

*3 tablespoons yellow corn meal*
*⅓ cup dark molasses*
*3 cups milk, scalded*
*½ cup sugar*
*1 egg, beaten*
*1 tablespoon butter*
*¼ teaspoon salt*
*½ teaspoon ground ginger*
*½ teaspoon cinnamon*
*1 cup cold milk*

Preheat the oven to 300°.

Scald the milk in a saucepan and stir in the corn meal and molasses. Cook over low heat until mixture thickens, stirring constantly.

Remove saucepan from heat and add the sugar, egg, butter, salt, ginger and cinnamon.

Pour into a buttered baking dish or casserole and bake for 30 minutes. After 30 minutes, pour cold milk into baking dish. Do not stir. Continue baking for 2 more hours. Serve warm with lightly sweetened whipped cream.

# RHUBARB PIE

serves 8

*2 cups rhubarb, cut up*
*1½ cups sugar*
*½ teaspoon salt*
*1½ tablespoons cornstarch*
*1 egg, beaten*
*2 tablespoons butter*
*2 pastries for 9-inch pies*

Preheat the oven to 425°.

Cut the rhubarb into 1-inch pieces. Do not peel. Place the pieces in a bowl and cover with boiling water for 1 minute. Drain and reserve.

Combine the sugar, salt, and cornstarch together in a mixing bowl. Add the egg. Add the rhubarb.

Place 1 of the pastries into a 9-inch pie pan. Fit well and crimp. Fill the shell with the rhubarb mixture and dot with butter.

Cut strips of dough with a sharp knife or pastry wheel from the second pastry. Make a lattice across the top of the pie pan and crimp the edges.

Bake for 35 to 40 minutes or until rhubarb is tender. Cool before serving.

# PUMPKIN PIE

yields 3 pies

3 eggs, beaten
1 cup sugar
3 cups purée of pumpkin or canned pumpkin
½ teaspoon salt
1 teaspoon cinnamon
½ teaspoon ground ginger
½ teaspoon grated nutmeg
2 tablespoons brandy
2 cups milk
3 pastries for 9-inch pies

To purée the pumpkin, stew it, drain well, and mash through a sieve.

Preheat the oven to 375°.

In a large bowl mix the beaten eggs, sugar, salt, cinnamon, ginger, nutmeg, milk, and brandy. Stir well.

To this mixture add the pumpkin. Stir until thoroughly combined.

Pour the pumpkin mixture into 3 9-inch pie plates lined with the pastries and bake for 40 to 45 minutes, or until a knife inserted halfway comes out clean. Cool before serving.

# BAY STATE PUMPKIN PIE

serves 8

1 cup purée of pumpkin, fresh or canned
3 eggs, separated
1 cup sugar
¾ cup milk
2 tablespoons melted butter
½ teaspoon salt
½ teaspoon ground ginger
¼ teaspoon grated nutmeg
1 teaspoon cinnamon
1 tablespoon unflavored gelatin
¼ cup cold water
1 pastry for 9-inch pie

Preheat the oven to 450°.

Place the pastry into a 9-inch pie pan. Crimp around the edges. Prick with a fork and bake for 10 minutes or until golden brown. When done, remove from oven and let cool.

Place the purée of pumpkin in the top of a double boiler. Beat the egg yolks and add to the pumpkin. Add ½ cup sugar, milk, butter, salt, ginger, nutmeg, and cinnamon. Cook, stirring constantly, until mixture thickens and reaches the consistency of custard. Remove from heat.

Soften the gelatin in cold water. Combine the gelatin with the pumpkin mixture and stir until dissolved. Chill until slightly thickened.

In a small bowl, beat the egg whites until they are stiff but not dry. Gradually beat in ½ cup sugar. Fold into pumpkin mixture.

Pour the mixture into the pastry shell. Chill for 3 hours or until firm. Serve with whipped cream.

# VERMONT CIDER PUDDING WITH HARD SAUCE

serves 8

½ cups almonds
¾ cup bread crumbs
4 eggs, separated
¾ cup sugar
1 teaspoon grated lemon peel
½ teaspoon cinnamon
¼ teaspoon grated nutmeg
¼ teaspoon salt
1½ cups apple cider
   Hard Sauce

Preheat the oven to 350°.

Grind the almonds and bread crumbs together in a blender or food processor.

In a mixing bowl, beat the egg yolks until light and fluffy. Add the sugar and beat until smooth and blended, about 3 minutes. Stir in the lemon peel, cinnamon, nutmeg, salt, and almond–bread crumb mixture. Blend well.

In a separate bowl, beat the egg whites until they are stiff but not dry. Fold them into the egg yolk mixture.

Pour the batter into a buttered 1½ quart casserole. Bake 25 to 30 minutes, or until brown and firm to the touch. Remove from oven.

Heat the cider thoroughly in a saucepan but do not boil. Pour the hot cider over the pudding while it is hot. Let stand for 10 minutes. Serve hot or cold with Hard Sauce.

# HARD SAUCE

⅓ cup buter, softened
1 cup confectioner's sugar
2 tablespoons dark rum

In a mixing bowl combine the butter and confectioner's sugar. Mix until well blended and smooth. Add the rum and stir well.

# BLUEBERRY PIE

serves 8

1 quart fresh blueberries
1 cup sugar
1 tablespoon flour
¼ teaspoon grated nutmeg
2 tablespoons butter, cut up
2 pastries for 9-inch pies

Preheat the oven to 450°.

Wash the blueberries and drain well.

Line a 9-inch pie pan with one of the pastries, trimming so that about ½ inch hangs over the edge. Reserve the second pastry for the top of the pie.

Mix 1 tablespoon sugar with the flour and sprinkle into the pie crust. Fill the crust with blueberries and sprinkle with nutmeg. Sprinkle with remaining sugar and dot with butter.

Place second pastry over top to cover. Tuck top crust under overlap of bottom crust and seal by crimping edges firmly together. Prick top of pie to let steam escape.

Place the pie on the lowest shelf of the oven for 10 minutes. Then move it to the middle shelf and lower the heat to 350°. Continue baking for about 30 minutes or until crust is golden.

## SHOOFLY PIE

serves 6 to 8

1 pastry for 9-inch pie
Crumb topping:
¾ cup flour
½ cup brown sugar, firmly packed
½ teaspoon salt
½ teaspoon cinnamon
⅛ teaspoon ground ginger
⅛ teaspoon grated nutmeg
2 tablespoons butter
Liquid mixture:
½ cup molasses
1 egg, beaten
½ teaspoon baking soda
¾ cup hot water

Preheat the oven to 400°.

Line a 9-inch pie pan with the pastry.

In a large mixing bowl combine the flour, brown sugar, salt, cinnamon, ginger, nutmeg, and butter. Blend well with fingers until crumbs begin to form.

In another mixing bowl combine the molasses, egg, baking soda, and hot water. Mix well. Pour the liquid into the prepared pie pan. Top with the crumbs.

Bake for 10 minutes. Then reduce oven heat to 325° and continue baking for about 30 minutes or until firm. Cool pie before slicing.

## APPLE PANDOWDY

serves 6 to 8

1½ cups flour
¼ teaspoon salt
½ cup butter
   ice water
¼ cup melted butter
Apple filling:
½ cup sugar
½ teaspoon cinnamon
¼ teaspoon salt
¼ teaspoon grated nutmeg
10 large apples, peeled, cored, and thinly sliced
½ cup Vermont maple syrup
3 tablespoons melted butter
¼ cup water

Combine the flour and salt in a large bowl. Cut in the butter with a pastry blender or two knives until the mixture is crumb-like. Sprinkle with just enough ice water to hold the mixture together.

Roll the dough out on a floured surface and brush with melted butter. Cut dough in half. Place halves on top of each other and cut again. Brush with melted butter. Cut pieces in half again. Brush with melted butter. Cut pieces in half yet again. There should now be 16 equal pieces. Brush all the pieces with butter again and stack them on top of each other. Wrap with plastic wrap and chill for at least 1 hour.

Roll the pastry and divide it into half. Use one portion to line a greased, deep, medium baking dish. Roll out and reserve the other portion for the top. Refrigerate the dish and the remaining dough while you make the filling.

*(continued on next page)*

Preheat the oven to 400°.

To make the filling, combine the sugar, cinnamon, salt, and nutmeg in a bowl. Add the apples to the bowl and mix thoroughly with the sugar mixture. Place this mixture into the pastry-lined baking dish.

In a bowl combine the maple syrup with the melted butter and water. Pour over the apples. Cover the pan with the reserved pastry and seal by crimping edges together. Place in the oven for 10 minutes; then reduce heat to 325°. At this time, make slits in the top crust with a sharp knife. Return to oven and bake for 1 hour. Serve hot with heavy cream.

# EARLY AMERICAN APPLE PIE

serves 6

*6 to 8 apples, peeled, cored, and thinly sliced*
*¼ cup sugar*
*¾ cup gingersnap crumbs*
*1 tablespoon flour*
*½ teaspoon cinnamon*
*⅛ teaspoon nutmeg*
*¼ teaspoon salt*
*½ cup chopped walnuts*
*¼ cup melted butter*
*½ cup Vermont maple syrup*
*1 pastry for 9-inch pie*

Preheat the oven to 350°.

Place half the sliced apples in the pastry shell.

In a mixing bowl combine the sugar, gingersnap crumbs, flour, cinnamon, salt, nutmeg, walnuts, and butter. Mix until well blended.

Sprinkle half this mixture over the apples in the pie shell. Place the remaining apple slices in a layer over the crumbs. Sprinkle with remaining crumbs.

Bake 45 minutes. Heat the maple syrup to boiling and pour evenly over the pie. Bake 15 to 20 minutes longer or until apples are tender.

# CRANBERRY SNOW

serves 8 (yields 1 quart)

*2 cups fresh cranberries*
*4 cups water*
*1½ cups sugar*
*1 teaspoon lemon juice*

Wash the cranberries. Place them in a 3-quart saucepan with the water and bring to a boil over high heat. Reduce the heat, cover the saucepan, and simmer for 10 to 12 minutes or until the cranberries can be easily mashed.

Purée the cranberries and their cooking liquid in a food mill, blender, or food processor. Alternatively, press them through a sieve with the back of a spoon.

Place the cranberry purée in a glass bowl and add the sugar and lemon juice. Stir well.

Remove the dividers from 2 ice-cube trays. Pour the mixture into the trays. Freeze the cranberry mixture for 3 to 4 hours, stirring with a fork every 5 minutes or so to break up the solid particles that form. Serve in individual dessert cups.

# HOLIDAY FRUITCAKE

serves 10 or more

   1 *pound seedless dark raisins*
   1 *pound seedless light raisins*
   1 *pound currants*
   1 *cup almonds*
   1 *cup pecans*
      *juice of ½ orange*
      *grated rind of ½ orange*
   2 *tablespoons flour*
   2 *tablespoons butter, softened*
   1 *cup butter*
1½ *cups sugar*
   6 *eggs, separated*
   2 *tablespoons Vermont maple syrup*
   2 *cups flour*
   1 *tablespoon brandy*
 ⅛ *teaspoon cinnamon*
 ¼ *teaspoon ground cloves*
 ¼ *teaspoon ground ginger*
 ¼ *teaspoon grated nutmeg*

Chop the dark raisins, light raisins, currants, almonds, and pecans finely and mix together in a bowl. Dredge with 2 tablespoons flour. Set aside.

Line a 9-inch ring-mold cake pan with wax paper. Butter the paper and sprinkle it with flour. Set aside.

Preheat the oven to 250°.

In a mixing bowl beat the butter until creamy. Add the sugar and beat until light, about 2 minutes. Add the egg yolks and beat with until fluffy.

In a separate bowl, beat the egg whites until they are stiff but not dry. Fold the egg whites into the butter and yolk mixture. Add the maple syrup.

Little by little, add the flour to the mixture. Beat well after each addition. Add the brandy and beat well. Next add the cinnamon, cloves, ginger, nutmeg, and fruit and nut mixture. Mix well. Pour into the cake mold.

Place the mold in a pan of water in the oven. Cover until the last half hour of baking, then uncover. Bake 4 hours or until a cake tester or toothpick comes out clean. Remove cake and cool completely. Wrap closely and put in a cool place until ready to use. Every 3 to 4 weeks, pour 2 ounces of Bourbon whiskey onto the cake to mellow it. This cake will keep for 9 months to 1 year, getting better all the time. Serve cut very thin.

# RICE PUDDING

serves 4

   3 *cups milk*
   1 *cup light cream*
   4 *teaspoons uncooked rice*
   2 *tablespoons water*
 ¼ *teaspoon salt*

Preheat the oven to 250°.

Pour the milk and cream into a lightly buttered medium baking dish or casserole. Stir in the rice, sugar, and salt.

Place the baking dish in the oven for 3 to 4 hours. Stir frequently, but not during the last 30 minutes of baking time. Test the rice for tenderness at the end of 3 hours. The pudding will be thin when it is taken from the oven.

Allow the pudding to cool before serving. It will thicken as it cools.

# PLAIN PASTRY

yields pastry for 1 2-crust 9-inch pie

2 cups flour
½ teaspoon salt
¾ cup butter, lard, or solid vegetable shortening
4 tablespoons cold water

Sift the flour with salt into a large mixing bowl. Cut in the shortening with a pastry blender, two knives, or your fingertips until mixture is crumbly.

Sprinkle cold water over flour mixture. Mix lightly with a fork until dough holds together. Press lightly into a ball. Chill in refrigerator for at least 1 hour.

Roll dough out on a lightly floured surface. Line a 9-inch pie plate with half the dough; trim the pastry so that ½ inch hangs over the edge. Use the other half of the dough for the top crust or for an additional pie.

Bake according to the instructions in the particular recipe.

If you do not need two crusts, either halve the recipe or make both crusts and freeze one for later use.

# Accents

# DUTCH GINGER PEARS

yields 3 to 4 pints

5 pounds hard pears
juice of 2 lemons
rind of 2 lemons
4 pounds dark brown sugar
¼ pound fresh ginger root

Peel and core the pears; cut into quarters. Cut the lemon rind into strings. Place the lemon rind, lemon juice, pears, brown sugar, and ginger root into a large pot.

Heat and cook slowly for 1 hour or until the syrup becomes clear. Spoon into sterilized glass jars. Seal and cool.

# DUTCH APPLE BUTTER

yields 4 pints

8 cups apple cider
3½ pounds apples, cut into eighths
3 cups sugar
½ teaspoon ground cloves
1 tablespoon cinnamon
¼ teaspoon salt

Place the apple cider in a large saucepan. Bring to a boil and boil for 15 minutes. Add the apples to the pot and cook until very tender.

When done, force the apples through a sieve with the back of a spoon. Put the sieved apples back into the saucepan; discard the peels and seeds in the sieve. Add the sugar, cloves, cinnamon, and salt. Simmer slowly until thick, stirring frequently to prevent burning. Pour into jars or crock.

# CANDIED CRANBERRIES

yields approximately 4 cups

4 cups fresh cranberries
2 cups sugar
¼ teaspoon salt
¼ teaspoon baking soda
1 cup water

Place the cranberries, sugar, salt, baking soda, and water into a large, heavy saucepan. Bring ingredients to a boil over medium heat. Cover and simmer gently for 15 minutes. Do not lift the cover during this time.

Cool, still leaving the cover on. Place in sterilized glass jars and close with screw lids. Store in refrigerator.

# ORANGE AND CRANBERRY RELISH

yields approximately 1 pint

3 small thin-skinned oranges, unpeeled
1 cup fresh cranberries
sugar to taste

Shred the oranges and cranberries by placing them in a blender or food processor for 10 to 15 seconds or by putting them through the coarse blade of a grinder.

Place the oranges and cranberries in a bowl. Add sugar to taste, but keep the mixture on the tart side.

Place in a covered jar and chill for 24 hours.

# CRANBERRY-PINEAPPLE RELISH

yields 1½ pints

1 cup water
4 cups fresh cranberries
1 cup dark raisins
2 cups sugar
½ teaspoon ground ginger
½ teaspoon cinnamon
¼ teaspoon salt
1 fresh pineapple, peeled and chopped

In a large saucepan, combine the water, cranberries, raisins, sugar, ginger, cinnamon, and salt. Mix well and cook over medium heat until the cranberries start to pop and the mixture begins to thicken, about 20 minutes.

Stir in the pineapple. Continue cooking for an additional 20 minutes, or until the sauce has reached the desired thickness. Cool relish and store in refrigerator. It will keep 1 to 2 weeks.

## SPICY PICKLED VEGETABLES

yields 3 to 4 quarts

  1  *pound small white onions*
12  *young, small cucumbers, washed and sliced but not peeled*
 ½  *hot red pepper*
  2  *small green peppers*
12  *small green tomatoes*
 ¼  *cup salt*
  1  *small head cauliflower, broken into flowerets*
  1  *teaspoon turmeric*
  4  *ounces dry mustard*
  1 to 2  *cups sugar*
 ½  *ounce mixed pickling spice (half a package)*
1½  *teaspoons celery seed*
 ¼  *cup olive oil*

Combine in a large bowl the onions, cucumbers, peppers, and tomatoes. Sprinkle with the salt and cover with water. Let stand overnight. Pour off the brine and rinse off the salt.

Blanch the cauliflower in boiling salted water for 1 minute.

Place the mustard and a little of the vinegar into a large pot. Add the vegetables. Add the remaining vinegar, sugar to taste, pickling spices, and celery seeds. Bring mixture to a boil. Cook until thickened, about 5 to 7 minutes. Taste and add more salt and sugar if desired. Stir in the olive oil.

Pour mixture into large sterilized glass jars. Seal and cool.

## RED AND GREEN PEPPER HASH

yields approximately 3 quarts

12  *green peppers*
12  *sweet red peppers*
12  *large onions*
  3  *tablespoons salt*
     *boiling water*
  2  *cups sugar*
  4  *cups vinegar*

Wash the peppers. Trim tops and remove the seeds and inner white membranes.

Coarsely chop the peppers and onions. Sprinkle with salt. Place peppers and onions in a large saucepan and cover with boiling water. Let stand 15 minutes. Drain well.

Add the sugar and vinegar to the peppers. Place the saucepan over heat and bring to a boil. Cook for 15 minutes.

Pour mixture into sterilized glass jars, cool, and seal.

# CHOW-CHOW

yields 7 to 8 quarts

  8  *quarts green tomatoes, stemmed and chopped*
  8  *large onions, chopped*
10  *green peppers, cleaned and chopped*
  3  *small hot red peppers, chopped*
  3  *tablespoons salt*
  1  *quart vinegar*
  1  *tablespoon cinnamon*
 ¼  *teaspoon ground cloves*
  3  *tablespoons dry mustard*
  2  *bay leaves*
  2  *cups sugar*
 ½  *cup horseradish*

In a large mixing bowl combine the tomatoes, onions, and peppers. Cover with salt and let stand overnight. Drain and place in a large pot.

Add the vinegar to the pot. Tie the cinnamon, cloves, mustard, and bay leaves into a piece of cheesecloth and add to the pot. Add the sugar and horseradish. Bring mixture to a boil and reduce heat. Simmer until ingredients are tender, stirring frequently, about 15 minutes.

Place the mixture into sterilized glass jars. Seal and cool.

In the days of the China trade, the New England men who sailed on the fast clipper ships discovered Oriental foods, including a fruit preserve they called chow-chow. Eventually, the word came to mean this particular relish.

# PEPPER CABBAGE RELISH

yields 3 pints

1 *cup celery, chopped*
2 *cups green peppers, chopped*
1 *medium head cabbage, cored and chopped*
2 *tablespoons cider vinegar*
 *salt and pepper to taste*

Place the celery, green peppers, cabbage, vinegar, salt, and pepper into a large saucepan. Cook over medium heat, stirring occasionally, until vegetables are tender.

Place mixture into sterilized glass jars, seal, and cool.

# SPICY PLUM JAM

yields 2 quarts or 12 8-ounce jars

6 *pound ripe plums*
9 *cups sugar*
½ *teaspoon cinnamon*
¼ *teaspoon ground cloves*
¼ *teaspoon ground ginger*
¼ *cup vinegar*

Halve and pit the plums. Do not peel. Place the plums in a large pot. Add the sugar, cinnamon, cloves, ginger, and vinegar. Bring slowly to the boil, stirring constantly. Simmer 40 to 45 minutes, stirring often.

When thickened, pour into hot sterilized glass jars. Seal and cool.

# GOLDEN JAM

yields 10 8-ounce jars

2 *large thin-skinned oranges*
6 *cups rhubarb, diced*
3 *cups raw carrots, ground*
4 *cups sugar*

Halve the oranges and remove the seeds. Grind oranges with peel.

In a large pot combine the oranges, rhubarb, carrots, and sugar. Let mixture stand overnight.

Place over heat and bring to a boil. Turn heat down and cook slowly until rhubarb is transparent and the mixture is thickened.

Pour into hot sterilized glass jars. Seal and cool.

## OLD-FASHIONED STRAWBERRY JAM

yields 4 8-ounce jars

6 *cups hulled strawberries*
3 *cups sugar*

Place the strawberries into a large, heavy pot and mash. Cook over moderate heat until fairly thick, stirring often. Gradually add the sugar. Continue cooking over low heat until the sugar is dissolved. Stir constantly. Bring mixture to a boil and boil rapidly for 15 to 20 minutes.

Skim the mixture and pour into hot sterilized glass jars. Seal and cool.

## STRAWBERRY-RHUBARB JAM

yields 2½ pints

3 *cups hulled strawberries*
3 *cups rhubarb, diced*
6 *cups sugar*

Wash and hull the strawberries. Place the strawberries into a large pot and mash them against the side of the pot with a wooden spoon. Cut the rhubarb into ½-inch pieces and add to pot. Mix with strawberries. Add 4 cups of sugar. Bring mixture to a rapid boil and boil for 4 minutes.

Add the remaining 2 cups of sugar and boil again for 4 minutes. Pour into hot sterilized glass jars. Seal and cool.

## CRABAPPLE JELLY

yields 4 8-ounce jars

5 *pounds crabapples*
8 *cups water*
  *sugar*
1 *teaspoon vanilla extract (optional)*

Wash the crabapples. Remove the stem and blossom ends and cut crabapples in half. Place the fruit in a large pot. Add water to cover and cook until fruit is very soft, about 10 minutes.

Strain the mixture through cheesecloth. Do not force juice through the cloth. Measure the juice; there should be about 7 cups. For every cup of juice, stir in ¾ cup sugar.

Place the sweetened juice in the pot and bring to a boil quickly. Cook rapidly until the juice begins to jell.

Skim off the foam, stir in vanilla, and pour into hot sterilized glass jars. Seal and cool.

## TARTAR SAUCE

yields 1 cup

1 *cup mayonnaise*
2 *tablespoons chopped pickle*
1 *tablespoon chopped green olives*
2 *teaspoons chopped onions*
1 *tablespoon chopped parsley*
1 *teaspoon mustard (optional)*

In a bowl combine the mayonnaise, pickle, olive, onions, parsley, and mustard. Combine thoroughly. Use immediately or refrigerate until needed.

# THE SOUTH

To speak of the South as one culinary region does disservice to the many strains and styles of cooking below the Mason-Dixon Line. From the she-crab soup of Charleston to the pompano of Florida, from the chilis and barbecues of Texas and New Mexico to the Creole and Cajun specialties of Louisiana, Southern cooking is one of the most diverse and satisfying native cuisines.

To sit down to a heap of crayfish in the bayou country is a treat few have experienced, but may be counted among the most heavenly of earthly diversions. To have a breakfast of ham and eggs made with real farm-cured Kentucky ham and new-laid eggs is to eat them for the first time. Yet too often, the best food in the South is to be found in private homes, not in restaurants. Even in its many forms and locales, Southern cooking is essentially created from what's available, prepared with care and simplicity—a cuisine of honest flavors.

The traditions of Southern hospitality go back, of course, to the days of the great plantations, but also, on a less mighty economic scale, to the honest neighborliness of the people. A stranger was always treated as an adopted family member, and in a few of the more rural communities, this tradition still persists. Though the staples of cornbread and bacon three times a day are luckily pretty much gone, the bounty of the land and sea are exploited with verve and imagination.

Brunswick stew, for example, was originally a way to combine whatever was at hand with the hunter's bag for the day: squirrel, possum, wild birds were chucked in along with vegetables and spices and simmered for long hours over an open fire to produce one of the most savory, if highly flavored, concoctions imaginable.

What was available in the inland regions was far less varied than the plenty of the coastal areas. Here, from the blue crabs and lobsters of the Carolinas to the shrimp and subtropical fish of the Gulf Coast—not to mention the crawfish, filé and fruits of the Louisiana bayous and Mobile Bay—was plenty for the taking.

Oranges, for example, were introduced by the Spanish and were utilized by the Seminoles and other tribes long before Florida became the playground of fun-seeking Northerners. Combined with local fish, they made a sweet and pungent stew. Today, of course, they are Florida's primary crop and are used in ways unimaginable a hundred years ago.

Unknown to most is that Mobile, Alabama, as well as New Orleans was originally a French settlement. The local cuisines echo that long-past influence. In Louisiana two distinct strains dominate the cooking: Creole and Cajun. Creole is the cuisine of New Orleans—the Frenchification of local ingredients with a spicy annointing. Cajun is essentially backwoods cuisine, brought from Acadia (hence the name) in Nova Scotia by the hearty pioneer stock whose descendants still hunt and fish the bayous today.

And it is the South which is the true home of the barbecue, originally a Caribbean feast, adapted to the celebratory community spirit of the area.

# Suggested Menus

### EASTER DINNER
for 6 to 8
Fried Okra Soup
Southern-Style Baked Ham
Peach Chutney or Mango Chutney
Collard Greens
Dirty Rice
Buttermilk Biscuits or
North Carolina Sweet Potato Biscuits
Pecan Pie
Beer, Iced Tea, or Sparkling Water
Wines: Beaujolais, Valpolicella,
or Cabernet Sauvignon

### SUNDAY FAMILY DINNER
for 6
Benne Biscuits and Cold Curry Soup
Southern Fried Chicken
Southwestern Cabbage Salad
Country-Style Potato Salad
Cornsticks or Hush Puppies
Georgia Pecan Pie or Dixie Brown Sugar Pie
Beer, Iced Tea, or Sparkling Water

### TEX-MEX BUFFET DINNER
for 6 to 8
Guacamole with Tortillas
Tamale Pie
Boiled Pinto Beans
Texas Green Bean Salad
Flan
Beer, Iced Tea, or Sparkling Water

### SUMMERTIME FISH DINNER PARTY
for 4 to 6
Gulf Crab Bisque
Pompano à lá Maitre d'Hotel
Fried Okra
Carolina Rice Pilau
Cold Kidney Bean Mix
Old-Fashioned Key Lime Pie
Beer, Iced Tea, or Sparkling Water
Wines: Frascati, Muscadet, Vouvray, Chenin Blanc

## SUNDAY BREAKFAST

(choose one or both menus)

for 4

MENU 1:
Orange or Grapefruit Juice
Hominy Grits with Butter and Cream
Brown Sugar Bread with
Old-Fashioned Blackberry Jam
Coffee or Tea

MENU 2:
Orange or Grapefruit Juice
Virginia Ham Omelet
Pecan-Corn Muffins
Coffee or Tea

## CREOLE DINNER PARTY

for 6 to 8

Eggplant Caviar with
Thinly Sliced Bread and Crackers
or Creole Canapés
Shrimp Creole or Shrimp Gumbo
Red Rice
Tossed Green Salad with Vinaigrette Dressing
Kentucky Bourbon Cake or Blackberry Cake
Beer, Iced Tea, or Sparkling Water
Wines: Muscadet, Frascati, or Chardonnay

## MID-WEEK LUNCHEON

(use one or both menus)

for 4

MENU 1:
She-Crab Soup
Florida Seafood Salad
Saffron Bread
Coconut Jumbles and Orange Sherbet
Coffee, Tea, or Sparkling Water

MENU 2:
Potage Crécy (New Orleans Carrot Soup)
Creole Omelet
Southern-Style Popovers
Herbed Bean Salad
Pound Cake
Coffee, Tea, or Sparkling Water

# ❧ ——Soups and Appetizers—— ❦

## WILLIAMSBURG CREAM OF PEANUT SOUP

serves 8

1 medium onion, finely chopped
½ cup celery, finely chopped
4 tablespoons butter
2 quarts chicken broth
1 cup smooth peanut butter
2 cups light cream
  salt and pepper to taste
  chopped peanuts for garnish

In a large skillet sauté the onion and celery in butter until soft but not browned. Add the flour and stir well. Pour in 1 cup chicken broth and bring to a boil, stirring frequently.

Remove the mixture from heat and place ½ cup at a time in a blender. Whirl until smooth. Return the blended mixture to the skillet and add the remaining chicken broth, the cream, and the peanut butter. Whisk while heating gently. Do not allow the mixture to boil. Season to taste with salt and pepper.

Serve hot or cold, garnished with chopped peanuts.

This dish is a specialty of the King's Arms Tavern at the Williamsburg restoration in Virginia. Diners there are served by waiters in authentic eighteenth-century garb.

## SHE-CRAB SOUP

serves 6 to 8

1 pound white crabmeat and roe (if possible)
6 tablespoons butter
1 tablespoon flour
2 cups milk
2 cups light cream
1 teaspoon freshly grated lemon rind
¼ teaspoon ground mace
1 teaspoon salt
¼ teaspoon pepper
3 tablespoons dry sherry
1 teaspoon parsley, finely chopped

Clean the crabmeat, checking for bits of shell or cartilage.

In the top of a double boiler over briskly boiling water, melt the butter. When melted, add the flour and blend well. Pour in the milk and light cream. Stir constantly. Add the grated lemon rind, mace, and crabmeat and roe. Stir well and continue cooking for 20 minutes. Add the salt and pepper.

Remove the mixture from the heat and allow it to stand over the hot water for 15 minutes. Stir in the sherry and serve. Garnish each bowl with chopped parsley.

George Washington was served this soup on a visit to Charleston, South Carolina in 1791. The soup need not be made with female crabs and their roe; any crabmeat will do.

# SOPA DE ARROZ (SHRIMP AND RICE SOUP)

serves 4

  2 tablespoons olive oil
  1 cup raw rice
  1 cup chopped tomatoes
  1 cup cooked shrimp, shelled and deveined
  3 cups hot water
  1 teaspoon salt
  1 teaspoon Tobasco sauce

Heat the olive oil in a heavy skillet until very hot. Add the rice and cook until it turns a deep golden brown. Stir constantly. Add the tomatoes, shrimp, water, salt, and Tabasco sauce. Cover and cook until rice is tender and has absorbed almost all the liquid, approximately 15 to 20 minutes.

This dish, adapted from Mexico by Texans, is really more of a stew than a soup, but it is traditionally served as a first course in the Southwest.

# BEEFY OKRA SOUP

serves 8

  2 pound lean chuck or other stewing beef,
      cut into 2-inch cubes
  8 tablespoons butter
  2 1-pound cans tomatoes
  1½ pounds fresh okra, thinly sliced
      boiling water
  2 cups cooked lima beans
  2 cups cooked chicken, diced
      salt and pepper to taste

Melt the butter in a large, deep pot. Add the meat and brown well on all sides. Add the tomatoes and okra. Add enough boiling water to cover the mixture completely and simmer, covered, for 1 hour. After the mixture has cooked for 1 hour, remove the cover. Add 4 cups of boiling water. Continue cooking until soup returns to the boil; lower heat and simmer, covered. Stir frequently. Skim the soup while it cooks. Simmer until okra and tomatoes are soft. Add the lima beans and chicken. Season to taste with salt and pepper.

# FRIED OKRA SOUP

serves 10

  2 cups fresh lima beans
  2 cups fresh corn, cut from the cob
  3 medium potatoes, peeled and diced
  ¼ teaspoon pepper
  ¼ teaspoon salt
  6 medium tomatoes, chopped
  2 medium onions, chopped
  ½ cup celery, chopped
  1 tablespoon sugar
  ¼ head cabbage, chopped
  ¼ pound bacon, diced
  4 cups fresh okra, sliced

Combine in a large pot the lima beans, corn, potatoes, pepper, salt, tomatoes, onions, celery, and sugar. Add enough water to cover.

Cover the pot and simmer until vegetables are almost tender, about 45 minutes. Add the cabbage. Remove pot from heat.

Fry the bacon in a skillet until brown. Add bacon to the soup; reserve the drippings.

Brown the okra in the bacon drippings. Add to the soup.

If the soup is too thick, add water. Simmer, covered, for 20 minutes longer. Serve hot.

# CREOLE SALPICON

serves 6

> meat from 24 crawfish, diced
> 3 tomatoes, skinned and finely chopped
> 1 dozen mushrooms, minced
> 2 tablespoons butter
> 3 tablespoons flour
> 2 cups boiling milk
> salt to taste
> 1 teaspoon grated nutmeg
> 12 black peppercorns
> 1 herb bouquet (1 bay leaf, ¼ teaspoon cloves, 1 sprig parsley tied in a cheesecloth bag)

Melt the butter in a saucepan. Add the flour and cook for 5 minutes, stirring constantly.

Gradually whisk in the boiling milk. Add the nutmeg, salt to taste, and peppercorns. Drop in the herb bouquet and cook over medium heat for 15 minutes.

Remove saucepan from heat. Discard the herb bouquet. Strain the milk mixture through a sieve and return it to the saucepan. Add the tomatoes, crawfish meat, and mushrooms. Return mixture to heat and cook for 5 minutes. Serve hot.

# POTAGE CRÉCY (NEW ORLEANS CARROT SOUP)

serves 4 to 6

> 4 large carrots, finely chopped
> 2 large onions, finely chopped
> 1 quart milk
> 1 medium turnip, finely chopped
> 2 stalks celery, finely chopped
> 1 teaspoon cornstarch
> 2 whole cloves
> 1 tablespoon butter
> ¼ teaspoon dried thyme
> salt and pepper to taste
> 3 pints water
> 2 quarts boiling water

Place the vegetables in a large pot with 3 pints water. Bring the water to a boil and cook until vegetables are tender, about 25 minutes.

When the vegetables are soft, drain and mash them. Press the mashed vegetables through a sieve with the back of a spoon.

Return the mashed vegetables to the pot and the 2 quarts boiling water. Cover and simmer gently for 15 minutes. Mix the cornstarch with 1 tablespoon milk and add to the pot after the first 5 minutes.

In a saucepan heat the remaining milk to the boiling point. Add the milk to the vegetables and cook for 3 minutes longer. Season with salt, pepper, and sugar to taste. Serve hot.

# GULF CRAB BISQUE

serves 4 to 6

    meat of 8 crabs or 1 7-ounce can of crabmeat
4 cups fish stock
1 cup bread crumbs
1 onion, thinly sliced
2 sprigs parsley
1 bay leaf
¼ teaspoon dried thyme
2 tablespoons butter, softened
1 cup heavy cream
    salt and pepper to taste
⅛ teaspoon cayenne pepper
2 tablespoons cooked shrimp, chopped
1 tablespoon sweet butter

Pick the meat from the crabs and chop very fine.

In a large saucepan mix together the fish stock, crabmeat, bread crumbs, onion, parsley, bay leaf, thyme, and a large piece of crab shell.

Bring the mixture to a boil. Lower the heat and simmer gently for 20 minutes.

Strain the soup through a sieve and return the liquid to the saucepan. Discard the solids in the sieve, including the crab shell. Add the softened butter and heat just to the boiling point. Add the cream and season with salt, pepper, and cayenne. Heat soup through, but do not boil.

Just before serving, stir in the shrimp and sweet butter. Serve hot.

# MULLIGATAWNY SOUP

serves 6

1 3-pound chicken, cut into serving pieces
4 tablespoons butter
½ cup carrots, chopped
½ cup green pepper, chopped
2 green apples, cored and chopped
1 tablespoon flour
2 teaspoons curry powder
8 cups chicken broth
2 whole cloves
¼ cup parsley, chopped
1 tablespoon sugar
¼ teaspoon pepper
1½ teaspoons salt

Melt the butter in a large saucepan. Add the chicken pieces and saute until well browned, about 5 to 8 minutes.

Add the carrots, green pepper, and apples. Stir well. Continue cooking until mixture is brown, about 8 minutes. Stir often.

Add the flour and curry powder. Mix well. Add the chicken broth, 1 cup at a time. Stir well. Add the cloves, sugar, pepper, and salt. Continue cooking until the mixture comes to a boil. Lower heat, cover saucepan, and simmer until chicken is very tender, about 30 to 35 minutes.

Remove the chicken from the soup and cool.

Strain the soup through a sieve. Push the vegetables through the sieve with the back of a spoon. Place the soup back in the saucepan and heat.

Remove the chicken from the bone, cut into small pieces, and add to the soup. Mix well and serve hot.

# COLD CURRY SOUP

serves 4

2 tablespoons butter
2 tablespoons curry powder
4 cups chicken broth
6 large egg yolks
½ cup light cream
½ cup heavy cream

In a large saucepan combine the butter and curry powder. Mix together and simmer over low heat for 5 minutes. Pour in the chicken broth and bring the mixture to a boil. Lower the heat and whisk in the egg yolks, light cream, and heavy cream. Stir constantly until the soup begins to thicken. Do not let the soup boil.

Chill and serve very cold.

# PICKLED SHRIMP

serves 6 to 8

2 pounds raw shrimp
¼ cup mixed pickling spices
1 cup vegetable oil
¾ cup white vinegar
1 teaspoon salt
¼ teaspoon pepper
2 teaspoons celery seed
1 teaspoon Tabasco sauce
1 large onion, chopped

In a saucepan combine the unshelled shrimp and pickling spices. Add enough water to cover the shrimp completely. Cover tightly, bring to a boil, reduce heat, and simmer 3 to 5 minutes. Remove from heat and allow the shrimp to cool. When completely cool, shell the shrimp.

In a small bowl, combine the vegetable oil, vinegar, salt, pepper, celery seed, and Tabasco sauce. Mix well.

Arrange layers of shrimp and chopped onion in a bowl. Add the oil-vinegar mixture, cover, and chill 8 hours or overnight.

# SHRIMP FRITTERS

serves 6

1 pound uncooked shrimp
1 cup flour
1 teaspoon baking powder
½ teaspoon salt
¼ teaspoon pepper
2 eggs, beaten
½ cup milk
⅓ cup onion, finely chopped
½ teaspoon Tabasco sauce
  oil for deep frying

Clean, peel, devein, and chop the shrimp.

In a mixing bowl combine the flour, baking powder, salt, and pepper. Stir in the eggs and sufficient milk to make a thick batter. Add the onion, Tabasco sauce, and shrimp. Mix until shrimp is well coated.

Heat the oil to 375° in a deep skillet. Drop the batter by teaspoons into the oil. Fry until golden brown, about 2 minutes.

Serve hot with cocktail sauce or tartar sauce.

# SHREVEPORT SHRIMP

serves 6

    2 pounds cooked shrimp, peeled and deveined
    ¾ cup white wine or dry vermouth
    ¼ teaspoon pepper
    ⅛ teaspoon cayenne pepper
    4 tablespoons butter
    1 cup bread crumbs
    2 cloves garlic, crushed
    ½ teaspoon salt

Preheat the oven to 350°.

Butter a 15-inch baking pan. Spread the shrimp over the bottom of the pan. Pour in the wine and sprinkle with pepper and cayenne. Dot the shrimp with 1 tablespoon of the butter cut into small pieces.

In a saucepan melt the remaining butter. Remove from heat and mix in the bread crumbs, garlic, and salt. Bake for 20 minutes. Serve hot.

# GULF CRAB SOUFFLES

serves 6

    1 pound fresh crabmeat
    2 tablespoons butter
    2 tablespoons flour
    ½ teaspoon salt
    ⅛ tespoon pepper
    1 cup milk
    2 eggs, separated
    1 cup heavy cream, whipped

Preheat the oven to 350°.

Clean the crabmeat and remove all cartilage and bits of shell.

In a saucepan, melt the butter and add the flour, salt, and pepper. Blend well. Slowly add the milk, stirring constantly. Cook until the mixture begins to thicken. Remove from heat.

In a separate bowl, add 1 tablespoon of the hot milk mixture to the egg yolks; stir yolks into the hot milk mixture. Add the crab meat and fold in the whipped cream.

In another bowl beat the egg whites until they are stiff but not dry. Fold into the crabmeat mixture.

Place the mixture into 6 buttered individual soufflé or casserole dishes. Set the dishes in a large pan of water. The water should come halfway up the sides of the dishes.

Bake for 40 minutes or until firm. Serve *immediately.*

# SEAFOOD PUFFS

serves 6 to 8

    1 cup beer
    8 tablespoons butter
    1 cup flour
    ½ teaspoon salt
    ¼ teaspoon pepper
    ½ pound cooked crabmeat, flaked, or finely
        chopped cooked shrimp

Preheat the oven to 450°.

Place the beer and butter in a saucepan. Bring mixture to a boil. When the butter is melted, add the flour, salt, and pepper. Stir until well blended. Cook over low heat until the mixture begins to pull away from the sides of the pan.

Remove saucepan from the heat and beat in the eggs, 1 at a time.

Drop the dough by heaping teaspoons 1 inch apart onto greased cookie sheets. Bake 10 minutes. Reduce heat to 350° and continue baking for 10 minutes longer or until golden brown. Cool slightly. Split puffs and fill with crabmeat or shrimp.

# DEEP-FRIED HOMINY BALLS

serves 6 to 8

2 cups water
½ teaspoon salt
½ cup quick-cooking hominy grits
1 cup grated sharp Cheddar cheese
¼ teaspoon cayenne pepper
¼ teaspoon grated nutmeg
2 eggs
1½ teaspoons olive oil
1½ cups bread crumbs
   oil for frying

In a saucepan, bring the water and salt to a boil. Slowly add the grits. Stir well. Bring the mixture back to a boil and reduce the heat. Cook grits for 3 to 5 minutes, stirring occasionally. Remove from heat and chill.

Place the chilled grits in a bowl and mash well with a fork. Stir in the grated cheese, cayenne, nutmeg, and pepper. Shape mixture into about 40 1-inch balls. (A melon baller is useful for this.)

In a small bowl beat together the eggs and olive oil. Dip the balls in the egg mixture and then in the bread crumbs.

Heat the oil to 375° in a deep skillet. Fry the balls until they are golden brown, about 2 minutes. Drain on paper towels and serve.

# BENNE BISCUITS

serves 6

2 cups flour
1 teaspoon salt
⅛ teaspoon cayenne pepper
¾ cup butter
¼ cup ice water
1 cup sesame seeds
   additional salt

Preheat the oven to 350°.

In a large bowl mix the flour, 1 teaspoon salt, and cayenne. With a pastry blender or two knives, cut in the butter. Add enough ice water to make a dough with the consistency of pie crust.

Place the sesame seeds in a shallow baking dish. Roast in the oven for 20 minutes or until well browned. Shake the pan during roasting to turn the seeds. Remove when done and lower temperature to 300°.

Add the sesame seeds to the dough mixture; stir well. On a lightly floured surface roll the dough out to ¼-inch thickness. Cut with a small round biscuit cutter. Place the rounds in muffin pans and bake for 20 to 30 minutes or until browned. Before removing from the pans, sprinkle with salt.

Store biscuits in tins. To crisp, heat them in a 300° oven before serving.

Benne, or sesame seeds, came to Ameria with slaves from Africa. Dishes made with benne are particularly associated with South Carolina and Charleston.

# CHEESE STRAWS

serves 6 to 8

1 cup freshly grated Parmesan cheese
1 cup flour
1 tablespoon butter, melted
1 egg yolk, beaten
   salt and cayenne pepper to taste

Preheat the oven to 450°.

Combine the flour and cheese in a mixing bowl. Add the salt and cayenne. Add the beaten egg yolk and the melted butter. Mix gently to form a paste.

Roll the dough out onto a lightly floured surface to ⅛-inch thickness. With a pastry wheel or sharp knife, cut the dough into strips 4 inches long. Place the strips on heavily greased cookie sheets and bake until light brown, about 5 to 7 minutes. Cool slightly and remove from sheets.

# EGGPLANT CAVIAR

serves 8

1 large eggplant
1 large onion, chopped
1 green pepper, chopped
½ cup olive oil
1 large clove garlic, chopped
2 tomatoes, peeled and chopped
   salt and pepper to taste
4 tablespoons white wine or dry vermouth

Preheat the oven to 400°.

Place the whole eggplant in a lightly oiled baking dish and bake until soft, about 1 hour.

In a skillet, sauté the onions and green pepper in the olive oil until soft but not brown. Add the garlic and cook 2 minutes longer. Do not brown.

When the eggplant is done, allow it to cool. Peel and chop the eggplant. Add it to the onion mixture. Add the chopped tomatoes. Season to taste with salt and pepper.

Add the wine and mix well. Cook until mixture is thick, about 25 to 30 minutes.

Cool and chill for 8 hours or overnight. Serve with bread or crackers.

# CREOLE CANAPÉS

serves 6

1 cup boiled ham, minced
1 medium onion, finely chopped
1 clove garlic, finely chopped
1 medium tomato, peeled and chopped
1 green pepper, finely chopped
   salt and pepper to taste
   cayenne pepper to taste
6 slices buttered toast, cut into strips
1 tablespoon butter
2 ounces freshly grated Parmesan cheese

In a skillet, sauté the ham, 1 tablespoon butter, onion, and garlic for 3 minutes. Add the green pepper and tomato. Continue cooking. Season to taste with salt, pepper, and cayenne pepper. Cook mixture until it is dry and thick, about 35 minutes.

Preheat the oven to 375°.

When ready to serve, place the spread on strips of buttered toast and sprinkle with cheese. Put strips on a cookie sheet and bake for 5 to 7 minutes. Serve hot.

# GUACAMOLE

2 large ripe avocados

1 large tomato, peeled, seeded, and finely chopped

1 hard-cooked egg, finely chopped

½ cup onions, finely chopped

2 canned green chilies, drained, seeded, and finely chopped

1 tablespoon lemon juice

1 teaspoon salt

Cut the avocados in half and remove the pits. Peel off the skin (this can easily be done with your fingers). In a bowl coarsely chop the avocados and then mash them with a fork or the back of a spoon until smooth. Add the tomato, egg, onions, chilies, lemon juice, and salt. Mix well.

Serve with chips or tostadas for dipping.

# —Salads—

# COLD KIDNEY BEAN MIX

serves 6

2 1-pound cans kidney beans, drained

1 cup scallions, finely chopped (about 6 scallions)

½ cup parsley, finely chopped

2 teaspoons pimientos, finely chopped

3 cloves garlic, finely chopped

6 tablespoons olive oil

3 tablespoons red wine vinegar

Drain the kidney beans and gently pat dry.

In a large bowl combine the kidney beans, scallions, parsley, and pimiento. Add the garlic, olive oil, and vinegar. Toss well. Chill in refrigerator for several hours. Remove 45 minutes before serving.

# TEXAS GREEN BEAN SALAD

serves 6

2 pounds whole fresh green beans

6 tablespoons wine vinegar

¾ cup olive oil

2 medium onions, finely chopped

salt and pepper to taste

½ pound salt pork, sliced

Trim the green beans and blanch in boiling salted water. Cook for 3 to 5 minutes. Drain and rinse with cold water.

In a small skillet cook the salt pork until well browned and crisp. Remove salt pork from skillet and crumble.

In a large bowl combine the wine vinegar, olive oil, onions, salt, and pepper. Add the green beans and toss well. Chill for 2 to 3 hours.

Drain the beans and place in a clean bowl. Add the crumbled salt pork. Toss well and serve.

# SOUTHWESTERN CABBAGE SALAD

serves 6

    1  large head cabbage, shredded and chilled
    1  green pepper, coarsely chopped
    ¼  cup mayonnaise
    ¼  cup sour cream
    3  tablespoons white wine vinegar
    3  tablespoons sugar
    ½  teaspoon chili powder
    ½  teaspoon salt
    ¼  teaspoon pepper
    ⅛  teaspoon cayenne pepper

Place the shredded cabbage in a large bowl and add the green pepper. Mix well and chill.

In a mixing bowl combine the mayonnaise, sour cream, vinegar, sugar, chili powder, salt, pepper, and cayenne. Blend well and chill for 2 hours.

Pour the dressing over the cabbage mixture and toss very well.

# SHRIMP AND BEAN SALAD

serves 4

    1  cup cooked or canned white beans
    1  cup cooked or canned kidney beans
    ¾  pound cooked shrimp, peeled and deveined
    1  cup green pepper, finely chopped
    1  tablespoon onions, chopped
    1  tablespoon pimiento, chopped
    ½  teaspoon salt
    ¼  teaspoon pepper
    ⅛  teaspoon cayenne pepper
    ¼  cup white wine vinegar
    ½  cup olive oil

If using canned beans, place them in a colander and rinse under cold running water. Drain well.

In a large bowl combine the beans, shrimp, green pepper, onions, and pimento. Sprinkle salt, pepper, and cayenne over the salad.

In a mixing bowl combine the vinegar and olive oil. Whisk until well blended. Pour only enough oil and vinegar over the salad to moisten it well. Toss. Chill for 1 hour and serve.

# FLORIDA SEAFOOD SALAD

serves 4

    1  cup cooked shrimp, peeled, deveined, and left whole
    ½  cup cooked lobster, coarsely chopped
    ½  cup cooked crabmeat, flaked
    ½  cup cooked scallops (cut in half if they are large)
    1  grapefruit, peeled and sectioned
    ½  cup black or green olives
    ½  cup olive oil
    1½ teaspoons white wine vinegar
    ½  teaspoon French-style mustard
    ¼  teaspoon salt
    ⅛  teaspoon pepper

Place the shrimp, lobster, crabmeat, and scallops in a bowl and chill.

Into a large bowl lined with lettuce or spinach leaves place the shrimp, lobster, crabmeat, and scallops. Add the grapefruit sections and olives.

In a small bowl combine the vinegar, mustard, salt, and pepper. Whisk in the oil until well blended. Pour dressing over salad and toss lightly. Serve immediately.

# PAPAYA SEAFOOD SALAD

serves 4

2 *ripe papayas, chilled*
2 *cups cooked shrimp, chopped, or crabmeat, flaked*
1 *cup celery, chopped*
½ *teaspoon curry powder*
½ *cup mayonnaise*
  *juice of 1 lime*
1 *lime, quartered*

Cut the papayas in half and scoop out the seeds.

In a bowl combine the shrimp, celery, curry powder, and mayonnaise. Fill each papaya half with the mixture. Sprinkle with the lime juice. Serve each papaya half with a lime wedge.

Papayas are low in calories but high in vitamins. They grow in the Caribbean and are extremely popular throughout the South and Southwest. Most well-stocked supermarkets carry papayas.

# SOUTHERN-STYLE POTATO SALAD

serves 6

6 *medium potatoes*
½ *cup sweet pickles, finely chopped*
1 *medium onion, finely chopped*
½ *cup cider vinegar*
½ *cup celery, finely chopped*
½ *teaspoon French-style mustard*
1 *teaspoon salt*
¼ *teaspoon pepper*
1½ *cups mayonnaise*

Place the potatoes in a pot with enough boiling salted water to cover. Cook, uncovered, until the potatoes are tender, about 40 minutes. Drain potatoes and allow to cool. When cool enough to handle, peel and dice into small cubes.

Place the diced potatoes in a large bowl. Add the cider vinegar and mix gently.

In a separate bowl combine the celery, onion, pickles, salt, pepper, mustard, and mayonnaise. Add the potato mixture and combine gently. Season to taste and let stand, covered, for 2 hours before serving to let flavors combine.

# TEXAS VEGETABLE SALAD

serves 4

1 *cucumber, peeled and sliced*
½ *cup cooked lima beans*
½ *cup cooked diced carrots*
6 *pimiento-stuffed olives, sliced*
¾ *cup mayonnaise*
1 *teaspoon chili sauce*
¼ *teaspoon sugar*
½ *teaspoon horseradish*
½ *teaspoon salt*
  *lettuce leaves*
2 *tablespoons olive oil*
1 *tomato, finely chopped*
4 *scallions, chopped*

In a large bowl combine the cucumber, lima beans, carrots, olives, mayonnaise, chili sauce, sugar, horseradish, and salt. Mix well.

Place 4 to 5 washed and drained lettuce leaves in a bowl. Add olive oil and toss.

Line a serving bowl with the lettuce leaves. Pour the vegetable mixture into the bowl. Top with the chopped scallions and chopped tomato. Serve immediately.

# HERBED BEAN SALAD

serves 6

  4 cups water
  1 cup dried navy or pea beans
  1 teaspoon salt
  1 tablespoon tarragon vinegar
  2 teaspoons French-style mustard
  ½ teaspoon Tabasco sauce
  ½ teaspoon pepper
  ⅓ olive oil
  2 tablespoons fresh basil, finely chopped,
    or 1 teaspoon dried, crumbled
  2 tablespoons chives or tops of scallions,
    finely chopped
  2 mint leaves, finely chopped, or ½ teaspoon dried,
    crumbled
  2 cloves garlic, finely chopped
  1 large tomato, peeled, seeded, and coarsely chopped

In a large saucepan bring the water to a rapid boil. Add the navy beans and boil, uncovered, for 3 minutes. Remove from heat and let beans cool in their water for 1 hour. Season water with salt and bring back to a boil. Lower heat and simmer beans, partially covered, for 1 hour or until tender. Remove from heat, drain, and cool.

In a mixing bowl, combine the vinegar, mustard, Tabasco, salt, and pepper. Add the olive oil in a steady stream and whisk the mixture until smooth.

In a large bowl combine the basil, chives, parsley, mint, and garlic. Mix well. Add the beans and tomatoes. Stir gently but thoroughly.

Pour the tomato-bean mixture into the dressing. Toss mixture until pieces are well coated. Cover bowl and place in refrigerator for 5 hours. Remove from refrigerator 1 hour before serving.

# SPICY CHICK PEA SALAD

serves 4

  1 1-pound can chick peas (garbanzos)
  1 small onion, finely chopped
  1 tablespoon parsley, finely chopped
  2 medium carrots, cooked and diced
  ¼ cup olive oil
  2 tablespoons cider vinegar
  1 teaspoon salt
  ½ teaspoon pepper
 1½ teaspoon hot red pepper flakes
  ⅛ teaspoons cayenne pepper
    lettuce leaves

Drain the chick peas and rinse under cold running water. Drain well.

Dice the carrots and cook in boiling water for 5 to 7 minutes. Drain well.

In a large bowl, mix together the chick peas, onion, parsley, carrots, oil, vinegar, and red pepper flakes. Add salt, pepper, and cayenne.

Chill in refrigerator for 1 to 2 hours. When ready to serve, line a large serving bowl with lettuce and spoon in the salad.

# Dairy Dishes

## CREOLE OMELET

serves 4

6 eggs
6 ripe medium tomatoes
2 medium onions
2 tablespoons ham, diced
1 tablespoon bread crumbs
1 tablespoon butter
½ clove garlic, finely chopped
   salt and pepper to taste
   cayenne pepper to taste
2 teaspoons butter

Pour boiling water over the tomatoes. Peel them and chop finely.

Chop the onions very finely and place in a bowl with the garlic and bread crumbs. Mix well.

Melt the butter in a skillet. Add the onions mixture and sauté until brown, about 8 minutes. Add the tomatoes. Season with salt, pepper, and cayenne to taste. Cover and simmer mixture for 1 hour.

Break the eggs into a mixing bowl and whisk until light. Add ham and whisk again.

Melt 1 teaspoon of butter in the skillet. Pour in the eggs. Cook omelet until bottom is lightly browned and top is creamy. As eggs begin to set, pour the tomato mixture into the center. Carefully fold the omelet and cook for 2 minutes longer. Turn out gently onto a serving dish and serve hot.

## LOUISIANA RUM OMELET

serves 4

6 eggs, separated
8 ounces dark rum
2 teaspoons milk
2 tablespoons butter
3 cubes white sugar

In a mixing bowl beat the egg yolks until they are thick and lemon-colored. Add the milk and mix well.

In another bowl beat the egg whites until they are stiff but not dry. Fold into the egg yolk mixture.

Melt the butter in a large skillet. Pour in the egg mixture and cook omelet until the bottom is lightly brown and the top is creamy. Life the edges while cooking to allow the uncooked parts to run into the skillet.

When omelet is done, fold and turn out onto a serving dish.

Place the sugar cubes on top of the omelet. Pour the rum over and around the omelet. Carefully light the rum, using a wooden kitchen match. With a long-handled spoon, pour the flaming rum over the omelet. Continue until sugar has melted and rum has evaporated and burned off. When flames have died away, cut omelet into portions and serve immediately.

## HUEVOS RANCHEROS (RANCH-STYLE EGGS)

serves 4

  1 clove garlic, finely chopped
  2 large onions, chopped
  3 tablespoons butter
  2 dried hot red peppers, crumbled, or 1½ teaspoons
    red pepper flakes
  1 28-ounce can whole tomatoes
    salt and pepper to taste
  8 eggs

Melt 2 tablespoons butter in a skillet. Add the garlic and onions and sauté until lightly browned, about 5 to 7 minutes. Add the hot peppers and tomatoes. Simmer, covered, for 45 minutes or until thick. Season to taste with salt and pepper.

Break the eggs into a bowl and beat well.

In another skillet, melt the remaining butter. Pour in the eggs and cook until bottom of omelet is lightly browned. Turn eggs over and cook until other side is lightly browned. Slide omelet onto a serving plate and pour sauce over it. Serve hot.

## HUEVOS FRITOS (DEEP-FRIED EGGS)

serves 4

  8 eggs
  1 cup flour
  1 cup bread crumbs
  2 eggs, beaten
    salt and pepper to taste
    olive oil for frying

Place the 8 eggs into a pot of boiling water. Cook for 4 minutes. Remove pot from heat. Run cold water over the eggs and peel carefully.

Place the flour, beaten eggs, and bread crumbs seasoned with salt and pepper into separate bowls. Dip the hard-cooked eggs first into the flour, then the beaten eggs, and then roll in the bread crumbs.

Heat a deep layer of olive oil in a deep skillet to 375° on a frying thermometer. Drop in the eggs and fry for 2 minutes, browning on all sides. Remove and drain on paper towels. Serve with a spicy tomato sauce if desired.

## FLORIDA EGG BAKE

serves 6

  3 tablespoons butter
  3 tablespoons flour
  2 cups canned tomato purée
  ½ teaspoon pepper
  1 teaspoon salt
  2 tablespoons scallions, chopped
  2 tablespoons sweet red pepper, chopped
  8 hard-cooked eggs, shelled and quartered
  ¾ cup grated Monterey Jack cheese
  8 strips bacon, diced

Preheat the oven to 375°.

In a saucepan combine the butter and flour. Blend well and cook for 3 minutes.

Slowly pour in the tomato purée. Add the salt and pepper. Cook the mixture until it begins to thicken, about 15 to 20 minutes. Add the scallions and red pepper. Continue cooking for 4 minutes longer.

Place the hard-cooked egg quarters in a buttered 1½-quart baking dish. Pour the tomato sauce over the eggs. Sprinkle with the grated cheese and bacon.

Bake for 20 to 25 minutes or until cheese is melted and bacon is crisp. Serve hot.

# NEW ORLEANS HERB OMELET

serves 2

4 eggs, very lightly beaten
4 tablespoons water
½ teaspoon salt
⅛ teaspoon pepper
½ teaspoon parsley, minced
½ teaspoon chives, minced
1 teaspoon watercress, minced
½ teaspoon chervil
2 tablespoons butter

Whisk together in a bowl the eggs, water, salt, pepper, parsley, chives, watercress, and chervil.

Melt the butter in a skillet over medium heat. Reduce heat slightly when butter is hot. Pour in the egg mixture and cook until lightly browned underneath and creamy on top. While cooking, lift edges of the omelet to allow the uncooked parts to run underneath. Fold and gently slide onto a plate. Serve hot.

Use only fresh herbs to make this omelet. Increase or decrease the amounts and vary the ingredients according to availability and taste. For more than 2 servings, do not multiply ingredients. Make separate batches instead.

# GEORGIA JELLY OMELET

serves 6

6 eggs, separated
½ teaspoon salt
⅛ teaspoon dried rosemary
¼ cup water
4 tablespoons blackberry jelly
1 teaspoon parsley, finely chopped

Preheat the oven to 400°.

In a bowl beat together the egg yolks, salt, and rosemary.

In a separate bowl beat the egg whites until they are stiff but not dry. Fold into the yolk mixture.

Lightly butter a 1-quart casserole or soufflé dish. Pour in a layer of the eggs and dot with jelly. Repeat 2 more times.

Place the casserole into a pan filled with hot water. The water should reach halfway up the sides of the dish. Bake for 20 minutes. Sprinkle with parsley and serve.

# KENTUCKY SCRAMBLE

serves 4

1 cup cooked fresh corn, cut from the cob
3 tablespoons bacon drippings
1 sweet red pepper, chopped
1 teaspoon parsley, chopped
6 eggs
1 teaspoon salt
¼ teaspoon pepper
⅛ teaspoon cayenne pepper

*(continued on next page)*

Heat the bacon drippings in a frying pan. Add the corn and sauté for 3 minutes. Stir in the red pepper and parsley. Cook 5 minutes longer.

In a bowl, beat the eggs, salt, pepper, and cayenne. Pour into the corn mixture and scramble until eggs are set but still moist. Serve immediately.

# GREEN CHILI AND CORN SOUFFLE

serves 6

6 egg whites
5 egg yolks
3 canned peeled green chilies
1 cup corn
½ teaspoon salt
1 teaspoon chili powder

Preheat the oven to 400°.

Place the egg yolks, chilies, corn, salt, and chili powder into the container of an electric blender. Blend for 1 minute. Pour into a large bowl.

In a separate bowl, beat the egg whites until stiff but not dry. Fold into chili-corn mixture. Pour into a heavily buttered 4½-cup soufflé or baking dish. Bake for 25 to 30 minutes or until firm.

Serve *immediately.*

# CHILALI

1 teaspoon melted butter
1 tablespoon sweet red pepper, chopped
1 tablespoon green pepper, chopped
½ cup chopped tomatoes
½ pound mild cheese, cut into ½-inch squares
½ teaspoon salt
1 teaspoon Tabasco sauce
1 egg, beaten
½ cup milk
4 to 6 slices toast

In a saucepan, combine the butter, green pepper, red pepper, onion, and tomatoes. Cook over low heat for 5 minutes. Stir in the cheese, salt, and Tabasco. Cook, stirring constantly, for 5 minutes.

Beat the egg into the milk. Pour the egg mixture into the saucepan and stir well. Heat thoroughly and spoon mixture over slices of toast.

This is a sort of Southwestern Welsh rabbit.

# VIRGINIA HAM OMELET

serves 4

6 eggs, slightly beaten
6 tablespoons water
¾ teaspoon salt
½ teaspoon pepper
3 tablespoons butter
¼ cup baked Virginia ham, finely chopped

In a bowl whisk together the eggs, water, salt, and pepper.

Heat the butter in a skillet. When butter begins to bubble, pour in the eggs.

Cook until omelet is lightly browned on the bottom and creamy on top. While cooking, lift the edges of the omelet to let the uncooked part run underneath.

When the omelet is creamy and begins to set, add the ham. Raise the heat slightly and cook 1 to 2 minutes. Make sure the omelet is not dry. Fold and gently roll out onto a serving dish.

## MISSISSIPPI "SHUSHED" EGGS

serves 4

8 *eggs*
4 *teaspoon butter*
  *salt and pepper to taste*

In a heavy skillet, melt the butter and let it brown slightly.

Break the eggs into a bowl and season to taste with salt and pepper. Beat only until yolks and whites are barely mixed. Do not overmix.

Pour the eggs into the brown butter. Stir, cooking only until the eggs are set, about 3 minutes. Serve hot.

## NEW MEXICO BAKED EGGS

serves 4

4 *tablespoons onion, chopped*
2 *cloves garlic, crushed*
2 *tablespoons olive oil*
1 *cup thinly sliced* chorizos (*Spanish sausage*)
2 *pimientos, minced*
2 *tomatoes, peeled and diced*
¼ *cup chicken broth*
¼ *cup water*
1 *teaspoon salt*
½ *teaspoon pepper*
8 *eggs*

Preheat the oven to 425°.

In a skillet, saute the onion and garlic in the olive oil until the onion begins to soften. Add the *chorizo* slices and brown. Stir in the pimientos, tomatoes, chicken broth, water, salt, and pepper. Simmer for 5 minutes.

Divide the mixture evenly among 4 lightly buttered individual casserole or soufflé dishes. Break 2 eggs into each dish and bake until the whites are set, about 5 to 8 minutes. Serve hot.

# Meat and Poultry

## SOUTHERN-STYLE BAKED HAM

serves 10 to 12

    1  10-pound fresh, uncooked ham
    1  tablespoon whole cloves
    1  stick cinnamon
    1  cup sugar
    1¼ cups white vinegar
    2  cloves garlic
    1  onion
    1  cup dark brown sugar
    2  teaspoons dry mustard
    ¾  cup water

Wash the ham and place it in a large saucepan with water to cover. Add the cloves, cinnamon stick, sugar, 1 cup vinegar, garlic, and onion. Bring the mixture to a boil, reduce the heat, and simmer for 2½ hours.

Remove the ham from the saucepan and let cool at room temperature for 3 hours.

Preheat the oven to 350°.

Remove the skin from the ham. Dry the ham gently but thoroughly.

In a small bowl combine the brown sugar and dry mustard. Rub the mixture into the ham. Place the ham in a baking dish and add the remaining vinegar and the water. Bake for 1 hour. After ham has cooked for 30 minutes, baste every 7 to 10 minutes.

## ROASTED PORK WITH TURNIPS

serves 4 to 6

    1  3½-pound smoked pork shoulder
    1½ pounds turnips, peeled and quartered
    2  tablespoons cider vinegar
       salt and pepper to taste

Preheat the oven to 325°.

Tie the pork tightly with string and place it in a lightly oiled roasting pan. Place in oven and roast for 1 hour.

After the pork has roasted for 50 minutes, begin to cook the turnips. Steam the turnips in a steamer or a little bit of water. Bring the water to a boil, then lower heat and simmer, covered, for 8 to 10 minutes.

When the pork has roasted for 1 hour, add the turnips to the roasting pan and mix with the pork drippings. Return pork to oven for 30 minutes.

Remove the pork to a cutting board. Pour the vinegar over the turnips in the roasting pan and mix well. Slice the pork and serve surrounded with turnips.

# SHERRIED SMITHFIELD HAM

serves 16 to 20

1  14-pound Smithfield ham
½  pound brown sugar
1  cup sherry

Wash the ham well and place it in a large pan, skin-side down. Cover the ham completely with cold water. Soak for 2 days, changing the water after the first day.

Drain the ham and place in a large, top-of-the-stove roasting pan. Cover completely with cold water. Heat and simmer 25 minutes per pound, about 4 hours. When ham is done, let it cool in its water. Remove skin.

Preheat the oven to 350°.

Dissolve the brown sugar in the sherry.

Place the ham in a baking dish and place in oven for 20 to 30 minutes, or until heated through. When ham is heated, poke holes with a skewer into the side where the skin was removed. Pour some of the sherry mixture into the holes. Return ham to the oven and continue to pour the sherry into the holes every few minutes until mixture is used up.

Remove ham from oven and allow to cool slightly. Slice as thinly as possible and serve.

Smithfield hams have been made in Tidewater Virginia for more than 350 years. These superb hams are made from peanut-fed pigs. The hams are cured in salt for 35 days, then set aside for another 21 days. They are then air-cured for 6 months or longer.

# CREOLE ROAST PORK

serves 6 to 8

1  6-pound loin of pork roast
1  teaspoon salt
½  teaspoon pepper
1  teaspoon dried sage
8  large tart apples, cored
4  sweet potatoes, peeled, quartered, and cooked
2  tablespoons brown sugar
¼  teaspoon grated nutmeg
¼  cup melted butter
¼  cup pure maple syrup

Preheat the oven to 300°.

Sprinkle the meat with the salt, pepper, and sage. Rub into the meat. Place the roast, fat-side up, on a rack in a baking pan. Roast for 3 hours.

With a sharp knife, remove enough pulp from the apples to make the core opening 1½ to 2 inches wide. Chop the removed pulp and reserve.

In a large bowl, mash the sweet potatoes. Add the apple pulp, brown sugar, nutmeg, and pepper.

In a small saucepan, heat the butter and maple syrup. Cook for 2 minutes. Spoon 1 teaspoon of the mixture into each of the apples. Reserve the leftover syrup.

Fill the apple openings with the sweet potato mixture until the apples are very full.

Remove the roast from the oven. Drain the fat from the pan and place the apples around the roast. Roast 1½ hours longer. Baste the apples frequently with the reserved syrup. When roast is done, place it on a serving platter and surround with apples.

# DOUBLE-DECK PORK TOSTADAS

serves 4

1 pound ground pork
1 medium onion, chopped
1½ teaspoons chili powder
1 teaspoon salt
¼ teaspoon ground cumin
1 clove garlic, finely chopped
1 15-ounce can kidney beans
½ cup water
8 6-inch corn tortillas
1 cup shredded lettuce
½ cup shredded mild cheese
1 tomato, chopped

Brown the pork and onion together in a large skillet, about 8 minutes. Pour off the fat. Add chili powder, salt, cumin, and garlic to pork.

Drain kidney beans, reserving ¼ cup liquid. Mash beans and add to pork. Stir in reserved bean liquid and water. Cook slowly for 15 minutes, stirring occasionally.

Heat the tortillas according to package directions.

Spread about ⅓ cup of the pork mixture on each of 4 tortillas; place ¼ cup of lettuce over each. Top each with a second tortilla. Spread each with an equal portion of the remaining pork mixture. Top with shredded cheese and chopped tomato.

Prepared tortillas are easily found in most supermarkets.

# BARBECUED SPARERIBS

serves 6

3 to 4 pounds spareribs, cut into strips between bones
1 cup onion, finely chopped
1 cup peach preserves
¼ cup Worcestershire sauce
¼ cup red wine vinegar
¼ cup brown sugar
¼ teaspoon Tabasco sauce
1 teaspoon dry mustard
2 cloves garlic, finely chopped
1 teaspoon salt
   pepper to taste
2 lemons, sliced

Preheat the oven to 325°.

Arrange the ribs, meaty side up, in a large shallow roasting pan.

In a saucepan combine the onions, peach preserves, Worcestershire sauce, vinegar, brown sugar, Tabasco, and dry mustard. Heat, stirring constantly, until mixture begins to boil. Reduce the heat and simmer for 5 minutes or until onions are soft.

Season the ribs with salt and pepper. With a pastry brush, spread the barbecue sauce on the ribs. Place lemon slices on top. Cover and place in the oven for 1½ hours. Remove from oven and skim fat from sauce. Turn oven up to 450° and brown ribs, uncovered, for 10 to 15 minutes.

# ORANGE GROVE PORK CHOPS

serves 4

4 center-cut pork chops (totaling about 2 pounds)
   salt and pepper to taste
   flour for dredging
3 tablespoons butter
1 large orange, peeled and cut into thin slices
½ cup orange juice
   watercress (optional)

Rub the pork chops with the salt and pepper. Dredge them in flour. Shake off excess.

Heat the butter in a large skillet. Add the chops and quickly brown over high heat, about 3 to 7 minutes per side. Remove the chops and transfer to a large shallow baking dish. The dish should be large enough to hold all the chops in one layer.

Preheat the oven to 350°.

Top each pork chop with 1 or 2 orange slices. Place a piece of aluminum foil over the dish and crimp so that the dish is tightly covered. Bake for 1 hour or until chops are tender. If desired, serve on a bed of watercress.

# CREOLE VEAL STEW

serves 6

4 pounds brisket of veal
½ pound ham, diced
2 large onions, chopped
2 sweet potatoes
2 dozen small fresh okra, very thinly sliced
6 medium tomatoes, chopped
2 cloves garlic, finely chopped
2 tablespoons butter
1 bay leaf
2 sprigs parsley
½ teaspoon dried thyme
   salt and pepper to taste
   cayenne pepper to taste

Cut the veal into pieces about 3 inches long and 2 inches wide. Season with salt, pepper, and cayenne.

Peel the sweet potatoes and cut into 1½-inch cubes.

Place 1 tablespoon butter in a large heavy pot and melt. Brown the veal in the butter, approximately 3 to 5 minutes per side. Add the ham and sweet potatoes and simmer gently for fifteen minutes.

Meanwhile, prepare the sauce. In a saucepan melt 1 tablespoon butter. Add the onions and brown. Stir in the bay leaf, parsley, and thyme. Add the tomatoes and cook for about 15 minutes.

Add sauce to veal. Mix thoroughly, cover tightly, and simmer slowly for about 2 hours.

Add the okra, simmer 30 minutes longer, and serve.

# CREOLE GRILLADES

serves 4 to 6

  1 to 1½ pounds beef round, approximately
      ½-inch thick
      salt and pepper to taste
⅛ teaspoon cayenne pepper
  2 tablespoons lard or olive oil
  1 small onion, thinly sliced
  2 cloves garlic, finely chopped
  1 large tomato, chopped

Trim the fat from the meat. Cut into 3- or 4-inch squares. Place the meat squares between two sheets of wax paper. Using a meat mallet, pound the squares until they are about ¼-inch thick. Rub the meat on both sides with salt, pepper, and cayenne.

In a large heavy skillet, heat the lard or oil. When hot, add the onion and garlic. Cook, stirring constantly, until brown, about 5 to 7 minutes. Stir in the tomato and cook 2 minutes.

Add the meat and stir well to coat on all sides. Cover the skillet and cook for 10 minutes or until beef is tender and well browned. Serve hot.

Traditionally served in New Orleans as a breakfast dish with grits, this is also a good main course when served with beans or rice.

# NEW MEXICO PICADILLO

serves 4 to 5

  2 tablespoons olive oil
  1 large onion, thinly sliced
  3 cloves garlic, finely chopped
½ pound ground lean beef
½ pound ground pork
      salt and pepper to taste
¼ teaspoon ground cumin
  1 bay leaf
½ cup red wine
  2 large tomatoes, peeled and chopped
¼ cup dark raisins, plumped
  1 sweet red pepper, cut into strips

In a large deep skillet heat the olive oil. Add the onion and garlic. Cook, stirring constantly, until they are soft and golden, about 5 to 7 minutes. Add the meat, salt, pepper, and cumin. Mix well. Cook over low heat, stirring constantly, until meat is well browned. Add the bay leaf, wine, tomatoes, and raisins. Mix well and cover skillet. Simmer mixture over low heat for 15 minutes, stirring frequently. If mixture is too wet, remove cover and continue cooking. Stir in the red pepper strips and cook 2 minutes longer.

Serve over rice or use mixture to fill taco shells.

The arguments about what constitutes the ingredients for *real* chili rage passionately. Some claim that venison is the correct meat; others say only jackrabbit should be used. Aficionados divide into armed camps over whether the mixture should contain tomatoes or not. Even the onion question is hotly debated. This recipe is not definitive; not even the annual World Championship Chili Cookoff, held in Terlingua, Texas since 1967, has come up with that.

# TEXAS CHILI CON CARNE

serves 6 to 8

4 tablespoons olive oil
2 cloves garlic, finely chopped
2 onions, chopped
2 pounds lean beef, cut into small cubes
4 tablespoons chili powder
1 teaspoon oregano
½ teaspoon ground cumin
½ teaspoon salt
10 dried chili peppers, boiled, seeded, and skinned
1 cup beef broth
1 cup water
1 cup pinto beans

Cook the pinto beans in a pot of lightly salted boiling water for 1½ to 2 hours. When done, drain and reserve the broth. Set the beans aside.

In a large skillet heat the olive oil. Add the onion and garlic and sauté for 2 minutes. Add the meat and brown, stirring frequently. Add the chili powder, oregano, cumin, salt, and dried chilies.

Cover the skillet and cook over low heat for 1 hour or until the meat is tender and the chili has thickened. If the chili gets too dry, add some of the water.

Just before serving, add the pinto beans and mix well. If the chili is too spicy, add some of the reserved bean broth.

# CALDILLO (SOUTHWESTERN BEEF STEW)

serves 4 to 6

1 pound stewing beef, cubed
¾ cup onion, diced
2 tablespoons bacon fat or olive oil
1½ cups tomatoes, diced
¾ cup sliced green chili peppers
¼ cup beef broth
¼ cup water
1 teaspoon salt
1 teaspoon pepper
2 gloves garlic, chopped
1 teaspoon ground cumin
1 pound potatoes, peeled and cubed

Heat the bacon fat or olive oil in a heavy skillet. Add the beef and onions. Sauté until onions are soft but not brown, about 5 to 8 minutes. Add the tomatoes, chilies, beef broth, water, salt, pepper, and cumin. Cook, covered, over low heat until meat is tender, about 2 hours. Add the potatoes after mixture has cooked for 1½ hours.

# DRIED BEEF AND GRAVY

serves 4 to 6

½ pound dried beef
water
2 tablespoons butter
2 tablespoons bacon fat
5 tablespoons flour
3 cups milk
4 potatoes, peeled, quartered, and boiled
1 cup potato water
salt and pepper to taste

Break the beef into small pieces and place them in a medium skillet. Add water to cover. Add the butter and bacon fat. Bring to a boil and cook until the water has been boiled away and the beef has been frizzled brown in the fat.

Lower the heat and stir in the flour, milk, and potato water. Continue cooking until mixture is thick and smooth.

Mash the boiled potatoes with butter and a little milk. Serve the beef over the potatoes.

# TAMALE PIE

serves 4

½ teaspoon salt
1 cup yellow corn meal
3 tablespoons butter or olive oil
1 medium onion, chopped
3 cups water
salt
1 clove garlic, chopped
1 small green pepper, chopped
1 pound ground chuck
1 teaspoon chili powder
4 medium tomatoes, sliced

Preheat the oven to 375°.

In a saucepan, bring 3 cups salted water to a boil. Slowly add the corn meal, stirring constantly. Lower the heat and cook for 10 minutes. Stir often.

In a skillet heat the butter or oil. Add the onion, green pepper, and garlic. Cook over low heat until soft but not brown, about 5 to 7 minutes. Add the ground chuck and brown. Pour off fat. Stir in the chili powder and salt. Remove skillet from heat.

Lightly oil a medium casserole dish. Spread half the cooked corn meal over the bottom and cover with a layer of sliced tomatoes. Add the meat mixture. Add a second layer of the corn meal and top with the tomatoes. Place in oven and bake for 25 minutes.

# LOUISIANA FROGS' LEGS

serves 4

12 pairs frozen frogs' legs, skinned and washed
   salt to taste
   flour for dredging
2 eggs, lightly beaten
   bread crumbs for dredging
2 cups olive oil
3 cloves garlic, crushed

If using frozen frog's legs, defrost thoroughly.

Season the frogs' legs with salt and dredge them in flour. Then dip the legs into the beaten eggs and roll in the bread crumbs.

In a large skillet, heat the olive oil until very hot. Add the garlic and then the frogs' legs, 2 at a time. Fry until golden brown on both sides, about 5 to 7 minutes.

Drain on paper towels and serve warm.

The French who settled Louisiana were delighted to find that the bayous were full of delicious frogs. Nowadays, most people get their frogs' legs in the frozen-foods section of well-stocked supermarkets. If you cannot find them, substitute chicken wings instead.

# GUMBO FILÉ

serves 4 to 6

1  5-pound chicken, cut into serving pieces
2  teaspoons salt
1  teaspoon pepper
1  clove garlic, chopped
3  tablespoons butter
2  medium onions, chopped
½  pound boiled ham, cut into strips
3  quarts water
½  teaspoon dried thyme
½  teaspoon dried rosemary
¼  teaspoon chili powder
1  cup canned tomatoes
1  cup fresh okra, sliced
24  oysters
1  tablespoon filé powder

Rub the salt, pepper, and garlic pieces into the chicken.

In a large saucepan, melt the butter. Add the onions and the chicken; cook until brown, about 8 minutes. Add the ham, water, thyme, rosemary, chili powder, and tomatoes. Cover and simmer for 2½ hours. Add the okra and cook 1 hour longer. Add the oysters. Bring the mixture to a boil and cook for 3 minutes.

Remove the saucepan from heat and stir in filé powder. Mix well. Do not allow the gumbo to boil. Do not reheat the gumbo after the filé powder has been added or the gumbo will become stringy. Serve hot in soup bowls.

A true gumbo must be made with filé powder, which gives it a slightly astringent flavor. This Cajun specialty from the bayous is made from sassafras leaves. Most well-stocked gourmet shops carry the powder.

# KENTUCKY BURGOO

serves 8 to 10

2½ tablespoons lard or olive oil
1 pound lean beef shank
1 pound beef bones
½ pound shoulder of veal
1 3-pound chicken, quartered
2 quarts water
1½ teaspoons salt
2 cups onions, chopped
1 clove garlic, chopped
1 cup potatoes, peeled and diced
4 stalks celery, diced with tops
1 20-ounce can tomatoes
3 carrots, diced
1 large green pepper, chopped
1 cup fresh butter beans or waxed beans
½ teaspoon crushed hot red pepper flakes
1 small onion
1 bay leaf
⅛ cup dark brown sugar
¼ teaspoon pepper
1 cup fresk okra, sliced
1½ cups fresh corn, cut from the cob
¼ cup butter
½ cup flour
½ cup parsley, finely chopped

In a large pot, heat ¼ tablespoon of the lard or oil. Add the beef shank, beef bones, and veal. Brown well for about 8 minutes.

Add the chicken, water, and salt. Cover and cook over low heat until very tender, about 30 to 40 minutes.

Remove the meat and chicken to a plate. When cool enough to handle, remove meat from bones. Cut it into small pieces and return to pot. Discard bones and chicken skin.

In a skillet, sauté the onion in the remaining lard or oil until soft but not brown, about 5 minutes. Add to the meat in the pot. Stir in the garlic, potatoes, celery, tomatoes, carrots, green pepper, beans, red pepper, whole onion, bay leaf, brown sugar, and ground pepper. Cook over low heat 2 hours. Stir occasionally.

After 2 hours, add the okra and corn. Cook 15 minutes longer.

In a small bowl, blend together the butter and flour. Add to the burgoo and cook, stirring constantly, until mixture thickens. Season to taste and sprinkle with chopped parsley before serving.

Although burgoo originated as a sort of thick porridge on board sailing vessels in the mid-1800s, it came to mean a thick meat stew as made in Kentucky. Burgoo is made in huge quantities for large events like Fourth of July picnics and Derby Day.

# JAMBALAYA

serves 8 to 10

3 3-pound chickens, cut into serving pieces
   flour for dredging
4 tablespoons lard or bacon fat
3 cups onions, chopped
2 cups sweet red pepper, chopped
1 scallion, thinly sliced
2 cloves garlic, chopped
½ pound lean baked ham, cut into ½-inch squares
1½ pound lean pork, trimmed of fat and cut into
   ½-inch cubes
6 hot sausages, sliced thin
½ pound cooked shrimp, peeled and deveined
3 teaspoons salt
1 teaspoon pepper
½ teaspoon Tabasco sauce
4 bay leaves
1½ cups raw long-grain rice
2 cups hot chicken broth
1 cup hot water

Wash the chicken pieces and remove all fat and skin. If breasts are very large, cut them in half. Dredge the chicken in flour and shake off excess.

In a large deep casserole, heat the lard or bacon fat. Add the chicken and quickly brown the pieces on all sides over high heat. Turn frequently, using tongs.

Remove the browned chicken pieces to a warm place. To the casserole add the onions, red pepper, scallions, garlic, ham, and pork. Reduce heat to medium and cook, stirring constantly, for 10 to 15 minutes, or until both vegetables and ham are browned. Add the sausage slices to the casserole. Stir in the salt, pepper, and bay leaves. Cook, stirring constantly, for 4 minutes.

Return the chicken pieces to the pot. Stir in the shrimp, raw rice, hot chicken broth, and hot water. Mix well. Raise the heat and bring the mixture to a boil. Immediately reduce heat to very low. Cover the pot and cook for 20 minutes, stirring occasionally. Uncover the casserole, raise the heat to medium, and cook 10 minutes longer, or until the rice is fluffy and dry. Stir often. Serve immediately.

This dish is best when made for a crowd. An amalgam of French and Spanish cooking traditions, jambalaya is a distinctively Cajun dish.

# BRUNSWICK STEW

serves 8

2  3-pound chickens, cut into serving pieces
2  pounds boneless shoulder of veal, in 1 piece
1  ham bone
3  quarts water
½  cup sugar
1  bay leaf
1  teaspoon dried basil
1  tablespoon fresh parsley, chopped
2  onions, sliced
4  cups tomatoes, peeled and chopped
2  cups celery, chopped with tops
2  cups butter or lima beans
4  cups fresh corn, cut from the cob
½  cup butter
1  teaspoon crushed hot red pepper flakes
4  medium potatoes, peeled, cooked, and mashed

In a large pot combine the chicken, veal, ham bone, water, sugar, bay leaf, basil, and parsley. Cook over low heat until the veal and chicken are tender and fall from bones, about 50 minutes.

Remove the veal and chicken from the broth and cool.

Add the onions, tomatoes, celery, and beans to the broth. Cook over low heat until beans are tender, about 15 minutes. Stir often.

Cut the veal into small pieces. Remove the chicken from the bone and cut into small pieces. Discard bones and skin. Return meat to the pot. Add the corn. Simmer stew for 10 minutes. Stir in the butter, red pepper flakes, and pepper. Season to taste with salt. Stir mashed potatoes into stew. Stir constantly for 15 minutes or until the stew thickens and the potatoes are absorbed. Serve hot.

The original recipe for Brunswick Stew called for squirrel instead of chicken. Brunswick County, North Carolina, and Brunswick County, Virginia still argue about which may lay claim to this stew.

# TURKEY BARBECUE

serves 10

1  10- to 12-pound fresh turkey
½  cup melted butter
½  cup olive oil
2  cups cider vinegar
1  cup tomato sauce
½  cup sugar
2  medium onions, chopped
¼  cup Worcestershire sauce
⅓  cup lemon juice
2  tablespoons dry mustard
3  tablespoons chili powder
2  teaspoons pepper
2  teaspoons salt
2  cloves garlic, crushed

Wash and clean the turkey. Gently pat dry.

In a saucepan, combine the melted butter, olive oil, cider vinegar, tomato sauce, sugar, onions, Worcestershire sauce, lemon juice, mustard, chili powder, pepper, salt, and garlic. Simmer sauce for 10 minutes.

Brush the entire turkey with the barbecue sauce.

Insert a spit rod through the turkey, running it through the tail and diagonally through the breastbone. Fasten the turkey with spit forks. Tie the wings and legs closely to the body with string.

Heat the charcoal until the coals turn gray. Heap the coals in the back of the firebox or to one side of the barbecue. Place the spit in its holders. Place a piece of aluminum foil under the turkey to catch the drippings.

While the turkey rotates on the spit, brush it with the barbecue sauce every 15 minutes. Add charcoal as needed to keep the temperature high.

Barbecue the turkey for about 20 minutes per pound. Remove the turkey from the spit and cool for 20 minutes before carving. Serve with any remaining barbecue sauce.

# GALLINA RELLENA (ROAST STUFFED TURKEY)

serves 12

1   12- to 13-pound fresh turkey
    salt
8   tablespoons butter
1   pound cooked beef, chopped
2   cups golden raisins
2   ounces unsweetened chocolate
1   cup pine nuts
1   cup beef broth
1   teaspoon cinnamon
1   teaspoon ground coriander
½   cup red wine

The night before the turkey will be cooked, clean it and rub the inside with salt and the outside with butter. Wrap in a clean, damp towel and refrigerate.

The next morning, remove the turkey from the refrigerator and set aside while stuffing is prepared.

Preheat the oven to 325°.

Roast the pine nuts in the oven for 12 minutes.

In a large saucepan over medium heat, melt the chocolate. Add the ground beef, raisins, pine nuts, beef broth, cinnamon, coriander, and salt. Mix well and simmer, stirring constantly, until mixture thickens, about 8 to 10 minutes. Add the wine and bring to a boil. Remove mixture from heat and cool.

Place the turkey, breast-side down, on a roasting rack in a baking pan. Stuff the cavity and close with thread or skewers. Immediately roast in oven for about 20 minutes per pound. When the turkey is half cooked, turn the bird and place the breast side up. Baste often with pan drippings. When done, remove from oven and cool slightly before carving.

# MALLARD DUCK AND TURNIP STEW

serves 4

1   mallard duck, jointed and cut into quarters
    oil, butter, or lard for frying
1   tablespoon flour
1   medium onion, finely chopped
2   cloves garlic, finely chopped
    salt and pepper to taste
    water
5   medium turnips, quartered
½   cup scallion greens, coarsely chopped

In a large skillet, heat about 2 teaspoons oil, butter, or lard. Add duck and sauté until brown on both sides, about 6 to 8 minutes. Remove the duck and set aside.

*(continued on next page)*

Add the flour to the fat in the skillet and stir until it forms a dark thick roux, about 3 minutes.

Add the onion, garlic, salt, and pepper. Mix well. Return the pieces of duck to the skillet and add enough water to cover them.

Cover the skillet and simmer 1 hour. Add the turnips and scallion greens and simmer until tender, about 35 to 45 minutes.

# NEW ORLEANS STEWED HEN

serves 6 to 8

    1  4- to 5-pound stewing hen
    1  stalk celery
    1  large carrot, cut in half
    2  sprigs parsley
    1  bay leaf
    6  medium onions
    ¾  teaspoon salt
    ¼  teaspoon pepper
    3  cups cooked ham, cut in ½-inch cubes
    1  pound fresh mushrooms, sliced
    ⅓  cup butter
    2  teaspoons curry powder
    2  tablespoons flour
    1  cup milk
    1  cup heavy cream
    ½  cup apple cider
    3  tablespoons lemon juice

Place the whole hen into a large deep pot. Add the celery, carrot halves, parsley, bay leaf, and 1 onion. Pour enough hot water over the hen to cover it halfway. Bring to a boil. Lower the heat and simmer, covered, for 2 to 2½ hours or until hen is tender. Cool hen in broth.

Remove the hen from the pot. Remove the meat from the bones. Discard the skin and bones. Cut the meat into ½-inch pieces.

Strain the chicken broth and place in a saucepan. Cook it over high heat until it is reduced to 2 cups. Set aside.

Chop the remaining onions. In a skillet, melt the butter. To this add the chopped onions, ham, and mushrooms. Sauté the mixture until the onions are tender but not brown. Stir in the curry powder and flour. Mix until smooth. Add the reserved broth, milk, and cream. Stir until well blended. Continue cooking over low heat for 10 minutes or until mixture just begins to thicken. Add the pieces of hen, salt, pepper, apple cider, and lemon juice. Cook 10 minutes longer. Serve hot.

# SOUTHERN FRIED CHICKEN

serves 6 to 8

    2  3-pound frying chickens, cut into serving pieces
    2  eggs
    1  cup milk
    2  teaspoons salt
    ½  teaspoon pepper
    1  cup flour
       shortening or oil for frying
    1  tablespoon flour
    1  cup light cream, scalded

Rinse and thoroughly dry the chicken pieces.

In a bowl beat the eggs until foamy. Add the milk, salt, and pepper. Mix well.

Dip the chicken pieces in the egg mixture. Make sure all pieces are covered and let stand in mixture for 10 minutes. Remove the chicken pieces and roll in flour. Make sure pieces are well coated and shake off excess.

In a deep skillet, heat the shortening or oil to 360° or 365° on a frying thermometer. Place a few pieces of chicken at a time into a frying basket and lower into hot shortening. Fry until golden brown on all sides, approximately 10 to 15 minutes. As the chicken pieces are cooked, keep them hot until all pieces are done.

To make a cream gravy, place 2 tablespoons of the shortening the chicken was fried in, into a saucepan and heat. Add 1 tablespoon flour and stir until mixture is smooth. Very slowly, add the scalded cream. Stir the mixture constantly until it reaches the boiling point. Remove from heat and season to taste. Serve over the chicken pieces.

# OVEN-FRIED CHICKEN

serves 6 to 8

2  2½- to 3-pound chickens, cut into serving pieces
1  tablespoon salt
1  tablespoon paprika
   pepper to taste
4  tablespoons butter, cut into small pieces

Preheat the oven to 400°.

Rinse the chicken pieces and dry them thoroughly. Season on all sides with the salt, pepper, and paprika.

In a shallow baking pan, place the chicken pieces in one layer. Use more than one pan if needed.

Place 2 tablespoons of butter pieces evenly over the chicken and cover the pan(s) with aluminum foil. Bake for 20 minutes.

Remove the foil and raise the oven temperature to 450°. Bake 30 minutes longer. Turn the chicken pieces, dot with remaining butter, and bake, uncovered, for 30 minutes longer. Remove from oven. Serve hot or cold.

# KEY WEST LIME CHICKEN

serves 4

½  cup fresh lime juice
½  teaspoon salt
1  teaspoon ground coriander
1  teaspoon ground cardamom
3  large chicken breasts, halved, skinned, and boned
   olive oil

Combine the lime juice, salt, coriander, and cardamom in a mixing bowl. Place the chicken breasts in the bowl and cover with the marinade. Marinate 2 hours.

Remove the chicken breasts from the bowl and reserve the marinade.

Brush each piece of chicken with olive oil and place the pieces in a large skillet. Pour the reserved marinade over the chicken. Simmer, covered, over low heat for 45 minutes or until chicken is tender.

# ROAST QUAIL

serves 6

6 quails
6 strips bacon
1 to 2 tablespoons butter
1 tablespoon water
  juice of 1 lemon
6 slices toast, buttered
  salt and pepper to taste
1 lemon, sliced
  watercress

Preheat the oven to 350°.

Clean and wash the quails. Pat dry thoroughly.

Butter the inside of each quail and sprinkle lightly with salt and pepper. Rub each quail lightly on the outside with butter. Truss each bird with string and wrap a strip of bacon around each. (Secure bacon with toothpicks if necessary.)

Place 1 tablespoon butter in a roasting pan and place the birds in the pan. Place in the oven for 20 to 30 minutes.

Place the slices of buttered toast on individual plates. When the quails are done, place one bird on each slice of toast.

Pour the pan juices from the roasting pan into a saucepan. Add 1½ teaspoons butter, the water, and lemon juice to the gravy. Cook for 3 to 4 minutes. Strain through a sieve and return gravy to saucepan. Simmer over low heat for 2 minutes longer. Pour gravy over breasts of quails so that it soaks into the toast. Garnish with watercress and lemon slices.

# QUAIL IN WINE

serves 4

½ cup butter, lard, or olive oil
2 small onions, chopped
8 peppercorns
2 cloves garlic, chopped
1 bay leaf
4 quails, cleaned and trussed
1½ cups white wine or dry vermouth
½ teaspoon salt
¼ teaspoon pepper
⅛ teaspoon cayenne
1 teaspoon chives, minced
2 cups light cream

Heat the butter, lard, or olive oil in a large heavy skillet. Add the onions, peppercorns, garlic, and bay leaf. Sauté for 3 minutes. Add the quail and brown on all sides. Add the wine or vermouth, salt, pepper, cayenne, and chives. Cover and cook over low heat for 30 minutes or until quails are tender.

When birds are done, place on a heated platter and set aside in a warm place.

Strain the liquid in the skillet through a sieve and return it to the skillet. Stir in the cream. Heat the mixture to the boiling point. Remove from heat, stir well, and pour over birds.

# ROAST LEG OF LAMB WITH SWEET POTATOES

serves 8 to 10

*¼ cup tarragon vinegar*
*2 tablespoons water*
*1½ cups water*
  *salt and pepper to taste*
*2 cloves garlic, finely chopped*
*¼ teaspoon dried dill*
*1 5½- to 6-pound leg of lamb, boned*
*½ cup apple cider*
*8 medium sweet potatoes*
*2 tablespoons butter*
*1 teaspoon freshly grated orange peel*
*2 teaspoons lemon juice*
*1 cup apples, peeled, cored, and chopped*
*½ cup pecans, chopped*
*3 tablespoons brown sugar*

In a mixing bowl, combine the vinegar, 2 tablespoons water, ½ teaspoon salt, pepper, garlic, and dill. Mix thoroughly.

Place the leg of lamb in a shallow dish. Pour the marinade over the lamb. Chill lamb 8 hours or overnight, turning occasionally.

Preheat the oven to 350°.

Remove the lamb from the marinade and place it in a baking dish. Bake for 2½ hours. Pour off the drippings in the pan and reserve.

Combine 1½ cups water and apple cider. Pour the mixture over the lamb and bake 30 minutes longer.

Bake the sweet potatoes in the oven with the lamb for 1 hour or until tender. Remove. When cool enough to handle, cut the sweet potatoes lengthwise and scoop out the pulp. Reserve the shells.

In a bowl, mash the sweet potatoes with the butter and orange peel. Combine the lemon juice and apples. Add to the sweet potato mixture. Stir in the pecans and mix well. Spoon the mixture back into the sweet potato shells. Sprinkle with brown sugar. If there is any sweet potato mixture left, stuff the lamb cavity with it.

Place the sweet potato halves into a shallow baking dish and bake for 15 to 20 minutes.

To make a gravy, skim the fat from the reserved pan drippings.

Serve lamb on a platter surrounded by sweet potato shells.

# BASQUE BARBECUED LAMB

serves 4 to 6

*1 7-pound leg of lamb, boned*
*1 strip pork tenderloin, cut to fit into the bone cavity of the leg of lamb*
*1 teaspoon dried rosemary*
*6 cloves garlic, minced*
  *salt and pepper to taste*
*¾ cup lemon juice*

Have the butcher bone the leg of lamb and cut the pork tenderloin so that it is the same length as the leg and is just enclosed by the cavity left by the bone.

Rub the inside of the lamb with rosemary, 3 cloves minced garlic, salt, and pepper.

Place the pork tenderloin on the inside surface of the lamb. Roll up and tie securely with string. Rub the outside of the lamb with the lemon juice and remaining garlic.

*(continued on next page)*

Place the lamb on a rack or spit and roast 4 inches above hot coals. If the lamb is on a rack, turn every 30 minutes. Barbecue for approximately 2 hours.

Many of the sheepmen of the Southwest are of Basque descent. A Basque barbecue always means lamb.

## LEG OF LAMB IN CAPER SAUCE

serves 4 to 6

1  5-pound leg of lamb
1  herb bouquet (2 sprigs parsley, ½ teaspoon dried thyme, and ½ teaspoon dried rosemary tied in a square of cheesecloth)
1  bay leaf
   salt and pepper to taste
   juice of 1 lemon
Caper sauce:
1½ ounces bread crumbs
½  cup cold water
1  tablespoon butter
1  cup heavy cream
6  peppercorns
   salt and pepper to taste
½  cup capers, finely chopped

Rub the lamb with salt and pepper.

Fill a large pot with water and bring to a boil. Add the herb bouquet, bay leaf, 1 teaspoon salt, and 1 teaspoon pepper.

Place the leg of lamb in the water, making sure that it is completely covered. Let it boil gently but steadily for 1¼ hours, or 15 minutes per pound.

When lamb is done, remove from pot and place on serving platter.

To make the sauce, place the bread crumbs in a saucepan with the water. Add the butter, salt, and peppercorns. Stir well. Cook for 5 minutes and add the cream. Stir well. Cook 5 minutes longer. Remove the peppercorns. Stir in the capers and season to taste.

Slice lamb, sprinkle with lemon juice, and serve with caper sauce.

## TENNESSEE SWEETBREADS

serves 6

1  pound veal sweetbreads
   salt
   white vinegar
2  tablespoons butter
2  tablespoons flour
1  teaspoon salt
¼  teaspoon pepper
2  cups milk
1  pound small fresh mushrooms
½  teaspoon salt
¼  cup fine bread crumbs
2  tablespoons butter

Place the sweetbreads into a large saucepan. Add enough water to cover. Add 1 teaspoon salt and 1 tablespoon vinegar for every quart of water. Simmer the sweetbreads for 20 minutes. Drain and place in a large bowl. Cover with cold water and chill until firm. When sweetbreads are firm enough to handle, remove all loose membranes.

Melt 1 tablespoon butter in a skillet. Add the sweetbreads and sauté for 3 to 5 minutes. Stir in 1 tablespoon flour. Add the salt, pepper, and 1 cup milk. Simmer until mixture begins to thicken. Lower heat.

Wash the mushrooms. Melt 1 tablespoon butter in a skillet. Add the mushrooms and sauté for 3 to 5 minutes. Stir in the remaining flour, ½ teaspoon salt, and 1 cup milk. Cook over low heat until mixture has thickened, about 5 minutes.

Preheat the oven to 400°.

Combine the mushroom mixture with the sweetbread mixture. Turn into a lightly buttered casserole. Top with bread crumbs and dot with 2 tablespoons butter. Brown for 5 to 8 minutes. Serve hot.

# LOUISIANA LIVER AND BACON

serves 4

1 pound fresh calf's liver
½ pound slab bacon
1 tablespoon flour
½ teaspoon salt
  pepper to taste
  parsley for garnish

Slice the liver into pieces about 3 inches long and ¼-inch thick. Slice the bacon very thin, making the same number of slices as there are pieces of liver.

Brown the bacon in a skillet. Remove and set aside in a warm place.

Season the flour with the salt and pepper. Dust the liver pieces with the flour. Sauté the liver in the bacon fat for about 2½ to 3 minutes per side.

Remove from pan and arrange on a serving platter in alternate slices with the bacon. Garnish with parsley and serve.

# CREOLE STYLE BREADED OX TAILS

serves 4

2 ox tails
1 cup bread crumbs
3 sprigs parsley, chopped
3 sprigs fresh thyme or ½ teaspoon dried
1 bay leaf
1 egg
  salt and pepper to taste
  cayenne pepper to taste
  oil

Wash the ox tails and cut them at the joints. Cut each piece into two pieces about 4 inches long.

Fill a saucepan with water and bring to a boil. Add the parsley, thyme, bay leaf, salt, pepper, and cayenne. Add the ox tails and boil until tender, about 2½ to 3 hours. Remove from heat and let the ox tails cool in their water.

In a mixing bowl, beat the egg. Dip the pieces of tail into the egg and then roll in the bread crumbs.

Place a layer of oil 1-inch deep into a deep skillet. Heat until very hot. Drop in the breaded ox tail pieces and fry until golden brown, about 5 to 7 minutes.

Remove from fat and drain on paper towels. Serve with tartar sauce if desired.

# Fish and Seafood

## GULF COAST SHRIMP

serves 4

2 pounds uncooked shrimp
3 cups beer
2 cloves garlic, chopped
1 teaspoon salt
½ teaspoon dried thyme
1 teaspoon celery seed
1 tablespoon parsley, finely chopped
½ teaspoon Tabasco sauce
2 tablespoons lemon juice
  melted butter

In a saucepan combine the shrimp, beer, garlic, salt, thyme, parsley, and Tabasco. Bring the mixture to a boil. Lower heat and simmer for 4 minutes or until the shrimp are pink.

Drain the shrimp and serve with melted butter.

## SHRIMP GUMBO

serves 4 to 6

1½ pounds uncooked shrimp, peeled and deveined
¼ cup butter
2 medium onions, finely chopped
1 clove garlic, finely chopped
3 green peppers, coarsely chopped
1 20-ounce can tomatoes
1 bay leaf
2 teaspoons salt
¼ teaspoon pepper
⅛ teaspoon cayenne pepper
1 teaspoon filé powder

Melt the butter in a large saucepan. Add the onions, garlic, and green peppers. Stir and cook over low heat until tender, about 5 to 8 minutes. Add the tomatoes with their liquid and the bay leaf. Stir. Simmer gently for 25 to 30 minutes. Season with salt, pepper, and cayenne.

Add the shrimp and cook 5 minutes longer. Stir in the filé well. Do not allow the mixture to come to a boil after filé has been added or it will become stringy. Serve immediately.

## SHRIMP CREOLE

serves 4 to 6

2 tablespoons butter
2 tablespoons flour
1 cup onion, chopped
⅓ cup green pepper, chopped
2 cloves garlic, chopped
3 cups canned tomatoes, with their liquid
1 pound fresh okra, sliced
2 bay leaves
  salt and pepper to taste
½ teaspoon Tabasco sauce
2 pounds uncooked shrimp, peeled and deveined

Melt the butter in a large skillet. Stir in the flour and cook over low heat, stirring constantly, until flour is a medium brown color. Add the onion, green pepper, and garlic. Cook, stirring occasionally, until onion is soft, about 5 to 8 minutes.

Stir in the tomatoes, okra, bay leaves, salt, pepper, and Tabasco. Bring the mixture to the boiling point and then lower heat. Cover the skillet and simmer for 30 minutes. Stir frequently.

Add the shrimp and cook 10 minutes longer. If mixture is too thick, thin with hot water.

# CREOLE BOILED SHRIMP

serves 6 to 8

100 uncooked shrimp
  3 tablespoons salt
  1 large head celery, with leaves, coarsely chopped
  1 teaspoon whole allspice
 ½ teaspoon whole mace
  6 whole cloves
  4 sprigs parsley
  4 bay leaves
 ½ teaspoon dried thyme
  1 dried hot red pepper pod
    salt and pepper to taste
    cayenne pepper to taste

Fill a very large pot with water and add the 3 tablespoons salt. Add the celery, allspice, mace, cloves, thyme, parsley, bay leaves, cayenne, and red pepper pod. Bring the water to a boil. Allow pot to boil for 3 minutes.

Drop all the shrimp into the pot. Boil for 10 minutes and remove pot from heat. Set aside and cool shrimp in their own water. Serve at room temperature.

# MARINATED BROILED SHRIMP

serves 6

 ½ cup olive oil
  2 teaspoons turmeric
  2 cloves garlic, crushed
 ½ teaspoon pepper
  2 teaspoons chili powder
  2 tablespoons red wine vinegar
  3 teaspoons dried basil
  2 pounds uncooked shrimp, peeled and deveined

In a mixing bowl combine the olive oil, turmeric, garlic, pepper, chili powder, wine vinegar, and basil. Add the shrimp to the bowl and mix well. Cover and let stand at room temperature for 3 hours.

Preheat the broiler.

Place the shrimp in a broiling pan and broil for 10 minutes. Baste often with the marinade. Serve hot.

# NEW ORLEANS STEAMED OYSTERS

serves 4

 48 fresh oysters
  1 tablespoon melted butter
    salt and pepper to taste
 ⅛ teaspoon cayenne pepper

Place a steaming basket or colander into a large pot. Add enough water to come up to the bottom of the basket. Bring water to a boil.

Scrub the oysters thoroughly.

*(continued on next page)*

Place the oysters in the steamer basket and cover the pot. Steam over the boiling water for 15 minutes or until the oyster shells open easily.

Place the oysters in a large dish and season with salt, pepper, and cayenne. Serve with melted butter.

# SOFT-SHELL CRABS A LA CREOLE

serves 6

12 soft-shell crabs
2 cups milk
4 tablespoons flour
½ cup melted butter
   salt and pepper to taste
2 lemons, quartered
   parsley for garnish

Clean the crabs and wash well in cold water. Dry with a clean towel and season generously with salt and pepper.

Season the milk with salt and pepper. Place the crabs in the milk and soak them for 30 minutes.

Remove the crabs from the milk and pat lightly with flour. Brush each crab with melted butter.

Preheat the broiler.

Place the crabs on a rack set in a broiler pan. Broil until crabs are a delicate brown, about 15 minutes. Turn crabs over after about 7 minutes.

Serve on a platter garnished with lemon quarters and parsley. Pour a little melted butter and chopped parsley over the crabs. Serve hot.

# BROILED CRAWFISH

serves 4 to 6

50 crawfish
 4 quarts water
   herb bouquet (one clove garlic, chopped, 1
   teaspoon whole allspice, and 6 whole cloves, tied in
   a square of cheesecloth)
½ gallon white wine or white wine vinegar
 3 tablespoons salt
 1 teaspoon cayenne pepper

Bring the water to a boil in a very large pot. Add the herb bouquet and boil for 3 to 5 minutes. Add the white wine or vinegar and 3 tablespoons salt. Add the cayenne.

Add all the crawfish to the pot. Boil for 20 minutes or until crawfish are bright red. Remove pot from heat and let crawfish cool in their own water.

Serve crawfish piled high on platter with salt, pepper, oil, and spiced vinegar.

Called crayfish everwhere but Gulf Coast kitchens, crawfish are freshwater crustaceans that resemble lobsters but are much smaller.

# CAROLINA CLAM FRITTERS

serves 4

2 cups fresh or canned clams, finely chopped
2 eggs, separated
1 cup fine bread crumbs
1 teaspoon salt
½ teaspoon pepper
1 tablespoon chives, chopped
⅓ cup milk
   olive oil

Drain the clams well and chop very fine.

In a mixing bowl beat the egg yolks until thick. Stir in the clams, bread crumbs, salt, pepper, and chives. Mix well. Add enough milk to form a heavy batter.

In a separate bowl, beat the egg whites until they are stiff but not dry. Fold whites into the batter.

Heat the olive oil in a heavy skillet. Drop the batter by teaspoons into the oil. Fry, turning once, until browned on both sides, about 5 to 8 minutes. Serve hot with lemon wedges or tartar sauce.

# LOUISIANA CRAB STEW

serves 4

  2  *tablespoons butter*
  1  *small onion, chopped*
  2  *cups mushrooms, thinly sliced*
  2  *tomatoes, peeled and chopped*
  1  *pound crabmeat, cooked and flaked*
  1  *teaspoon salt*
  ⅛  *teaspoon cayenne pepper*
  1  *cup heavy cream*
  ½  *cup light cream*
  2  *tablespoons parsley, chopped*
  1  *teaspoon chives, chopped*
  ¼  *cup brandy*

Melt the butter in a large skillet. Stir in the onion and cook over moderate heat for 2 minutes. Stir in the mushroom slices and continue cooking for 2 to 3 minutes. Add the tomatoes. Stir and cook for 5 minutes. Stir in the crabmeat, salt, cayenne, heavy cream, and light cream. Continue to cook until mixture comes to a boil.

Remove from heat. Stir in parsley, chives, and brandy. Serve hot with rice.

# CATFISH FRY

serves 3 to 4

  1½  *pounds catfish*
  1  *egg*
  2  *tablespoons water*
  ½  *cup flour*
  ½  *cup corn meal*
  1  *teaspoon salt*
  ⅛  *teaspoon pepper*
  ½  *cup olive oil*

Clean and skin the fish. Gently pat dry.

In a shallow dish, beat the egg slightly. Stir in the water and set dish aside.

In another shallow dish combine the flour, corn meal, salt, and pepper.

Dip the catfish in the egg and coat well. Dip the catfish in the flour mixture and coat well. Shake off excess.

Heat the oil in a skillet. Add the fish and brown on both sides. Cook until the fish flakes easily, approximately 10 to 12 minutes.

Drain on paper towels. Serve hot with tartar sauce or lemon wedges.

# ARKANSAS FRIED CATFISH

serves 4 to 5

  4  *pounds catfish*
     *salt and pepper to taste*
  ¼  *cup bacon drippings*
     *juice of 1 lemon*
  ¼  *cup parsley, chopped*

Clean and skin the fish. Gently pat dry.

*(continued on next page)*

Season fish well with salt and pepper.

In a large skillet heat the bacon drippings. When hot, add the fish. Cook over moderate heat until catfish is golden brown, about 12 to 15 minutes. Turn fish once while cooking.

Drain fish on paper towels. Sprinkle with lemon juice and parsley. Serve hot.

# GRILLED BASS WITH HERBS

serves 6

6 large bass fillets
1 cup white wine or dry vermouth
1/3 cup olive oil
1 cup fresh mushrooms, chopped
1/2 cup scallions, chopped
2 tablespoons lemon juice
2 teaspoons salt
1/4 teaspoon cayenne pepper
1/4 teaspoon dried tarragon, crumbled

Heat the coals in a barbecue until gray and very hot.

Cut 6 pieces of heavy aluminum foil (or doubled regular aluminum foil) into 18-inch squares. Lightly oil the foil.

In a large bowl combine the wine or vermouth, olive oil, mushrooms, scallions, lemon juice, salt, pepper, and tarragon. Mix well.

Place 1 fillet on each piece of foil. Pour the dressing over the pieces. Wrap the fish in the foil and seal. Place the packages on the grill, about 6 inches from the coals.

Grill 20 to 25 minutes or until fish flakes easily when tested with a fork. Serve hot.

# POMPANO A LA MAITRE D'HOTEL

serves 4

4 pounds pompano, either one large fish or
   several small ones
1 tablespoon olive oil
1 tablespoon butter
   juice of 1 lemon
1 lemon, sliced
   salt and pepper to taste
   parsley for garnish
Maitre d'hôtel sauce:
1 tablespoon butter
1 tablespoon flour
   juice of 1/2 lemon
1 tablespoon parsley, chopped
2 cups fish broth, chicken broth, or water
1 egg yolk, beaten

Preheat the broiler.

Clean the fish. If the fish are large, split down the back; if small, broil whole.

Season the fish with salt, pepper, and olive oil.

Put the fish in a broiler pan and broil until well browned, about 10 to 12 minutes per side. Turn fish once.

When done, remove to a heated serving platter and dot with butter. Sprinkle with the lemon juice.

To make the maitre d'hôtel sauce, place the butter and flour in a saucepan. Heat and stir until well blended. Do not burn. Continue mixing over low heat and add fish broth. Stir well. Add the lemon juice and chopped parsley. Bring the sauce to a boil and let it boil for about 15 minutes. Remove from heat. Stir in beaten egg yolk. Mix until well blended. Serve with broiled fish.

# NEW ORLEANS POMPANO EN PAPILLOTE

serves 4

    4 squares parchment paper
    8 pompano fillets
    1½ teaspoons butter
    1½ teaspoons flour
    ½ cup white wine
        salt and pepper to taste
    8 large shrimp, cooked and chopped
    ½ cup crabmeat, cooked and chopped

Preheat the oven to 450°.

Cut the parchment paper into squares big enough to fold around 2 fillets. Place 2 fillets on each piece.

In a saucepan, melt the butter. Stir in the flour. Slowly add the white wine and cook over low heat. Stir constantly and continue cooking until the mixture is smooth and thick. Season to taste with salt and pepper.

Spoon the sauce over the fish. Top with the chopped shrimp and crabmeat. Fold parchment paper over the fish.

Place in the oven for 15 minutes or until the paper is puffed and browned. Serve immediately in the paper.

# DEEP-FRIED PORGY

serves 4

    3 pounds porgy or butterfish, filleted but not skinned
    2 teaspoons salt
    ½ teaspoon pepper
    1 cup yellow corn meal
        lard or oil for deep frying

Wash and dry the fillets. Score on the fleshy side with a sharp knife, making approximately 3 small slashes per fillet.

Season the fillets well with salt and pepper on both sides. Dip them into the corn meal. Make sure the fillets are coated evenly. Gently shake off the excess corn meal.

In a large deep skillet heat a ½-inch layer of oil or lard. When very, hot add the fish. Fry for 4 minutes on the first side. Turn fillets carefully and fry 3 to 4 minutes longer or until fish is golden brown. Drain fish on paper towels and serve hot.

# BROILED MACKEREL

serves 6

    3 pounds mackerel fillets or steaks
    6 tablesoons melted butter
    ½ teaspoon salt
    ¼ teaspoon pepper
    ⅛ teaspoon cayenne
        juice of 2 limes
    1 tablespoon French-style mustard
    ¼ teaspoon ground fennel

Preheat the broiler.

Lightly butter a baking dish. Place the fillets skin-side down in the dish. Brush with 2 tablespoons melted butter. Season with salt, pepper, and cayenne.

Broil for 5 minutes.

In a small bowl, mix the remaining butter, lime juice, mustard, and fennel. Combine thoroughly. Pour sauce over fish and broil 5 minutes longer, or until fish flakes easily. Serve hot.

# SAUCY CREOLE FISH

serves 6

    4 tablespoons butter
    2 tablespoons onion, chopped
    4 tablespoons celery, chopped
    2 tablespoons sweet red pepper, chopped
    2 tablespoons flour
    1/2 cup light cream
    1/2 cup fine bread crumbs
    1/4 teaspoon dried rosemary
    1 cup cooked crabmeat
    1 cup cooked shrimp, coarsely chopped
    1/4 cup parsley, chopped
    1/4 teaspoon salt
    1/4 teaspoon pepper
    1 1/2 teaspoons Worcestershire sauce
    1/2 teaspoon Tabasco sauce
    6 fillets of sole or flounder
    3 tablespoons melted butter
Creole sauce:
    4 cups canned tomatoes
    2 tablespoons butter
    2 cloves garlic, chopped
    1 bay leaf
    1 teaspoon salt
    1/4 teaspoon pepper
    1/8 teaspoon cayenne pepper
    1 tablespoon flour

Preheat the oven to 350°.

In a saucepan melt the butter. Add the onion, celery, and red pepper. Cook until tender, about 5 to 8 minutes. Carefully stir in the flour. Stir until mixture is smooth. Add the light cream and continue cooking until mixture has thickened.

Remove saucepan from heat. Stir in the bread crumbs, rosemary, crabmeat, shrimp, parsley, salt, pepper, Worcestershire sauce and Tabasco.

Place the 6 fillets flat on a work surface. Place a heaping tablespoon of the filling on each fillet. Roll up the fillet and secure with a toothpick.

Place the fillets into a baking dish about 1 to 2 inches apart. Brush with the melted butter and sprinkle with salt. Place in the oven and bake 15 minutes. Pour Creole sauce over fish. Reduce temperature to 325° and bake 30 minutes longer.

To prepare the Creole sauce, in a saucepan combine the tomatoes, half the butter, garlic, bay leaf, salt, pepper, and cayenne. Cook over moderate heat, stirring occasionally, until the mixture is reduced to about half, about 20 to 30 minutes.

In a small saucepan, melt the remaining butter. Stir in the flour and continue cooking until lightly browned.

Add the flour mixture to the tomatoes. Cook for 2 to 3 minutes. Remove sauce from heat and strain through a sieve. Pour over fish and continue baking.

# BROILED TROUT

serves 6

6 trout fillets
2 tablespoons melted butter
1 lemon, sliced
    salt and pepper to taste
1 tablespoon olive oil
    parsley for garnish

Preheat the broiler.

Wash and dry the fillets. Season fillets by rubbing well with salt, pepper, and olive oil.

Place fillets in a broiler pan. Broil for 3 to 5 minutes on the first side. Turn fillets and brush with melted butter. Broil 5 to 8 minutes longer, depending on the thickness of the fillets.

Remove from broiler. Garnish with parsley and serve with lemon slices.

# RED SNAPPER WITH CHILI PEPPER

serves 4

4 red snapper fillets
2 tablespoons olive oil
1 clove garlic, chopped
½ cup onion, chopped
½ cup pimiento-stuffed green olives, sliced
¼ cup sweet red pepper, chopped
1 teaspoon coriander, chopped
1 dried hot red chili pepper, seeded and crushed
6 tablespoons lemon juice
6 tablespoons orange juice
½ teaspoon salt
¼ teaspoon pepper

Preheat the oven to 375°.

Wash and dry fillets. Place in a lightly buttered shallow baking dish.

In a skillet, heat the olive oil. Add the garlic and onion and sauté until the onion is soft. Add the sliced olives, sweet red pepper, coriander, and crushed chili pepper. Stir constantly and cook for 3 minutes. Add the orange juice, lemon juice, salt, and pepper. Stir until well blended.

Pour the mixture over the fillets and bake, uncovered, for 15 to 20 minutes or until fish flakes easily.

Remove fish from oven and place on a platter. Pour pan juices over the fish and serve.

# RED SNAPPER TEXAS GULF–STYLE

serves 4

2 pounds red snapper steaks or fillets
    salt and pepper to taste
2 tablespoons butter, softened
½ cup carrot, chopped
1 stalk celery, chopped
2 tablespoons parsley, chopped
6 uncooked shrimp, peeled and chopped
1 cup white wine or dry vermouth
¼ teaspoon dried basil

Preheat the oven to 400°.

Pat the fish dry. Rub with salt and pepper and place into a heavily buttered deep casserole or baking dish.

In a bowl, combine the butter, carrots, celery, parsley, shrimp, white wine, and basil. Mix well. Pour sauce over the fish. Bake fish for 30 minutes or until it flakes easily. Serve hot in the baking dish.

## LEMON-LIME RED SNAPPER

serves 4

4 red snapper fillets, unskinned
½ cup scallions, finely chopped
¼ cup lime juice
2 teaspoons freshly grated lemon peel
1 teaspoon salt
¼ teaspoon grated nutmeg

In a shallow baking dish, combine the scallions, lime juice, lemon peel, and salt. Mix well.

Add the fillets to the baking dish and turn to coat. The fillets should fit in one layer. Place the fillets skin-side up and marinate for 30 minutes at room temperature.

Preheat the oven to 400°.

Turn the fillets so that the skin side is down. Sprinkle with nutmeg and pepper. Bake the fish for 10 to 12 minutes or until fish flakes. Baste frequently. Serve hot from baking dish.

## BAKED REDFISH

serves 4 to 5

1 4-pound redfish
3 to 4 tablespoons butter
  salt and cayenne pepper to taste
6 shrimps, cooked and coarsely chopped
¼ cup capers, chopped
  lemon wedges for garnish

Preheat the oven to 400°.

Clean, scale, wash, and dry the fish.

Place 2 tablespoons of butter, cut up into small pieces, inside the fish. Dot the outside of the fish with the remaining butter. Season fish with salt and cayenne pepper.

Place the fish in a well-buttered shallow baking dish. Cover with a piece of well-buttered brown paper cut to fit. Bake for 40 minutes or until fish flakes.

Five minutes before the fish is ready, remove it from the oven. Sprinkle the capers and shrimp around the fish. Return to the oven for 5 minutes.

Serve surrounded with shrimp and capers and garnished with lemon wedges.

## SOUTHERN SMOKED FISH

serves 4

1 4-pound redfish
2 cloves garlic, crushed
  salt and pepper to taste
  rind of 1 lemon, freshly grated
  juice of 3 lemons
¼ pound melted butter
2 tablespoons Worcestershire sauce
½ teaspoon Tabasco sauce
1 teaspoon parsley, chopped

Clean and wash fish. Pat dry. Rub the fish with the garlic, pepper, and lemon rind.

In a small bowl combine the lemon juice, butter, Worcestershire sauce, Tabasco, and parsley. Mix well.

Cover the head and tail of the fish with pieces of aluminum foil.

Place the fish on a grill over low flame. Cover grill and smoke fish for about 1 hour or until fish flakes. Do not overcook. Baste with the sauce every 15 minutes. Cool before serving.

# ALABAMA STUFFED POMPANO

serves 4

4 1-pound pompanos
1 pound cooked shrimp, peeled and deveined
1 egg, well beaten
½ teaspoon salt
¼ teaspoon pepper
⅛ teaspoon cayenne
3 tablespoons sherry or madeira
1 cup light cream

Preheat the oven to 350°.

Clean and wash the fish. Split the fish, leaving the heads and tails intact.

Place the pompano in a large, oiled shallow baking dish. The dish should be large enough to hold all the fish in one layer.

Chop the shrimp finely in a blender, food mill, or food processor. In a small bowl, combine the shrimp, egg, salt, pepper, cayenne, sherry and ½ cup light cream.

Stuff the cavities of the fish with the shrimp mixture. Pour the remaining cream over the fish and bake for 40 minutes. Baste occasionally. Remove fish and serve hot with pan juices.

# ·Vegetables·

# NEW MEXICO CORN BAKE

serves 6

1 tablespoon olive oil
1 onion, finely chopped
2 cups canned tomato purée
2 tablespoons celery, diced
2 tablespoons chili powder
2 tablespoons butter
3 cups fresh corn, cut from the cob
 (approximately 4 ears)
1 teaspoon salt
½ teaspoon pepper

Heat the olive oil in a heavy skillet. Add the onion and sauté until golden, about 5 to 8 minutes. Add the tomato purée, celery, chili powder, butter, corn, salt, and pepper. Mix well and remove from heat.

Butter a 1-quart casserole dish. Pour in the corn mixture and bake, uncovered, for 30 minutes. Serve hot from dish.

# FRIED CORN

serves 4

3 cups fresh corn, cut from the cob
½ cup boiling water
⅓ cup milk
2 tablespoons bacon drippings
1 teaspoon salt
½ teaspoon sugar
¼ teaspoon pepper
1 tablespoon flour
2 tablespoons cold water
1 teaspoon butter

In a saucepan combine the boiling water, milk, bacon drippings, salt, sugar, and pepper. Add the corn and stir. Bring the mixture to a boil over low to medium heat. When corn begins to boil, cover and cook for 10 minutes or until corn is tender. Stir occasionally.

In a small bowl combine the flour and the water. Blend until smooth. Add to the corn mixture. Stir and cook 1 minute longer or until corn begins to thicken. Remove from heat. Stir in butter and serve.

This popular dish, which is actually stewed, is misleadingly called fried corn throughout the South.

# FRIED OKRA

serves 6

1½ pounds fresh okra
½ teaspoon salt
¼ teaspoon pepper
½ cup yellow corn meal
1 tablespoon flour
3 tablespoons bacon drippings or lard

Wash the trim and okra. Cut into ½-inch slices and sprinkle with salt and pepper.

In a shallow bowl, combine the corn meal and flour. Roll the okra slices in the mixture until well coated. Shake off excess.

Heat the bacon drippings in a skillet. When hot, add the okra and fry until golden brown, about 2 to 5 minutes. Drain on paper towels and serve hot.

# CORN AND OKRA MIX

serves 4 to 6

4 strips bacon
4 tablespoons bacon drippings
1 onion, finely chopped
1 cup fresh okra, thinly sliced
3 cups fresh corn, cut from the cob
3 large tomatoes, peeled and diced
1 teaspoon sugar
   salt and pepper to taste
¼ teaspoon Tabasco sauce

In a large skillet, fry the bacon until it is crisp and brown. Drain on paper towels and reserve. Discard all but 4 tablespoons of the bacon drippings.

Add the corn, okra, and onion to the hot bacon drippings. Sauté for 10 minutes, stirring constantly. Add the tomatoes, sugar, salt, pepper, and Tabasco. Cover skillet and simmer over low heat for 25 minutes. Stir occasionally.

Remove skillet from heat. Season to taste and sprinkle with crumbled bacon.

# CREOLE-STYLE STEWED OKRA

serves 6 to 8

    3 to 4 dozen fresh okra
    1 tablespoon butter
    3 tomatoes, finely chopped, with their juice
    1 onion, minced
    1 green pepper, minced
    1 clove garlic, chopped
      salt and pepper to taste
      cayenne pepper to taste
    1 teaspoon parsley, chopped

Wash and trim the okra. Set aside.

In a saucepan melt the butter and add the onion, garlic, and green pepper. Stir well and sauté for 5 to 8 minutes. Add the tomatoes and their juice. Season to taste with salt, pepper, and cayenne. Add the parsley. Add the okra and simmer slowly for 20 minutes. Remove from heat and serve hot.

# SUMMER SQUASH CASSEROLE

serves 6 to 8

    3 cups zucchini and/or yellow summer squash,
      coarsely chopped
    ½ teaspoon salt
    ¼ teaspoon pepper
    3 tablespoons butter
    ½ cup sour cream
    1 small onion, finely chopped
    2 eggs beaten
    ¼ teaspoon grated nutmeg
    ¼ teaspoon crushed hot red pepper flakes
    2 cups bread crumbs

Preheat the oven to 350°.

Steam the squash until tender, about 3 to 5 minutes. Drain and place squash in a mixing bowl and season with salt, pepper, and butter. Add the sour cream, onion, eggs, nutmeg, and red pepper. Mix well.

Lightly butter a 1½-quart casserole dish. Place a layer of half the squash mixture into the dish. Add 1 cup bread crumbs in a layer. Then add the rest of the squash mixture and top with the remaining crumbs.

Bake, uncovered, for 30 minutes. Serve hot.

# SMOTHERED PARSNIPS

serves 4 to 6

    6 to 8 small parsnips
    2 tablespoons butter
      salt and pepper to taste
      chopped parsley for garnish

Wash and gently scrape parsnips. Boil in lightly salted water for 45 minutes to 1 hour, depending on size.

Drain parsnips and cool. Cut lengthwise into strips approximately ½-inch thick.

Melt the butter in a large skillet. Add the parsnips. Sprinkle with salt and pepper. Cover the skillet and cook until parsnips are lightly browned on both sides, about 8 minutes. Stir often.

Remove parsnips to serving dish, sprinkle with parsley, and serve hot.

# COLLARD GREENS

serves 6

2 pounds collards
½ pound salt pork, chopped
1 gallon water
4 medium potatoes, peeled
   salt and pepper to taste

Wash the collards thoroughly. Cut off and discard any tough stems and discolored leaves.

In a very large pot, combine the salt pork and water. Bring to a boil and cook 20 to 30 minutes. Add the collards. Cover the pot and simmer for 1 to 1½ hours. Add the potatoes and cook 30 minutes longer or until potatoes are tender. Season to taste with salt and pepper. Serve hot.

Collard greens are a type of kale.

# CANDIED VIRGINIA SWEET POTATOES

serves 4 to 6

6 sweet potatoes
½ teaspoon salt
1 cup dark brown sugar, firmly packed
½ cup water
4 tablespoons butter
1 tablespoon lemon juice

Place the unpeeled sweet potatoes into a pot of boiling salted water. Cook until almost tender, approximately 15 to 20 minutes.

Drain the sweet potatoes. When cool enough to handle, peel them and cut into ½-inch slices.

Preheat the oven to 375°. Butter a shallow baking dish. Place the sweet potato slices into the dish and season with salt.

In a saucepan combine the brown sugar, water, and butter. Mix well. Cook over moderate heat for 2 minutes. Stir in the lemon juice. Remove from heat and pour over sweet potatoes.

Bake for 20 to 25 minutes, basting occasionally. Serve hot.

# BRANDIED SWEET POTATOES

serves 6

4 cups hot mashed sweet potatoes
4 tablespoons butter, softened
1 tablespoon butter, melted
¼ cup sugar
¼ teaspoon ground ginger
¼ teaspoon grated nutmeg
½ teaspoon salt
¼ cup brandy
2 tablespoons light cream

Preheat the oven to 375°.

In a large bowl combine the sweet potatoes, butter, sugar, nutmeg, ginger, and salt. Mix well. Stir in the brandy and the cream. Combine thoroughly.

Butter a 1-quart casserole. Turn the sweet potato mixture into the casserole and brush with melted butter.

Bake for 30 to 40 minutes or until brown. Serve hot in baking dish.

# SOUTHWESTERN SWEET POTATO PIE

serves 8

1 cup sifted flour
1/8 teaspoon baking powder
1/4 teaspoon salt
1/3 cup lard or vegetable shortening
3 tablespoons ice water
3/4 cup butter
3/4 cup sugar
1 1/2 cups sweet potato, peeled and grated
1/3 cup milk
3/4 teaspoon ground ginger
2 tablespoons freshly grated orange rind

Into a bowl sift the flour, baking powder, and salt. Cut in the shortening with a pastry blender or two knives until the mixture resembles a coarse meal. Add the water, a little at a time. Toss lightly with a fork until the dough forms a ball. Wrap in plastic wrap and refrigerate for 2 hours.

Roll the dough out onto a lightly floured surface. Line an 11-inch unbuttered pie tin with the dough. Place the tin in the refrigerator.

Preheat the oven to 300°.

In a mixing bowl cream the butter. Add the sugar and continue to cream until mixture is light and fluffy. Gradually add the sweet potatoes and milk alternately. Beat well after each addition. Add the ginger and orange rind and beat well.

Pour mixture into the prepared pie tin. Bake for 45 minutes or until lightly browned. Serve hot from pie tin.

# HOPPIN' JOHN

serves 6 to 8

1 cup dried blackeye peas
  water
1 teaspoon salt
1 medium onion, diced
2 ounces salt pork, diced
1/4 teaspoon pepper
1/8 teaspoon cayenne pepper
1 cup raw long-grain rice
1 tablespoon butter

Place the blackeye peas in a colander and rinse well. Put in a bowl with 3 cups cold water and soak 8 hours or overnight.

Drain the blackeye peas and reserve the water. Add enough water to the reserved water to make 3 cups.

Place the water, blackeye peas, salt, onion, and salt pork into a large pot. Cover and bring the mixture to a boil. Lower heat and simmer 1 1/4 hours or until peas are tender. There should be very little water left in the pot. Season with pepper and cayenne.

Bring 1 1/2 cups water to a boil in a saucepan. Add the rice and cook, covered, for 18 minutes or until water is absorbed. Add butter and toss.

Add the rice to the blackeye peas and cook for 2 to 3 minutes to blend flavors. Serve hot.

Hoppin' John is a traditional New Year's Day dish throughout the South.

## GLAZED TURNIPS

serves 6

1½ pounds turnips
4 tablespoons butter
1½ teaspoons sugar
¼ teaspoon grated nutmeg

Peel and quarter the turnips.

Melt the butter in a large heavy skillet. Add the turnips and cook over moderate heat for 3 minutes. Stir constantly.

Combine the sugar and nutmeg. Sprinkle over the turnips and mix well.

Cover the skillet and cook over low heat for 10 minutes or until the turnips are tender. Remove turnips to a serving dish and serve hot.

## TURNIP GREENS AND HAM HOCK

serves 6 to 8

1  1¾-pound ham hock
2  quarts water
2  bunches turnip greens with turnips
1  teaspoon salt
1  tablespoon sugar
   pepper to taste

Wash the ham hock and place it in a large heavy pot. Add the water and bring to a boil. Lower heat and simmer gently for 35 to 45 minutes or until the ham hock is tender.

Wash and trim the turnip greens. Discard any discolored leaves. Peel the turnips and cut them in half.

Add the turnip greens, turnips, salt, and sugar to the pot with the ham hock. Bring to a boil. Lower the heat and simmer 35 to 45 minutes or until the greens and turnips are tender.

Remove from heat. Season to taste with pepper. Spoon greens and turnips into a serving bowl and serve hot.

## MUSTARD GREENS WITH NEW POTATOES

serves 6

2  ounces salt pork
   boiling water
12  small new potatoes
2  pounds fresh mustard greens
1½  teaspoons salt
½  teaspoon sugar
¼  teaspoon pepper

Slice the salt pork thinly. Place in a large skillet filled with boiling water to a depth of 1 inch. Cover and simmer for 40 to 50 minutes or until pork is tender.

Wash the potatoes. Add to the pork and cook 5 to 7 minutes. Add more water if necessary.

Wash and trim the mustard greens and cut into pieces 2 to 3 inches long. Add greens to the pork and potatoes. Season with salt and sugar. Cover and cook over medium heat for 15 minutes or until greens are tender. Do not overcook. Season with pepper and toss well. Serve hot.

# Grains and Beans

## MEXICAN RICE

serves 4

1 cup onions, chopped
⅓ cup olive oil
1 cup raw long-grain rice
1 teaspoon salt
1 tablespoon chili powder
2 to 3 cups tomato juice
1 cup beef or vegetable broth
½ cup sliced chorizo (Spanish sausage)

Heat the oil in a large skillet. Add the onion and sauté for 2 to 3 minutes. Stir in the rice, salt, chili powder, tomato juice, beef broth, and *chorizo.* Bring the mixture to a boil. Cover and lower the heat. Simmer for 20 to 25 minutes or until the rice is tender. Remove from heat and serve hot.

## DIRTY RICE

serves 6 to 8

1½ cups brown rice
3½ cups water
1½ teaspoons salt
2 onions, finely chopped
2 green peppers, finely chopped
4 stalks celery, with leaves, finely chopped
1 clove garlic, finely chopped
2 tablespoons bacon drippings
½ pound chicken giblets, chopped
   Tabasco sauce to taste
   Worcestershire sauce to taste
   salt and pepper to taste
   cayenne pepper to taste

Bring the water and salt to a boil in a medium saucepan. Add the rice, cover tightly, and lower heat. Cook 50 minutes or until all the water is absorbed. Set rice aside.

In a skillet heat the bacon drippings. Add the onions, peppers, celery, and garlic. Sauté approximately 30 minutes or until most of the liquid is gone. Stir often.

Add the chopped chicken giblets (gizzards, livers, and hearts) and sauté until browned. Add the Tabasco, Worcestershire sauce, salt, cayenne, and pepper to taste. Mix in the rice. Combine and heat thoroughly, then serve.

## SOUTHERN RICE

serves 4

1 cup raw long-grain rice
1½ cups cold water
2 tablespoons butter
1 teaspoon lemon juice
1 teaspoon salt

Place the rice in a colander and rinse under cold running water for 2 to 3 minutes. Stir often while rinsing.

Place 1½ cups water in a saucepan. Add the butter, lemon juice, and salt. Bring to a boil over high heat. Stir in the rice, cover saucepan, and reduce heat. Cook until the rice is tender and all the water is absorbed, about 20 minutes.

Remove from heat and let stand, covered, for 5 to 10 minutes. Fluff with a fork and serve.

# CAROLINA RICE PILAU

serves 4 to 6

- *1 cup raw long-grain rice*
- *1 cup water*
- *1 cup chicken broth*
- *¼ cup pistachio nuts, shelled*
- *½ cup pine nuts or toasted slivered almonds*
- *3 tablespoons butter*
- *1 teaspoon powdered mace*
- *½ teaspoon salt*

Place the chicken broth and water in a saucepan. Bring to a boil and add rice. Stir and cover saucepan. Reduce the heat and simmer until rice is done and all the liquid is absorbed, about 20 minutes.

While the rice cooks, melt the butter in a heavy skillet. Add the pistachio and pine nuts and cook for several minutes, stirring frequently. The nuts will become golden in color.

Add the rice to the skillet. Season with the mace and salt. Stir until well blended and heated through. Serve immediately.

# RICE FRITTERS

serves 4

- *2 eggs, separated*
- *1 cup sugar*
- *1 cup cooked rice*
- *2 cups flour*
- *2 teaspoons baking powder*
- *oil for frying*
- *confectioner's sugar (optional)*

In a large bowl mix together the egg yolks, sugar, rice, flour, and baking powder.

In a separate bowl, beat the egg whites until stiff but not dry. Fold them into the rice mixture.

In a large deep skillet heat the oil until very hot, 370° on a deep-fat thermometer. Drop the rice mixture by tablespoons into the oil and fry until golden, about 3 to 4 minutes.

Remove from oil and drain on paper towels. Dust with confectioner's sugar and serve hot.

# RED RICE

serves 4

- *6 slices bacon*
- *1 cup onions, finely chopped*
- *½ cup sweet red pepper, finely chopped*
- *1 cup raw long-grain rice*
- *⅛ teaspoon Tabasco sauce*
- *1 teaspoon paprika*
- *1 teaspoon sugar*
- *1 teaspoon salt*
- *2 medium tomatoes, peeled, seeded, and coarsely chopped*
- *1½ cups cold water*

Fry the bacon in a heavy skillet until brown and crisp. Drain on paper towels. Crumble and set aside.

Discard all but 4 tablespoons of the bacon fat. Add the onions and red pepper. Sauté, stirring frequently, until the onions are soft but not brown, about 5 minutes. Add the rice and stir until the grains are well coated. Stir in the Tabasco, paprika, sugar, salt, tomatoes, and water.

Bring the mixture to a boil over high heat. Cover the skillet, reduce the heat, and simmer for 20 minutes or until rice is tender. Remove from heat and let stand, covered, for 5 to 10 minutes. Place rice in a serving bowl, sprinkle with crumbled bacon, and serve.

# CALAS (DEEP-FRIED RICE BALLS)

serves 6 to 8

½ package active dry yeast
½ cup very warm water (105° to 115°)
1½ cups very soft cooked rice
3 eggs, beaten
1¼ cups flour
¼ cup sugar
½ teaspoon salt
¼ teaspoon grated nutmeg
confectioner's sugar (optional)
oil for deep frying

Place the very warm water into a bowl. Sprinkle in the yeast and let stand for a few minutes, then stir until completely dissolved.

Place the cooked rice in a mixing bowl. Mash the cooked rice and let it cool until lukewarm. Stir the yeast mixture into the rice and mix well. Cover the bowl and let rise overnight.

Add the eggs, flour, sugar, salt, and nutmeg to the risen mixture. Beat mixture until smooth. Let stand in a warm place for 30 minutes (an oven that has been heated and then turned off is ideal).

Heat the oil in a large deep skillet until very hot, 360° on a deep-fat thermometer.

Drop the rice mixture by tablespoons into the oil. Fry until golden, about 3 minutes.

Remove from oil and drain on paper towels. Dust with confectioner's sugar and serve hot.

# HOMINY

serves 4

2 cups whole hominy
3 cups water
2 teaspoons salt
½ cup light cream
½ cup butter

Place the whole hominy in a large bowl. Cover with warm water and soak overnight.

Drain the soaked hominy and place in a large pot. Add the water and the salt. Simmer 6 hours or until the hominy is barely tender. Add more water if necessary.

Add the cream and butter and simmer 1½ to 2 hours longer. Stir occasionally.

Whole or big hominy is hulled, dried corn.

# HOMINY GRITS

serves 4 to 6

5 cups water
1 teaspoon salt
1 cup regular white hominy grits
1 tablespoon butter
salt and pepper to taste

*(continued on next page)*

In a heavy saucepan bring the water and salt to a boil. Slowly stir in the grits. Stir constantly to form a smooth mixture. Lower the heat and cover the saucepan. Cook 25 to 35 minutes, stirring occasionally. Stir in the butter and season with salt and pepper to taste.

Hominy grits are hominy ground into a coarse meal. Grits are often served as a side dish with butter or gravy or as a breakfast cereal with butter and cream.

# FRIED GRITS

serves 4 to 6

　5 cups water
　1 teaspoon salt
　1 cup regular white hominy grits
　1 tablespoon butter
　2 eggs, beaten
　1 cup bread crumbs or flour
　4 tablespoons bacon fat or butter

In a heavy saucepan bring the water and salt to a boil. Slowly stir in the grits. Stir constantly to make a smooth mixture. Lower the heat and cover the saucepan. Cook 25 to 35 minutes, stirring occasionally. Stir in the butter.

Heavily butter a 9 × 13-inch loaf pan.

Pour the cooked grits into the loaf pan. Cool and cover pan with plastic wrap. Refrigerate 6 hours or overnight.

Carefully unmold the chilled grits and cut into 12 slices. Dip the slices into the beaten eggs and then the bread crumbs.

Heat the bacon fat in a skillet. When hot add the grits and fry until golden brown, about 3 minutes on each side. Turn carefully.

Drain grits on paper towels. Serve hot with maple syrup.

# GRITS AND CHEESE CASSEROLE

serves 4 to 6

　5 cups water
　1 teaspoon salt
　1 cup regular white hominy grits
　½ cup butter, cut into small pieces
　2 cups sharp Cheddar cheese, grated
　3 eggs, beaten
　¼ teaspoon Tabasco sauce
　　salt and pepper to taste

In a heavy saucepan bring the salt and water to a boil. Slowly stir in the grits. Stir constantly to form a smooth mixture. Lower the heat and cover. Cook for 25 to 35 minutes. Stir occasionally.

Preheat the oven to 350°.

Remove saucepan from heat and stir in the butter and cheese. Cool mixture to lukewarm.

When grits are cooled stir in the eggs, Tabasco, salt, and pepper.

Heavily butter a 1½-quart casserole. Turn grits into the casserole and bake 30 to 40 minutes or until golden brown. Remove from oven. Serve hot as a side dish.

# FRIJOLES REFRITOS (REFRIED BEANS)

serves 4 to 6

*2 cups dried pinto or kidney beans*
*6 cups water*
*1 cup onions, coarsely chopped*
*1 medium tomato, peeled, seeded, and coarsely chopped*
*3 cloves garlic, chopped*
*8 tablespoons lard*
*1 teaspoon salt*

Rinse the beans under cold running water. In a heavy saucepan, combine the beans, water, ½ cup chopped onions, ¼ cup tomatoes, garlic, and 1 tablespoon lard. Bring to a boil over high heat. Reduce heat and simmer the mixture, partially covered, for 1½ hours. Stir in the salt and continue to simmer, partially covered, for 30 to 40 minutes longer, or until a bean can be easily mashed against the side of the saucepan. Stir occasionally as beans cook and add water, ¼ cup at a time, as necessary. Drain the bean and reserve the liquid.

Melt 2 tablespoons lard in a heavy skillet. When hot, add the remaining onions and cook, stirring frequently, for 5 minutes or until onions are soft but not brown. Add the remaining chopped tomatoes, stir, and cook for 2 to 3 minutes. Reduce heat to low.

Add ½ cup of the beans to the skillet. Mash them with a fork and stir in 1 tablespoon lard. Repeat, alternating 1 cup of beans with 1 tablespoon lard, until all the beans and lard are mashed together. The mixture should be creamy yet slightly crisp. If the beans seem too dry, add some of the reserved bean liquid, 1 tablespoon at a time. Serve hot.

# BOILED PINTO BEANS

serves 8

*2 cups dried pinto beans*
*6 cups water*
*1 medium onion*
*2 cloves garlic, crushed*
*1 teaspoon salt*
*¼ teaspoon sugar*

Rinse the dried beans well under cold running water. Place in a large bowl with 6 cups cold water and soak overnight.

Drain the soaked beans and place in a large saucepan. Add 6 cups water, the whole onion, and garlic. Bring the water to a boil over high heat. Reduce the heat and simmer 3½ to 4 hours, partially covered.

Add the salt and sugar. Continue to simmer 30 minutes longer or until beans are tender but still intact. Drain the beans and serve hot.

# Breads

## SOUTHERN-STYLE POPOVERS

yields 12 popovers

1½ cups flour
¼ teaspoon salt
2 eggs, lightly beaten
1½ cups milk
2 tablespoons melted butter

Preheat the oven to 425°.

In a large bowl sift together the flour and salt. Add the eggs, milk, and butter. Blend well to make a smooth batter.

Beat the batter with an electric mixer for 3 minutes.

Lightly butter 1 12-cup muffin tin or 2 6-cup tins that have been warmed in the oven for 5 minutes. Fill the cups two-thirds full with the batter.

Bake for 30 minutes. Do not open the oven while popovers bake. They will brown and pop when done. Serve hot.

## BUTTERMILK BISCUITS

yields 12 to 14 biscuits

2 cups flour
1 teaspoon baking powder
½ teaspoon baking soda
1 teaspoon salt
4 tablespoons butter, softened
1 cup thick buttermilk

Sift the flour, baking powder, baking soda, and salt into a mixing bowl. Cut in the butter with a pastry blender or two knives until the mixture resembles a coarse meal. Add enough of the buttermilk to make a soft dough. Mix lightly.

Turn the dough out onto a lightly floured surface. Knead for about 5 minutes.

Preheat the oven to 450°.

Roll out the dough on a floured surface to ½-inch thickness. Cut the dough with a 2-inch floured biscuit cutter.

Place the biscuits on lightly greased cookie sheets. Bake for 10 to 12 minutes. Remove from oven and serve hot.

## PECOS RIVER PECAN BREAD

yields 1 loaf

3½ cups flour
1 cup sugar
1 teaspoon salt
3 teaspoons baking powder
1 cup milk
2 cups chopped pecans
¼ cup melted butter or lard
1 egg

Preheat the oven to 350°.

In a large bowl combine the flour, sugar, salt, and baking powder. Mix well. Add the milk, egg, and melted butter. Stir until well blended and batter is smooth. Stir in the pecans.

Butter a 9 × 5 × 3-inch loaf pan. Pour batter into the pan and bake for 1 hour or until cake tester inserted into the middle comes out clean.

Remove from oven. Cool in the pan for 10 minutes. Then turn loaf out onto a rack and cool completely. Serve when cooled.

# CREOLE HONEY BREAD

yields 1 loaf

2 cups flour
1 teaspoon baking soda
1 teaspoon baking powder
1 teaspoon salt
1 teaspoon ground ginger
½ teaspoon cinnamon
1 cup milk
1 cup honey
1 egg, slightly beaten

Preheat the oven to 375°.

Into a large bowl sift the flour, baking soda, baking powder, salt, ginger, and cinnamon. Stir in the milk, honey, and egg. Place in the bowl of an electric mixer and beat for 20 minutes or until all ingredients are well blended and the batter is smooth.

Pour into a buttered 9 × 5 × 3-inch loaf pan. Bake for 45 minutes or until bread tests done when a cake tester is inserted in the middle.

Remove bread from the oven and cool in pay for 10 minutes. Turn out onto a rack and continue cooling. Serve bread sliced thin.

# APPLE-NUT BREAD

yields 1 loaf

2 cups flour
¾ cup light brown sugar, firmly packed
3 teaspoons baking powder
1 teaspoon cinnamon
1 teaspoon salt
½ teaspoon baking soda
1 cup chopped walnuts or pecans
¾ cup unsweetened applesauce
¼ cup apple cider or applejack
2 tablespoons melted butter
1 egg, beaten

Preheat the oven to 350°. Butter a 9 × 5 × 3-inch loaf pan and set aside.

In a large bowl combine the flour, brown sugar, baking powder, cinnamon, salt, baking soda, and nuts. Stir until thoroughly mixed.

In another bowl combine the applesauce, apple cider or applejack, melted butter, and egg. Stir mixture until well blended.

Stir the dry ingredients into the applesauce mixture a little at a time. Continue stirring until well blended.

Pour batter into the loaf pan and bake for 1 hour or until a cake tester inserted into the center of the bread comes out clean.

Remove bread to a cooling rack. Cool in the pan for 15 minutes. Then turn bread out and cool completely.

# SPOON BREAD

serves 4 to 6

    1 cup white corn meal
    ½ teaspoon salt
    1½ cups boiling water
    2 eggs, separated
    1 tablespoon melted butter
    1 cup buttermilk
    ½ teaspoon baking soda

Preheat the oven to 325°.

In a large bowl mix the corn meal and salt. Add the water and egg yolks. Mix well. Add the butter and buttermilk. Stir until well blended.

In a separate bowl beat the egg whites and the baking soda until stiff but not dry. Fold into batter.

Grease a 1½- or 2-quart baking dish. Pour the batter into the dish. Bake for 45 minutes. Remove from oven and serve immediately.

# HUSH PUPPIES

yields 12 hush puppies

    1½ cups white corn meal
    ½ cup flour
    ⅛ teaspoon salt
    2 tablespoons baking powder
    ½ teaspoon baking soda
    1 egg
    1 cup buttermilk
    1 onion, finely chopped
    4 tablespoons melted bacon drippings, lard, or
      vegetable oil

In a large bowl combine the flour, salt, baking powder, and baking soda. Mix well. Stir in the corn meal. Add the egg and beat mixture with a wooden spoon until it is smooth.

Pour in the buttermilk and stir until it is absorbed by the corn meal mixture. Stir in the onion.

In a deep skillet heat the bacon drippings until very hot, 375° on a deep-frying thermometer. The fat should be to a depth of 2 to 3 inches in the skillet.

Drop the hush puppies by rounded teaspoons into the fat. Fry, turning frequently, until golden, about 3 minutes.

Serve warm with butter

Hush puppies are the perfect accompaniment to fried fish.

# NORTH CAROLINA SWEET POTATO BISCUITS

yields 10 to 12 biscuits

    1 small sweet potato
    2 tablespoons butter
    1 cup flour
    1 teaspoon baking powder
    ½ teaspoon salt
    1 to 3 tablespoons milk

Preheat the oven to 425°.

Wrap the sweet potato in aluminum foil and bake for 40 to 45 minutes or until soft. Turn oven down to 400°.

When potato has cooled, peel and dice it.

Sift the flour, baking powder, and salt together into a large bowl. Cut the sweet potato pieces and butter into the mixture, using a pastry blender or two knives. Add the milk and stir until well blended.

Turn the dough out onto a lightly floured surface and knead for 2 minutes. Roll to ½-inch thickness. Cut the dough with floured 2-inch biscuit cutter.

Place the biscuits onto a greased cookie sheet and bake for 12 minutes or until golden. Remove from oven and serve hot.

# LOUISIANA CHEESE BISCUITS

serves 6 to 8

*¼ pound butter*
*1 cup flour*
*¾ cup grated Swiss cheese*
*½ tablespoon French-style mustard*
*2 egg yolks, beaten*
*⅛ teaspoon cayenne pepper*

Preheat the oven to 300°.

In a bowl beat the butter until very creamy. Add the egg yolks and mix well. Add the grated cheese, mustard, and cayenne. Gradually stir in the flour. Mix thoroughly to make a stiff dough.

Roll out the dough on a lightly floured surface. Cut with a floured 1-inch biscuit cutter.

Place the biscuits on a greased cookie sheet and bake for 20 minutes or until golden. Remove from oven and serve hot.

# SOPAPILLAS

yields 36 *sopapillas*

*4 cups flour*
*2 teaspoons salt*
*4 teaspoons baking powder*
*¼ cup lard or vegetable shortening*
*1 to 1½ cups warm water*
*lard or vegetable oil for frying*

Sift the flour, salt, and baking powder together in a large bowl. Add the lard or shortening and work with the fingers until the mixture resembles a coarse meal. Add just enough warm water to hold the dough together. Place the dough in the refrigerator for 10 minutes.

Roll the dough out onto a lightly floured surface to ⅛-inch thickness. With a pastry wheel or sharp knife cut the dough into 3-inch squares.

Heat a 3-inch layer of the lard or vegetable oil in a deep skillet. When the lard is very hot (400° on a deep-frying thermometer) add the *sopapillas*, as many as will fit at one time, and fry 2 to 3 minutes per side. When they are crisp on both sides remove and drain on paper towels. Serve hot.

*Sopapillas*, or "sofa pillows," are a Southwestern specialty. Only Yankees butter them. For a sweet bread, roll the *sopapillas* in sugar and brown cinnamon after frying.

# SAFFRON BREAD

yields 2 loaves

¼ teaspoon crumbled saffron threads
½ cup boiling water
2 cups milk
¼ pound melted butter
1 package active dry yeast
2 tablespoons warm water
1 cup sugar
½ teaspoon salt
½ teaspoon nutmeg
6 to 6½ cups sifted flour
 rinds of 2 lemons, grated
2 cups currants
1 tablespoon melted butter

Steep the saffron in the boiling water for 1 hour. Strain and reserve the saffron liquid.

In a saucepan, scald the milk and place it in a large mixing bowl. Add the saffron liquid and the melted butter. Stir well.

Dissolve the yeast in the warm water. Stir it into the warm milk mixture. Add the sugar, salt, and nutmeg. Sift in the flour and mix well. Add the grated lemon rind and the currants. Mix dough until well blended. The dough should be stiff.

Cover the mixing bowl with a clean towel. Let rise in a warm place until doubled in bulk, about 1½ hours.

Remove the dough from the bowl. Punch down. Knead on a lightly floured surface until smooth, about 2 minutes.

Butter 2 9 × 5 × 3-inch loaf pans.

Divide the dough and shape each half into a loaf. Place in loaf pans. Let dough rise a second time, about 50 to 60 minutes.

Preheat the oven to 350°.

Bake the loaves for 1 hour or until they are golden and sound hollow when tapped.

Remove the pans to cooling racks and brush the tops of the loaves with melted butter. Cool in the pans for 10 minutes. Turn loaves out onto racks and continue cooling. Cool completely before slicing.

# CORNSTICKS

yields 12 cornsticks

1½ cups corn meal
½ cup flour
1 teaspoon baking soda
1 teaspoon baking powder
2 teaspoons sugar
2 eggs, beaten
2 cups buttermilk
3 tablespoons melted butter

Preheat the oven to 425°.

In a large bowl combine the flour, baking soda, salt, baking powder, and sugar. Stir in corn meal.

In another bowl combine the eggs, buttermilk, and melted butter. Add to the flour mixture and beat well.

Butter the molds of a 12-stick cast-iron cornstick pan. Spoon the batter into the molds, filling them two-thirds full.

Bake for 20 to 25 minutes or until golden brown. Remove from oven and serve at once.

# CORN BREAD

yields 1 corn bread

1½ cups corn meal
1½ teaspoons baking powder
  3 tablespoons flour
  ½ teaspoon salt
1½ cups milk
  1 egg
  2 tablespoons bacon fat or butter

Preheat the oven to 450°.

Melt the butter in a heavy 12-inch iron skillet.

In a mixing bowl combine the corn meal, flour, salt, and baking powder. Add the milk and egg. Mix well.

Add the melted butter and stir to blend. Pour the batter into the hot iron skillet.

Place the skillet in the oven and bake 20 to 25 minutes or until golden brown. Serve warm with butter.

Although this bread can be made in a baking dish, for true authenticity it must be made in a cast-iron skillet.

# HOECAKES

yields 8 hoecakes

  1 cup white corn meal
  ½ teaspoon salt
  ¾ cup boiling water
  1 to 2 tablespoons bacon fat or butter

In a mixing bowl combine the corn meal and the salt. In a slow, continuous stream, pour in the boiling water; stir constantly. Beat until the batter is smooth.

To form the hoecakes, scoop up approximately 2 tablespoons of the batter and gently pat it into a flat circle about 3½ to 4 inches in diameter.

Heat 1 tablespoon bacon fat in a heavy skillet. When the fat is very hot, lower the heat and add 4 hoecakes. Fry for about 2 minutes per side or until golden brown. Turn carefully.

Remove the fried hoecakes. Add the remaining 4 hoecakes and fry. Add the remaining fat if needed. Serve hoecakes hot.

# RICE BREAD

yields 1 loaf

  1 cup cooked cold rice, pushed through a sieve
  2 cups white corn meal
  3 eggs
  1 tablespoon melted butter
2½ teaspoons baking powder
2¼ cups milk
  1 teaspoon salt

Preheat the oven to 400°.

In a bowl beat the eggs lightly. Gradually pour in the milk and mix well.

In another bowl combine the corn meal, salt, and baking powder. Add to egg mixture and beat well. Add the melted butter and sieved rice. Beat until the batter is very light.

Butter a shallow 9 × 9-inch baking pan and fill with the batter. Bake for 30 minutes or until golden. Serve hot with butter.

# Desserts

## GEORGIA PECAN CAKE

yields 1 10-inch cake

3¾ cups flour
1 teaspoon baking powder
4 teaspoons grated nutmeg
4 cups chopped pecans
5 cups golden raisins
1 cup dark raisins
½ pound butter, softened
2 cups sugar
6 eggs
½ cup brandy

Preheat the oven to 275°. Butter a 10-inch tube pan and set aside.

In a large bowl stir together the flour, baking powder, and nutmeg.

Remove ½ cup of the flour mixture and add it to the pecans and raisins in a separate bowl. Mix and set aside.

Cream the butter and sugar until light and fluffy. Add the eggs, 2 at a time. Beat thoroughly after each addition.

Add the flour mixture to the creamed butter alternately with the brandy. Mix after each addition until well blended. Add the pecan-raisin mixture and mix thoroughly.

Turn the batter into the tube pan. Bake in the center of the oven for 2 hours.

Remove to a cooling rack. Cool in the pan for 15 minutes. Turn cake out and cool completely on rack.

## POUND CAKE

yields 2 loaf cakes

1 pound butter
1 pound sugar
10 eggs, separated
4 cups flour
½ teaspoon salt
1 teaspoon baking powder
1 teaspoon vanilla
2 tablespoons freshly grated lemon rind

Butter 2 12-inch loaf pans and dust lightly with flour. Set aside.

In a large bowl cream the butter. Gradually add the sugar and continue creaming until the mixture is light and fluffy.

In a separate bowl beat the egg yolks. Add the yolks to the butter mixture, beating constantly.

In a bowl or on a large sheet of wax paper, sift together the flour, salt, and baking powder 4 times.

Gradually add the flour to the butter mixture. Mix thoroughly. Add the vanilla and lemon rind. Mix thoroughly.

Preheat the oven to 300°.

In a small bowl beat the egg whites until they are stiff but not dry. Fold into the batter.

Pour half the mixture into each of the loaf pans. Bake for 1 to 1¼ hours or until a cake tester inserted into the middle of the loaf comes out clean.

Remove to cooling racks. Cool 10 minutes in the pan. Then turn out onto racks and cool completely.

A traditional pound cake such as this one calls for 1 pound each of the major ingredients. Ten eggs weigh about 1 pound.

# SOUTHERN RUM PIE

serves 6 to 8

1 *pastry for 2-crust, 9-inch pie*
1 *cup light brown sugar*
¾ *teaspoon cinnamon*
¼ *cup flour*
⅛ *teaspoon salt*
6 *cups apples, peeled, cored, and thinly sliced*
2 *tablespoons butter, cut into small pieces*
2 *tablespoons dark rum*

Preheat the oven to 425°.

Roll out the pastry on a lightly floured surface. Fit into a 9-inch pie plate.

In a small bowl combine the sugar, cinnamon, flour, and salt.

Place the sliced apples in a large bowl. Add the sugar mixture and mix lightly. Place apple-sugar mixture into pie plate and dot with butter.

Roll out the remaining pastry on a lightly floured surface. Make slits in the center and adjust over filling. Seal the edges together, trim, and flute.

Bake for 45 to 50 minutes or until crust is golden. Remove from oven to a cooling rack. Pour rum through center slits. Cool on rack until warm and serve.

# CHARLESTON TORTE

serves 8 to 10

3 *eggs*
1½ *cups sugar*
¼ *cup flour*
1 *teaspoon baking powder*
¼ *teaspoon salt*
1 *cup apples, peeled, cored, and finely chopped*
1 *cup finely chopped pecans*
1 *teaspoon vanilla extract*
1 *cup heavy cream, chilled*
2 *tablespoons chopped pecans*

Preheat the oven to 400°. Generously butter a 12 × 8 × 2-inch baking pan. Set aside.

Sift together the flour, baking powder, and salt. Set aside.

Beat the eggs briefly. Then add the sugar and vanilla and beat until mixture is thick, about 4 to 5 minutes.

Beat in the flour mixture until well blended. Add the chopped apples and 1 cup chopped pecans. Mix gently but thoroughly into the batter with a rubber spatula.

Turn batter into the pan and bake for 30 to 35 minutes or until a cake tester inserted into the center comes out clean.

Remove from oven and cool slightly.

Beat the cream in a chilled mixing bowl until stiff. Transfer to a serving bowl and sprinkle with 2 tablespoons chopped pecans. Serve cake directly from the pan while still warm. Serve whipped cream on the side.

# KEY LIME PIE

serves 6 to 8

1 cup and 2 tablespoons sugar
⅓ cup cornstarch
¼ cup cold water
½ teaspoon salt
1½ cups hot water
6 tablespoons fresh lime juice
3 eggs, separated
3 tablespoons butter
1 tablespoon grated lime rind
1 9-inch pastry shell
6 tablespoons sugar
⅛ teaspoon salt
1 lime, sliced, for garnish

Preheat the oven to 450°.

Roll out the pastry onto a lightly floured surface. Fit into a 9-inch pie plate. Prick shell with a fork and bake for 12 to 15 minutes. Cool completely. Reduce oven temperature to 300°.

In a saucepan combine 1 cup and 2 tablespoons sugar, the cornstarch, ½ teaspoon salt, and cold water. Mix well. Add the hot water and cook over very low heat. Stir mixture constantly until very thick. Remove from heat and stir in lime juice. Return to low heat and cook until thickened.

In a small bowl lightly beat the egg yolks. Beat in 1 teaspoon of the sugar mixture.

Remove sugar mixture from heat and slowly stir in the egg yolks. Return saucepan to heat and cook 2 minutes, stirring constantly. Add the butter and the grated lime rind. Stir well. Remove from heat and cool.

Pour the cooled filling into the pie shell.

In a small bowl beat the egg whites until stiff but not dry. Gradually beat in the 6 tablespoons sugar and the salt. Beat until well blended.

Spread the meringue over the top of the pie and bake for 20 minutes. Cool before serving.

# PECAN PIE

serves 8

4 eggs
2 cups dark corn syrup
2 tablespoons butter, melted and cooled
1 teaspoon vanilla extract
1 9-inch pastry shell
1½ cups pecan halves

Preheat the oven to 400°.

On a lightly floured board roll out the pastry for 1 9-inch pie crust. Fit into pie plate. Line the pastry with a buttered sheet of aluminum foil pressed gently into the shell. Bake for 10 minutes. Remove foil and bake 2 minutes longer. Remove from oven and cool.

In a large bowl whisk the eggs for about 30 seconds or until smooth. Continue whisking and pour in the corn syrup in a slow continuous stream. Add the vanilla and melted butter. Continue to whisk until ingredients are well blended.

Pour the mixture into the cooled pie shell and top with the pecan halves.

Bake on the middle shelf of the oven for 35 to 40 minutes or until firm. Serve warm with whipped cream.

# DIXIE BROWN SUGAR PIE

serves 6 to 8

*1 cup brown sugar, firmly packed*
*1 egg, slightly beaten*
*2 tablespoons flour*
*3 tablespoons milk*
*1 teaspoon vanilla*
*2 tablespoons melted butter*
*1 pastry for 9-inch pie*

Preheat the oven to 350°.

Roll the dough out onto a lightly floured surface. Fit into pie shell and flute edges. Set aside.

In a large bowl combine the brown sugar, egg, flour, milk, vanilla, and melted butter. Mix until well blended.

Pour mixture into the pie shell. Bake for 15 minutes or until set. Remove from oven and let cool. Serve warm.

# HUCKLEBERRY PIE

serves 6 to 8

*1 quart fresh huckleberries*
*3 tablespoons quick-cooking tapioca*
*1 cup sugar*
*¼ teaspoon salt*
  *juice of 1 lemon*
*1 pastry for 2-crust 9-inch pie*
*1 tablespoon butter, cut into pieces*

Preheat the oven to 450°.

In a large bowl combine the huckleberries, tapioca, sugar, salt, and lemon juice. Set aside.

Roll the pastry out onto a lightly floured surface. Use half to line the pie plate. Fit well and trim edges.

Pour the berry mixture into the pie shell. Dot with butter.

Cover the pie with the remaining pastry. Moisten the edges with a little water and flute to seal. Cut several vents in the top.

Bake for 10 minutes. Reduce heat to 350° and bake for 30 to 35 minutes longer. Serve warm or cold.

Huckleberries have a stronger flavor than blueberries, but are otherwise much the same.

# OSGOOD PIE

serves 6 to 8

*½ cup butter*
*1 cup sugar*
*2 eggs, separated*
*½ cup pecans, chopped*
*½ cup raisins*
*½ teaspoon ground cloves*
*½ teaspoon cinnamon*
*2 teaspoons cocoa*
*1 teaspoon vinegar*
*1 pastry for 9-inch pie*

Preheat the oven to 375°.

Roll the pastry out onto a lightly floured surface. Fit into a 9-inch pie plate and flute edges. Set aside.

In a large bowl cream the butter and sugar together until light and fluffy. Beat the egg yolks and add them to the creamed mixture. Blend well.

*(continued on next page)*

Stir in the pecans, raisins, cloves, cinnamon, cocoa, and vinegar. Mix well.

In a small bowl, beat the egg whites until stiff but not dry. Fold the egg whites into sugar mixture.

Turn mixture into the unbaked pie shell and bake for 10 minutes. Reduce heat to 325° and bake 30 minutes longer. Cool before serving.

# KENTUCKY BOURBON CAKE

yields 1 10-inch cake

1½ cups butter, softened
 2 cups sugar
2¼ cups light brown sugar, firmly packed
 6 eggs
5½ cups flour
 ¼ teaspoon salt
 1 teaspoon grated nutmeg
 2 cups Bourbon whiskey
3½ cups coarsely chopped pecans

Preheat the oven to 300°. Heavily grease a 10-inch tube pan. Flour lightly and shake out excess. Set aside.

In a very large mixing bowl cream the butter until soft.

In a medium bowl combine the sugar and brown sugar. Mix well. Add half the sugar mixture to the butter and cream until it is very smooth.

In another bowl beat the eggs until light and fluffy. Slowly beat in the remaining sugar mixture. Continue beating until mixture is smooth and creamy. Add to the butter mixture and stir until thoroughly combined.

Sift the flour, salt, and nutmeg together. Add the flour and Bourbon alternately to the batter, beginning and ending with the flour. Mix thoroughly. Stir in the pecan pieces.

Turn batter into the tube pan and bake for 1½ to 1¾ hours or until the cake begins to shrink from the pan.

Remove from oven and cool in pan for 15 minutes. Turn out onto rack and cool completely. This cake improves with age. Wrap tightly in aluminum foil and store.

# BLACKBERRY CAKE

serves 10 to 12

1½ cups sugar
 ½ cup butter
 2 eggs
 1 cup fresh blackberries, cleaned and washed
 2 cups flour
 ½ teaspoon baking powder
 1 teaspoon grated nutmeg
 ½ teaspoon cinnamon
 ⅔ cup buttermilk
 1 teaspoon baking soda

Preheat the oven to 350°. Butter and flour a 13 × 9 × 2-inch baking pan. Set aside.

In a mixing bowl combine the sugar, butter, eggs and blackberries. Beat mixture with an electric mixer at medium-high for 2 minutes.

In a separate bowl combine the flour, baking powder, nutmeg, and cinnamon.

Combine the buttermilk and baking soda. Add alternately with the flour mixture to the berries. Beat for 2 minutes.

Pour batter into the pan and bake for 25 to 30 minutes or until a cake tester inserted into the center of the cake comes out clean.

Remove and let cool. Serve from baking pan.

# JAM CAKE

yields 1 cake

> ¾ cup butter, softened
> 1 cup sugar
> 3 eggs
> 3 cups flour
> 2 teaspoons baking powder
> 1 teaspoon baking soda
> ¼ teaspoon salt
> 1 teaspoon ground cinnamon
> ½ cup buttermilk
> 1 cup thick blackberry jam

Preheat the oven to 350°. Grease 2 9-inch round cake pans. Set aside.

In a large mixing bowl cream the butter and sugar until light and fluffy. Add the eggs and beat well.

In a bowl or on a large sheet of wax paper, sift together the flour, baking powder, baking soda, and cinnamon 3 times.

Add the flour mixture to the creamed mixture alternately with the buttermilk. End with the flour. Fold in the jam.

Turn the batter into the prepared cake pans. Distribute evenly. Bake for 35 to 45 minutes or until golden brown.

Remove to cooling racks and cool in the pans for 10 minutes. Turn out onto racks and continue cooling.

Frost with Fruit Frosting (see below).

Jam cake is a favorite in Kentucky and Tennessee. Use only berry jam.

# FRUIT FROSTING

yields enough for 1 2-layer cake

> ½ cup pitted dates
> 1½ cups raisins
> 1 orange, peeled
> 1 lemon, peeled
> ⅓ cup sugar

Grind the dates and raisins together and place in a saucepan.

Peel the orange and lemon. Cut into pieces and remove all seeds. Grind the pieces together and add to the saucepan.

Add the sugar to the saucepan and cook over medium heat until mixture thickens. Stir constantly. Spread over cake while still warm.

To frost the jam cake, place one cake layer top-side down on a serving plate. Brush off any crumbs. Spread with about one-third the frosting mixture. Place the second layer, top-side up, on top. Frost the sides of both layers and then frost the top. Smooth the frosting.

Allow the frosting to set for a few hours before cutting the cake.

## PECAN BUTTER BALLS

yields approximately 36 cookies

½ cup butter
1 cup flour
2 tablespoons sugar
1 teaspoon vanilla extract
⅛ teaspoon salt
1 cup finely ground pecans
  confectioner's sugar

Preheat the oven to 375°.

In a large bowl cream the butter and sugar together until light and fluffy. Add the vanilla and mix well.

Combine the flour and salt. Add to the creamed mixture and mix well. Add the nuts and stir until thoroughly combined.

Place batter by well-rounded teaspoons on ungreased cookie sheets. Bake for 20 minutes.

Remove from oven and cool for 1 minute on the cookie sheets. Roll each ball in confectioner's sugar and continue cooling.

## KENTUCKY BOURBON BALLS

yields approximately 50 balls

1 6-ounce package semisweet chocolate pieces
½ cup sugar
2 tablespoons light corn syrup
⅓ cup Bourbon whiskey
1 7-ounce package vanilla wafers, finely ground
1 cup finely chopped walnuts
1 cup finely ground pecans or almonds

In the top of a double boiler over hot but not boiling water, melt the chocolate pieces.

Remove from heat and stir in sugar, corn syrup, and Bourbon.

In a mixing bowl combine the wafer crumbs and the walnuts. Stir in the chocolate mixture. Blend well.

Immediately shape the mixture into 1-inch balls and roll them in the ground pecans.

Store in an airtight container for at least 7 days before serving.

## FLAN

serves 4

¼ cup sugar
½ cup sugar
3 eggs
3 cups milk
½ teaspoon vanilla extract

Preheat the oven to 350°.

In a saucepan heat ¼ cup sugar until it becomes a light brown syrup. Coat the sides and bottom of a custard dish or medium soufflé dish with the syrup. Set aside to cool.

In a mixing bowl beat the eggs and ½ cup sugar. Add the milk and vanilla. Beat well.

Pour mixture into the custard dish. Set the dish into a pan of hot water and bake for 30 minutes or until a knife inserted into the center comes out clean.

Flan is favorite Southwestern and Mexican dessert. It is sometimes called baked custard by Yankees.

# Accents

## BRANDIED WHOLE PEACHES

yields approximately 6 pints

4 pounds sugar
4 pounds peaches
2 cups brandy

In a large pot place the sugar and add enough water to dissolve. Bring to a boil. When syrup begins to boil, add peaches and cook for 5 minutes.

Remove peaches and boil syrup 15 minutes longer. Stir in the brandy. Remove pot from heat.

Place the peaches into 6 1-pint sterilized jars. Pour the syrup over them. Seal, cool, and store.

## PICKLED PEACHES

yields 2 quarts

12 peaches (about 3 pounds)
12 whole cloves
4½ cups sugar
    water
3 cups cider vinegar
4 cinnamon sticks, coarsely broken

In a large pot boil enough water to cover the peaches. When the water boils, add the peaches, 4 at a time, and let boil for 2 to 3 minutes. Drain peaches and rinse with cold water.

Peel the peaches with a sharp knife. Stick a clove into each peach and put peaches into large sterilized jars.

Place the sugar, vinegar, and cinnamon in a large saucepan. Bring the mixture to a boil. Stir only until the sugar dissolves. Remove from heat and carefully spoon syrup over peaches, a little at a time. Allow syrup to settle before adding more.

Cover jars tightly and cool to room temperature. Refrigerate for 4 or more days before serving.

## PICKLED FIGS

yields 8 pints

1 gallon water
1 tablespoon baking soda
6 pounds fresh figs, stemmed and washed
3 pounds sugar
2 cups white wine vinegar
1 tablespoon cinnamon
1½ teaspoons whole cloves
2 lemons, thinly sliced

Bring the water to a boil in a large pot. Add the baking soda and dissolve. Remove from heat. Add the figs and let them soak for 10 minutes.

Drain the figs and rinse in cold water.

In another pot place the sugar, vinegar, cinnamon, cloves, and lemons. Add the figs and bring the mixture to a boil. Cook until liquid is clear.

Remove the figs and place them in sterilized jars. Boil the syrup until it thickens. Pour the syrup over the figs. Seal the jars, cool, and store.

# MIXED CHUTNEY

yields approximately 3 quarts

*1 quart white vinegar*
*1 pound mangos, peeled and sliced*
*3 pounds apples, peeled, cored, and sliced*
*1 pound dark brown sugar*
*1 ounce fresh chili peppers, finely chopped*
*1 cup seedless golden raisins*
*½ pound finely cut dried lemon peel*
*½ pound candied ginger*
*2 cloves garlic, crushed*
*2 ounces mustard seed*
*2 teaspoons salt*
*2 teaspoons confectioner's sugar*

In a large pot bring the vinegar to a boil. Add the mangos and apples. Cook until soft, about 20 to 25 minutes.

Add the brown sugar, chili pepper, raisins, lemon peel, ginger, and garlic. Add the mustard seeds, salt, and sugar. Mix well and cook for 15 minutes.

Remove from heat and pour into hot sterilized jars. Seal, cool, and store.

# PEACH CHUTNEY

yields 4 pints

*4 quarts peaches, chopped*
*1 cup onion, chopped*
*1 clove garlic, chopped*
*1 hot red pepper pod*
*1 cup raisins*
*1 quart vinegar*
*2 tablespoons ground ginger*
*¼ cup mustard seeds*
*3 cups brown sugar*
*2 teaspoons salt*

Place the chopped peaches into a large pot. Add the onion, raisins, vinegar, brown sugar, and salt. Mix well.

Combine the garlic, hot pepper, ginger, and mustard seeds. Place them into a square of doubled cheesecloth and tie with string.

Bring the peach mixture to a boil. When mixture begins to boil, add the bag with the spices. Lower heat and cook, stirring frequently, until thick, about 40 minutes.

Remove bag with spices. Pour peach mixture into hot sterilized jars. Seal, cool, and store.

# CHILI RELISH

yields 2 pints

*2 quarts tomatoes, peeled and chopped*
*1 cup scallions, chopped*
*½ cup green pepper, finely chopped*
*½ cup sweet red pepper, finely chopped*
*1 teaspoon crushed hot red pepper flakes*
*1 cup sugar*
*1½ teaspoons salt*
*1½ teaspoons mustard seed*
*½ teaspoon cinnamon*
*1¼ cups white vinegar*

Into a large pot place the tomatoes, scallions, green pepper, red pepper, hot red pepper, sugar, salt, mustard seed, cinnamon, and vinegar. Stir well.

Bring the mixture to a boil. Reduce heat to medium-low and simmer, stirring frequently, until the mixture is thick, about 3 to 4 hours.

Pour into hot sterilized jars. Seal, cool, and store.

# GREEN CHILI SAUCE

yields approximately 2 cups

*3 fresh or canned green chili peppers,
  with seeds, chopped*
*4 medium green tomatoes, chopped*
*2 medium onions, chopped*
*1 cup boiling water*
*1 clove garlic, crushed*
*1 teaspoon dried oregano*
  *salt to taste*

Place the chopped chilies in a saucepan.
Add enough water to cover and bring to
a boil. Cook chilies for 10 minutes.
Remove from heat and drain.

Return chilies to the saucepan and add
the tomatoes, onions, and boiling water.
Simmer over medium heat for 20
minutes.

Remove from heat and press mixture
through a sieve. Discard any solids
remaining in the sieve. Add the garlic,
oregano, and salt. Stir well. The mixture
should be very thick.

Store tightly covered in the refrigerator.

# SOUTHERN-STYLE TARTAR SAUCE

yields 1½ cups

*1 cup mayonnaise*
*6 shallots, finely chopped*
*1 tablespoon chives, chopped*
*¼ cup dill pickle, finely chopped*
*1 tablespoon parsley, chopped*
*1 teaspoon capers, finely chopped*
*2 tablespoons tarragon vinegar*
*1 teaspoon dry mustard*
*⅛ teaspoon cayenne pepper*

In a bowl combine the vinegar and
cayenne. Whisk until cayenne dissolves.
Add the pickles, shallots, chives, parsley,
and capers. Stir well. Beat in the
mayonnaise and mustard.

Cover and refrigerate for 3 hours before
serving. This sauce will keep for up to 2
days in the refrigerator.

# SOUTHERN-STYLE GREEN TOMATO RELISH

yields approximately 2 to 2½ pints

*4 to 5 pounds green tomatoes, chopped*
*2 medium onions, chopped*
*2 quarts cold water*
*½ cup salt*
*1½ cups white vinegar*
*½ cup boiling water*
*1½ cups sugar*
*1½ teaspoons celery seeds*
*½ teaspoon cinnamon*
*½ teaspoon ground turmeric*
*¼ teaspoon dry mustard*

Place the tomatoes and onions in a large
bowl. Pour the cold water over them and
sprinkle with the salt. Soak for 3 hours.

Drain the tomatoes and onions in a
colander. Rinse well with cold water.

In a saucepan combine the vinegar,
boiling water, sugar, celery seeds,
cinnamon, turmeric, and mustard. Bring
to a boil and boil for 3 minutes. Add the
tomatoes and the onions and bring to a
boil again. Lower heat and simmer,
uncovered, for 10 minutes. Remove from
heat.

Carefully spoon mixture into hot
sterilized jars. Seal, cool, and store.

# CAROLINA MINT RELISH

½ cup fresh mint leaves
3 large tart apples, cored
1½ cups seedless raisins
12 tomatoes
2 sweet red peppers, seeded
4 large onions
2 tablespoons mustard seeds
½ cup salt
2 cups sugar
6 cups cider vinegar

Coarsely chop the mint, apples, raisins, tomatoes, pepper, and onions in a food chopper, blender, or food processor. Place the mixture in a bowl. Stir in the mustard seeds, salt, sugar, and vinegar. Mix well.

Place the mixture into a crock or well-sealed glass container for 10 days. Stir occasionally.

After 10 days, spoon the mixture into hot sterilized jars. Seal, cool, and store.

# CITRUS CONSERVE

yields approximately 3½ pints

6 oranges
5 cups water
6 cups sugar
¼ cup fresh lime juice
1 2-inch cinnamon stick
½ cup seedless raisins

Wash and quarter the oranges. Remove the peel. Cut the pulp finely, discarding the membranes and seeds.

Chop the peel finely in a food chopper, blender, or food processor. Place the peel in a saucepan. Cover with the water and bring to a boil. Lower heat to medium and cook until peel is tender, about 20 minutes. Add the orange pulp and juice and cook 20 minutes longer or until the mixture has cooked down to half its original volume.

Add the sugar, lime juice, cinnamon, and raisins. Cook, stirring constantly, until the sugar is totally dissolved, about 30 minutes.

Remove from heat. Carefully spoon mixture into hot sterilized jars. Seal, cool, and store.

# OLD-FASHIONED BLACKBERRY JAM

yields 5 cups

5 cups fresh ripe blackberries
½ cup water
4 cups sugar

Wash the berries and discard any unripe or damaged fruit.

Place the berries into a heavy pot. Add the water and sugar and bring to a boil. Stir until the sugar dissolves. Reduce heat to medium-low and cook, uncovered, until jam reaches 221° on a candy thermometer. Stir occasionally.

Remove from heat. Skim the top of the mixture. Carefully spoon the jam into hot sterilized jars. Seal, cool, and store.

THE BOUNTY OF THE AMERICAN HARVEST

SHRIMP
CREOLE

AVOCADO SPREAD AND SACRAMENTO SALAD

CABBAGE SALAD AND TEXAS CHILI CON CARNE

PACIFIC MUSSEL SOUP (left)            CREOLE BOILED SHRIMP

VEAL SCALLOPS WITH LEMON SAUCE,
MINNESOTA WILD RICE AND MUSHROOMS,
AND BUTTERMILK BISCUITS

SAN FRANCISCO GLAZED DUCK WITH SAGE RICE

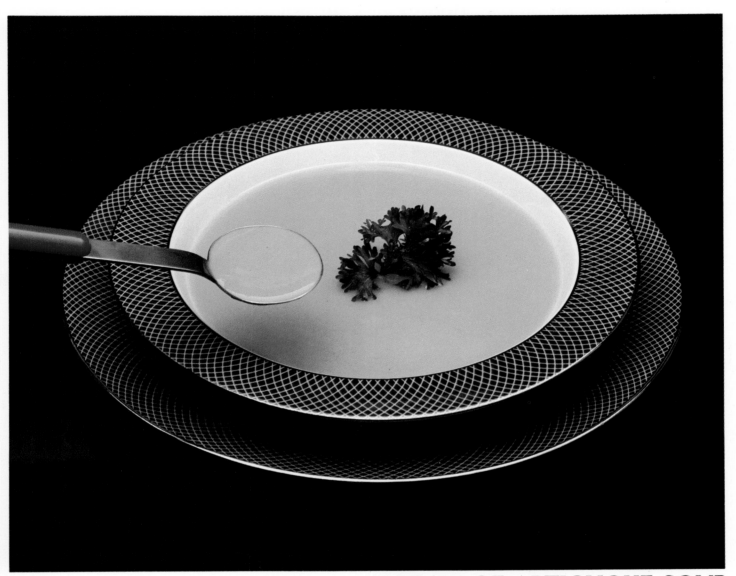

CREAM OF ARTICHOKE SOUP

HEARTLAND VEGETABLE SOUP(left)

BARBECUED SPARERIBS AND CORN BREAD

PEACH PIE

LEMON MERINGUE PIE AND EARLY AMERICAN APPLE PIE

FRESH SCALLOPS, OYSTERS (top inset) AND CLAMS (bottom inset)

# FAVORITE AMERICAN BREADS
*Including Anadama bread, Swedish Rye Bread, Old-Fashioned Oatmeal Bread, and San Francisco Sourdough Bread.*

# THE HEARTLAND

Gone are the thundering herds of buffalo, the endless, uninterrupted prairies, the skies shadowed with vast flocks of game birds. Yet the states encompassing the Midwest and bordering on the South and the Rockies are, in their ways, the most traditionally American of all. Not in their Anglo-Saxon heritage, but in their complete acceptance of the melting-pot theory of the country. Germans, Swedes, French, Poles, Basques . . . they have all done much to preserve the ethnic identities of their immigrant forbears.

If grilled buffalo tongue (the tenderest part of that shaggy beast) no longer graces picnic menus, and if spits groaning with wild ducks and geese are almost so rare as not to exist, the American Heartland still sets a table of extraordinary bounty and variety, far too underrated by the rest of the country.

After all, this is the most fertile grain-producing area of the world, and with it comes vast herds of livestock. The region produces most of our bread and meat, the mainstays of the American diet. But here too are splendid lake and river fish, from Coho salmon to whitefish and pike to the lowly but increasingly popular catfish. Fruits and vegetables grow large and juicy. What the region may lack in exotics, it more than makes up for in the bounty and quality of its produce. Dairy products, especially from the upper Midwest, are an international commodity.

The cooking of the Heartland tends to be hearty fare, suited to the robust climate and traditionally hard-working termperament of the people. Stews, roasts, the sizzling prime steak, steaming bowls of fresh vegetables and mountainous desserts are common. But there are unexpected subtleties also: the fish stews of Northern Minnesota (derived from the original French trappers of the area), the variants on Scandinavian salads brimming with tender whitefish, the native rabbit grilled over wood fires, as well as the traditional fish fry of the Mississippi River's northern reaches.

Amongst the hopping rabbits and fields of corn, though, are some of the great dessert cooks of America. The great flour-milling concerns are here, and thousands of recipes for cakes, pies, breads and muffins, cookies and other confections have spilled forth into the rest of the country. With church sales, state fairs and bake-offs held on a regular basis, the best cooks' creations have received wider attention than they might otherwise have done.

Finally, the Heartland is incredibly rich in the products of dairy farming: cheeses by the score, butter, cream. They have all played a vital role in the development of the region's cuisine. Perhaps, with our concern for lower cholesterol and lighter cooking, they have gone too far out of fashion. Who could resist a fresh-baked cherry pie covered with thick, fresh cream, or the new vegetables of spring gently sautéed in sweet butter from the creamery?

Though the Heartland may lack the spiciness of the Southwest, the variety of the West or the sobriety of the East, its cooking is the melding of dozens of ethnic traditions into a satisfying whole.

# Suggested Menus

### FOURTH OF JULY
### CELEBRATION DINNER
for 6 to 8
Chilled Blackberry Soup
Lake Erie Coho Salmon
Summer Squash Relish
Roasted Corn
Colorful Cabbage Salad
Drop Biscuits
South Dakota Apple Crumb Pie or Streusel
Beer, Iced Tea, or Sparkling Water

### SMALL DINNER PARTY
for 4
Black Walnut Soup
Roast Wild Duck
Minnesota Wild Rice and Mushrooms
Simmered Radishes
Wilted Lettuce
Old-Fashioned Nut Cookies
Wines: Beaujolais, Valpolicella,
Vouvray, or Pinot Noir

### FAMILY DINNER
for 4
Oven-Fried Catfish
Kale with Onions
Hoosier Baked Tomatoes
Raw Fried Potatoes
Midwestern Buttermilk Raisin Cake or
Apple Spice Cake
Beer, Coffee, Tea, or Sparkling Water

### WINTERTIME BUFFET DINNER
for 6 to 8
Wisconsin Cheddar Cheese Squares and
Danish Stuffed Cherry Tomatoes
Danish Pork and Prunes
Walnut Sweet Potatoes or Mashed Turnips
Wisconsin Blue Cheese Salad
Sour Cream Biscuits
Wisconsin Raisin Pie
Wines: Cabernet Sauvignon, Pommard,
Burgundy, or Valpolicella

# SATURDAY LUNCHEON

(choose one or both menus)

for 4

**MENU 1:**
Frukt Soppa (Swedish Fruit Soup)
Scandinavian Herring Salad
Limpa (Swedish Rye Bread)
Scandinavian Raisin Ring or Peach Squares
Coffee, Tea, or Sparkling Water

**MENU 2:**
Tossed Green Salad with Vinaigrette Dressing
Idaho Potato Omelet
Old-Fashioned Muffins with
Walnut Grape Conserve
Norwegian Spritz Cookies
Coffee, Tea, or Sparkling Water

# SPRINGTIME CELEBRATION DINNER

for 6

Heartland Vegetable Soup
Braised Short Ribs
Wisconsin Baked Beans
Spinach Ring
Spiced Apple Bread
Walnut-Chocolate Drops and Honey Custard
Beer, Iced Tea, or Sparkling Water
Wines: Valpolicella, Cabernet Sauvignon,
or Burgundy

# HEARTY WEEKEND BREAKFAST

(choose one or both menus)

**MENU 1:**
Orange Juice
Buckwheat Pancakes
Fried Bacon
Old-Fashioned Oatmeal Bread with
Pear Marmalade
Coffee, Tea, or Milk

**MENU 2:**
Orange Juice
Dakota Eggs
Quick Oatmeal Muffins with
Spicy Blackberry Jam
Coffee, Tea, or Milk

# ⸙ ——Soups and Appetizers —— ⸙

## HEARTLAND VEGETABLE SOUP

serves 8 to 10

  5  pounds beef shank, with bone
  1  tablespoon salt
  2  quarts water
  1  clove garlic, crushed
  ⅓  cup pearl barley
  2  cups onion, chopped
3½  cups or 1 28-ounce can tomatoes, chopped
  ½  cup butter
1½  cups celery, diced
  1  cup carrots, diced
  1  cup potatoes, diced
  1  cup fresh green beans, sliced
  1  cup cabbage, finely chopped
  2  cups fresh peas
  1  cup fresh spinach, chopped
     salt and pepper to taste

Have the butcher cut the beef shank into 3 pieces.

In a large pot place the beef shank, 1 tablespoon salt, water, garlic, barley, and chopped onion. Bring the mixture to a boil. Lower heat and cover. Simmer for 3 hours or until the meat is tender. Skim the soup when the beef is done. Remove the meat and bones. Reserve.

Stir the tomatoes into the soup. Continue to cook over low heat.

In a saucepan melt the butter. Add the celery, carrots, potatoes, green beans, and cabbage. Cook for 7 minutes, stirring frequently. Add mixture to the soup. Cover the pot and simmer for 20 minutes.

Cut the reserved meat into small cubes. Add the meat, peas, and spinach to the pot. Cover and simmer 10 minutes longer.

Season to taste with salt and pepper. This soup will gain flavor as it ages.

## CREAMY CARROT SOUP

serves 6

  ½  cup onion, chopped
  6  tablespoons butter
  2  cups carrots, thinly sliced
  1  teaspoon salt
  3  cups chicken broth
  ¼  cup raw long-grain rice
  1  cup milk
  1  cup light cream

Heat the butter in a saucepan. Add the onions and sauté until lightly browned, about 5 to 7 minutes. Add the carrots and salt. Mix well to coat the carrots with the butter and onion mixture. Cover and simmer over low heat for 20 minutes. Stir occasionally. Stir in the chicken broth and the rice. Cover and simmer for 1 hour. Stir occasionally.

Place the soup in the container of a blender or food processor. Blend until smooth.

Return soup to the saucepan. Stir in the milk and cream. Continue stirring until soup is heated through. Remove from heat and serve.

# WISCONSIN CHEDDAR CHEESE SOUP

serves 6

3 tablespoons butter
4 tablespoons flour
4 cups chicken broth
2 cups milk
½ onion, finely chopped
¾ pound Cheddar cheese, grated
1 cup light cream
1 teaspoon salt
⅛ teaspoon cayenne pepper

Melt the butter in a saucepan. Stir in the flour and blend until smooth. Very slowly stir in the chicken broth. Continue stirring until mixture is smooth.

Add the milk and stir. Add the onion. Continue cooking over low heat for 5 minutes. Add the cheese and cook until cheese is melted. Stir and remove from heat.

Stir in the light cream, salt, and cayenne. Serve hot.

# IOWA CORN CHOWDER

serves 4 to 6

½ cup bacon, finely chopped
1 onion, chopped
½ cup celery, sliced
1½ cups potatoes, diced
2 cups water
1 bay leaf
1 teaspoon salt
¼ teaspoon pepper
2 cups milk
½ cup light cream
2 cups fresh corn, cut from the cob
    (about 2 or 3 ears)

In a saucepan, sauté the bacon until well browned. Stir in the onion and continue cooking for 2 minutes longer. Add the green pepper, potatoes, water, bay leaf, and salt. Simmer gently until potatoes are tender, about 20 to 30 minutes.

Meanwhile, remove the corn from the cob with a sharp knife. Gently scrape the cob with the back of the knife to remove all the kernel. Set aside.

In a small bowl mix the flour with 1 tablespoon milk. Stir until smooth. Add to the potato mixture. Add the remaining milk and stir. Heat until soup thickens.

Slowly stir in the cream and corn. Heat the mixture gently but thoroughly.

Season with pepper. Stir. Remove from heat and serve.

# CHESTNUT SOUP

serves 6

1 cup cooked chestnuts, mashed
1 cup cooked lentils, mashed
1 cup light cream
5 cups beef broth
1 cup smoked beef sausage, diced
1 tablespoon flour
1 teaspoon cold milk
1 tablespoon onion, chopped
½ tablespoon parsley, chopped
½ cup celery, chopped
2 tablespoons butter
1 teaspoon salt

Melt the butter in a large saucepan. Add the celery and cook for 5 minutes, stirring frequently. Add the onion and cook 5 minutes longer.

Add the mashed chestnuts, mashed lentils, parsley, sausage, and beef broth to the saucepan. Heat and let simmer, covered, for 20 minutes.

In a small bowl dissolve the flour in the cold milk. Add to the saucepan and mix well. Let the mixture come to a boil, uncovered. Add the salt and cream and stir. Heat until soup thickens. Remove from heat and serve hot.

# MICHIGAN YELLOW PEA SOUP

serves 6

  2  *pounds pork butt*
  3  *quarts water*
  2  *tablespoons bacon drippings*
  2  *medium onions, finely chopped*
  1  *medium carrot, finely chopped*
  1  *celery stalk, finely chopped*
  1  *pound yellow split peas*
     *salt and pepper to taste*
 ¼  *teaspoon grated nutmeg*

Rinse the peas under cold running water. Drain and set aside.

In a large pot place the pork and water. Bring to a boil. Lower the heat and cover. Simmer over low heat until pork is tender, about 1½ hours.

Remove the pork from the pot and set aside. Skim the cooking water, place water in a bowl, and set aside.

In the same pot heat the bacon drippings. Stir in the onions, carrot, and celery. Cook for 3 minutes, stirring constantly.

Pour the reserved water back into the pot and add the peas. Add the salt, pepper, and nutmeg. Cover the pot and simmer for about 1 hour.

Cut the pork butt into very small cubes. Add to the soup and cook 30 minutes to 1 hour longer. Serve hot.

# BLACK WALNUT SOUP

serves 4

  3  *tablespoons butter*
  3  *tablespoons flour*
  4  *cups beef broth*
 ½  *teaspoon dried marjoram*
  1  *teaspoon salt*
 ⅛  *teaspoon cayenne pepper*
  1  *cup black walnuts, crushed*
 ½  *cup sour cream*
 ½  *cup heavy cream*

Melt the butter in a large pot. Add the flour and stir until blended and smooth. Slowly pour in the beef stock. Stir well. Add the marjoram, salt, and cayenne. Stir again.

In a small bowl combine the walnuts and sour cream. Add to the soup pot and stir. Cook for 2 minutes. Remove from heat and stir in the cream. Serve immediately.

One recommended way of cracking black walnuts is to place them on a cement driveway and run them over with a car. The black stains they leave on your hands will eventually wear away. The drawbacks of black walnuts are offset by their rich flavor. However, they are sometimes difficult to obtain. Regular brown-shelled walnuts may be substituted.

# RUTABAGA-POTATO SOUP

serves 6

    1  1-pound rutabaga, peeled and cut into small pieces
    1  teaspoon salt
1½  cups water
    3  medium potatoes, peeled and thinly sliced
    2  cups milk
¾  teaspoon sugar
    1  cup chicken broth
    2  tablespoons butter
       salt and pepper to taste

Place the rutabaga pieces, salt, and water in a saucepan. Cover and cook over medium heat for 15 to 20 minutes. Add the potatoes and cook 10 minutes longer or until rutabaga and potatoes are tender.

Remove the saucepan from the heat and mash the vegetables. Do not drain. Add the milk, sugar, chicken broth, butter, salt, and pepper. Return to heat and cook until heated through. Serve hot.

Rutabagas were a staple of the first settlers in the Plains states. They are also called yellow or Swedish turnips.

# MASHED POTATO SOUP

serves 4

    4  potatoes, peeled and cut into eighths
    1  large onion, peeled and quartered
    3  stalks celery, cut into thirds
1½  cups water
    1  quart milk
    1  teaspoon butter
       salt and pepper to taste

In a saucepan, combine the potatoes, onion, and celery. Add the water. Bring the mixture to a boil. Cover and lower the heat. Cook until the vegetables are soft, about 30 minutes.

Remove the saucepan from the heat and mash the vegetables. Do not drain. Add the milk, butter, salt, and pepper.

Return the soup to the heat. Heat gently but thoroughly. Remove from heat and serve.

# NORTH DAKOTA BARLEY SOUP

serves 6

    3  tablespoons butter
½  cup pearl barley
    1  large onion, minced
    1  stalk celery, minced
    1  large carrot, minced
    1  tablespoons flour
    8  cups chicken broth
       salt and pepper to taste
    1  cup light cream

In a large saucepan melt the butter. Add the barley, onion, celery, and carrot. Cook over medium heat, stirring constantly, for 5 minutes or until barley is lightly browned and the vegetables soft.

Add the flour. Stir and cook for 1 minute longer. Add the chicken broth and stir. Cover the pot and simmer for 30 minutes or until the barley is tender. Season to taste with salt and pepper.

Add the cream and stir just until heated through. Do not allow the soup to boil. Remove from heat and serve immediately.

# CREAM OF TURNIP SOUP

serves 6

1½ cups beef stock or beef broth
10 small white turnips, peeled and coarsely grated
 1 teaspoon salt
 ½ teaspoon pepper
 1 tablespoon flour
 1 tablespoon butter
 1 cup light cream

In a large pot combine the beef broth, turnips, salt, and pepper. Cover and simmer for 15 minutes.

In a small saucepan, melt the butter. Stir in the flour and combine until well blended. Add the mixture to the soup. Stir until smooth and cook 2 minutes longer.

Remove pot from heat. Stir in the cream. Season to taste and serve hot.

# FRUKT SOPPA (SWEDISH FRUIT SOUP)

serves 6 to 8

 2 quarts water
 1 cinnamon stick
 4 cups mixed dried fruits (apricots, prunes, raisins)
 1 tablespoon cornstarch
 1 teaspoon water
 ¼ cup quick-cooking tapioca
 ¼ cup sugar
 1 tablespoon lemon juice

Place the water, cinnamon, and fruit into a pot. Bring to a boil and boil for 5 minutes.

Add 1 teaspoon water to the cornstarch and mix well to form a thin paste. Add the cornstarch mixture and the tapioca to the fruit mixture. Stir well and cook for 10 minutes.

Add the sugar. Stir and cook 2 to 3 minutes longer. Add the lemon juice and stir.

Remove the cinnamon stick and serve hot.

The Scandinavian heritage of many Midwesterners is evident in the many fruit soups of the region.

# CHILLED BLUEBERRY SOUP

serves 6

 1 package unflavored gelatin
 ¼ cup cold water
 4 cups orange juice
 3 tablespoons lemon juice
 ¼ cup sugar
 2 cups fresh blueberries

In a small bowl soften the gelatin in the cold water. Place the bowl in a pan of hot water until the mixture melts. It is ready for use at that point.

In a bowl combine the orange juice, lemon juice, sugar, and melted gelatin. Stir the mixture until both the sugar and the gelatin are dissolved. Place in the refrigerator for 15 to 30 minutes or until mixture begins to thicken.

Fold the blueberries into the mixture and chill until ready to serve.

# CHERRY SOUP

serves 4 to 6

2 pounds tart red cherries, pitted
2 cups water
½ cinnamon stick
2 whole cloves
¼ teaspoon salt
2 cups red wine, port, or medium-dry sherry
2 egg yolks, well beaten

Place the cherries in a pot with the water, cinnamon, cloves, and salt. Bring the mixture to a boil. Lower the heat and cook the cherries until they are very soft, about 20 to 30 minutes.

When the cherries are done remove the cinnamon and cloves. Place the cherries in a blender or food processor along with ¼ to ½ cup of the cooking liquid. Blend until smooth, adding more cooking liquid if necessary.

Return the blended cherries to the pot. Add the red wine.

In a small bowl mix 1 tablespoon of the soup with the egg yolks. Stir into the soup and heat the mixture. Stir constantly until the soup begins to thicken.

Remove from heat and cool. Chill for at least 2 hours before serving.

# WISCONSIN CHEDDAR CHEESE SQUARES

yields approximately 14 dozen

1 loaf sliced stale or day-old bread
¼ pound melted butter
¼ pound Cheddar cheese, grated

Preheat the oven to 300°.

Trim the crusts from the bread. Cut each slice into strips 2 inches wide. Cut each strip into 4 squares.

Dip each square into the melted butter. Coat each evenly with the grated cheese.

Place the squares on a cookie sheet lined with aluminum foil. Bake for 10 to 15 minutes or until golden. Serve hot.

# FISKEKROKETER (SWEDISH FISH CROQUETTES)

yields about 4 to 5 dozen

2 tablespoons butter
¼ cup flour
1 teaspoon salt
⅛ teaspoon pepper
1 cup light cream
3 cups flaked cooked fish
   (cod, sole, whitefish, or trout)
1 egg yolk, beaten
2 eggs, slightly beaten
1 cup bread crumbs or flour
   oil for deep frying

Fill a deep pan or electric deep-fryer with oil until it is halfway to two-thirds full. Heat the oil to 350° on a deep-fat thermometer.

Melt the butter in a saucepan. Over low heat, stir in the flour, salt, and pepper.

Mix until well blended. Heat the mixture until it begins to bubble. Slowly add the cream, stirring constantly.

Cook over medium heat until mixture thickens, stirring constantly. Remove from heat and cool.

Add the flaked fish to the cooled mixture. Add the beaten egg yolk. Stir well.

Shape the mixture into 1-inch balls.

Dip the fish balls into the beaten eggs. Roll them in the bread crumbs or flour, coating evenly.

Place the fish balls into the hot oil. Fry as many at a time as will fit easily in one layer. Do not crowd. Fry the balls, turning often, until lightly brown, about 2 minutes.

Remove balls from oil with a slotted spoon and drain on paper towels.

# DANISH STUFFED CHERRY TOMATOES

serves 6

1 quart large cherry tomatoes
¼ pound smoked salmon, chopped
1 onion, chopped
½ teaspoon dried dill
⅛ teaspoon pepper

Wash the tomatoes and carefully cut off the tops. Scoop out the tomato pulp and the seeds and reserve. Set tomatoes aside.

In a bowl combine the smoked salmon, onion, dill, pepper, and tomato pulp. Mix until thoroughly combined. Adjust seasonings.

Carefully fill the tomatoes with the salmon mixture. Chill for at least 1 hour before serving.

# Salads

# WILTED LETTUCE

serves 4

6 slices bacon, diced
⅓ cup cider vinegar
2 heads lettuce, torn into medium-small pieces
¼ cup scallions, chopped
¼ teaspoon salt
¼ teaspoon pepper
2 hard-cooked eggs, chopped

Sauté the bacon pieces in a large skillet. When the bacon is crisp, add the vinegar to the skillet. Cook over very low heat until heated through.

Remove skillet from heat and add the lettuce, scallions, salt, and pepper. Toss 1 to 2 minutes or until lettuce is wilted. Add the chopped eggs and toss again. Place in a bowl and serve immediately.

## MACARONI SALAD

serves 4

4 ounces elbow macaroni
1 tablespoon olive oil
1 tart apple, peeled, cored, and diced
1 tablespoon lemon juice
1 small onion, minced
½ cup mayonnaise
   salt
   paprika

Cook the macaroni until tender in boiling salted water. Drain, rinse with cold water, and drain well.

Place the macaroni in a bowl and toss with the olive oil. Allow macaroni to cool to room temperature.

Combine the macaroni with the apples, lemon juice, onion, and mayonnaise. Season to taste. Toss well and serve.

## WYOMING BEAN SALAD

serves 4

2 cups any mixed boiled beans
1½ tablespoons olive oil
1 teaspoon cider vinegar
1 teaspoon Worcestershire sauce
½ teaspoon dry mustard
½ teaspoon sugar
½ teaspoon salt
⅛ teaspoon cayenne pepper
1 tablespoon cucumber, chopped
1 tablespoon sweet red pepper, chopped
1 tablespoon onion, chopped
   lettuce leaves

In a large bowl whisk the olive oil and vinegar until well blended. Add the cucumber, red pepper, onion, Worcestershire sauce, dry mustard, sugar, salt, and cayenne. Mix very well.

Add the beans and stir well. Let salad stand for 1 hour at room temperature before serving.

Toss again and serve on lettuce leaves.

## SCANDINAVIAN HERRING SALAD

serves 4 to 6

2 salt herrings
2 small apples, peeled, cored, and cut into small pieces
2 cups cooked beets, finely chopped
½ cup onion, minced
¼ cup dill pickle, chopped
2 hard-cooked eggs, chopped
   olive oil
   cider vinegar
   lettuce leaves

Place the salt herrings in a bowl of cold water to cover. Soak for 2 hours. Drain and carefully flake the meat.

Place the herring meat in a mixing bowl. Add the apples, beets, onions, and pickle. Dress with oil and vinegar to taste. Toss well. Chill for 2 hours.

Remove salad from refrigerator 45 minutes before serving. Toss again, sprinkle with chopped eggs, and serve on lettuce leaves.

# CREAMY POTATO SALAD

serves 4 to 6

6 *large potatoes*
¾ *cup heavy cream*
4 *tablespoons cider vinegar*
1 *tablespoon vegetable oil*
1½ *teaspoons salt*
¼ *teaspoon pepper*
1 *medium onion, halved and thinly sliced*
8 *radishes, thinly sliced*

Place the potatoes, unpeeled, into a pot of boiling salted water. Cook until tender, about 30 to 40 minutes. Drain and let cool slightly.

When potatoes are cool enough to handle, peel and dice.

In a small bowl combine the cream, vinegar, oil, salt, and pepper. Whisk until well blended.

Pour dressing over warm potatoes and toss gently. Add the onion, pulling layers apart. Add the radishes. Toss well.

Let the salad stand at room temperature for 45 minutes before serving.

# POTATO AND BACON SALAD

serves 6

6 *medium potatoes*
4 *slices bacon, diced*
1 *medium onion, chopped*
½ *cup cider vinegar*
½ *cup water*
1 *teaspoon salt*
1 *teaspoon sugar*
  *pepper*

Place the potatoes, unpeeled, into a pot of boiling salted water. Cook until tender, about 30 to 40 minutes. Drain and cool.

When potatoes are cool enough to handle, peel and cut into thin slices. Place slices into a serving bowl.

Sauté the bacon in a skillet until crisp. Add the onions and sauté for 2 minutes. Do not allow onion to brown. Add the salt, pepper, sugar, vinegar, and water. Bring mixture to a boil. Remove from heat and pour over potatoes. Toss gently but thoroughly. Garnish with parsley and serve.

# INLAGD RÖDBETOR (PICKLED BEET AND ONION SALAD)

serves 6 to 8

5 *medium beets*
  *water*
1 *medium onion, thinly sliced*
¾ *cup cider vinegar*
¾ *cup reserved beet liquid*
1 *whole clove*

Scrub the beets thoroughly. Cut off the leaves, but leave a 2-inch stem and the root end. Place the beets in a large saucepan with water to cover. Bring the water to boil. Reduce heat and simmer, covered, for 30 to 45 minutes or until tender. Drain and reserve liquid.

Immerse the beets into cold water. Peel off the skin, stem, and root end. Cut the beets into ¼-inch slices.

*(continued on next page)*

Slice the onion very thinly. Separate the slices into rings.

Place a layer of beets in a serving bowl. Top with a layer of onion rings. Repeat until beets and onions are used up. End with a layer of beets.

In a small bowl mix together the vinegar, beet liquid, and clove. Pour over the beets and onions.

Cover bowl and chill salad for 4 to 5 hours to allow flavors to blend.

# COLORFUL CABBAGE SALAD

serves 6

*1 medium onion, chopped*
*2 cups red cabbage, finely shredded*
*2 cups green cabbage, finely shredded*
*¼ cup vegetable oil*
*2 tablespoons cider vinegar*
*¼ teaspoon celery seed*
*1 teaspoon salt*
*½ teaspoon sugar*
*¼ teaspoon pepper*

In a bowl combine the vinegar, celery seeds, salt, sugar, and pepper. Whisk to blend. Slowly pour in the oil and whisk until well blended. Chill for 10 minutes.

Place the red cabbage and green cabbage in a large bowl. Remove dressing from refrigerator, whisk again, and pour over cabbage. Toss well.

# APPLE COLESLAW

serves 6

*2 cups cabbage, finely shredded*
*2 cups apples, unpeeled, cored, and diced*
*½ cup sour cream or plain yogurt*
*¾ teaspoon dried dill*
*½ teaspoon salt*
*1 teaspoon lemon juice*
*¼ teaspoon pepper*
*½ teaspoon sugar*
*1 apple, unpeeled and thinly sliced*

In a large bowl combine the cabbage, apples, sour cream or yogurt, dill, salt, lemon juice, pepper, and sugar. Toss gently but thoroughly.

Serve garnished with apple slices.

# WISCONSIN BLUE CHEESE SALAD

serves 6 to 8

*½ cup olive oil*
*2 tablespoons tarragon or cider vinegar*
*4 tablespoons blue cheese, crumbled*
*½ teaspoon salt*
*¼ teaspoon pepper*
*1 head romaine lettuce*
*1 head chicory*

Thoroughly wash and dry the lettuce leaves. Tear ito small pieces and place in a large serving bowl.

In a bowl whisk together the vinegar, blue cheese, salt, and pepper. Add the oil to the bowl in a thin, steady stream. Whisk until mixture is well blended.

Pour dressing over lettuce and toss well. Serve at once.

# Dairy Dishes

## DAKOTA EGGS

serves 4

½ pound unsliced bacon, cubed
4 ears fresh corn
3 eggs, beaten
1 teaspoon salt
½ teaspoon pepper

With a sharp knife cut the kernels of corn from the cob. Scrape the cob with the back of the knife to remove all the kernel. Set aside.

In a skillet fry the bacon cubes until brown and crisp. Pour off all but 2 tablespoons fat.

In a bowl beat together the eggs and corn. Add the salt and pepper. Pour mixture over the bacon cubes and cook until eggs are set and lightly browned underneath. Slide eggs onto plate and serve.

This dish originated with the Indians of the Dakota territories.

## IDAHO POTATO OMELET

serves 4 to 6

4 tablespoons butter
8 eggs, slightly beaten
8 tablespoons water
1 teaspoon salt
½ teaspoon pepper
2 cups cooked potatoes, cubed and still warm

Melt the butter until very hot in a large omelet pan.

In a mixing bowl beat the eggs, water, salt, and pepper. Pour the eggs into the omelet pan. Cook over medium heat. As omelet cooks, lift the edges to allow the uncooked parts to run underneath.

When omelet is almost done, place the warm potatoes in the center. Carefully fold over the eggs and brown.

Turn omelet onto a plate and serve.

## POACHED EGGS WITH CHICKEN LIVERS

serves 4

2 tablespoons olive oil
6 to 8 small chicken livers
2 tablespoons onion, minced
salt and pepper to taste
6 tablespoons tomato juice
¼ cup dry white wine
4 eggs

Heat the oil in a skillet. Add the chicken livers, onion, salt, and pepper. Sauté over low heat for 5 minutes. Stir in the tomato juice and wine. Cook 5 minutes longer.

Very carefully break 1 egg at a time into the skillet onto the livers and sauce. Do not break yolks. Cover the skillet and cook 3 minutes or until eggs are set. Serve hot with warm biscuits, toast, or toasted English muffins.

# EGGS AND CREAM

serves 4

4 tablespoons butter
3 medium onions, thinly sliced
3 tablespoons flour
1 cup light cream, heated
1 cup milk, heated
  salt and pepper to taste
⅛ teaspoon grated nutmeg
8 hard-cooked eggs, sliced ½-inch thick

Melt the butter in a heavy saucepan. Add the onions and cook, stirring constantly, until onions are soft but not brown, about 5 to 8 minutes. Stir in the flour. Slowly stir in the heated cream and milk. Add the salt, pepper, and nutmeg. Cook over very low heat for 7 to 10 minutes. Stir frequently.

Add the sliced eggs. Heat but do not allow mixture to boil. Transfer eggs and sauce to a serving dish. Serve with toast or corn bread.

# OMELET SCHNITZEL

serves 4

4 slices bacon, diced
½ slice ham, diced
4 eggs
4 small onions, diced
1 cup milk
  toast

Sauté the bacon in a skillet until crisp. Add the ham and sauté until lightly browned.

Take 1 tablespoon of fat from the skillet and place it in another skillet. Heat the fat and add the onions. Cook, stirring frequently, until brown, about 10 to 12 minutes. Add the onions to the skillet with the ham and bacon.

Beat the eggs and milk together. Pour the eggs over the bacon and ham. Cook for 3 minutes, stirring. Remove from heat.

Serve on slices of toast.

# PIPERADE

serves 6

⅓ cup bacon drippings
4 medium onions, thinly sliced
4 medium tomatoes, peeled and coarsely chopped
3 large green peppers, seeded and sliced
  salt and pepper to taste
¼ teaspoon dried marjoram
7 eggs, beaten

In a heavy skillet heat the bacon drippings until very hot. Lower the heat and add the onions. Cook, stirring frequently, for 5 to 10 minutes or until onions are soft but not brown. Stir in the tomatoes, peppers, salt, pepper, and marjoram.

Cover the skillet and cook over low heat for 15 minutes. Stir frequently. The vegetables are done when they resemble a purée.

Add the beaten eggs to the vegetables. Scramble gently until eggs set. Remove from heat and serve.

# BAKED APPLE OMELET

serves 4

3 tablespoons flour
1/4 teaspoon baking powder
1/8 teaspoon salt
2 egg whites
3 tablespoons sugar
4 tablespoons heavy cream
2 egg yolks, well beaten
1 tablespoon lemon juice
1 large apple, peeled, cored, and thinly sliced
1/4 cup sugar
1/8 teaspoon grated nutmeg

Preheat the oven to 375°.

Into a bowl sift the flour, baking powder, and salt.

In another bowl, beat the egg whites until they are stiff but not dry.

Beat the cream and the egg yolks into the flour mixture. Continue beating until smooth. Fold in the egg whites and add the lemon juice.

Generously butter a 10-inch cast-iron skillet. Heat the skillet until hot. Pour the batter into the pan. Place the apple slices on top and sprinkle with sugar and nutmeg.

Place skillet in oven and bake for 10 minutes or until sugar has melted. Remove and serve from skillet.

# RUTABAGA SOUFFLE

serves 4 to 6

1 cup cooked rutabaga, mashed
1/2 cup hot mashed potatoes
1 cup milk
2 tablespoons cornstarch
1/2 teaspoon salt
1 tablespoon light brown sugar
1/8 teaspoon grated nutmeg
1/8 teaspoon pepper
3 eggs, separated
2 tablespoons bread crumbs
2 tablespoons grated Parmesan cheese
1 tablespoon butter

Preheat the oven to 325°.

Place the rutabaga and potatoes in a bowl and beat together. Set aside.

In a saucepan combine the milk and cornstarch. Heat the mixture to the boiling point. Lower the heat and cook, stirring constantly. Stir in the salt, brown sugar, nutmeg, and pepper.

Beat the egg yolks slightly. Add the hot milk mixture to the egg yolks. Stir constantly. Add egg mixture to the rutabaga and potatoes and beat until well blended.

In a separate bowl beat the egg whites until they are stiff but not dry. Fold into egg yolk and vegetable mixture. Turn the mixture into a lightly buttered 1½-quart soufflé or casserole dish.

Combine the bread crumbs, cheese, and butter. Sprinkle on top of the soufflé.

Bake for 50 minutes or until a knife inserted halfway into the center comes out clean. Remove from oven and serve *immediately*.

# SPINACH SOUFFLE

serves 4

1½ pounds fresh spinach
3 tablespoons butter
3 tablespoons flour
1 cup light cream
   salt and pepper to taste
⅛ teaspoon grated nutmeg
1 cup Swiss cheese, grated
4 eggs, separated

Preheat the oven to 325°.

Thoroughly wash the spinach in cold running water. Remove any tough stems and blemished leaves. Tear large leaves into smaller pieces.

Place the spinach in a saucepan. Do not add water; the spinach will cook in its own liquid. Cover and cook over high heat for 3 minutes or just tender. Drain the spinach and squeeze out all the moisture. Set aside.

Heat the butter in a large saucepan. Add the flour and cook for 2 minutes, stirring constantly. Stir in the cream and cook over low heat, stirring constantly, until smooth and thick. Stir in the cheese; continue stirring until melted. Add the spinach to the saucepan and mix well. Remove from heat and cool slightly.

Beat the egg yolks in a bowl until thick and lemon-colored. Add the yolks to the cooled spinach mixture and beat.

In a separate bowl beat the egg whites until stiff but not dry. Fold whites into the spinach mixture.

Turn the spinach mixture into a well-buttered 2-quart soufflé or casserole dish. Bake for 30 minutes or until a knife inserted halfway into the center comes out clean. Serve *immediately*.

# GINGER SQUASH SOUFFLE

serves 4

1½ cups cooked acorn squash, mashed
3 eggs, separated
3 tablespoons ground hazelnuts
1½ teaspoons molasses
¼ teaspoon ground ginger
¼ teaspoon grated nutmeg
¼ teaspoon salt
¼ teaspoon freshly grated lemon peel
⅛ teaspoon pepper

Preheat the oven to 375°.

In a mixing bowl combine the mashed squash, molasses, ginger, nutmeg, salt, lemon peel, and pepper. Beat the egg yolks and add them to the mixture. Combine well.

Beat the egg whites in a separate bowl until they are stiff but not dry.

Fold the ground nuts and the egg whites into the squash mixture. Mix gently but thoroughly.

Turn the mixture into a buttered 2-quart soufflé or casserole dish. Place the dish in a pan of hot water and bake for 35 to 40 minutes or until the top surface is nicely browned and a knife inserted halfway into the center comes out clean. Remove from oven and serve *immediately*.

# WISCONSIN CHEESE RABBIT

serves 4 to 6

3½ cups milk
1 pound sharp Cheddar cheese, grated
4 eggs, slightly beaten
1 teaspoon paprika
2 teaspoons salt
1 teaspoon pepper

Preheat the oven to 300°.

Place the milk in the top of a double boiler. Heat over hot water. Add the cheese and stir.

In a bowl combine the eggs, salt, pepper, and paprika. Beat well and stir into the cheese-milk mixture.

Remove from heat and turn the mixture into a generously buttered 2-quart casserole or soufflé dish. Place the dish in a pan of hot water and bake for 30 minutes or until set.

Remove from oven and serve immediately.

# Meat and Poultry

# BUCK STEW

serves 4 to 6

3 pounds venison, elk, or antelope, cubed
    dry red wine
2 teaspoons salt
1 teaspoon pepper
    flour
½ cup vegetable oil
1 cup carrots, coarsely chopped
1 cup onion, coarsely chopped
1 cup celery, coarsely chopped

Place the meat in a shallow glass dish and add enough red wine to cover almost completely. Cover dish with aluminum foil and marinate for 36 to 48 hours. Turn the meat occasionally.

Drain the meat and reserve the wine. Season the meat cubes with salt and pepper. Dredge in flour.

Heat the oil in a heavy skillet. When oil is hot, add the meat and brown on all sides. Remove meat from skillet and set aside. Add the vegetables to the skillet. Pour in the reserved wine and add enough water to cover vegetables. Cook over low heat until vegetables are tender, about 10 to 15 minutes. Return the meat to the skillet and continue to cook, covered, over low heat. Simmer until stew is thickened and heated through, about 2 to 2½ hours. Serve hot.

# BRAISED TONGUE WITH RAISIN SAUCE

serves 6

1  3- to 4-pound fresh tongue
    cold water
2  carrots, sliced
1  small onion
2  stalks celery
6  peppercorns
1  bay leaf
1  teaspoon salt
Raisin sauce:
2  tablespoons butter
2  tablespoons flour
1  cup beef broth
1  cup white wine or dry vermouth
½  cup seedless raisins
½  teaspoon freshly grated lemon peel
3  whole cloves
4  gingersnaps, crushed
¼  cup dark brown sugar

Wash and scrub the tongue with warm water. Place tongue in a large pot and add enough cold water to cover. Add the carrots, onion, celery, peppercorns, bay leaf, and salt. Bring mixture to a boil. Reduce heat and simmer for 2 to 4 hours, depending on the size of the tongue.

Remove tongue from water and immediately immerse in cold water. Peel off the skin and trim. Slice the tongue thinly and arrange on serving platter. Top with raisin sauce.

To make the raisin sauce, melt the butter in a saucepan. Add the flour and stir until thoroughly combined. Stir in the beef broth and the wine. Cook, stirring constantly, until thick and smooth.

Stir in the raisins, lemon peel, cloves, gingersnaps, and brown sugar. Blend well. Cover and cook over low heat until the raisins are plumped, about 30 to 45 minutes. Serve hot with tongue.

# BATTER-FRIED LIVER

serves 4

1⅓  cups flour
  2  tablespoons baking powder
  1  teaspoon salt
⅔  cup milk
  1  egg, beaten
     boiling water
  1  pound fresh calf's liver
     salt and pepper to taste
     oil for frying

Combine the flour, baking soda, and salt in a bowl. Add the milk and beaten egg. Mix well.

Cut the liver into small pieces. Pour boiling water over the pieces and let them soak for 5 minutes. Drain, pat dry, and remove the thin outer membrane.

Sprinkle the liver pieces with salt and pepper. Dip the pieces in the batter and roll until coated.

Heat a 2-inch layer of oil in a deep skillet until it registers 375° on a deep-fat thermometer. Add the liver pieces to the oil and fry, turning often, until well browned, about 3 to 4 minutes.

Remove liver pieces from the skillet with a slotted spoon and drain on paper towels. Serve hot.

# HASENPFEFFER (CREAMY RABBIT STEW)

serves 4 to 6

2  2-pound rabbits, cut into sixths
6  tablespoons butter
¾  cup bacon, chopped
2  carrots, chopped
2  onions, chopped
1  bay leaf
1  clove garlic
   salt and pepper to taste
2  cups dry white wine or dry vermouth
1  cup sour cream

Wash and dry the rabbit pieces. Place in a bowl of salted water and soak for 1 hour. Drain pieces and discard liquid.

In a skillet, heat the butter. Add the bacon and cook until brown. Add the rabbit pieces and brown quickly on both sides, about 2 minutes per side. Add the carrot, onion, bay leaf, garlic, salt, and pepper. Stir in the wine and cover.

Simmer over low heat until rabbit is tender, about 1 hour.

Just before serving, remove from heat and stir in the sour cream.

# RABBIT FRICASSEE

serves 4

1  3-pound rabbit, cut into eighths
   flour
¼  cup butter
   salt and pepper to taste
1  medium onion, finely chopped
1½  cups red wine
   rind from ½ lemon
3  sprigs parsley
2  stalks celery, with leaves, cut in thirds
1  bay leaf
1  tablespoon flour
1  tablespoon butter

Wash the rabbit pieces and gently pat dry. Dust pieces with flour.

In a large skillet heat the butter. When butter begins to melt, add the rabbit pieces and season with salt and pepper. Fry the pieces until golden brown on all sides, about 3 to 5 minutes. Add the onion. Stir well and cook 2 minutes longer. Add the wine and stir well.

Place the lemon rind, parsley, celery, and bay leaf into a square of cheesecloth. Tie the square closed with string and add the bag to the skillet. Tightly cover the skillet and simmer until rabbit is tender, about 1 hour.

Remove the rabbit from the skillet onto a serving plate. Discard the cheesecloth bag.

In a small bowl mix the flour and butter together with the back of a spoon until well blended. Add to the skillet and cook, stirring constantly, until sauce thickens and begins to bubble.

Remove from heat. Pour sauce over rabbit and serve.

# SAVORY RABBIT

serves 4

2 2-pound rabbits, quartered
6 tablespoons flour
½ teaspoon salt
¼ teaspoon pepper
3 tablespoons olive oil
2 slices bacon, finely chopped
1 medium onion, coarsely chopped
2 cloves garlic, chopped
1 stalk celery, with leaves, chopped
1 cup dry sherry
½ cup tomato juice
½ cup chicken broth
10 whole mushrooms

Combine the flour, salt, and pepper on a plate. Dredge the rabbit pieces in the flour. Coat evenly.

Heat the olive oil in a skillet. Add the rabbit pieces and brown on all sides, about 2 minutes per side. Remove the rabbit and reserve.

Add the bacon, onion, garlic, and celery to the skillet. Sauté for 5 minutes. Add the sherry, tomato juice, and chicken broth. Return the rabbit to the skillet. Quickly bring the liquid to a boil, then reduce heat and cover. Simmer for 1 hour or until rabbit is tender. Stir occasionally. Five minutes before serving, add the mushrooms. Serve hot.

# MICHIGAN BOOYAW

serves 6 to 8

1 pound pickled pork, cubed
2 2-pound rabbits, cut into serving pieces
1 yellow turnip, cubed
2 large onions, sliced
6 carrots, cut into 1-inch pieces
6 large potatoes, cubed
2 stalks celery, chopped
  salt and pepper to taste

Place the pork and rabbit into a large pot. Add enough water to cover. Bring to a boil. Reduce the heat and cover. Simmer until meats are tender, about 1 to 1½ hours.

Add the vegetables. Cover the pot and cook 20 to 30 minutes longer or until vegetables are tender. Season to taste and serve.

# HOOSIER PORK CHOPS

serves 4

4 pork chops, 1½ inches thick
1 onion, thinly sliced
  salt and pepper to taste
  flour
2 potatoes, sliced
1 carrot, sliced
1 cup fresh green peas
1 14-ounce can tomatoes
  oil for frying

Trim the fat from the pork chops and place the fat in a deep skillet. Melt the fat. Add the onion slices and sauté until slices are brown, about 7 to 10 minutes. Remove onion from pan and drain fat.

Heat the oil in the pan until it begins to bubble. Season the pork chops with salt and pepper and dredge in flour.

Add the pork chops to the hot oil and brown on both sides, about 2 to 3 minutes per side. Add the vegetables and season to taste with salt and pepper. Bring mixture to a rapid boil. Boil for 5 minutes. Reduce heat and simmer, covered, for 1½ hours or until meat and vegetables are tender.

# OHIO PORK CASSEROLE

serves 6

2 onions, sliced
¼ cup butter
2⅓ cups fresh tomatoes or 1 20-ounce can
2 teaspoons sugar
   salt and pepper to taste
⅛ teaspoon oregano
1 cup bread crumbs
2 cups unsweetened applesauce
¼ cup horseradish
2 cups sauerkraut, rinsed and drained
6 large lean pork chops
1 tablespoon oil

Preheat the oven to 350°.

Melt the butter in a saucpean. Add the onions to the butter and sauté until brown, about 8 to 10 minutes. Add the tomatoes, sugar, salt, pepper, oregano, bread crumbs, applesauce, horseradish, and sauerkraut. Mix well with the onions. Pour mixture into a shallow baking dish approximately 12 × 16 inches.

Heat the oil in a skillet. Add the pork chops and brown on both sides. Sprinkle with salt and pepper. Place in baking dish on top of applesauce and sauerkraut mixture. Cover dish with aluminum foil and bake for 1¾ hours. Serve hot.

# GLAZED LOIN OF PORK

serves 6

1 5-pound loin of pork
   flour
   salt and pepper to taste
Glaze:
1 cup sugar
⅓ cup cider vinegar
½ cup boiling water
1 teaspoon salt
3 cloves garlic, crushed

Preheat the oven to 450°.

Score the fat on the roast and rub the entire surface with flour, salt, and pepper. Place the pork on a rack in a shallow roasting pan. Roast for 15 minutes. Reduce oven temperature to 350°. Roast 2½ to 2¾ hours longer. Baste frequently with the glaze.

To make the glaze, heat the sugar in a heavy skillet over medium heat until it becomes a golden-colored liquid. Pour in the boiling water, a little at a time. Cook, stirring constantly, until all the sugar is dissolved and mixture is smooth.

Measure out ½ cup of the syrup and mix it with the vinegar, salt, and garlic. Mix well. Use to baste pork.

# PORK AND CABBAGE STEW

serves 6

> 3 tablespoons butter
> 1 large onion, chopped
> 2½ pounds lean pork shoulder, cut into small pieces
> 2 cups beef broth
> 1½ cups red cabbage, shredded
> 1 large tart apple, peeled, cored, and diced
> ¾ cup light cream
> ¾ teaspoon salt
> ¼ teaspoon pepper

Melt the butter in a deep skillet. Add the onion and pork. Sauté until the meat is lightly browned all over, about 5 to 8 minutes. Add the beef broth, cabbage, and apple. Bring the mixture to a boil. Reduce heat and simmer, covered, for 2 hours.

Uncover the skillet and raise the heat to medium high. Cook until liquid is almost absorbed. Stir frequently.

Stir in the cream and season with salt and pepper. Heat through but do not boil. Serve hot accompanied with mashed potatoes.

# STUFFED PORK SHOULDER

serves 8

> 1 6-pound pork shoulder roast
> ¼ pound bacon, diced
> ½ cup celery, diced
> ½ cup onion, chopped
> 2 cups tart apples, diced
> ½ cup sugar
> 1 cup bread crumbs
> ½ teaspoon salt
> ⅛ teaspoon pepper
> ½ cup French-style mustard

Have the butcher remove the bones from the roast.

Preheat the oven to 350°.

Sauté the bacon in a saucepan until crisp. Remove the bacon and add the celery and onion. Cook until onion is yellow and tender, about 5 minutes. Add the apples and sugar to the pan. Cover and cook until apples are tender, about 15 to 20 minutes.

In a large bowl combine the bread crumbs, salt, pepper, and bacon. Add the apple mixture and mix well.

Stuff the cavity of the pork roast with the mixture. Close the cavity with skewers or poultry pins.

Place the pork on a rack in a roasting pan. Season with salt and pepper. Roast for 3 to 3½ hours or until pork is done.

When half the roasting time is done, remove the pork. Spread with mustard. Return to oven and continue cooking.

Remove pork and cool slightly before slicing.

# BAKED LAMB CHOPS

serves 4

4 shoulder lamb chops, trimmed of fat
2 tablespoons butter
8 medium potatoes, thinly sliced
4 medium onions, thinly sliced
  salt and pepper to taste
4 apples, peeled, cored, and quartered
1 tablespoon flour
1¼ to 1½ cups beef broth
½ cup apple cider

Preheat the oven to 375°.

Heat the butter in a large deep skillet. When butter has melted, add the lamb chops and brown quickly, about 2 minutes per side. Remove chops from skillet and keep warm.

Add the potatoes and onions to the skillet. Cook until golden brown, about 5 to 8 minutes.

Butter a baking dish that is approximately 12 × 16 inches. Place a layer of the onion and potato mixture into the bottom of the dish. Top with lamb chops and cover the chops with the remaining vegetables. Season with salt and pepper.

Arrange the apple quarters on top of the dish.

Add the flour to the skillet. Add the beef broth and bring the mixture to a boil. Stir constantly. Pour in the apple cider, stir, and remove from heat. Strain the mixture into the baking pan. Bake for 1 hour or until the lamb chops are tender. Serve from the baking dish.

# LAMB STEW

serves 6

1 cup dried lima beans
4 cups water
2½ pounds boneless leg of lamb, cut into small cubes
1½ tablespoons butter
¾ teaspoon salt
¼ teaspoon pepper
¼ teaspoon dried rosemary
2 large onions, quartered
3 small potatoes, peeled and quartered
6 carrots, halved
3 tablespoons flour

Place the beans in a pot with enough salted water to cover. Bring the mixture to a rapid boil and boil for 2 minutes. Remove from heat and let beans soak for 1 hour. Drain and set aside.

Melt the butter in a large skillet. Add the lamb cubes and brown on all sides, about 2 to 3 minutes per side. Add the beans, 4 cups water, salt, pepper, and rosemary. Reduce the heat and cover. Simmer for 1½ hours or until the lamb and beans are almost tender.

Preheat the oven to 350°.

Add the onions, potatoes, and carrots to the pot. There should be enough liquid to cover the vegetables; if not, add more water to the pot. Sift the flour evenly over the meat.

Place the pot, uncovered, into the oven and bake until vegetables are tender, about 1 hour. Serve hot.

# STUFFED LAMB SHANKS

serves 4

4 lamb shanks
2 tablespoons butter
3 cups water
1 teaspoon salt
¼ teaspoon pepper
½ teaspoon dried rosemary
1 cup pearl barley
1 tablespoon flour
½ cup water

In a large skillet, melt the butter. Add the lamb shanks and brown well on all sides, about 2 to 3 minutes per side.

Add the water, salt, pepper, rosemary, and barley. Cover the skillet and simmer over low heat until lamb is tender, approximately 1½ hours. Add additional water if needed.

Remove the lamb from the skillet and allow it to cool. When cool enough to handle, remove the bones.

Continue cooking the barley until it is done, about 30 minutes longer. Remove the barley from the skillet and stuff the cavities in the lamb shanks with it.

In a small bowl combine the water and flour. Stir well. Add to the lamb broth and stir constantly until the sauce begins to thicken. Return the shanks to the skillet and spoon the sauce over them. Cover and heat through over low heat for 15 minutes.

Remove shanks and serve with gravy.

# SWEDISH MEATBALLS

serves 8

2 pounds ground beef chuck
1 pound ground pork
2 eggs, well beaten
1 cup mashed potatoes
1 cup bread crumbs
1 teaspoon brown sugar
1 teaspoon pepper
2 teaspoons salt
½ teaspoon ground ginger
¼ teaspoon grated nutmeg
¼ teaspoon ground allspice
1 cup milk
  flour
¼ cup butter or oil
2 cups light cream

In a large bowl combine the beef, pork, eggs, potatoes, bread crumbs, brown sugar, pepper, salt, ginger, nutmeg, and milk. Mix very well and shape into meatballs 1½ to 2 inches in diameter. The mixture will be quite soft. Roll each meatball lightly in flour and set aside.

Preheat the oven to 325°.

In a large skillet heat the butter or oil. Add the meatballs, a few at a time, and brown well on all sides. Transfer the meatballs into a large baking dish or casserole. Pour the cream over them and bake for 40 minutes. Serve from the dish.

## THREE-MEAT STEW WITH BUTTERMILK DUMPLINGS

serves 6

¾ pound stewing beef, cut into 1-inch cubes
½ pound pork, cut into 1-inch cubes
½ pound beef liver, cut into 1-inch cubes
2 quarts boiling water
2 small onions, sliced
1 teaspoon salt
¼ teaspoon pepper
¼ cup flour
¼ cup water
Buttermilk dumplings:
  1 cup buttermilk
  ¼ teaspoon baking soda
  1½ teaspoons baking powder
  ½ teaspoon salt
  1 egg, well beaten
  1¼ to 1½ cups flour

Place the beef, pork, and liver into a large deep saucepan. Pour in the boiling water. Bring mixture to a boil. Reduce heat, cover, and simmer for 1½ hours. Add the onion, salt, and pepper. Simmer for 30 minutes longer.

Meanwhile, prepare the buttermilk dumplings. In a large bowl combine the buttermilk, baking soda, and baking powder. Stir well until mixture begins to bubble. Add the salt, egg, and enough of the flour to make a soft, workable dough. Set dough aside for a few minutes.

In a small bowl combine ¼ cup flour and ¼ cup water. Mix well and stir into the stew.

## VEAL STEW WITH DUMPLINGS

serves 4

2 pounds stewing veal, cubed
2 onions, coarsely chopped
½ cup parsley, chopped
1 teaspoon salt
½ teaspoon pepper
  water
Dumplings:
  2 cups flour
  2 teaspoons baking powder
  1 teaspoon salt
  1 cup milk

Place the veal, onions, and parsley in a large deep skillet. Add the salt and pepper. Add just enough water to cover. Quickly bring the mixture to a boil. Lower the heat, cover, and simmer for 1 to 1½ hours or until veal is tender.

Meanwhile, make the dumplings. In a mixing bowl combine the flour, baking powder, and salt. Add the milk and stir until well blended.

Drop the dumplings by rounded teaspoons onto the top of the simmering stew. Cover the pot and simmer for 15 minutes longer or until the dumplings are done.

Remove stew from heat and serve.

# BRAISED SHORT RIBS

serves 4

3 pounds beef short ribs
1 teaspoon salt
½ teaspoon pepper
  flour
  vegetable or olive oil
1 carrot, thickly sliced
1 turnip, peeled and thickly sliced
1 onion, thickly sliced and pulled apart into rings
1 green pepper, thinly sliced
1 stalk celery, thinly sliced
3 sprigs parsley, coarsely chopped
2 cups boiling water
4 medium potatoes, peeled and halved
2 tablespoons flour
1 to 2 tablespoons water

Preheat the oven to 400°.

Heat the oil in a large skillet. Season the ribs generously with salt and pepper. Dredge in enough flour to coat them lightly. Add the ribs to the hot oil and brown on all sides, about 2 to 3 minutes per side.

Transfer the browned ribs to a roasting pan. Surround the ribs with the vegetables, pour the water over the mixture, and cover. Bake for 2 hours.

Add the potatoes to the roasting pan and bake, uncovered, for 40 minutes longer, or until meat and potatoes are tender and well browned.

Remove the meat and potatoes to a serving plate. In a small bowl mix together the flour and a little water until they form a smooth mixture.

Heat the gravy in the roasting pan on top of the stove. Stir in the flour mixture and bring to a boil. Cook, stirring constantly, until gravy is thick. Pour over ribs and serve.

# OHIO FLANK STEAK

serves 6

3 pounds flank steak
2 tablespoons flour
2 tablespoons butter
1 teaspoon salt
¼ teaspoon pepper
1 stalk celery, coarsely chopped
1 carrot, finely chopped
2 medium onions, finely chopped
  juice of ½ lemon
½ cup tomato sauce
2 teaspoons cider vinegar
1 teaspoon sugar

Score the steak on both sides with a sharp knife. Dust with flour.

Melt the butter in a large skillet. Add the steak and sauté until well browned on both sides, about 3 minutes per side. Add the salt, pepper, celery, carrot, and onion. Mix well. Stir in the tomato sauce, lemon juice, vinegar, and sugar.

Cover the skillet and simmer over low heat until the steak is tender, about 1 to 1½ hours.

Remove the steak from the skillet; keep warm. Reduce sauce by cooking, uncovered, for several minutes. Stir constantly. Serve with the steak.

# KANSAS CITY PICKLED BEEF

serves 6 to 8

*2 cups cider vinegar*
*4 pounds round steak, boned*
*2 onions, thinly sliced*
*1 lemon, sliced*
*1 teaspoon peppercorns*
*1 teaspoon juniper berries*
*1 bay leaf*
*2 tablespoons butter or olive oil*
*2 teaspoons salt*
*1 cup red wine*

Place the meat in a large glass bowl. Pour the vinegar over the meat. Add the onions, lemon slices, peppercorns, juniper berries, and bay leaf. Cover bowl and let mixture marinate in the refrigerator for 2 days. Turn meat twice a day.

Remove the meat from the marinade. Strain the liquid and reserve.

Heat the butter or oil in a large skillet. Dry the meat and place it in the hot butter. Slowly brown the meat on all sides, about 3 minutes per side.

Add 1 cup of the reserved marinade to the meat. Add the salt and wine and cover the skillet. Simmer over low heat for 2 hours or until meat is tender.

Remove meat from skillet and cool slightly before slicing. If desired, thicken the pan juices with a little flour and pour over the meat. Serve hot.

# ST. LOUIS SAUERBRATEN

serves 6

*1 4-pound pot roast*
*2 cloves garlic, halved*
*2 teaspoons salt*
*¼ teaspoon pepper*
*2 cups cider vinegar*
*2 cups water*
*2 onions, thinly sliced*
*2 bay leaves*
*1 teaspoon peppercorns*
*¼ cup sugar*
*2 tablespoons lard*

Rub the meat with the cut surfaces of the garlic cloves. Season with salt and pepper and rub well. Place the meat in a deep casserole or baking dish.

In a saucepan combine the vinegar, water, onions, bay leaves, peppercorns, and sugar. Heat the mixture just to the boiling point. Remove from heat and pour over the meat. Cover the dish and refrigerate. Allow meat to marinate for 3 to 4 days. Turn daily.

Remove the meat. Strain the marinade and reserve the liquid.

Heat the lard in a deep skillet. Add the meat and brown evenly on all sides, about 2 to 3 minutes per side. Add the reserved marinade and cover. Simmer over low heat until meat is tender, about 2 to 3 hours. Add hot water if additional liquid is needed.

Remove the meat from the skillet and let cool slightly. Slice meat and serve.

# STANDING RIB ROAST

serves 8

1 6-pound standing rib roast (about 3 ribs)
1½ teaspoons salt
⅛ teaspoon pepper

Have the butcher cut the ribs near the backbone so that they will be easy to remove later on.

Preheat the oven to 325°.

Place the roast, fat-side up, in a shallow roasting pan. Rub with salt and pepper. For rare meat, roast for 2½ hours; for medium meat, roast for 3½ hours.

Remove the roast from the oven and let cool slightly before carving.

Serve pan drippings on the side.

# BROWN BEEF STEW

serves 6 to 8

3 pounds beef chuck, cut into 1- to 1½-inch cubes
    flour
4 to 6 tablespoons bacon drippings
2 cups water
1 medium onion, quartered
    salt and pepper to taste
⅛ teaspoon ground allspice
4 large potatoes, peeled and cut into 1½-inch slices
4 large carrots, cut into 1-inch slices
8 small white onions, unpeeled

Trim the beef of fat. Dredge the cubes in flour until they are thickly coated.

In a large skillet, heat the bacon drippings. Add the meat, a few pieces at a time, and brown quickly until crusty.

After pieces are browned, transfer them to a deep pot or casserole.

Add the water to the pot or casserole. Add the onions and bring the mixture quickly to a boil. Lower heat and cover. Simmer for 1 to 1½ hours, stirring occasionally. Check the gravy. If it is too thick, add water, a tablespoon at a time.

Add the salt, pepper, and allspice. Simmer 30 minutes longer.

Add the potatoes and carrots. Cover the pot and simmer until the vegetables are tender, about 20 to 30 minutes. Add more water if necessary.

Meanwhile, cook the unpeeled white onions in boiling water until just tender, about 20 minutes. Drain and rinse in cold water. Peel the onions and add them to the stew. Mix well and cook 15 minutes longer.

# MINNESOTA ROAST DUCK

serves 4

1 4-pound duck
2 cups cold cooked rice
1 cup tart apple, peeled, cored, and grated
½ cup raisins
⅛ teaspoon ground cardamom
½ teaspoon freshly grated orange peel
    salt
2 tablespoons onion, minced
2 tablespoons melted butter
⅓ cup flour
2 cups water

Preheat the oven to 350°.

In a large bowl combine the cooked rice, grated apple, raisins, minced onion, orange peel, cardamom, and ¼ teaspoon salt. Mix well. Add the melted butter and stir until well blended.

Wash the duck and pat dry. Stuff the duck with the rice and apple mixture, packing it lightly into the cavity. Skewer or sew the duck closed. Place the duck on a rack in a roasting pan. Bake for 1 hour to 1 hour 20 minutes or until done.

Remove from the oven to a platter. Remove the skewers or thread.

Skim the fat from the pan drippings; reserve ½ cup fat. Mix the fat with the flour and blend until smooth. Combine the pan drippings and water. Add to the flour and fat mixture. Cook over medium heat until thick and smooth. Season with salt if desired.

Scoop the stuffing out of the duck. Cut the duck into serving pieces. Serve with stuffing and gravy on the side.

Duck prepared in this way reflects the Swedish heritage of many Minnesotans.

# WILD DUCK IN WINE

serves 4

2 *wild ducks*
  *salt and pepper to taste*
8 *tablespoons butter*
2 *cups red wine*

Clean and wash the ducks. Pat dry. Season inside and out with salt and pepper.

Melt the butter in a large skillet. Add the ducks and brown. Turn the ducks breast-side down in the skillet. Add 1 cup wine and cover. Simmer for 1 hour over low heat.

Turn the ducks breast-side up. Add 1 cup wine and cover. Simmer until ducks are tender, about 1½ hours.

Remove ducks from skillet. Cut them into quarters or halves and serve. Serve the pan gravy on the side.

# ROAST WILD DUCK

serves 4

2 *wild ducks*
  *salt*
1 *onion, halved*
½ *apple, halved*
1 *stalk celery, chopped*
2 *sprigs parsley*
¼ *cup olive oil*
¼ *cup sweet vermouth*

Preheat the oven to 475°.

Clean and wash the ducks. Pat dry. Rub inside and out with salt. Stuff each duck with ½ onion, ¼ apple, several pieces of celery and 1 sprig parsley. Skewer or sew the ducks closed.

Place the ducks on a roasting rack in shallow pan and roast for 20 to 25 minutes per pound. Baste the duck every 10 minutes with a combination of the olive oil and vermouth.

Remove the duck from the oven. Remove the skewers or thread. Quarter or halve the ducks and serve.

# HOOSIER CHICKEN PIE

serves 6

1  4- to 5-pound chicken
1  cup chicken broth
3  cups water
1  stalk celery
1  sprig parsley
1  scallion
2  teaspoons salt

Gravy:

¼  cup butter
¼  cup flour
3  cups chicken broth
2  egg yolks
½  cup light cream

Biscuits:

2  cups flour
3  teaspoons baking powder
½  teaspoon salt
½  cup butter
⅔  cup sour cream

Cut the chicken into 6 pieces.

In a large skillet, combine the chicken, chicken broth, water, celery, parsley, scallion, and salt. Bring the mixture quickly to a boil. Skim the foam from the top and lower the heat. Cover and simmer for 2 to 2½ hours, or until chicken is tender.

Remove chicken from the broth. Strain and reserve the broth. Remove the meat from the bones. Discard bones and skin. Place the chicken into a lightly buttered, shallow 2½-quart baking pan.

Preheat the oven to 425°. Prepare the gravy and the biscuits.

To make the gravy, in a small saucepan melt the butter. Stir in the flour and blend well. Add 3 cups of the reserved chicken broth. Cook until mixture is thick and smooth.

Combine the eggs and cream in a separate bowl. Remove saucepan with broth mixture from heat and stir in eggs and cream. Pour over the chicken in the baking dish.

To make the biscuits, sift the flour, baking powder, and salt together into a large bowl. Add the butter and blend well. Stir in the sour cream.

Transfer the dough to a lightly floured board and knead several times.

Drop the dough by tablespoons on top of the chicken and gravy. Bake, uncovered, for 15 to 20 minutes or until chicken is heated through and biscuits are brown. Remove and serve hot.

# GREAT LAKES BAKED CHICKEN

serves 4

1 2½- to 3-pound broiling chicken, cut into serving
    pieces
    salt and pepper to taste
¼ cup flour
¼ pound butter
¼ cup boiling water
¼ teaspoon Tabasco
Gravy:
3 tablespoons flour
1 cup chicken broth
½ cup heavy cream

Preheat the oven to 400°.

Wash and dry the chicken pieces and place them in one layer in a 13 × 9-inch baking dish. Season with salt and pepper. Sprinkle with the flour on all sides. Top with half the butter cut into small pieces. Bake for 10 minutes.

In a small bowl combine the remaining butter with the boiling water and Tabasco. Baste the chicken with this mixture every 5 minutes, baking for 20 minutes longer or until chicken is golden brown and tender.

Remove the chicken from the oven and place on a plate. Set aside and keep warm.

To make the gravy, pour all but 3 tablespoons of fat from the baking dish. Place the dish on the top of the stove. Add the 3 tablespoons of flour and mix well. Scrape in the brown bits stuck to the pan. Cook, stirring constantly, for 2 to 3 minutes. Add the chicken broth and cream. Cook, stirring constantly, for 4 minutes longer. Pour gravy over chicken and serve hot.

# PHEASANT AND APPLE CASSEROLE

serves 4

½ cup flour
½ teaspoon salt
⅛ teaspoon pepper
1 pheasant
¼ cup butter
½ teaspoon salt
½ teaspoon dried thyme
⅛ teaspoon pepper
2 tart apples, peeled, cored, and sliced
1 cup apple cider
2 tablespoons wine vinegar

Preheat the oven to 350°.

Clean and wash the pheasant. Dry and cut into serving pieces.

In a small bowl combine the flour, salt, and pepper. Roll the pheasant pieces in the mixture and coat thoroughly.

Heat the butter in a large skillet. When the butter has melted, add the pheasant pieces and brown thoroughly on all sides, about 2 to 3 minutes per side.

Place the pheasant pieces into a 3-quart baking or casserole dish. Season the pheasant again with salt, pepper, and thyme. Place the apples into the dish and mix lightly. Pour the apple cider and vinegar over the mixture. Cover and bake for 1¼ hours.

Remove from the oven and serve directly from the dish.

# MICHIGAN FROGS' LEGS

serves 4

12 large frogs' legs
   salt and pepper to taste
½ cup butter
2 cloves garlic, crushed
   juice of ½ lemon
2 tablespoons parsley, chopped
2 tablespoons chives, chopped
1 teaspoon dried tarragon
2 tablespoons brandy
¼ cup dry white wine, sherry, or vermouth

Rinse the frogs' legs in cold water. Dry well. Season to taste with salt and pepper.

Heat the butter in a large skillet until foamy. Add the garlic, lemon juice, and frogs' legs.

Sauté over moderately high heat until legs are golden brown on both sides. Add the parsley, chives, and tarragon. Cook for 1 minute.

Pour in the brandy. Heat for 10 seconds and carefully flame. After flame dies away, add the wine or sherry and cook for another minute. Serve immediately.

The state of Michigan borders on 4 of the 5 Great Lakes. The Upper Peninsula area has many marshy bogs that abound in frogs. If there are no frogs' legs in the supermarket frozen-foods section, substitute large chicken wings.

# ⟫ — Fish and Seafood — ⟪

# PAN-FRIED TROUT

serves 4

4 ½-pound trout
2 teaspoons salt
¼ teaspoon pepper
½ cup yellow corn meal
½ cup flour
3 tablespoons butter
6 tablespoons vegetable oil
1 lemon, quartered

Clean and wash the trout, but leave the heads and tails intact. Pat dry. Rub the fish inside and out with the salt and pepper.

In a large bowl combine the flour and corn meal. Roll the trout, one at a time, in the mixture until well coated. Shake off excess.

Heat the butter and oil together in a large skillet. When very hot, add the coated trout. Fry the fish until golden brown, about 4 to 5 minutes per side.

Carefully remove from skillet and drain briefly on paper towels. Serve hot with lemon.

# BUTTER-STUFFED TROUT

serves 4

1 4-pound lake trout
2 tablespoons dry sherry
¾ cup butter
1 scallion, minced
2 tablespoons parsley, minced
½ cup mushrooms, finely chopped
1 clove garlic, crushed
1 teaspoon salt
  pepper to taste
1 cup dry white wine
1 cup heavy cream
2 egg yolks
¼ cup brandy, heated

Clean and rinse the fish. Pat dry. Brush the inside of the fish with sherry. Place in the refrigerator for 2 hours.

Preheat the oven to 375°.

In a small bowl cream the butter and scallion together. Add the parsley, mushrooms, garlic, and 1 teaspoon salt. Mix until well combined.

Remove fish from refrigerator and place in a flat baking pan. Spread the inside of the fish with three-quarters of the butter mixture. Spread the remaining mixture on the outside of the fish. Pour the wine over the fish and bake for 45 minutes. Baste frequently.

Remove the fish from the oven and carefully transfer it to a heat-proof serving dish.

Strain the liquid in the baking pan into a saucepan. Simmer the liquid until it is reduced by half.

In a small bowl combine the cream and egg yolks. Slowly beat the hot liquid into the egg mixture. Cook over low heat for 2 to 3 minutes. Stir constantly. Season with salt and pepper to taste.

Pour the heated brandy over the fish. Carefully light the brandy and baste the fish with the spirit until the flame dies out.

Pour the cream sauce over the fish and serve immediately.

# POACHED TROUT WITH SCALLIONS

serves 4

4 ½-pound brook trout
1 cup dry white wine
1 cup water
⅛ teaspoon salt
¾ cup scallions, chopped
1 tablespoon butter
3 tablespoons flour
2 cups milk
1 teaspoon salt
½ teaspoon pepper
⅛ teaspoon cayenne
1 egg yolk, beaten

Clean the trout. Remove the tails and fins but leave the heads intact.

In a large saucepan combine the water, ⅛ teaspoon salt, and wine. Bring to a boil. Add the fish and lower heat slightly. Cover the saucepan and poach the fish for 3 minutes on each side.

*(continued on next page)*

Melt the butter in a skillet. Add the scallions and sauté for 2 to 3 minutes. Add the flour. Stir well and cook for 5 minutes longer. Add the milk, salt, pepper, and cayenne. Stir until well blended.

Remove skillet from heat and stir in the egg yolk. Do not return skillet to heat.

Remove the trout from the water and place them on a platter. Pour the sauce over the fish and serve.

# BAKED PIKE IN DILL SAUCE

serves 6

  1  3-pound pike
  1  tablespoon salt
  1  egg
  1  tablespoon water
     bread crumbs
  2  strips bacon, halved
  2  cups light cream

Preheat the oven to 425°.

Clean and wash the fish.

In a small bowl combine the egg with 1 tablespoon water and beat lightly.

Rub the inside of the fish with salt. Brush on the outside with egg mixture. Roll the fish in the bread crumbs and place in a lightly buttered, shallow baking dish. Cut 4 small slashes along the fish and place a piece of bacon in each one.

Bake fish for 40 minutes. Baste with the light cream every 5 to 8 minutes until fish begins to brown.

Remove fish from oven and transfer to a platter. Serve with dill sauce.

# DILL SAUCE

yields 1 cup

       yolk of 1 hard-cooked egg
  ½  cup vegetable oil
  1½  teaspoons cider vinegar
  ¼  teaspoon Worcestershire sauce
  ½  teaspoon dry mustard
  ½  teaspoon sugar
  ¼  teaspoon salt
  ¼  teaspoon pepper
  ¼  teaspoon dried dill or 1 teaspoon fresh
  ¼  cup heavy cream

Press the egg yolk through a sieve into a bowl. Beat in the vegetable oil. Add the vinegar, Worcestershire sauce, mustard, sugar, salt, pepper, and dill. Beat until well combined.

Whip the heavy cream until it is thick and can hold its shape. Fold into the egg yolk mixture. Combine thoroughly and refrigerate until ready to use.

# SAUTEED PICKEREL

serves 4

  2  pounds pickerel fillets
  5  tablespoons lemon juice
  ⅔  cup yellow corn meal
  3  tablespoons grated sharp Cheddar cheese
  1  teaspoon crushed fennel seeds
     salt and pepper to taste
  2 to 3  tablespoons olive oil
  2 to 3  tablespoons butter
  2  lemons, sliced

Wash and pat dry the fillets.

Place the fillets in the lemon juice and soak for 10 minutes.

In a small bowl combine the corn meal, grated cheese, fennel, salt, and pepper.

Dip the fillets in the mixture and roll until well coated. Shake off excess.

Heat the butter and oil together in a large skillet. Add the fillets and sauté gently over medium heat until golden brown, about 6 minutes per side. Add additional oil and butter if necessary.

Remove fillets from skillet and serve with lemon slices.

# GREAT LAKE SMELTS

serves 4

16 smelts
 1 teaspoon salt
½ teaspoon pepper
½ cup yellow corn meal
½ cup flour
½ cup butter
 3 tablespoons bacon drippings

Clean the fish but leave the heads intact. Wash and pat dry. Rub fish with salt and pepper.

In a large bowl combine the flour and corn meal. Roll the fish, one at a time, in the mixture. Coat well and shake off any excess.

In a large skillet, heat the butter together with the bacon drippings. When the fat is very hot, add the smelts, 3 at a time. Fry, turning once, until golden brown, about 3 minutes per side

Carefully remove fish from pan and drain on paper towels. Serve hot.

# PAN-FRIED SMELTS

serves 4

 2 pounds smelts
   beer
½ cup flour
¼ cup almonds, finely ground
½ teaspoons salt
½ teaspoon pepper
¼ pound butter
   lemon wedges

Clean the smelts but leave the heads intact. Wash and dry the fish. Place them in a large bowl and pour in enough beer to cover completely. Refrigerate for 2 hours.

Remove fish from beer and pat dry.

In a bowl combine the flour, ground almonds, salt, and pepper. Roll the smelts, one at a time, in the mixture until lightly coated.

Melt the butter in a deep skillet. When hot, open the fish and add them to the skillet, slit-side down. Fry until crisp. Turn the fish and brown the skin sides. This will take about 5 to 8 minutes depending on the size of the fish.

Fry as many fish as will fit into the skillet comfortably at one time. Add more butter if necessary.

Remove fish from skillet. Drain briefly on paper towels and serve with lemon wedges.

# WHITEFISH WITH WALNUT SAUCE

serves 4

  1  *3-pound whitefish*
     *salt to taste*
  1  *carrot, thinly sliced*
  1  *leek, sliced*
  2  *onions, chopped*
     *celery leaves*
  ½  *teaspoon parsley, chopped*
  4  *cloves garlic, chopped*
Walnut sauce:
  1  *cup walnuts*
  2  *tablespoons flour*
  1  *teaspoon sugar*
  ½  *clove garlic, crushed*
     *cold water*
  ½  *teaspoon pepper*

Clean and bone the fish. Leave the head and tail intact. Rub the fish inside and out with salt and let stand for 1 hour.

Place the onions, carrot, leek, celery leaves, parsley, and chopped garlic in a pot with enough water to cover. Bring to a boil and boil for 45 minutes.

Cut the whitefish into pieces that are 1½ inches wide. Place the pieces into boiling water and vegetables and simmer over low heat for 10 minutes. Remove from heat and let cool.

Grind the walnuts very finely. Combine in a bowl with the flour and ½ clove chopped garlic. Mix well. Add enough cold water to make a thick paste. Add pepper, sugar, and enough of the fish water to give the mixture the consistency of a sauce. Transfer mixture to a saucepan and cook for 30 minutes or until creamy but not thick.

Remove fish pieces from pot and place on a platter. Arrange pieces to re-form the shape of the fish. Surround the fish with some of the vegetables from the pot. Pour the walnut sauce over the fish and serve.

# PLANKED MICHIGAN WHITEFISH

serves 4

  1  *3-pound whitefish*
     *salt and pepper to taste*
     *paprika*
  ¼  *pound melted butter*
     *juice of 1 lemon*
     *lemon slices*

Preheat the oven to broil.

Place a thick oak or maple plank under hot running water. Run water over plank until it is heated.

Split the whitefish in half and remove the backbone. Place the fish on the plank, skin-side down.

Season fish with salt and pepper. Sprinkle with paprika. Brush with a little melted butter and place plank under broiler.

Broil for 30 minutes or until fish is tender. Baste with a mixture of the butter and lemon juice every 7 to 8 minutes.

When fish is done, remove from broiler and serve on the plank surrounded by lemon slices.

# BOILED MIDWESTERN CRAYFISH

serves 4 to 6

> 2 *pounds live crayfish*
> 2 *quarts boiling water*
> 2 *tablespoons salt*
> 1 *tablespoon caraway seeds*
> 1 *teaspoon chopped fresh dill or* ½ *teaspoon dried*

In a large pot, bring the water to a boil. Add the salt, caraway seeds, and dill. Boil for 1 minute.

Drop the live crayfish into the boiling water. Cook for *exactly* 5 minutes.

Drain the crayfish, chill for 1 hour, and serve.

Crayfish are found in the freshwater streams of the Midwest. The head, body, and legs are usually discarded; only the tail is eaten.

# OVEN-FRIED CATFISH

serves 6

> 2 *pounds catfish fillets*
> 1 *cup dry sherry*
> 1 *tablespoon salt*
> 1 *cup bread crumbs*
> ⅓ *cup vegetable oil*
> 2 *lemons, sliced*

Preheat the oven to 450°.

Wash and pat dry the fillets. If the fillets are very large, cut into smaller pieces.

Place the bread crumbs in a baking dish and toast in oven for 1 minute. Remove and mix with salt.

Dip the fillets, one at a time, into the sherry and then into the bread crumbs. Coat evenly with the crumbs.

Place the fillets onto a well-oiled cookie sheet. Sprinkle the fish with the remaining oil and wine. Bake for 15 minutes. Remove fillets from oven and serve with lemon slices.

# NORWEGIAN FISH STEW

serves 4

> 2 *pounds fresh pickerel or pike*
> 3 *cups water*
> ¼ *cup vinegar*
> ½ *teaspoon salt*
> 1 *bay leaf*
> 2 *whole cloves*
> 1½ *cups milk*
> 1½ *cups light cream*
> 1 *tablespoon butter*
> 1 *tablespoon flour*
> 4 *boiled potatoes*
> 1 *teaspoon fresh dill, chopped, or* ½ *teaspoon dried*

Clean the fish and cut into serving pieces.

In a large pot combine the vinegar, salt, bay leaf, cloves, and water. Bring the water to a boil and add the fish. Reduce the heat and simmer until the fish flakes easily, about 10 minutes. Remove from heat and set aside.

Combine the milk and cream in a saucepan. Heat only until lukewarm and then add to fish mixture. Stir gently.

In a bowl mix the flour and butter until well blended. Add to the fish mixture. Stir gently. Add the boiled potatoes and continue to cook until heated through. Serve hot.

## LAKE ERIE COHO SALMON

serves 8

1  8-pound fresh salmon
½  cup celery
½  cup onion, chopped
¼  cup butter
1  teaspoon salt
½  teaspoon dried sage
½  teaspoon pepper
½  pound cooked crabmeat
2  cup sunflavored croutons
   olive oil

Clean and rinse the salmon. Pat dry. Season with salt and set aside.

Preheat the oven to 350°.

Melt the butter in a saucepan. Add the celery and onion. Sauté until tender but not brown, about 5 minutes.

Remove saucepan from heat. Add the salt, sage, pepper, and crabmeat. Add the croutons and toss until well coated.

Fill the cavity of the salmon with the crabmeat mixture. Close cavity with skewers or sew with kitchen string. Brush the outside of the fish generously with olive oil.

Place the salmon in a shallow baking dish and bake for 1 to 1½ hours or until fish flakes when tested with a fork. Baste with the pan drippings 3 times as it bakes.

Remove fish from oven. Remove skewers or string. Carve fish and serve.

## LAKSLODA (SWEDISH POTATO AND SMOKED SALMON CASSEROLE)

serves 4

1  tablespoon butter, softened
4  tablespoons melted butter
3  medium potatoes, peeled and thinly sliced
4  tablespoons onions, finely chopped
½  pound smoked salmon, very thinly sliced
1½ cups light cream
¼  teaspoon grated nutmeg
   pepper to taste

Preheat the oven to 325°.

Heavily butter a 1-quart casserole, using 1 tablespoon butter.

Place one-third of the sliced potatoes in the casserole. Sprinkle with 2 tablespoons onions. Top with half the salmon. Add another third of the potatoes, the remaining onions, and the rest of the salmon. Top with the remaining potato slices.

Pour the cream down the sides of the casserole. Pour the melted butter over the top and sprinkle with the nutmeg and pepper.

Bake for 1 hour or until the potatoes are tender. Remove from oven and serve hot from casserole dish.

# · Vegetables ·

## COUNTRY FRIED POTATOES

serves 6

6 *slices bacon*
6 *potatoes, cooked and chilled*
4 *cups bacon drippings*
¾ *teaspoon salt*
⅛ *teaspoon pepper*

Fry the bacon in a skillet until brown and crisp. Remove and drain on paper towels. Drain off all but ¼ cup of the bacon drippings. Reserve.

Peel and slice the chilled potatoes.

Heat the reserved drippings in the skillet. Add the potato slices and season with salt and pepper. Fry the potatoes over medium heat, turning frequently, until the potatoes are nicely browned, about 10 minutes.

Crumble the bacon slices into the potatoes. Mix well. Remove from heat and serve.

## WALNUT SWEET POTATOES

serves 6

9 *medium sweet potatoes*
¾ *teaspoon salt*
6 *tablespoons butter*
½ *cup heavy cream*
¾ *cup chopped walnuts*
1 *tablespoon butter, cut into small pieces*

Preheat the oven to 400°.

Wash the sweet potatoes and bake for 1 hour or until tender.

Remove sweet potatoes from oven. When cool enough to handle, peel the sweet potatoes and mash. Add the salt, butter, and cream. Beat the mixture until is is very fluffy. Gently fold in the nuts.

Turn the mixture into a buttered 1½-quart casserole dish. Dot with butter and bake, uncovered, for 20 minutes or until butter has melted and potatoes are heated through. Remove from oven and serve hot.

## SWEET POTATO AND APPLE BAKE

serves 4

4 *large sweet potatoes*
4 *tart apples*
5 *tablespoons butter, cut into pieces*
  *sugar*
  *grated nutmeg*

Preheat the oven to 400°.

Wash the sweet potatoes and bake for 1 hour or until tender.

Peel, core, and thinly slice the apples.

Remove sweet potatoes from oven when they are ready. Turn the oven down to 350°. When the sweet potatoes are cool enough to handle, peel and cut them into ½-inch slices.

Place a layer of sweet potatoes in a buttered 1½- or 2-quart casserole. Sprinkle lightly with sugar and nutmeg. Dot with some pieces of butter. Place a layer of apple slices over the sweet potatoes. Sprinkle lightly with sugar and nutmeg. Continue making layers until sweet potatoes and apples are used up. End with a layer of sweet potatoes.

Cover the casserole and bake for 30 to 35 minutes. Remove and serve hot.

# KANSAS CORN OYSTERS

serves 6

    3 cups corn, cut from the cob
    3 eggs, well beaten
 1½ teaspoons baking powder
    ½ teaspoon salt
    ¼ teaspoon pepper
    3 tablespoons light cream
    ⅓ cup flour
      butter

In a large bowl combine the corn, eggs, baking powder, salt, pepper, cream, and flour. Beat mixture until well blended.

Melt 1 tablespoon butter on a griddle. When hot, drop the corn mixture by rounded tablespoons onto the griddle. Fry until golden brown on both sides, about 3 to 4 minutes a side. Fry only as many corn oysters as will fit easily on the griddle at one time. Add more butter as needed. Serve hot.

# MISSOURI BAKED CORN

serves 6

 12 ears fresh corn
      salt and pepper
    1 tablespoon sugar
    2 tablespoons water
    ¼ cup heavy cream

Preheat the oven to 350°.

Cut the kernels from the ears of corn with a sharp knife. Scrape the cobs with the back of the knife to remove all of the kernels.

Place the corn kernels in a mixing bowl. Season with salt and pepper. Add the sugar and water. Stir well.

Turn the corn into a lightly buttered, shallow baking dish. Bake for 30 minutes.

Remove dish from oven and stir in the cream. Serve immediately.

# HOOSIER FRIED TOMATOES

serves 4

 4 *firm ripe tomatoes*
   *corn meal*
   *salt and pepper to taste*
   *bacon drippings*
   *sugar*

Remove the stem ends of the tomatoes and cut the tomatoes into ½-inch slices.

Pour some corn meal onto a plate and season with salt and pepper. Combine well.

Coat the tomato slices with the corn meal mixture.

In a skillet heat the bacon drippings. When hot, add the coated tomato slices. Fry the tomatoes slowly, turning once, until browned, about 4 to 5 minutes per side. Sprinkle each slice with ½ teaspoon sugar before removing from skillet. Serve at once.

# HOOSIER BAKED TOMATOES

serves 6

 6 *firm ripe tomatoes, halved crosswise*
 1 *cup bread crumbs*
 ¼ *cup ground hazelnuts*
 2 *teaspoons salt*
 2 *teaspoons sugar*
 ¼ *teaspoon dried rosemary*
   *pepper*
 ¼ *cup butter, softened*
 2 *tablespoons parsley, chopped*

Preheat the oven to 325°.

Butter a shallow baking dish and place the tomatoes in it, cut-side up.

In a small bowl combine the bread crumbs, hazelnuts, salt, sugar, rosemary, pepper, butter, and parsley. Combine well. Cover the tops of the tomatoes with the mixture. Bake for 15 to 20 minutes.

# TURNIP CASSEROLE

serves 8

 3 *pounds turnips*
   *cold water*
 4 *tablespoons butter*
 1½ *teaspoons sugar*
 1 *teaspoon salt*
   *pepper*
 3 *eggs*
 1 *cup bread crumbs*
 1½ *teaspoons lemon juice*

Preheat the oven to 375°.

Peel the turnips and cut them into small cubes. Place the turnips in a large pot and cover with cold water. Add the salt to the water and bring to a boil. Cook for 20 to 30 minutes or until turnips are soft. Drain well and place in a large mixing bowl.

Add the butter, sugar, salt, and pepper. Beat mixture until smooth. Add the eggs, 1 at a time, beating well after each addition. Stir in the bread crumbs and lemon juice.

Turn the mixture into a buttered 2-quart rectangular casserole dish. Bake, uncovered, for 50 minutes.

# RUTABAGA WITH BACON

serves 4

    4 cups rutabaga, peeled and cubed
        water
    ¼ pound slab bacon, finely chopped
    1 onion, minced
        salt and pepper to taste

Place the rutabaga cubes in a large pot and add water to cover. Bring to a boil. Reduce heat and cook for 25 to 35 minutes or until rutabaga is tender. Drain well and set aside.

Sauté the bacon in a skillet until crisp and brown. Add the onion and cook for 2 to 3 minutes longer. Stir in the rutabaga. Cook for 5 minutes, stirring frequently to brown evenly. Season to taste with salt and pepper. Remove from skillet and serve.

# SWEDISH-STYLE RUTABAGAS

serves 4

    1 medium rutabaga, peeled and thinly sliced
    1 teaspoon salt
    6 tablespoons butter
    1 cup fresh mushrooms, coarsely chopped
    ½ teaspoon pepper

Place the rutabaga slices in a large pot and add enough water to cover. Add salt to the water and bring to a boil. Reduce heat, cover, and simmer rutabaga for 25 to 35 minutes or until tender. Drain well.

Place rutabaga in a mixing bowl. Add 3 tablespoons butter and mash well until smooth.

Heat the remaining butter in a saucepan. Add the chopped mushrooms and sauté until brown, about 8 to 10 minutes.

Add the mushrooms to the mashed rutabaga. Season with salt and pepper and mix well. Serve hot.

# SIMMERED RADISHES

serves 6

    4 cups fresh small red radishes
        water
    2 tablespoons butter
    ¼ teaspoon salt

Wash and trim the radishes. Leave whole.

Place the radishes in a pot with enough water to cover. Cook, covered, over low heat for 30 minutes or until tender. Drain well and place radishes in serving bowl. Add butter and salt. Toss well and serve.

# RED RIVER GLAZED SQUASH

serves 4

    1 3-pound butternut squash
    ¾ cup dark brown sugar, firmly packed
    ¼ cup butter
    1 tablespoon water

Preheat the oven to 350°.

Bake the whole squash for 1 hour or until tender. Remove from oven. When just cool enough to handle, carefully remove the rind. Do not cut squash.

In a small saucepan mix the brown sugar, butter, and water. Combine until well blended. Place over moderate heat and cook for 3 to 4 minutes or until syrupy.

Place the squash in a baking dish. Spoon the thick, hot syrup all over the squash. Bake for 15 to 20 minutes or until squash is well glazed. Remove from oven, slice, and serve.

# SUMMER SQUASH CASSEROLE

serves 6

3 tablespoons butter
½ cup scallions, chopped
¾ cup celery, diced
3 cups yellow summer squash, sliced
1½ cups cherry tomatoes
1 teaspoon salt
  pepper to taste
1 teaspoon fresh basil, chopped, or ¼ teaspoon dried

Preheat the oven to 300°.

In a large skillet melt the butter. Add the scallions and celery. Sauté until the scallions are transparent, about 3 to 5 minutes. Add the squash and stir well.

Turn the mixture into a buttered shallow baking dish. Top with the cherry tomatoes. Sprinkle with salt, pepper, and basil.

Cover the dish and bake for 30 minutes. Serve hot.

# BAKED CABBAGE

serves 4

1 medium head cabbage, cored and cut into eighths
  boiling water
3 tablespoons melted butter
4 tablespoons cider vinegar
1 teaspoon salt
½ teaspoon pepper

Preheat the oven to 325°.

Place the cabbage in a large pot and cover with boiling water. Cook over medium heat for 15 minutes or until tender. Drain well and cool.

Chop the cabbage finely and place in a large mixing bowl. Add the melted butter, cider vinegar, salt, and pepper. Mix well.

Turn mixture into a buttered baking dish and heat for 20 to 30 minutes. Remove from oven and serve hot.

# CREAMED CABBAGE

serves 4

1 medium head cabbage, cored and quartered
  boiling water
1 tablespoon salt
2 tablespoons butter
1 cup light cream
  salt and pepper to taste
  grated nutmeg to taste

In a large pot, bring the water and salt to a boil.

Chop the cabbage quarters finely. Add the cabbage to the boiling water. Cook, uncovered, for 3 minutes. Drain well.

*(continued on next page)*

Place cabbage in a clean towel and squeeze to extract as much water as possible.

In a large saucepan, heat the butter. Add the cabbage and mix well. Pour in the cream and season with salt, pepper, and nutmeg. Stir well. Cover and simmer for 5 minutes. Stir frequently. Serve cabbage very hot.

# OHIO BRAISED CELERY

serves 6

  2 large red onions
    salt and pepper to taste
  ¼ cup butter
  4 cups celery, cut diagonally into ½-inch slices
  2 cups beef broth
  2 tablespoons water
  1 tablespoon cornstarch

Preheat the oven to 325°.

Peel the onions and slice very thinly. Place the slices into a buttered 1½-quart casserole dish. Season with salt and pepper.

In a skillet, heat the butter. Add the celery and cook over moderate heat until lightly browned, about 5 minutes. Stir often.

Heat the beef broth in a saucepan.

Combine the cornstarch and water in a small bowl. Blend until smooth. Add to the broth. Bring the broth to a boil and cook, stirring constantly, 3 to 5 minutes or until the sauce is thick and smooth.

Add sauce to the celery and mix well. Spoon the mixture over the onions in the casserole dish. Bake for 1 hour. Serve hot.

# SAUTEED PARSNIPS

serves 4 to 6

  2 pounds parsnips
    boiling water
  4 tablespoons butter
    salt and pepper to taste

Trim and peel the parsnips. Cut into matchsticks.

Place the parsnips in a pot and cover with boiling water. Cook, uncovered, for 3 minutes, or until parsnips are cooked but still slightly crisp. Drain well.

In a skillet heat the butter. Add the parsnips and sauté over medium heat until golden brown, about 3 to 5 minutes. Stir constantly. Season to taste with salt and pepper and serve hot.

# KALE WITH ONIONS

serves 4 to 6

  1 large bunch kale
  1 large onion, thinly sliced
  1 clove garlic, crushed
  2 tablespoons butter
  1 tablespoon French-style mustard

Thoroughly wash and trim the kale. Remove the roots, stalks, and any wilted or blemished leaves. Chop coarsely.

Place the kale in a large skillet filled with ½ to 1 inch of water. Cover and steam the kale for 25 minutes. Drain well.

In a large saucepan melt the butter. Add the garlic and onions and cook until lightly browned, about 5 minutes. Add the kale and stir. Add the mustard and stir well. Heat through and serve.

# Noodles, Grains, and Beans

## WILD RICE CASSEROLE

serves 4

    1 cup raw wild rice
    ¼ cup butter
    3 tablespoons onion, chopped
    3 tablespoons green pepper, chopped
    ½ cup slivered almonds
    2 cups hot chicken broth
    1 cup hot water

Preheat the oven to 325°.

Rinse the wild rice well with cold water and drain well.

In a skillet melt the butter. Add the wild rice, onions, green pepper, and almonds. Cook over low heat until the rice begins to turn yellow. Stir constantly.

Spoon the mixture into a lightly buttered 1½-quart casserole. Add the hot chicken broth and hot water. Cover and bake for 1½ hours or until all the liquid has been absorbed and the wild rice is tender. Remove from oven and serve from casserole.

## MINNESOTA WILD RICE AND MUSHROOMS

serves 4

    ½ pound fresh mushrooms, sliced
    2 tablespoons onions, finely chopped
    ¼ cup butter
    1 cup wild rice, cooked, well-drained, and hot
    ⅓ cup melted butter

Melt the ¼ cup butter in a skillet. Add the mushrooms and onions and sauté until lightly browned, about 8 minutes.

Cook the wild rice according to package directions. Do not overcook. Place the cooked and drained wild rice into a serving bowl. Add the mushrooms and onions. Add the melted butter. Mix gently but thoroughly. Serve at once.

## CHEESY RICE

serves 6

    4 cups cooked rice
    ½ cup beef stock
    1½ cups sharp Cheddar cheese, grated
    ¼ sweet red pepper, diced
    ¼ green pepper, diced
    1 teaspoon salt
    ¼ to ½ teaspoon dried thyme

Preheat the oven to 350°.

In a large saucepan combine the rice and beef broth. Stir and heat gently. Remove from heat. Add the cheese, red pepper, green pepper, salt, and thyme. Mix well.

Turn mixture into a buttered 2-quart casserole and bake, covered, for 20 to 30 minutes or until the cheese melts and the rice is heated through. Remove from oven and serve directly from casserole.

# SCANDINAVIAN APPLE BEANS

serves 6

    1 pound fresh snap beans
    1 cup boiling water
1¼ teaspoons salt
    3 tablespoons butter
    3 medium tart apples
    2 tablespoons flour
    2 tablespoons sugar
1½ tablespoons lemon juice

Wash and drain the beans. Cut into 1-inch pieces.

Peel and core the apples. Cut into ½-inch slices.

In a saucepan combine the beans, boiling water, and 1 teaspoon salt. Cook over moderate heat until tender, about 8 minutes. Drain and reserve the liquid.

Pour the bean liquid into a bowl and add enough water to make 1¼ cups. Reserve.

Return the beans to the saucepan.

In a skillet melt 2 tablespoons butter. Add the apples and simmer, covered, for 5 minutes or until the apples are tender. Add the apples to the saucepan and combine with the beans.

Add the remaining butter to the skillet. Add the flour and stir well. Pour in the reserved bean liquid and bring to a boil, stirring constantly. Lower heat and simmer for 5 minutes. Stir in the sugar and lemon juice. Pour the mixture over the beans and apples. Season with remaining salt and mix well. Heat briefly and serve.

# WISCONSIN BAKED BEANS

serves 6 to 8

    4 cups dried pea beans
    1 tablespoon salt
1½ cups apple cider
      water
      boiling water
    1 cup dark molasses
    2 teaspoons dry mustard
¼ teaspoon ground ginger
½ cup tomato sauce
    2 tablespoons cider vinegar
    1 teaspoon sugar
½ slab bacon, cut into 2-inch cubes

Place the pea beans in a large pot and add enough cold water to cover. Soak the beans for 8 hours or overnight.

Drain the beans and season with salt. Return beans to the pot. Add the apple cider and enough cold water to cover. Add the onion and quickly bring to a boil. Reduce the heat, cover, and simmer gently for 45 to 55 minutes or until beans are tender.

Drain the beans and reserve the liquid. Discard the onion.

In a bowl combine the molasses, mustard, ginger, tomato sauce, vinegar, sugar, and 2 cups of the reserved bean liquid.

Place the bacon cubes in a colander and pour boiling water over them. Pat dry.

In the bottom of a heavy bean pot, place 2 pieces of the bacon. Add the beans and top with the remaining bacon. Pour in the molasses mixture and add enough water to cover the beans. Let pot stand for 10 to 12 minutes.

Preheat the oven to 325°.

Place bean pot in oven and bake for 2 hours. Remove and serve.

# SPLIT PEAS AND NOODLES

serves 4

1 cup yellow split peas
4 tablespoons onion, minced
4 tablespoons celery, minced
½ teaspoon garlic, chopped
½ teaspoon salt
¼ teaspoon pepper
2 cups water
2 cups cooked thin egg noodles
2 tablespoons parsley, chopped
4 tablespoons sour cream
1 cup tomato, peeled and chopped

In a large pot combine the peas, onion, celery, garlic, salt, pepper, and 2 cups water. Bring to a boil. Reduce the heat and cook, partially covered, for 30 minutes or until the peas are tender. Add more water if needed.

Remove from heat and stir in the noodles, parsley, sour cream, and chopped tomatoes. Return pot to heat and cook until heated through. If mixture becomes too thick, thin with a little water or dry white wine. Season to taste.

# BRUNA BÖNER (SWEDISH BEANS)

serves 6

1¼ cups dried kidney beans
1½ quarts cold water
1 tablespoon salt
2 tablespoons cider vinegar
2 tablespoons molasses
1 tablespoon dark brown sugar
1 tablespoon butter
1 tablespoon cornstarch
  water

Place the beans in a large pot and cover with the cold water. Soak overnight.

Cook the beans in the soaking water. Add the salt to the water and bring to a boil. Reduce the heat, cover, and simmer for 2 hours or until beans are just tender. Add additional water if needed.

Add the vinegar, molasses, brown sugar, and butter to the beans. Stir to combine and cook 10 minutes longer.

In a small bowl combine the cornstarch with a little cold water (about 1 teaspoon or more). Blend to make a smooth paste. Add to the beans and stir well. Cook the beans 2 to 3 minutes longer or until the liquid begins to thicken. Serve hot.

# Breads

## WISCONSIN HICKORY NUT BREAD

yields 2 loaves

      2  packages active dry yeast
  1½  cups very warm (105° to 115°) water
      1  teaspoon sugar
  1½  teaspoons salt
      2  cups or more flour
      ½  cup light brown sugar, firmly packed
      ¼  cup butter
      ½  cup boiling water
      4  cups or more graham or whole wheat flour
  1½  cups coarsely broken hickory nuts

Sprinkle the yeast into the very warm water in a bowl. Let stand for 2 minutes and then stir until yeast is dissolved. Add the sugar and proof. Let stand for 5 minutes more.

Transfer the yeast to a large mixing bowl. Add the salt and flour and beat until well combined. Let the mixture rise in a warm place until light and bubbly, about 30 minutes.

In a small bowl combine the brown sugar, butter, and boiling water. Stir to dissolve. When the mixture has cooled to lukewarm, add it to the yeast and flour mixture. Add the graham flour and nuts. Mix well.

Turn the dough out onto a lightly floured surface. Knead for approximately 10 minutes or until dough is smooth and elastic.

Place the dough in a bowl and cover with a damp towel. Let the dough rise in a warm place until doubled in bulk, about 1½ hours.

Turn the dough out onto a lightly floured surface. Divide in half. Cover halves and let rest for 10 minutes.

Butter 2 8 × 4 × 2-inch loaf pans.

Shape each dough half into a loaf and place in the pans. Cover and let rise until doubled in bulk, about 50 minutes.

Preheat the oven to 350°.

Bake the loaves for 50 minutes or until done. Remove from oven and cool in pans for 5 minutes. Turn out onto cooling racks and cool completely.

## OLD-FASHIONED OATMEAL BREAD

yields 2 loaves

  ¾  cup milk
  1  package active dry yeast
  1  cup quick-cooking oatmeal
  1¼  cups boiling water
  1½  teaspoons salt
  ½  cup molasses
  1  tablespoon butter
  5  cups flour
      melted butter

Heat the milk in a saucepan until a thin skin forms on top. Remove saucepan from heat and skim.

When the milk has cooled to lukewarm, stir in the yeast.

In a large mixing bowl combine the oatmeal, boiling water, salt, molasses, and melted butter. Stir to mix well. Cool to lukewarm. Stir in the flour and the milk and yeast mixture. Mix thoroughly with hands.

Cover the bowl with a clean towel and let stand in a warm place until doubled in bulk, about 1½ hours.

Turn the dough out onto a lightly floured surface and knead gently for 3 minutes. Divide dough into halves and shape each half into a loaf. Place into 2 buttered 9 × 5 × 3-inch loaf pans and cover with clean towels. Let dough rise until doubled in bulk, about 50 to 60 minutes.

Preheat the oven to 350°.

Bake loaves for 1 hour or until well browned. Remove from oven and brush tops with melted butter. Cool in the pans for 15 minutes. Turn out onto cooling racks and cool completely.

# PUMPERNICKEL

yields 2 loaves

    2 packages active dry yeast
1½ cups very warm water
  ½ cup dark molasses
    2 tablespoons caraway seeds
    1 tablespoon salt
    2 cups rye flour
    4 cups flour
    3 tablespoons butter, softened

Add the yeast to the warm water in a bowl. Let stand for 2 minutes and then stir to dissolve.

In a large bowl combine the yeast, molasses, caraway seed, and salt. Stir to mix well. Add the rye flour and 2 cups flour. Beat until well mixed. Add the butter and beat well. Stir in the remaining flour. Turn the dough out onto a lightly floured surface and knead until smooth, about 5 to 7 minutes.

Place the dough in an oiled bowl. Cover with a clean towel and let rise in a warm place until doubled in bulk, about 2 hours.

Turn dough out onto a lightly floured surface. Divide into halves and let rest, covered with a clean towel, for 10 minutes. Shape each half into a loaf.

Butter 2 9 × 5 × 3-inch loaf pans. Place the dough into the pans and cover. Let rise until doubled in bulk, about 50 minutes.

Preheat the oven to 450°.

Bake the loaves for 10 minutes. Lower the temperature to 350° and continue baking for 30 minutes.

Remove from oven to cooling racks. Cool in the pan for 10 minutes. Turn out onto racks and cool completely.

# LEFSE (SWEDISH POTATO BREADS)

yields approximately 30 *lefse*

6 medium potatoes, peeled and halved
¼ cup butter
¼ cup milk
1½ teaspoons salt
1 teaspoon sugar
⅛ teaspoon pepper
2½ to 3 cups flour
   butter, softened

Place the potatoes in a skillet with enough water to cover. Cook, covered, for 20 minutes or until potatoes are tender. Drain well. Return potatoes to skillet and dry over low heat, shaking skillet back and forth.

Mash the potatoes thoroughly. Add the ¼ cup butter, milk, salt, sugar, and pepper. Whip until light and fluffy. Place in refrigerator and chill for 4 hours.

Heat a large griddle over very low heat until it is very hot.

Remove the potatoes from the refrigerator. Add about half the flour and beat until smooth. Beat in enough of the remaining flour to form a soft dough. Form the dough into a ball and turn out onto a lightly floured surface. Roll out into a round sheet about ⅛-inch thick. Cut 24 to 30 6-inch rounds out of the dough.

Place a round on the very hot griddle. Cook until lightly browned. This will take only a moment or two. Turn round and brown the other side. Brown the rest of the rounds.

Transfer the rounds to a clean towel as they are cooked. Cool completely. Serve spread with softened butter and loosely rolled.

# LIMPA (SWEDISH RYE BREAD)

yields 2 round loaves

2 packages active dry yeast
½ cup warm water
½ cup dark brown sugar, firmly packed
⅓ cup molasses
2 tablespoons butter
1 tablespoon salt
3 tablespoons freshly grated orange rind
¾ teaspoon anise seed
1½ cups hot water
2½ cups medium rye flour
3½ to 3 cups unbleached flour
   cornmeal
   milk

Add the yeast to the warm water and allow it to soften for 2 minutes. Stir to dissolve. Set aside.

In a large bowl combine the brown sugar, molasses, butter, salt, orange rind, and anise seed. Pour in the hot water and mix well. Let mixture cool to lukewarm.

Add 1 cup rye flour to the mixture and beat until smooth. Add the yeast and stir. Slowly add the rest of the rye flour. Beat well. Add enough unbleached flour to make a soft dough, about 2½ to 3 cups. Beat until the dough starts to come away from the side of the bowl.

Turn the dough out onto a lightly floured surface and let rest for 8 to 10 minutes.

Knead in enough additional unbleached flour to make a smooth dough that does not stick. Shape the dough into a ball and place in a well-oiled deep bowl. Cover with a clean towel and let rise in a warm place until doubled in bulk, about 2 hours.

Punch down the dough and remold it into a ball. Turn completely over in the bowl. Cover and let rise again until almost doubled in bulk, about 1 hour.

Punch down the dough and turn out onto a lightly floured surface. Divide dough into halves and shape each half into a well-rounded, smooth ball.

Grease a cookie sheet and sprinkle it with corn meal. Place the loaves on the sheet and cover with a clean towel. Let dough rise again until doubled in bulk, about 30 minutes.

Preheat the oven to 375°.

Bake the loaves for 25 to 30 minutes. Remove loaves from oven and transfer to cooling racks. Brush immediately with milk. Cool completely.

# HUCKLEBERRY BREAD

yields 1 loaf

2 eggs
1 cup sugar
3 tablespoons melted butter
1 cup milk
3 cups flour
1 teaspoon salt
4 teaspoons baking powder
1 cup fresh huckleberries
½ cup chopped walnuts

Preheat the oven to 350°.

In a large bowl beat the eggs. Gradually add the sugar and continue beating for 1 minute. Add the butter and milk. Stir until well blended.

In a bowl combine the huckleberries and the chopped nuts.

Combine the flour with salt and baking powder. Add to the huckleberries and nuts and stir gently. Add the mixture to the egg and milk mixture. Stir only until dry ingredients are moistened.

Turn dough into a buttered 5 × 12-inch loaf pan. Bake for 50 to 60 minutes or until a cake tester inserted into the center comes out clean.

Remove to a cooling rack and cool in the pan for 10 minutes. Turn out onto rack and cool completely.

# BLACK WALNUT BREAD

yields 1 loaf

3 cups flour
4½ teaspoons baking powder
½ cup sugar
1 teaspoon salt
1 cup chopped black walnuts
¼ cup melted butter
2 eggs
1 cup milk

Preheat the oven to 350°.

In a large mixing bowl combine the flour, baking powder, sugar, and salt. Add the chopped nuts and stir.

*(continued on next page)*

In a bowl combine the eggs, milk, and melted butter. Beat until well blended. Add to the flour mixture. Stir until well blended. Do not try to break up the lumps.

Gently spoon the batter into a buttered 9 × 5 × 3-inch loaf pan. Bake for 1 hour or until cake tester inserted into the center comes out clean.

Remove from oven to a cooling rack. Cool in pan for 10 minutes. Turn out onto cooling rack and cool completely.

## SPICED APPLE BREAD

yields 1 loaf

    1  cup flour
    1  teaspoon baking soda
    1  teaspoon cinnamon
    ¼  teaspoon salt
    ¼  teaspoon grated nutmeg
    ¼  teaspoon ground cardamom
    ⅓  cup butter, softened
    1  egg, beaten
    ¾  cup honey
    ½  teaspoon vanilla extract
    2  medium tart apples, peeled, cored, and thinly sliced
    ¼  cup ground hazelnuts

Preheat the oven to 350°.

In a bowl combine the flour, baking soda, cinnamon, salt, nutmeg, and cardamom. Set aside.

In a large mixing bowl cream the butter. Add the egg, honey, and vanilla. Cream until well blended. Add the apples and ground hazelnuts. Stir well until combined. Stir in the flour mixture. Mix well until thoroughly blended.

Pour the batter into a buttered 9 × 5 × 3-inch loaf pan.

Bake for 30 minutes. Lower temperature to 325° and bake 20 minutes longer or until a cake tester inserted into the center comes out clean.

Remove from oven to a cooling rack. Let cool in the pan for 10 minutes. Turn out onto the rack and cool completely.

## BUCKWHEAT PANCAKES

serves 4

    ¾  cup buckwheat flour
    ¾  cup flour
    ½  teaspoon salt
    3½ teaspoons baking powder
    2  tablespoons sugar
    1  egg beaten
    3  tablespoons melted butter
    1¼ cups milk
    1  tablespoon light molasses

In a large bowl combine the buckwheat with the flour, baking powder, salt, and sugar.

In a mixing bowl combine the egg, butter, milk, and molasses. Beat until well blended. Add the flour mixture to the egg mixture and stir gently until well mixed.

Heat an ungreased griddle over medium heat. Drop the batter by teaspoons onto the griddle. Cook about 1 minute on each side. Turn when pancakes are bubbly on top and dry around the edges.

Serve hot with butter and honey.

# MINNESOTA APPLE PANCAKES

serves 6 to 8

4 eggs
½ cup light cream
1 cup milk
½ teaspoon salt
9 tablespoons sugar
2 cups flour
3 tablespoons butter, cut into small pieces
3 tart apples, peeled, cored, and thinly sliced
3 tablespoons cinnamon
1 tablespoon light brown sugar

Preheat the oven to 375°.

In a large bowl beat the eggs until light and fluffy. Add the cream, milk, salt, and 2 tablespoons sugar. Beat until well blended. Add the flour and beat well. Set aside.

Generously butter 2 9-inch round cake pans. Sprinkle each pan with 1 tablespoon sugar. Arrange the apples slices in circles in the pans.

In a small bowl combine the remaining 5 tablespoons sugar, cinnamon, and brown sugar. Sprinkle the mixture over the apples. Dot the apples with pieces of butter.

Pour the batter evenly into both pans. Bake for 30 minutes or until pancakes are golden and set. Remove from oven and slice into wedges. Serve immediately with smoked sausages.

# SOUR CREAM BISCUITS

yields 1 dozen

2 cups flour
2 teaspoons baking powder
½ teaspoon baking soda
1 teaspoon salt
1 tablespoon butter
1 cup plus 2 tablespoons sour cream

Preheat the oven to 450°.

Combine the flour with the baking powder, baking soda, and salt in a large bowl. Cut in the butter with a pastry blender or two knives until the mixture resembles a coarse meal. Stir in the sour cream and mix well to form a soft dough.

Roll the dough out on a lightly floured surface to form a 6 × 8-inch rectangle that is ¾-inch thick. Cut approximately 12 rounds from the dough with a lightly floured 2-inch biscuit cutter.

Place the rounds on a greased baking sheet and bake for 12 to 15 minutes or until golden. Serve hot.

# DROP BISCUITS

yields 1 dozen

2 cups flour
2 teaspoons baking powder
1 teaspoon salt
4 tablespoons butter
1 cup milk

Preheat the oven to 450°.

*(continued on next page)*

Combine the flour with the baking powder and salt in a large bowl. Cut in the butter with a pastry blender or two knives until the mixture resembles a coarse meal. Add the milk and stir to form a soft dough.

Drop the dough by well-rounded tablespoons onto a lightly buttered cookie sheet. There should be 12 biscuits.

Bake for 12 to 15 minutes or until golden. Serve hot.

# MOLASSES SPICE MUFFINS

yields 1 dozen

 2 cups flour
 1/2 teaspoon baking soda
 1 teaspoon baking powder
 1/2 tablespoon ground ginger
 1/2 teaspoon cinnamon
 1/2 teaspoon salt
 1/2 teaspoon pepper
 1/4 teaspoon ground cloves
 2 tablespoons butter
 3/4 cup sugar
 2 eggs, well beaten
 1/3 cup dark molasses
 1/4 cup buttermilk

Preheat the oven to 350°.

In bowl combine the flour, baking soda, baking powder, ginger, cinnamon, salt, pepper, and ground cloves.

Cream the butter and sugar together in a mixing bowl until light and fluffy. Beat in the eggs. Add the molasses. Stir until blended. Add the flour mixture and the buttermilk alternately. Stir well after each addition.

Spoon the batter into 12 buttered muffin cups. Bake for 25 to 30 minutes or until a cake tester inserted into the center of a muffin comes out clean. Serve warm.

# OLD-FASHIONED MUFFINS

yields 1 dozen

 2 cups flour
 1 tablespoon baking powder
 1 tablespoon sugar
 1/2 teaspoon salt
 1 egg, lightly beaten
 1 cup milk
 1/4 cup melted butter

Preheat the oven to 425°.

In a large bowl combine the flour, baking powder, sugar, and salt.

In a small bowl combine the egg, milk, and butter. Stir gently.

Make a well in the middle of the flour mixture and pour the egg and milk mixture into it all at once. Stir gently but quickly with a fork. The batter should be lumpy.

Lightly butter the bottoms of 12 muffin cups. Spoon the batter into each cup until two-thirds full.

Bake for 20 minutes or until golden brown. Serve hot.

# QUICK OATMEAL MUFFINS

yields 1 dozen

1 cup quick-cooking oats
1 cup buttermilk
1 cup flour
1 teaspoon baking powder
½ teaspoon salt
½ teaspoon baking soda
1 egg, slightly beaten
⅓ cup light brown sugar, firmly packed
⅓ cup vegetable oil

Preheat the oven to 400°.

Place the oats in a mixing bowl and pour the buttermilk over them. Let soak for 15 minutes.

In a bowl combine the flour with baking powder, salt, and baking soda. Stir into the oats and buttermilk mixture. Stir in the egg, brown sugar, and vegetable oil. Mix until just blended.

Spoon the batter into 12 buttered muffin cups. Bake for 20 to 25 minutes or until golden. Serve hot or allow to cool.

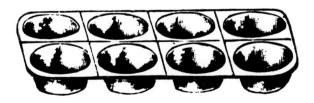

# ALL-PURPOSE DUMPLINGS

yields 2 dozen

2 cups flour
5 teaspoons baking powder
1 teaspoon salt
1 egg
1 egg yolk
½ cup milk
1½ teaspoons dried dill

Into a large bowl sift the flour together with the baking powder and salt. Repeat twice.

In a mixing bowl combine the egg, egg yolk, milk, and dill. Beat until well blended. Add to the flour and stir only until mixed. If the dough is too thick, add more milk, 1 tablespoon at a time, until a fairly stiff dough is formed.

Drop the dumplings by rounded tablespoons into the simmering broth, soup, or stew. Cover the pot tightly as soon as all the dumplings have been added.

Cook, tightly covered, for 15 to 18 minutes. Be certain that the heat is low and that the cooking liquid is just simmering.

Remove the cover and serve.

# Desserts

## BUTTERNUT SQUASH PIE

yields 1 9-inch pie

1 *butternut squash*
1 *cup boiling water*
1 *cup heavy cream*
1 *cup sugar*
3 *eggs, slightly beaten*
¼ *cup brandy*
1 *teaspoon grated nutmeg*
1 *teaspoon cinnamon*
¾ *teaspoon ground ginger*
½ *teaspoon salt*
1 *egg white, slightly beaten*
1 *pastry for 9-inch pie crust*

Cut the butternut squash in half. Save one half for some other use. Seed, peel, and cut into pieces the other half. Place the pieces in a pot with 1 cup boiling water. Cook, covered, for 10 minutes or until squash is tender. Drain well and mash. Add the cream, sugar, eggs, brandy, nutmeg, cinnamon, ginger, and salt. Mix until well blended.

Preheat the oven to 400°.

Fit the pastry into a pie pan and brush with the egg white. Pour the squash mixture into the pie pan and bake for 5 minutes.

Lower the heat to 300° and continue to bake for 40 to 50 minutes or until a knife inserted into the center comes out clean.

Remove from oven and let cool slightly. Serve while still hot or warm.

## BLACKBERRY PIE

yields 1 9-inch pie

6 *cups fresh blackberries*
1 *cup sugar*
¼ *teaspoon grated nutmeg*
1 *tablespoon flour*
¼ *cup butter, cut into pieces*
1 *pastry from 2-crust 9-inch pie*

Preheat the oven to 400°.

Roll out half the pastry onto a lightly floured surface. Fit the pastry into a deep 9-inch pie pan.

Add the berries to the pie shell.

In a small bowl combine the sugar, nutmeg, and flour. Sprinkle mixture over the berries and dot with the butter pieces.

Fit the second crust over the top of the pie. Seal and flute the edges. Cut steam vents in the top.

Bake for 15 minutes. Reduce heat to 350° and bake for 20 to 30 minutes longer. When the filling boils up through the vents, the pie is done.

Remove from oven and cool.

This pie is best when made with freshly gathered wild blackberries. The basic recipe may be used for huckleberries, blueberries, raspberries, or plums.

# PEACH PIE

yields 1 9-inch pie

*7 fresh peaches, peeled and sliced*
*1 cup sugar*
*⅓ cup flour*
*¼ teaspoon salt*
*1 cup sour cream*
*¼ teaspoon cinnamon*
*2 tablespoons sugar*
*1 pastry for 2-crust 9-inch pie*

Preheat the oven to 425°.

Roll out half the pastry onto a lightly floured surface. Fit into a 9-inch pie pan.

Arrange the sliced peaches in the pie crust.

In a small bowl combine the flour, sugar, and salt. Mix well. Add the sour cream and stir well. Pour mixture over the peaches.

Roll out the other half of the pastry. With a pastry wheel or sharp knife, cut it into strips. Arrange the strips over the peach mixture in a lattice. Sprinkle the top of the pie with cinnamon and 2 tablespoons sugar.

Bake for 15 minutes. Reduce heat to 350° and bake 40 minutes longer. Remove from oven and cool.

# OHIO LEMON PIE

yields 1 9-inch pie

*2 lemons*
*2 cups sugar*
*4 eggs*
*1 pastry for 2-crust 9-inch pie*

Preheat the oven to 450°.

Slice the lemons as thinly as possible. Remove the pits and put the slices in bowl. Add the sugar and mix well. Let stand for 2 to 3 hours.

Roll out half the pastry on a lightly floured surface. Fit the pastry into a 9-inch pie pan. Roll out the remaining pastry for a top, cut a slit in it, and set aside.

In a small bowl beat the eggs until foamy. Add to the bowl with the lemon slices and mix well. Pour the mixture into the pie pan. Cover with the top, fit well, seal, and flute.

Bake for 15 minutes. Reduce temperature to 350° and bake 45 minutes longer. Remove from oven and serve warm.

# SOUTH DAKOTA APPLE CRUMB PIE

yields 1 9-inch pie

*1 large lemon*
*4 cups apples, peeled and shredded (about 5 to 6 large apples)*
*3 egg yolks*
*½ cup sugar*
*2 tablespoons heavy cream*
*⅓ cup golden raisins*
*⅓ cup slivered almonds*
*⅛ teaspoon ground cloves*
*⅛ teaspoon cinnamon*
*⅛ teaspoon ground ginger*
*½ cup ground almonds*
*1 pastry for 9-inch pie shell*

Topping:
*½ cup light brown sugar, firmly packed*
*¼ cup melted butter*
*⅓ cup flour*

*(continued on next page)*

Preheat the oven to 425°.

Roll out the pastry onto a lightly floured surface. Fit into a 9-inch pie pan, flute edges, and set aside.

Grate the rind of the lemon and set aside. Squeeze the juice of the lemon into a bowl. Add the apples to the bowl and mix well to coat with lemon juice. Pour off any liquid remaining in the bowl.

In a large bowl combine the egg yolks, sugar, and cream. Beat until well blended. Add the lemon rind, raisins, slivered almonds, cloves, cinnamon, and ginger. Stir to mix well. Add the apples and lemon juice. Mix well.

Spread the ground almonds over the bottom of the pie shell. Pour in the apple filling. Level off the top.

Bake for 25 minutes.

In a bowl combine the flour, brown sugar, and melted butter. Mix until crumbs form. Remove the pie from the oven and sprinkle the crumbs on top. Return pie to the oven and bake 20 minutes longer or until top is golden.

Remove and cool 30 minutes before serving.

# RHUBARB CUSTARD PIE

yields 1 9-inch pie

2 to 2½ cups diced rhubarb
3 eggs
1 cup sugar
½ cup milk
1 pastry for 9-inch pie crust

Preheat the oven to 450°.

Roll the pastry out onto a lightly floured surface. Fit into a 9-inch pie pan and flute the edges. Prick all over with a fork and bake for 4 to 5 minutes. Remove and set aside. Lower oven temperature to 350°.

In a large bowl, combine the eggs and sugar. Beat together with an electric mixer set on high for 4 to 5 minutes. Pour in the milk and continue beating until the milk is thoroughly incorporated.

Sprinkle the rhubarb evenly over the bottom of the pie pan. Pour the egg mixture over it.

Bake for 20 to 25 minutes or until a knife inserted into the center of the pie comes out clean.

Remove from oven and cool.

# GREAT PLAINS CARROT PIE

yields 1 9-inch pie

1½ cups cooked carrots, puréed
½ cup light brown sugar
1 tablespoon cornstarch
½ teaspoon salt
½ teaspoon cinnamon
½ teaspoon ground ginger
¼ teaspoon grated nutmeg
1½ cups milk
2 eggs, well beaten
½ teaspoon vanilla extract
1 pastry for 9-inch pie crust

Roll out the pastry on a lightly floured surface. Fit into a 9-inch pie pan and flute high edges.

Preheat the oven to 350°.

In a large bowl combine the carrots, brown sugar, cornstarch, salt, cinnamon, ginger, nutmeg, milk, eggs, and vanilla. Beat with a electric mixer at medium-high speed until well blended.

Turn the mixture into the pie pan and bake for 50 to 60 minutes or until set.

Remove from oven and cool completely.

# SCANDINAVIAN RAISIN RING

yields 1 ring

1 package active dry yeast
¼ cup very warm water (105° to 115°)
3 cups flour
¾ cup sugar
1 teaspoon salt
¾ cup butter
¼ cup melted butter
1 cup light cream
3 egg yolks
  rind of 1 small lemon, freshly grated
2 tablespoons cinnamon
½ cup golden raisins
½ cup diced citron
1 egg white, slightly beaten
  chopped almonds
  Confectioner's Icing

Sprinkle the yeast into a bowl with the warm water. Set aside for 2 minutes and then stir to dissolve.

In a large bowl combine the flour, ¼ cup sugar, and salt. Cut in ¾ cup butter with a pastry blender or two knives until the mixture resembles a coarse meal. Add the yeast, cream, egg yolks, and lemon rind. Beat well. Wrap dough in plastic wrap and refrigerate overnight.

Remove dough from refrigerator and turn out onto a lightly floured surface. Roll out into a 16 × 12-inch rectangle. Brush with ¼ cup melted butter and sprinkle with ½ cup sugar and the cinnamon. Sprinkle with the raisins and citron.

Roll up the dough and place it on a buttered baking sheet. Join the ends to form a ring. With sharp scissors, cut all the way through the ring from the edge three-quarters of the way to the center. Make cuts at 1½-inch intervals. As pieces are cut, lift each up slightly and place on its side, turning every other piece in the opposite direction. Press the ring to flatten the dough pieces and make them all the same height. Cover and let rise until doubled in size, about 1 to 2 hours.

Preheat the oven to 350°.

Brush the ring with the egg white and sprinkle with almonds. Bake for 30 minutes.

Remove from oven and cool completely. Frost with Confectioner's Icing (see below).

# CONFECTIONER'S ICING

yields ⅓ cup

1 tablespoon boiling water
½ teaspoon lemon juice
¾ cup confectioner's sugar

Mix the boiling water and lemon juice in a bowl. Add the confectioner's sugar and mix well. Drizzle or spread on completely cooled cake.

# STREUSEL

yields 1 cake

1½ cups flour
 3 teaspoons baking powder
 ¼ teaspoon salt
 ¾ cup sugar
 ¼ cup butter
 1 egg
 ⅓ cup milk
 1 teaspoon vanilla extract

Filling:

2½ cups light brown sugar
 2 teaspoons flour
 2 teaspoons cinnamon
 2 teaspoons melted butter
 ½ cup chopped walnuts

Preheat the oven to 350°.

Combine the flour with the baking powder, salt, and sugar in a large bowl. Cut in the butter with a pastry blender or two knives until the mixture resembles a fine meal. Add the egg, milk, and vanilla. Stir until well mixed.

To make the filling, combine the brown sugar, flour, cinnamon, melted butter, and chopped nuts in a bowl. Mix well.

Butter an 8-inch square baking pan. Pour half the batter into the pan and sprinkle with half the filling. Add the remaining batter and top with the remaining filling.

Bake for 20 to 30 minutes.

Remove from oven and cool before serving.

# MIDWESTERN BUTTERMILK RAISIN CAKE

yields 1 cake

 ½ cup butter
 1 cup sugar
 3 eggs, separated
 ½ cup buttermilk
 2 tablespoons prune juice
 2 cups flour
 ½ teaspoon baking soda
 1 heaping cup raisins, chopped

Preheat the oven to 350°.

In a mixing bowl cream the butter and sugar together until light and fluffy.

In a separate bowl beat the egg yolks. Stir into the butter and sugar mixture. Add the buttermilk and prune juice. Stir until well mixed. Add the flour and baking soda.

In a small bowl beat the egg whites until stiff but not dry. Fold gently into the batter. Stir in raisins.

Turn the batter into a buttered 9-inch square baking pan. Bake for 35 to 40 minutes or until a cake tester inserted into the center comes out clean.

Remove from oven and cool.

# APPLE SPICE CAKE

yields 1 cake

 4 cups tart apple pieces, peeled (about 3 large apples)
  rind of 1 large lemon, grated
  juice of 1 large lemon
 ½ cup butter
 ⅔ cup sugar
 1 egg beaten
 1½ cups flour
 1 teaspoon baking soda
 ¼ teaspoon salt
 ½ teaspoon cinnamon
 ½ teaspoon ground ginger
 ⅛ teaspoon grated nutmeg
 ½ cup milk
 ⅔ cup chopped walnuts

Preheat the oven to 350°.

Place the apple pieces in a bowl. Add the lemon rind and lemon juice. Mix until the apples pieces are well coated. Set aside.

In a mixing bowl cream the butter until soft and light. Beat in the sugar, a little at a time. Beat in the egg.

Combine the flour with baking soda, salt, cinnamon, ginger, and nutmeg. Add to the butter mixture alternately with the milk. Beat well after each addition. Add the apple pieces and any juice in the bowl. Add the nuts. Mix well.

Turn mixture into a heavily buttered 9-inch square baking pan. Level and smooth the top of the cake.

Bake for 45 to 50 minutes or until the cake begins to pull away from the sides of the pan.

Remove from the oven and serve warm with heavy cream, or cool completely.

# SCANDINAVIAN WALNUT HONEY CAKE

yields 1 loaf

 ½ cup butter
 ⅓ cup sugar
 ⅔ cup honey
 1 tablespoon anise seeds, crushed
 2 cups flour
 2 teaspoons baking soda
 ⅔ cup finely chopped walnuts
 ½ cup boiling water

Preheat the oven to 350°.

In a saucepan combine the butter, sugar, and honey. Cook over low heat until melted. Add the crushed anise seeds and stir. Remove from heat and set aside.

Combine the flour and baking soda in a bowl. Add the chopped walnuts and stir.

Add the flour and nut mixture to the honey mixture. Stir until well blended. Stir in the boiling water.

Butter a 9 × 5 × 3-inch loaf pan. Line it with wax paper and butter again. Pour in the batter.

Bake for 30 minutes or until a cake tester inserted into the middle of the loaf comes out clean.

Remove cake from oven and cool in the pan. When completely cool, turn loaf out and peel off wax paper.

# BUCKEYE MAPLE CAKE

yields 1 cake

⅓ cup butter
½ cup sugar
¾ cup pure maple sugar
2¼ cups flour
3 teaspoons baking powder
¼ teaspoon salt
½ cup milk
3 egg whites
¾ cup chopped walnuts
Maple Icing

Preheat the oven to 350°.

Combine the flour with the baking powder and salt in a bowl. Set aside.

In a mixing bowl cream the butter until soft. Gradually add the sugar and beat until light and fluffy. Stir in the maple syrup. Add the flour mixture alternately with the milk. Stir until well combined.

In a separate bowl beat the egg whites until stiff but not dry. Fold into the batter.

Butter a 9-inch square baking pan. Line it with wax paper and butter again. Pour in the batter.

Bake for 35 minutes. Remove to a cooling rack. Cook cake in pan for 5 minutes. Turn out onto a rack and remove wax paper. Turn cake right-side up and cool completely. When cool frost with Maple Icing.

# MAPLE ICING

yields approximately 2 cups

2 cups pure maple syrup
2 egg whites
⅛ teaspoon salt

In a bowl beat the egg whites and salt until stiff but not dry.

Boil the maple syrup in a saucepan until it registers 232° on a candy thermometer or spins a soft thread.

Pour the syrup slowly over the egg whites and beat with a whisk or electric mixer until the mixture forms soft peaks.

Spread the sides and top of the cooled cake with icing. Sprinkle with the chopped walnuts.

# OLD-FASHIONED NUT COOKIES

yields 48 cookies

1½ cups sugar
1 cup butter
3 eggs, well beaten
½ cup molasses
1½ cups raisins
½ cup finely chopped hickory nuts
2 cups flour
1 teaspoon baking soda
½ teaspoon cinnamon
¼ teaspoon ground cloves
⅛ teaspoon salt

Preheat the oven to 350°.

Combine 1 cup flour, the baking soda, cinnamon, cloves, and salt in a bowl. Set aside.

In a large bowl cream the butter and sugar together until light and fluffy. Add the eggs and molasses. Beat well. Stir in the raisins and nuts. Mix well. Add the flour mixture and stir. Add enough additional flour to make a soft dough, about 1 cup.

Chill the dough for 10 minutes or until it is easy to handle.

Roll the dough out thinly on a lightly floured surface. Cut with cookie cutter.

Transfer the cookies to a buttered cookie sheet and bake for 10 to 12 minutes.

Remove from oven and transfer cookies with a spatula to cooling racks.

# NORWEGIAN SPRITZ COOKIES

yields 48 cookies

1 cup butter, softened
1 cup sugar
2 egg yolks
1 teaspoon almond extract
2½ cups flour

Preheat the oven to 350°.

In a large bowl cream the butter and sugar together until light and fluffy. Beat in the egg yolks. When yolks are well blended, add the almond extract. Sift the flour into the mixture, a little at a time. Beat well after each addition.

Place the dough into a cookie press fitted with any shape. Press the shapes out 1 inch apart onto ungreased cookie sheets.

Bake for 10 minutes or until lightly browned.

Remove from oven and transfer to cooling racks with a spatula. Cool completely. Store in tightly covered container.

# WALNUT-CHOCOLATE DROPS

yields 48 cookies

1¾ cups flour
½ teaspoon baking soda
½ teaspoon baking powder
¼ teaspoon salt
½ cup butter
1 cup sugar
1 egg
1 egg yolk
3 ounces unsweetened chocolate, melted
1 teaspoon vanilla extract
½ cup milk
1 cup raisins
1 cup coarsely chopped walnuts

Preheat the oven to 350°.

Combine the flour with the baking soda, baking powder, and salt in a bowl.

In a mixing bowl cream the butter until light and fluffy. Beat in the sugar gradually. Add the egg and egg yolk. Beat well. Add the melted chocolate and vanilla. Stir until well blended. Add the flour alternately with the milk. Stir in the raisins and nuts.

Drop the batter by teaspoons onto a buttered cookie sheet. Bake for 12 to 14 minutes.

Remove from oven and transfer to cooling racks. Store in an airtight container.

# CRULLERS

yields approximately 30 crullers

1 package active dry yeast
1/4 cup very warm water (100° to 115°)
3/4 cup scalded milk, cooled to lukewarm
4 cups flour
10 tablespoons sugar
1/2 cup butter
1 egg
2 egg yolks
1 teaspoon salt
1/2 teaspoon grated nutmeg
   vegetable oil for deep frying
   confectioner's sugar

Sprinkle the yeast into a bowl with the warm water. Let sit for 2 minutes; then stir to dissolve yeast.

Add the yeast to the cooled milk. Stir. Add 1 cup flour and 2 tablespoons sugar. Beat until thoroughly blended. Set aside in a warm place until mixture is light and fluffy, about 45 minutes.

In a large bowl cream the butter until light and fluffy. Gradually add 8 tablespoons sugar. Beat until well blended. Beat in the egg and egg yolks one at a time. Beat well after each addition.

Beat the butter mixture, salt, nutmeg, and remaining 4 cups flour into the yeast mixture. Place the dough in an oiled bowl, cover with a clean towel, and let rise until almost doubled in bulk, about 1 to 1 1/2 hours.

Turn the dough out onto a lightly floured surface. Roll dough out 1/2-inch thick.

With a pastry wheel or sharp knife cut the dough into 1/2 × 8-inch strips. Fold each strip in half the long way. Twist the strips and pinch the ends together. Cover and let rise until light, about 35 to 45 minutes.

Heat the oil in a deep skillet until it is very hot, 370° on a deep-fat thermometer. Fry the crullers, a few at a time, until golden brown, about 3 minutes per side.

Remove from oil and drain on paper towels. Dust with confectioner's sugar and serve.

# APPLE DUMPLINGS

serves 6

2 1/2 cups flour
3 teaspoons baking powder
1 teaspoon salt
3 tablespoons sugar
2/3 cup butter
1/2 cup milk
2 tablespoons butter
2/3 cup light brown sugar
3/4 teaspoon cinnamon
1/4 teaspoon freshly grated lemon peel
6 medium apples, peeled and cored

Preheat the oven to 350°.

In a large bowl combine the flour with the baking powder, salt, and sugar. Cut in 2/3 cup butter with a pastry blender or two knives until the mixture resembles a coarse meal. Add the milk gradually. Mix gently and shape the dough into a ball.

In a small bowl combine the 2 tablespoons butter, the brown sugar, cinnamon, and lemon peel.

Turn the dough out on a lightly floured surface and roll into a 13 × 20-inch rectangle. With a pastry wheel or sharp knife, cut the dough into 6¼-inch squares.

Place an apple in the center of each square. Spoon the brown sugar mixture evenly into the cored centers. Moisten the edges of the pastry and bring the 4 corners up and over the apples. Press corners together to secure. Cut small gashes into the sides of the pastry.

Place the encased apples into a buttered baking dish. Bake for 40 to 45 minutes or until the pastry is golden. Remove from oven and serve warm with whipped cream.

## IOWA APPLE FRITTERS

serves 6 to 8

1 cup flour
2 tablespoons sugar
¼ teaspoon salt
⅔ cup milk
2 eggs, separated
2 tablespoons melted butter
6 large apples, peeled and cored
3 tablespoons lemon juice
    oil for deep frying
    confectioner's sugar

In a mixing bowl combine the flour, sugar, and salt.

In a small bowl combine the milk, egg yolks, and melted butter. Stir gently until mixed. Beat into flour mixture. Beat until mixture is smooth.

In another bowl beat the egg whites until stiff but not dry. Gently fold into the batter.

Cut the apples into ½-inch slices. Place in a small bowl and sprinkle with the lemon juice. Toss gently to coat evenly. Dip each apple slice into the batter.

In a deep skillet heat the oil until very hot, 365° on a deep-fat thermometer. Add the apples slices, a few at a time, and fry until golden, about 3 to 4 minutes per side.

Remove the apple slices from the oil with a slotted spoon. Drain on paper towels. Dust with confectioner's sugar before serving.

## CRUSTLESS BLACK WALNUT PIE

yields 1 9-inch pie

4 egg whites
1 teaspoon cream of tartar
1 cup sugar
1 teaspoon vanilla extract
8 unsalted soda crackers, finely crushed
½ cup chopped black walnuts or regular walnuts

Preheat the oven to 275°.

In a mixing bowl beat the egg whites until just stiff. Sift in the cream of tartar and blend in gently. Gradually add the sugar and beat until the mixture is very stiff but not dry. Add the vanilla. Gently fold in the cracker crumbs and chopped walnuts.

Turn the mixture into a buttered 9-inch pie pan. Pile it in lightly.

Bake for 45 to 55 minutes or until top is dry.

Remove from oven and serve warm, preferably with ice cream or fresh berries.

# BLACKBERRY FLUMMERY

serves 8

2 quarts fresh blackberries
½ cup water
1 cup sugar
⅛ teaspoon ground cinnamon
1 tablespoon freshly grated lemon rind
2 tablespoons cornstarch
3 tablespoons water

Wash the berries and place them in a saucepan. Stir in ½ cup water, the sugar, cinnamon, and lemon rind. Quickly bring the mixture to a boil. Reduce the heat, cover lightly, and continue cooking for 5 minutes.

In a small bowl combine the cornstarch and 3 tablespoons water. Blend to form a smooth paste. Slowly stir the paste into the blackberry mixture. Continue cooking for 3 to 5 minutes or until thickened. Stir constantly.

Remove blackberry mixture from heat and turn into a serving bowl. Allow to cool before serving or chill briefly in the refrigerator. Serve with heavy cream.

# HONEY CUSTARD

serves 6

2 cups milk
4 tablespoons honey
3 eggs
¼ teaspoon salt
   grated nutmeg

Preheat the oven to 375°.

Place the milk in a saucepan and scald. Remove from heat and stir in honey.

In a small bowl beat together the eggs and salt. Gradually beat in 1 to 2 tablespoons of the milk and honey mixture. Add the eggs to the milk and honey in the saucepan and combine.

Pour the mixture into 6 small custard cups. Sprinkle each cup with nutmeg. Place cups in a pan of hot water. Bake for 30 to 40 minutes or until a knife inserted into the center of the custard comes out clean.

Remove from oven and from pan of hot water. Cool completely and chill before serving.

In colonial and pioneer times refined sugar was scarce and expensive. This recipe, which uses honey for the sweetening, is very old.

# PERSIMMON PUDDING

serves 4 to 6

3 very ripe persimmons
¾ cup light brown sugar, firmly packed
1 cup milk
¼ cup melted butter
1 cup flour
2 teaspoons baking powder
¼ teaspoon salt
¼ teaspoon cinnamon

Preheat the oven to 325°.

Wash and peel the persimmons. Blend in an electric blender or push through a sieve to yield 1 cup of persimmon pulp.

In a bowl combine the persimmon pulp, brown sugar, milk, and butter. Stir until well blended.

Combine the flour and baking powder, salt, and cinnamon in a bowl. Add to the persimmon mixture and stir until smooth.

Turn the mixture into a buttered 1½-quart baking dish. Bake for 1 hour or until pudding begins to come away from the sides of the dish.

Remove from oven and serve warm or cold, with or without whipped cream.

Be certain to use only very ripe persimmons—the astringent taste of an unripe persimmon is very unwelcome.

## MISSOURI APPLE NUT PUDDING

serves 4 to 6

 ¼ cup flour
1¼ teaspoons baking powder
 ⅛ teaspoon salt
 1 egg
 ¾ cup sugar
 ½ cup chopped walnuts
 ½ cup apple, chopped
 1 teaspoon vanilla extract

Preheat the oven to 350°.

In a small bowl combine the flour, baking powder, and salt. Stir to mix thoroughly.

In a large bowl combine the egg and sugar. Beat together until mixture is smooth and well blended. Add the flour mixture to the egg mixture. Stir to blend. Add the chopped walnuts, apple, and vanilla. Mix well.

Pour mixture into a buttered 8-inch pie pan. Bake for 35 minutes or until a knife inserted into the center comes out clean.

Remove from oven. Cool slightly and serve warm or chill for several hours. Serve with whipped cream or ice cream.

## INDIANA CANTALOUPE BALLS

serves 4 to 6

 1 large ripe cantaloupe
 ½ cup sugar
1½ teaspoons cornstarch
 ⅛ teaspoon salt
 ¾ cup water
 12 large fresh mint leaves
 1 tablespoon butter

Using a small melon baller form the cantaloupe into balls. Place in a large bowl and refrigerate for 2 hours.

Combine the sugar, cornstarch, and salt in a saucepan. Add the water and mint leaves. Stir, crushing the mint leaves against the side of the saucepan with the back of a spoon. Bring mixture to a boil, stirring constantly. Continue cooking until mixture begins to thicken.

Remove from heat. Cool for 15 minutes and strain through a sieve. Add the butter and chill.

Combine the chilled melon balls and the mint sauce in a bowl. Mix well. Serve icy cold.

# Accents

## CORN AND PEPPER SALAD

yields approximately 3 quarts

24 *ears fresh corn*
1 *medium head cabbage*
2 *onions*
3 *green peppers*
3 *sweet red peppers*
2 *cups sugar*
2 *tablespoons salt*
3 *tablespoons mustard seed*
5 *cups distilled white vinegar*

Cut the corn from the cobs with a sharp knife.

Finely chop the cabbage, onions, green peppers, and red peppers.

Place the corn and chopped vegetables into a large saucepan. Add the sugar, salt, mustard seed, and vinegar. Bring to a boil. Reduce the heat and simmer for 20 minutes.

Remove from heat and spoon into hot sterilized jars. Seal, cool, and store.

## CUCUMBER SLICES

yields approximately 1½ quarts

6 *cups cucumbers, sliced*
1 *cup onions, thinly sliced*
1 *cup green pepper, chopped*
2 *cups sugar*
1 *cup distilled white vinegar*
1 *teaspoon salt*

In a large bowl combine the cucumber slices, onion slices, and green pepper.

In a small bowl combine the sugar, vinegar, and salt. Pour over the cucumber mixture and toss until well mixed.

Transfer to a large jar and store, tightly covered, for 1 to 2 weeks in refrigerator.

## APPLE-TOMATO RELISH

yields approximately 3 to 4 pints

4 *medium tart apples, cored and cut into eighths*
3 *medium onions, quartered*
1 *stalk celery, sliced*
4 *large ripe tomatoes, peeled, seeded, and cut into eighths*
1 *sweet red pepper, diced*
2½ *cups white vinegar*
3 *cups light brown sugar*
¾ *cup seedless raisins*
2 *tablespoons mustard seed*
1 *tablespoon ground ginger*
2 *ounces candied ginger, finely chopped*
1 *tablespoon salt*

Coarsley chop the apple pieces, onions, and celery. Place in a large saucepan. Add the tomatoes, vinegar, brown sugar, raisins, mustard, ground ginger, candied ginger, and salt. Mix well. Bring the mixture to a boil. Reduce heat and simmer, uncovered, for 1¾ hours. Stir often.

Add the red pepper and continue to simmer for 15 minutes longer. Stir often.

Carefully spoon mixture into hot sterilized jars. Seal, cool, and store.

# SWEET AND SOUR APPLE RELISH

yields approximately 2 quarts

12 *tart apples, peeled, cored, and chopped*
 1 *onion, coarsely chopped*
 2 *green peppers, coarsely chopped*
 1 *cup seedless raisins*
 1 *cup sugar*
 2 *cups cider vinegar*
 1 *lemon, thinly sliced and seeded*
1½ *teaspoons salt*
1½ *teaspoons ground ginger*

In a large saucepan combine the chopped apples, onions, green pepper, raisins, vinegar, sugar, lemon slices, salt, and ginger. Stir to mix. Bring the mixture to a boil. Reduce the heat and simmer, covered, for 2 hours or until mixture is thick. Stir frequently.

Carefully spoon the mixture into hot sterilized jars. Seal, cool, and store.

# INDIA RELISH

yields approximately 3 pints

12 *large green tomatoes*
 1 *sweet red pepper*
 1 *green pepper*
 4 *large onions*
 1 *cup distilled white vinegar*
 1 *cup sugar*
 1 *tablespoon mustard seed*
 1 *tablespoon celery seed*
 1 *tablespoon salt*

Coarsely chop the tomatoes, red pepper, green pepper, and onion. Place vegetables in a colander and drain thoroughly.

Place drained vegetables into a large saucepan. Stir in the vinegar, sugar, mustard seed, celery seed, and salt. Bring the mixture to a boil. Reduce heat and simmer for 15 minutes or until the vegetables are tender and the relish begins to thicken. Stir frequently.

Carefully spoon mixture into hot sterilized jars. Seal, cool, and store.

# SUMMER SQUASH RELISH

yields approximately 3 pints

 2 *pounds yellow summer squash or zucchini*
 2 *small onions*
   *water*
¼ *cup salt*
 2 *cups distilled white vinegar*
 2 *cups sugar*
 1 *teaspoon celery seed*
 1 *teaspoon turmeric*
 2 *teaspoons mustard seed*

Wash, dry, trim, and thinly slice the squash. Peel and quarter the onions and cut into thin slices. Combine squash and onion together in a bowl. Pour in enough water to cover and add the salt. Let soak for 2 hours. Drain in a colander. Return vegetables to the bowl.

In a saucepan combine the vinegar, sugar, celery seed, turmeric, and mustard seed. Bring to a boil. Remove from heat and pour over vegetables. Let soak for 2 hours.

Turn the mixture into a large saucepan and bring to a boil. Boil for 15 minutes. Remove from heat and spoon into hot sterilized jars. Seal, cool, and store.

# PEAR AND PEPPER RELISH

yields approximately 2½ pints

6 firm fresh pears, cored
3 onions
3 green peppers
1 sweet red pepper
2 tablespoons salt
½ teaspoon crushed hot red pepper flakes
1 cup white vinegar
1 cup sugar

Coarsely chop the pears, onions, green peppers, and red pepper. Add the crushed hot red pepper flakes.

Place the mixture into a bowl. Season with the salt and let stand for 2 hours. Empty bowl into a colander and drain well.

In a large saucepan combine the vinegar and sugar. Add the vegetables. Stir. Bring the mixture to a boil. Reduce the heat and simmer for about 15 minutes. Stir frequently.

Carefully spoon the mixture into hot sterilized jars. Seal, cool, and store.

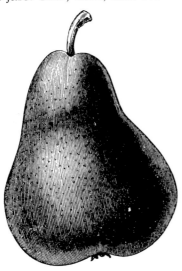

# BLUEBERRY RELISH

yields 1½ cups

1½ quarts fresh blueberries or 2 10-ounce packages frozen
1 apple, peeled, cored, and finely chopped
½ cup sugar
1 cinnamon stick
1 teaspoon whole cloves
4 teaspoons lemon juice
2 teaspoons cider vinegar
½ teaspoon Angostura bitters

Place the blueberries into a large saucepan. Stir in the apple, sugar, cinnamon, and cloves. Bring the mixture to a boil. Reduce the heat and simmer for 3 to 4 minutes. Add the lemon juice, vinegar, and bitters. Stir until just mixed. Remove from heat and cool.

When the mixture has cooled completely, pour into a strainer. Reserve the syrup. Discard the cinnamon stick and cloves. Chill the solid relish left in the strainer. It will keep well for 7 to 10 days in the refrigerator. Use the syrup to glaze a small ham.

# WALNUT GRAPE CONSERVE

yields 8 6-ounce jars

4 pounds Concord grapes
5 cups sugar
freshly grated rind of 2 oranges
juice of 2 oranges
⅛ teaspoon salt
1 cup seedless raisins
1 cup finely chopped walnuts

Wash the grapes and remove stems. Peel the grapes by pinching the end opposite the stem and squeezing grape out. Put the grape skins into a bowl and the peeled grapes into a saucepan. Cook over low heat for 5 to 8 minutes. Remove from heat. Press grapes through a sieve with the back of a spoon. Discard the seeds and solids left in the sieve.

Place the grape pulp back into the saucepan. Add the sugar, orange rind, orange juice, salt, and raisins. Mix well. Cook over low heat, stirring constantly, until sugar has dissolved. Raise the heat and bring mixture to a boil. Stir constantly until mixture is thick. Add the skins to the saucepan and cook 5 minutes longer or until very thick. Remove from heat and stir in walnuts.

Carefully spoon the mixture into 8 6-ounce hot sterilized jars. Seal, cool, and store.

# TOMATO GINGER MARMALADE

yields 1½ pints

9 medium ripe tomatoes (approximately 3 pounds)
    boiling water
2½ cups sugar
¼ cup lemon juice
    peel of 7 to 8 lemons
½ cup candied ginger, finely chopped

Cut the lemon peels into strips about ⅛ inch wide and 1 inch long. There should be about 1 cup.

Put the whole tomatoes into a pot of boiling water. Boil for 10 to 12 seconds. Drain and rinse tomatoes in cold water. Using a small paring knife, peel the tomatoes. Coarsely chop the tomatoes.

Place the tomato pieces into a large bowl. Add the sugar and mix gently. Let mixture stand for 1 hour, uncovered.

In a large saucepan combine the sugar and tomato mixture, the lemon juice, lemon peel, and candied ginger. Quickly bring the mixture to a boil, stirring constantly. Reduce heat and simmer until thick and solid, about 1 hour. Stir often.

Skim the top of the marmalade. Carefully spoon into hot sterilized jars. Seal, cool, and store.

# SPICY BLACKBERRY JAM

yields approximately 2 to 2½ pints

4 cups canned natural blackberry pulp
¼ teaspoon grated nutmeg
¼ teaspoon ground cloves
½ teaspoon ground cinnamon
3 cups sugar
1 tablespoon lemon juice

Place the blackberry pulp into a large saucepan and bring to a boil. Boil for 15 minutes.

Stir in the nutmeg, cloves, cinnamon, and sugar. Continue to boil rapidly for 45 minutes or until the mixture forms thick drops that stick to a spoon. Remove from heat and stir in the lemon juice.

Cool for 30 minutes. Stir and carefully spoon into hot sterilized jars. Seal, cool, and store.

# GINGER RHUBARB JAM

yields 3 cups

8 *cups fresh rhubarb, cut into ½-inch pieces (about 4 pounds)*
8 *cups sugar*
½ *cup water*
4 *ounces candied ginger, finely chopped*
½ *cup lemon juice*
¼ *cup lemon peel, finely chopped*

In a large saucepan combine the rhubarb, sugar, and water. Cook over low heat until the sugar is dissolved and the rhubarb is slightly soft. Stir constantly.

Raise the heat and bring the mixture to a boil. Cook, uncovered, over medium-high heat until the jam reaches the temperature of 221° on a candy thermometer. As jam starts to thicken, stir constantly and lower the heat slightly.

Remove the saucepan from the heat and add the ginger, lemon juice, and lemon peel. Skim the top of the jam.

Carefully spoon the jam into hot sterilized jars. Seal, cool, and store.

# BLACKBERRY VINEGAR

yields approximately 2 quarts

2 *quarts fresh blackberries*
1 *quart white wine vinegar*
  *sugar*

Place 4 cups of the blackberries into a deep jar or bowl. Pour the vinegar over them and let stand for 24 hours.

Strain the mixture through a double thickness of clean cheesecloth. Discard the blackberries. Add the remaining 4 cups blackberries to the strained mixture. Let stand for 24 hours.

Strain the mixture through a double thickness of clean cheesecloth. Put the berries back into the strained liquid and let stand 24 hours longer. Repeat the straining and standing process twice more, letting mixture stand 24 hours each time.

Measure the total amount of the strained liquid. Add 1 pound of sugar for each pint of liquid. Discard the remaining blackberries.

Place the liquid and sugar in a large saucepan and bring to a boil. Boil for 30 minutes, stirring frequently. Remove from heat and cool completely.

Bottle the vinegar and keep it in a cool place. It will keep for years, improving with age. Currant and cherry vinegar can be made using the same technique.

# THE WEST

When most people think of the West Coast, the most common images are of stunning scenery on one hand and movie stars on the other. Of course, what's really there is another matter altogether, but Americans like their myths reinforced. In actual fact, the cooking of the West Coast states is among the most original and constantly evolving of all.

Coming comparatively late into the Union, the West Coast states were originally outposts of Spain, Russia and England. As such, much of the south of the border touch is in evidence, especially in Southern California. But it is evidenced in dishes that have virtually no recognizable counterpart in Mexico itself. Chili con carne is a prime example of a distinctly American dish, yet one with undeniable Mexican roots.

In the Northwest, Russian methods of smoking fish and several unusual fish chowders have left their marks. And all along the coast, the many fishermen who naturally migrated to the bounteous Pacific waters brought their native foods with them, to be modified by time and the contents of the river. Cioppino, the pungent fish stew of the Portugese fishermen of San Francisco Bay, is one "new" dish of this provenance.

The immensely fertile valleys of the West Coast have allowed the cultivation of crops that have changed more than just the region's cooking. Almonds, avocados, grapes, citrus fruits, artichokes and herbs in abundance have, since the development of transcontinental shipping, made for more varied tables across the nation.

All those prunes and apricots have brought an astringently sweet tang to the nation's breakfast tables and desserts. And the California wine industry, in the short years since Prohibition, has made the drinking of wine—both American and imported—a far, far more common occurance than it had been.

But it is in California that the most exciting new cooking is being developed. Here, amidst the good life, a new generation of chefs are sparking a renaissance in the subtle and imaginative use of native products in unusual combinations. Chefs such as Alice Waters and Wolfgang Puck have created international reputations by taking simple ingredients of the best quality and bringing out their native characteristics to the full. Essentially a fresh, simple approach to eating, the "new" California cuisine has converted thousands to its healthful approach.

Lifestyles play a major role in what people eat. Gone are the salt pork and 'taters of grandfathers' days. We are all trying to eat more healthfully and stay more youthful. The West Coast region, despite its hearty approach, is filled with people who spend much of their days in the sun, who may well be fitter, livelier and more prone to vanity. No wonder the food revolution started there, albeit influenced by European chefs of the nouvelle cuisine. The melting pot gets clarified!

# Suggested Menus

## SUMMER BARBECUE
for 6
Pasta Salad with
Broccoli, Tomatoes, and Olives
Grilled Chicken Halves
Grated Zucchini
Spinach Salad
Apricot Walnut Bars or
Fig and Nut Squares
Beer, Lemonade, Iced Tea, or Sparkling Water
Wines: Chardonnay or Chenin Blanc

## AFTER-SKI BUFFET DINNER
for 4 to 6
Hot Buttered Rum
San Francisco Lentil Salad
Veal Stew with Sweet Potato Dumplings
Hawaiian Ginger Carrots
Pecan Coffee Cake
Beer or Sparkling Water
Wines: Chenin Blanc or Chardonnay

## SPRINGTIME DINNER PARTY
for 6 to 8
West Coast Cucumber Bisque
Columbia River Baked Salmon
Green Beans with Dill Sauce
Lemon Rice
Sacramento Salad
Mocha Café Soufflé
Sparkling Water or Iced Tea
Wines: Chardonnay or Chenin Blanc

## FAMILY DINNER
for 6
Portland Leek and Potato Soup
Roast Lamb
California Relish
Turnips with Coriander
Baked Rice and Onions
Tossed Green Salad with Vinaigrette Dressing
Chocolate Triple Layer Cake or
Chocolate Yogurt Cheesecake
Iced Tea, Beer, or Sparkling Water
Wines: Cabernet Sauvignon, Zinfandel, or Pinot Noir

## SUNDAY LUNCHEON

(choose one or both menus)

for 4

MENU 1:
Fennel Salad
Goat Cheese Soufflé
Sweet Walnut Bread
Blueberry Butter Cake
Coffee, Tea, or Sparkling Water
Wines: Chenin Blanc or Chardonnay

MENU 2:
Chilled Avocado Soup
Crabmeat Salad with Hot Caper Dressing
Orange Grove Rye Bread
Hazelnut Cookies or Coconut Pecan Squares
Coffee, Tea, or Sparkling Water
Wines: Chenin Blanc or Chardonnay

## WEST COAST CHRISTMAS DINNER

for 6

Paté-Stuffed Mushrooms
Honeyed Duck
Pineapple and Raisin Chutney
Sautéed Leeks
Marinated Fried Mushrooms
Ensalada de Verdolaga (Purslane Salad)
Sourdough Rolls
Fresh Fruit Tart and Lemon Sorbet
Wines: Gamay Beaujolais, Chardonnay, or Pinot Noir

## RELAXING SATURDAY BREAKFAST

(choose one or both menus)

for 4

MENU 1:
Valley Fruit Salad
Seattle Puff Pancakes with
Lemon Butter and Peach Honey or
Pear Syrup
Willamette Valley Apple Bread
Coffee, Tea, or Milk

MENU 2:
Orange or Grapefruit Juice
Western Omelet
Buttered Toast with
Tomato Ginger Preserves
Coffee, Tea, or Milk

# Soups and Appetizers

## CHILLED AVOCADO SOUP

serves 4 to 6

2 ripe avocados, peeled and mashed
2 cups chicken broth
1 teaspoon salt
1 teaspoon dried tarragon, crumbled
¼ teaspoon Tabasco sauce
1 tablespoon lemon juice
1 cup light cream
  fresh chives, chopped

Place the avocados and the chicken broth in the container of an electric blender or food processor. Blend until smooth. Add the salt, tarragon, Tabasco, and lemon juice. Blend again. Add the cream and blend until just mixed.

Chill in refrigerator for at least 1 hour. Serve in chilled bowls garnished with fresh chives.

## WEST COAST CUCUMBER BISQUE

serves 8

2 large cucumbers
1 small clove garlic, crushed
1 teaspoon salt
½ teaspoon dried dill
1 tablespoon chives, chopped
1 teaspoon lemon juice
2 cups sour cream
2 cups half-and-half
1 to 2 cups milk
8 cucumber slices, unpeeled

Peel and seed the cucumbers. Place cucumbers into the container of an electric blender or food processor. Add the garlic, salt, dill, chives, and lemon juice. Blend mixture until smooth.

Empty the container into a large mixing bowl. Add the sour cream, half-and-half, and enough milk to produce the desired thickness. Stir until well blended.

Chill in the refrigerator for 4 to 5 hours.

Serve in chilled bowls garnished with cucumber slices.

## CREAM OF ARTICHOKE SOUP

serves 4

1½ tablespoons butter
 1 tablespoon flour
 ½ teaspoon salt
 ⅛ teaspoon cayenne pepper
 ⅛ teaspoon grated nutmeg
 3 cups water
 4 cooked artichoke hearts, mashed
 ½ cup heavy cream
 1 egg yolk, beaten
 3 tablespoons dry white wine

Melt the butter in a medium saucepan. Stir in the flour, salt, cayenne, and nutmeg. Slowly stir in the water. Continue stirring and add the artichokes. Cook for 2 minutes.

In a small bowl combine the heavy cream, egg yolk, and wine. Mix until well blended.

*(continued on next page)*

Slowly add the cream mixture to the artichoke mixture. Stir constantly. Continue cooking until the soup is just under the boiling point. Do not let soup boil.

Remove from heat and serve.

# L.A. GAZPACHO

serves 4 to 6

      3 *pounds tomatoes*
      2 *cucumbers*
      2 *cloves garlic, finely chopped*
    ½ *cup green pepper, chopped*
    ½ *cup onion, chopped*
      2 *cups chilled tomato juice*
    ⅓ *cup olive oil*
      3 *tablespoons vinegar*
    ¼ *teaspoon Tabasco*
        *salt and pepper to taste*

Peel, seed, and finely chop the tomatoes. Save as much of the juice as possible. Place the tomatoes in a large bowl. Add the garlic.

Peel, seed, and finely chop the cucumbers. Add to the tomatoes, along with the green pepper, onion, and tomato juice. Stir. Add the olive oil, vinegar, Tabasco, and salt and pepper to taste. Stir until well blended.

Cover the bowl and chill in the refrigerator for 3 to 4 hours. Remove and season to taste with salt and pepper.

Serve in chilled bowls garnished with croutons or chopped raw vegetables.

# PORTLAND LEEK AND POTATO SOUP

serves 4

      5 *leeks, thinly sliced (white parts only)*
      3 *tablespoons butter*
      4 *cups potatoes, peeled and diced*
      4 *cups chicken broth*
    1½ *teaspoons salt*
    ⅛ *teaspoon cayenne pepper*
        *grated nutmeg*

Melt the butter in a saucepan. Add the leeks and sauté until soft but not brown, about 5 minutes. Stir in the potatoes, chicken broth, salt, and cayenne. Cook over moderate heat until the potatoes are soft, about 15 to 20 minutes.

Remove from heat. Mash the potatoes thoroughly and strain the liquid to remove any remaining solids. Return mixture to the saucepan and reheat for 2 minutes. Serve hot garnished with grated nutmeg.

# BAJA CREAM OF ALMOND SOUP

serves 4 to 6

    1½ *cups whole blanched almonds*
      6 *cups chicken broth*
      1 *small onion*
      2 *bay leaves*
      3 *tablespoons butter*
      2 *tablespoons flour*
      1 *cup milk*
      1 *cup heavy cream*
    ⅛ *teaspoon ground cardamom*
        *salt and pepper to taste*

In a blender or food processor, grind the almonds finely. There should be approximately 2½ cups

Place ground almonds in a saucepan. Add the chicken broth, onion, and bay leaves. Bring to a boil. Reduce heat to very low, cover, and simmer for 30 minutes. Remove from heat and keep warm. Remove bay leaves.

Melt the butter in a saucepan. Add the flour and stir. Cook over low heat for 2 minutes. Stir constantly; do not brown. Stir in the milk and continue cooking, stirring constantly, until sauce is smooth and thick. Add sauce to the almond mixture and stir to blend.

Cook the soup over low heat for 5 to 6 minutes, stirring constantly. Remove from heat and stir in cream and cardamom. Add salt and pepper to taste. Return to heat and cook until heated through. Do not allow soup to boil.

Serve hot or chill for 3 to 4 hours and serve cold.

## SPIKED CRABMEAT SOUP

serves 6 to 8

1 *small head cauliflower*
2 *zucchini, sliced*
1 *onion, thinly sliced*
1 *cup light rum*
7 *cups chicken broth*
1 *bay leaf*
  *salt and pepper to taste*
1 *cup cooked crabmeat*

Wash the cauliflower and break into flowerets.

In a large saucepan combine the cauliflower, zucchini, onion, rum, and chicken broth. Add the bay leaf and simmer, uncovered, for 15 to 20 minutes or until vegetables are tender.

Remove the bay leaf and season to taste with salt and pepper. Stir in the crabmeat and simmer until piping hot. Serve at once.

## FISHERMAN'S WHARF HALIBUT BROTH

serves 4

2 *pounds fresh halibut, cleaned, boned, and cut into pieces*
1 *cup dry white wine*
4 *cups water*
1 *teaspoon lemon juice*
1 *clove garlic, crushed*
1 *bay leaf*
2 *tablespoons olive oil*
1 *teaspoon salt*
½ *teaspoon pepper*
  *freshly grated Parmesan cheese*

In a large pot, combine the halibut, white wine, water, lemon juice, garlic, bay leaf, olive oil, salt, and pepper. Bring mixture to boil. Reduce the heat and simmer, covered, for 30 minutes.

Remove from heat and serve immediately. Sprinkle with Parmesan cheese.

# DUNGENESS CRABMEAT BISQUE

serves 6

4 tablespoons butter
½ cup onions, finely chopped
½ stalk celery, finely chopped
2 tablespoons flour
¼ teaspoon paprika
1 teaspoon salt
⅛ teaspoon pepper
2 cups milk
2 cups heavy cream
2 cups cooked Dungeness crabmeat
¼ cup dry sherry

Melt the butter in a large saucepan. Add the celery and onion and cook over moderate heat for 5 minutes or until the vegetables are tender but not brown. Stir often. Stir in the flour, paprika, salt, and pepper. Mix well.

Whisk in the milk and cream, pouring them in a slow, thin stream. Quickly bring the mixture to a boil. Stir constantly to be sure that soup is smooth. Reduce heat and simmer gently for 3 minutes.

Add the crabmeat. Stir well and simmer 3 minutes longer or until mixture is heated through. Stir in the sherry, a little at a time. Remove from heat and serve at once.

Dungeness crabs are large crustaceans found all along the Pacific coast.

# PACIFIC MUSSEL SOUP

serves 6 to 8

50 mussels
1 quart water
1 onion, coarsely chopped
2 bay leaves
3 tablespoons olive oil
1 leek, finely chopped (white part only)
½ pound raw rice
¼ teaspoon saffron
1 tomato, coarsely chopped

Scrub and debeard the mussels. Put the mussels in a large pot with the water, onion, and bay leaves. Cook until the mussels open, about 5 minutes. Drain and reserve the both. Shell the mussels and set aside.

Heat the olive oil in a saucepan. Add the chopped leek and sauté until golden brown, about 8 to 10 minutes.

Add the mussel broth, rice, and saffron. Simmer until the rice is tender, about 20 minutes. Stir in the mussels and the chopped tomato. Boil for 1 minute. Remove the bay leaves and serve hot.

# CHICKEN LIVER SPREAD

serves 4

2 tablespoons butter
1 medium onion, minced
½ pound fresh chicken livers
⅓ cup sherry
salt and pepper to taste
¼ teaspoon Tabasco sauce
2 tablespoons brandy

Trim the chicken livers and cut into pieces.

Melt the butter in a skillet. Add the onion and sauté until soft and golden brown, about 6 to 8 minutes.

Add the chicken livers, sherry, salt, pepper, and Tabasco. Simmer gently, uncovered, for 15 to 20 minutes.

Place the mixture in the container of a blender or food processor. Blend until smooth. Turn out into a bowl.

Stir in the brandy, 1 tablespoon at a time. Serve with crackers or bread.

# HAWAIIAN SHRIMP BALLS

serves 4 to 6

- 2 cups cooked shrimp, chopped
- 2 eggs, beaten
- 1 clove garlic, crushed
- ¼ cup bread crumbs
- ⅛ teaspoon pepper
- ½ teaspoon salt
- 1 tablespoon fresh parsley, chopped, or 1 teaspoon dried
- ⅛ teaspoon grated nutmeg
  vegetable oil for frying

In a large bowl combine the shrimp, eggs, garlic, bread crumbs, pepper, salt, parsley, and nutmeg. Mix well. Form the mixture into balls approximately 1 to 1½ inches in diameter.

In a deep skillet heat the oil until it is very hot, 365° on a deep-fat thermometer. Fry the balls until golden brown, about 3 to 4 minutes. Turn often to brown evenly. Remove from the oil with a slotted spoon and drain on paper towels. Serve hot.

# ALMOND-AVOCADO BUTTER

serves 6 to 8

- 3 medium avocados
- 2 tablespoons lemon juice
- 1 cup butter, softened
- ½ teaspoon Worcestershire sauce
- ⅛ teaspoon cayenne pepper
- ½ cup chopped almonds

Preheat the oven to 375°.

Spread the almonds evenly in a metal pan and toast in oven for 3 to 5 minutes. Remove from oven and cool.

Halve the avocados. Remove the pits and discard. Scoop the pulp out of the halves and reserve the skins.

In a large mixing bowl combine the avocado pulp, lemon juice, butter, Worcestershire sauce, and cayenne. Blend until smooth. Stir in almonds and mix well.

Spoon mixture into the reserved avocado skins. Serve at room temperature with crackers and bread.

# CALIFORNIA WALNUT SPREAD

serves 6 to 8

- 2 hard-cooked eggs
- ½ cup finely chopped walnuts
- 1 cup sharp Cheddar cheese, grated
- ½ cup scallions, finely chopped
- ¼ cup green olives, pitted and finely chopped
- 3 tablespoons chili sauce

*(continued on next page)*

Preheat the oven to 375°.

Spread the chopped walnuts evenly in a metal pan and toast in oven for 3 to 5 minutes. Remove from oven and cool.

In a bowl chop the hard-cooked eggs as finely as possible. Add the walnuts, cheese, scallions, olives, and chili sauce. Mix until well blended.

Cover and chill for 3 to 4 hours. Serve with crackers or bread.

## PICKLED SALMON

serves 6

1 cup distilled white vinegar
1 cup water
2 tablespoons olive oil
1 small onion, thinly sliced
1 bay leaf
1 teaspoon mustard seed
1 teaspoon whole cloves
1 teaspoon white peppercorns
1 teaspoon black peppercorns
2½ pounds fresh salmon, boned, skinned, and cubed
1½ teaspoons salt

In a large saucepan, combine the vinegar, water, olive oil, onions, bay leaf, mustard seeds, cloves, white peppercorns, and black peppercorns. Quickly bring the mixture to a boil. Reduce the heat and simmer, loosely covered, for 45 minutes.

In the meantime, place the salmon pieces on a piece of wax paper. Season with salt and let stand for 30 minutes at room temperature. Transfer pieces to a colander and rinse thoroughly with cold water. Drain well and gently pat dry.

Place the salmon pieces in glass jars or crocks. Pour the hot vinegar mixture over the salmon, a little at a time. Always allow the liquid to settle to the bottom before adding more.

Cool the salmon to room temperature. Cover jars tightly with aluminum foil and refrigerate for at least 24 hours. Salmon will keep well in refrigerator for 1 week.

## SAN FRANCISCO CHICKEN WINGS

serves 4 to 5

3 pounds chicken wings
½ cup butter
1 cup soy sauce
1 cup light brown sugar, firmly packed
¾ cup water
½ teaspoon dry mustard
¼ teaspoon cinnamon

Place the wings in a shallow 11 × 7 × 2-inch baking pan.

In a saucepan combine the butter, soy sauce, sugar, water, mustard, and cinnamon. Cook over moderate heat until the butter melts and the sugar dissolves. Remove from heat and cool completely.

Pour mixture over chicken wings and marinate for 2 to 2½ hours. Turn occasionally.

Preheat the oven to 375°. Bake wings for 1½ hours, turning every 20 minutes. Remove from oven, drain briefly on paper towels, and serve.

# Salads

## MARINATED ARTICHOKE HEARTS

serves 4

4 large artichokes
1 lemon, halved
cold water
⅓ cup olive oil
¼ cup distilled white vinegar
10 whole black peppercorns
2 cloves garlic, sliced
2 bay leaves
1 teaspoon sugar
1 teaspoon dried basil
½ teaspoon salt
5 thin lemon slices

Cut off the stems of the artichokes and discard. Snap off the outer leaves, breaking them close to the base, and discard. Continue to remove and discard leaves until the inner pale leaves are exposed. Trim the bases and sides of the artichokes. Cut off the top ½ inch of the hearts.

Cut the hearts lengthwise into 8 pieces. With a spoon, carefully remove the chokes and discard. Rub the pieces with 1 of the lemon halves. Place the pieces into a bowl of cold water. Add the juice of the remaining lemon half.

Combine the oil, vinegar, peppercorns, garlic, bay leaves, sugar, basil, salt, and lemon slices in a saucepan. Quickly bring the mixture to a boil. Reduce the heat, cover, and simmer for 10 minutes.

Drain the artichoke hearts and add them to the simmering mixture in the saucepan. Loosely cover the saucepan and simmer for 30 to 40 minutes longer or until the hearts are just tender.

Remove from heat and allow the hearts to cool in the liquid. Refrigerate for at least 1 hour. Serve chilled.

## ENSALADA DE VERDOLAGA (PURSLANE SALAD)

serves 6 to 8

2 pounds purslane
4 tablespoons olive oil
1 tablespoon tarragon or red wine vinegar
½ teaspoon salt
pepper to taste
1 medium onion, sliced

Wash, drain, and dry the purslane.

In a large salad bowl combine the oil, vinegar, salt, and pepper. Whisk together until well blended.

Add the sliced onions and purslane to the dressing. Toss well. Refrigerate until ready to serve.

*Verdolaga* or purslane grows wild in many parts of southern California. Good substitutes are chicory, watercress, or dandelion leaves.

# SACRAMENTO SALAD

serves 4

8  *large romaine lettuce leaves*
1  *large clove garlic, halved*
1  *stalk celery, chopped*
1  *bunch watercress, chopped*
2  *cups black olives, pitted and chopped*
3  *tablespoons olive oil*
1  *tablespoon red wine vinegar*
1  *teaspoon salt*
   *pepper to taste*
2  *small ripe tomatoes, sliced*

Wash, drain, and gently dry the lettuce leaves.

Rub a large wooden salad bowl with the garlic halves. Discard garlic.

In the salad bowl combine the lettuce, celery, watercress, olives, oil, vinegar, salt, and pepper. Toss until well mixed. Add the sliced tomatoes. Mix gently but thoroughly. Avoid breaking the tomato slices. Serve at once.

# CAESAR SALAD

serves 4 to 6

 2  *heads romaine lettuce*
 2  *cups unflavored croutons*
¾  *cup olive oil*
 3  *garlic cloves, crushed*
 1  *teaspoon salt*
15  *anchovy fillets, finely chopped*
 2  *tablespoons lemon juice*
 1  *egg*
    *pepper to taste*
¾  *cup freshly grated Parmesan cheese*

Wash and dry the lettuce. Chill in refrigerator.

In a skillet heat ¼ cup of the olive oil with the garlic cloves. When oil is hot add the croutons. Sauté briefly. Remove and drain on paper towels.

Remove the lettuce from the refrigerator. Tear into bite-size pieces and place in a chilled large salad bowl. Add the remaining olive oil and toss until lettuce is well coated. Add the croutons, salt, anchovies, pepper, and lemon juice.

Break the egg into the salad bowl. Toss until well blended. Add the grated cheese and serve at once.

# SPINACH SALAD

serves 4

1  *pound fresh spinach*
4  *slices bacon*
¼  *cup olive oil*
¼  *cup red wine vinegar*
2  *tablespoons lemon juice*
½  *teaspoon sugar*
1  *teaspoon salt*
   *pepper to taste*

Thoroughly wash the spinach. Discard any tough stems and blemished leaves. Pat the spinach dry and tear into bite-size pieces. Place in a salad bowl and set aside.

Fry the bacon in a skillet over moderate heat until slices are brown and crisp. Remove from skillet and drain on paper towels. When drained and cool, crumble.

Pour off the bacon drippings from the skillet and add the olive oil. Add the crumbled bacon bits to the skillet and cook briefly over high heat for 2 to 3 seconds. Stir constantly.

Remove from heat. Add the vinegar, lemon juice, sugar, salt, and pepper to the skillet and whisk. Pour the dressing over the spinach and toss well. Serve immediately.

# SAN FRANCISCO LENTIL SALAD

serves 4 to 6

  2 *cups dried lentils*
    *water*
    *salt*
  1 *onion*
  1 *bay leaf*
  1 *teaspoon dried thyme*
1½ *cups scallions, finely chopped*
 ½ *cup olive oil*
  1 *clove garlic, finely chopped*
  4 *tablespoons wine vinegar*
1½ *teaspoons pepper*
 ½ *cup parsley, chopped*

Place the lentils in a pot and add enough cold water to cover. Salt the water and add the onion, bay leaf, and thyme. Quickly bring lentils to a boil. Reduce the heat and simmer, covered, until lentils are just tender, about 45 to 50 minutes. Do not overcook. Discard the onions and bay leaf. Drain lentils well and place in a mixing bowl.

Add the scallions, olive oil, garlic, vinegar, and pepper. Toss well and allow the salad to cool. Add the parsley and adjust the seasonings. More oil and vinegar may be needed. Serve on crisp lettuce leaves. This salad ages well, but the parsley should be added immediately before serving.

# HOT POTATO SALAD WITH LEMON DRESSING

serves 4

  8 *small new potatoes, quartered*
    *boiling water*
  1 *teaspoon salt*
  1 *medium red onion, thinly sliced and separated into rings*
  3 *tablespoons lemon juice*
 ½ *cup olive oil*
 ½ *cup celery, sliced*
 ¼ *cup parsley, chopped*

Place the potatoes in a saucepan and cover with 1 inch of boiling water. Add ½ teaspoon salt and quickly bring the mixture to a boil. Reduce the heat, cover, and simmer for 20 minutes or until potatoes are just tender. Drain well.

As potatoes cook, crisp the onion rings in cold water for 10 to 12 minutes. Drain well.

In a large bowl combine the lemon juice, ½ teaspoon salt, pepper, olive oil, celery, parsley, and onion rings. Mix well. Add the hot potato pieces and toss gently to blend well. Serve at once while hot.

# FENNEL SALAD

serves 4

1 medium fennel
4 radishes, thinly sliced
2 oranges, peeled and sectioned
4 black olives, pitted and halved
4 tablespoons onion, minced
    several torn feathers from fennel
6 tablespoons olive oil
3 tablespoons cider vinegar
1 teaspoon Pernod or anisette
½ teaspoon salt
⅛ teaspoon cayenne pepper

Slice the bulb and stalks of the fennel into rings. Place in a serving bowl. Arrange the radishes, orange sections, olive, onion, and torn fennel feathers around the fennel.

In a mixing bowl whisk together the oil, vinegar, Pernod, salt, and pepper. Pour over the salad and serve.

# KOREAN SALAD

serves 4

1 cup bean sprouts
2 bunches watercress
2 tablespoons soy sauce
2 tablespoons rice wine vinegar or lemon juice
4 tablespoons scallions, chopped
4 tablespoons sesame seeds, toasted
1 teaspoon sesame oil
    salt and pepper to taste

Blanch the bean sprouts for 1 minute in a pot of boiling water. Drain well.

Trim the tough stems from the watercress. Combine with bean sprouts in a bowl.

Preheat the oven to 375°.

Place the sesame seeds in a metal pan and toast in oven for 3 to 5 minutes or until golden. Remove and cool.

In a mixing bowl combine the soy sauce, rice wine vinegar, scallions, sesame seeds, and sesame oil. Whisk until well blended.

Pour dressing over bean sprouts and watercress. Season to taste and chill before serving.

# PASTA SALAD WITH BROCCOLI, TOMATOES, AND OLIVES

serves 4

1 pound corkscrew-shaped pasta
1 tablespoon olive oil
1 head broccoli, broken into flowerets
2 large tomatoes, peeled, seeded, and chopped
1 cup black olives, pitted and sliced
Dressing:
2 tablespoons red wine vinegar
2 cloves garlic, finely chopped
4 tablespoons fresh basil, chopped
1 teaspoon salt
½ teaspoon pepper
4 tablespoons olive oil
½ cup freshly grated Parmesan cheese

Cook the pasta in a large pot of salted boiling water for 10 minutes or until tender. Drain, rinse with cold water, and drain well again.

Cook the broccoli flowerets in a saucepan with 1 inch of boiling water, or steam them for 5 minutes, until just cooked but still crisp. Drain and rinse in cold water.

In a large bowl, combine the vinegar, garlic, basil, salt, and pepper. Slowly whisk in the olive oil. Add the cheese and continue to whisk.

Place the broccoli, pasta, tomatoes, and olives in a large bowl. Slowly add the dressing and toss. Serve at room temperature.

# CRABMEAT SALAD WITH HOT CAPER DRESSING

serves 4

*5 cups romaine lettuce, torn into bite-size pieces*
*1 cup warm cooked crabmeat*
*½ cup olive oil*
*3 tablespoons red wine vinegar*
*3 tablespoons drained capers*
*½ teaspoon salt*
*½ teaspoon dried oregano*
*¼ teaspoon pepper*

Place the romaine lettuce and the crabmeat in a salad bowl. Set aside.

In a saucepan combine the olive oil, vinegar, capers, garlic, salt, oregano, and pepper. Heat just to the boiling point.

Remove from heat and pour dressing over the lettuce and crabmeat. Toss well and serve at once.

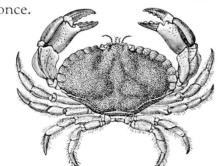

# PEAR SALAD

serves 4

*4 Bartlett pears*
*1 clove garlic, crushed*
*1 teaspoon salt*
*1½ teaspoons sugar*
*½ teaspoon dried tarragon, crumbled*
*½ teaspoon dried basil, crumbled*
*¼ cup red wine vinegar*
*¼ cup olive oil*
*¼ cup water*
*1 tablespoon sherry*
*1 cup celery, coarsely chopped*
*1 cup green pepper, coarsely chopped*
*½ cup scallions, sliced*
*2 large ripe tomatoes, finely chopped*
*4 romaine lettuce leaves, chilled*

Wash the pears and refrigerate.

In a bowl mix together the garlic, salt, and sugar. Add the tarragon, basil, vinegar, oil, water, and sherry. Whisk until well blended. Transfer to a 16-ounce jar, cover, and let stand for 1 to 1½ hours.

Place the celery, green pepper, scallions, and tomatoes into a bowl. Chill for 1 hour.

Remove the vegetables and pears from the refrigerator. Shake the dressing to mix well. Pour half the dressing over the vegetables and toss.

Place 1 lettuce leaf on each of 4 serving plates.

Halve and core the pears. Arrange 2 pear halves, cut-side up, on each lettuce leaf. Top with the dressed vegetables. Spoon the remaining dressing over the pears and serve.

# FRESH TUNA SALAD

serves 6 to 8

       1 cup white wine vinegar
       2 garlic cloves, crushed
       1 tablespoon hot red pepper flakes
       1 tablespoon pepper
    1½ cups olive oil
       1 onion, thinly sliced
       2 bay leaves
       2 pounds tuna fillet, cubed
       2 cups canned chick peas, rinsed and drained
      20 brine-cured black olives

Combine the vinegar, garlic, red pepper flakes, and pepper in a mixing bowl. Slowly whisk in 1 cup olive oil. Continue whisking until dressing is well blended.

Add the onion, bay leaves, and tuna. Stir the mixture and marinate the tuna in the bowl overnight in the refrigerator. Cover bowl with aluminum foil. Stir occasionally.

When ready to serve, drain the tuna and reserve the marinade. Remove the bay leaves and discard.

Combine the tuna and chick peas in a bowl.

In a small bowl combine ¼ cup of the reserved marinade. Whisk in the remaining ½ cup olive oil until the mixture is well blended. Season to taste with salt and pepper.

Pour the dressing over the tuna mixture and toss well. Transfer salad to a serving dish and garnish with olives. Serve at once.

# CALIFORNIA CHICKEN SALAD

serves 4

    2 cups cold cooked chicken breast, cubed
    ½ cup celery, finely chopped
    ⅓ cup black olives, pitted and sliced
    2 tablespoons lemon juice
      salt and pepper to taste
      Tabasco sauce to taste
    2 large ripe avocados

In a bowl combine the chicken, celery, and sliced olives. Add the lemon juice, salt, pepper, and Tabasco. Stir to mix well.

Halve the avocados. Remove the pits and scoop out the avocado pulp. Reserve the avocado shells. Dice the pulp and add to the chicken mixture. Stir carefully to mix well.

Fill each avocado shell with chicken salad and serve.

# ·Dairy Dishes·

## WESTERN OMELET

serves 4

8 eggs
1 teaspoon salt
¼ teaspoon pepper
6 tablespoons cold water
1 cup bacon, diced
½ cup onions, chopped
1 large green pepper, diced

In a bowl beat the eggs together with the salt, pepper, and water.

Fry the bacon in a large skillet for about 5 minutes. Pour off most of the bacon drippings, leaving the bacon pieces in the skillet. Add the onions and green pepper. Cook, stirring occasionally, for 10 minutes. Add the eggs and cook over very low heat. Lift the edges of the omelet as it cooks to allow the uncooked portions to run underneath. When omelet is set turn it out of the skillet onto a serving plate.

Cut omelet into four portions and serve.

## SAN DIEGO OMELET

serves 4

4 cups potatoes, peeled and thinly sliced
4 cups cold water
1 teaspoon salt
½ cup olive oil
¾ cup ham, chopped
6 eggs, beaten

Place the potatoes in a large bowl. Cover with the cold water and salt. Soak for 4 hours. Drain well and pat dry.

In a large skillet heat the oil. Add the potatoes and sauté until lightly browned, about 5 to 8 minutes. Smooth the potatoes into an even layer. Sprinkle evenly with the ham and add the eggs. Reduce heat and cook until the bottom of the omelet is golden brown. Place a large plate over the pan and turn the omelet onto the plate. Slide the uncooked side of the omelet back into the pan. Continue to cook until golden brown. Serve hot.

## DRIED BEEF WITH EGGS

serves 4

1 pound dried chipped beef, shredded
   cold water
6 tablespoons olive oil
1 small onion, minced
1 clove garlic, minced
1 teaspoon vinegar
4 tablespoons canned tomatoes, chopped
2 eggs, lightly beaten

Soak the dried beef in cold water to cover for 1 hour. Drain well and pat dry.

Heat the olive oil in a large skillet. Add the beef, onion, garlic, and vinegar. Fry the mixture until the beef is brown, about 5 to 8 minutes. Add the tomatoes and continue cooking over low heat until the mixture is almost dry, about 10 to 15 minutes. Stir in the eggs and cook for 4 minutes or until the eggs are creamy.

Serve on toast or with tortillas.

# SPANISH OMELET

serves 4

½ cup green pepper, finely chopped
¾ cup onion, finely chopped
2 tablespoons butter
4 tablespoons olive oil
1 cup fresh mushrooms, sliced
2 cups canned tomatoes, drained
1 clove garlic, finely chopped
1 teaspoon salt
1 teaspoon pepper
¼ teaspoon Tabasco sauce
8 eggs
2 tablespoons butter

In a skillet heat the olive oil and 2 tablespoons butter. Add the green pepper and onion. Cook until soft but not brown, about 3 to 5 minutes. Stir in the mushrooms, tomatoes, and garlic; continue cooking for 5 minutes longer. Add the salt, pepper, and Tabasco sauce. Simmer until the mixture is well blended and thickened, about 15 to 20 minutes.

In a bowl beat 4 eggs until foamy.

Melt 1 tablespoon butter in a skillet. When butter is hot pour in the eggs and cook over moderate heat. Lift the edges of the omelet to allow the uncooked portions to run underneath. When omelet is lightly browned on the bottom and set on the top, spoon in half the filling. Carefully fold the omelet and slide it out of the pan. Repeat with the remaining eggs and filling to make a second omelet. Each omelet serves 2.

For a spicier omelet with a Mexican touch, add some chopped green chilies to the filling.

# SPINACH FRITTATA

serves 4

2 cloves garlic, minced
1 onion thinly, sliced
4 tablespoons olive oil
2 cups spinach, cooked, chopped, and well drained
   (2 pounds fresh spinach or 3 packages frozen, thawed
   and pressed dry)
1 teaspoon salt
½ teaspoon pepper
¼ teaspoon nutmeg
8 eggs, lightly beaten
½ cup freshly grated Parmesan cheese

In a large skillet heat the olive oil. Add the garlic and onion and sauté until onion is just limp, about 2 to 3 minutes. Add the spinach and cook until heated through. Stir to blend. Add the salt, pepper, and nutmeg.

Pour the eggs over the mixture in the skillet. Cook over medium heat until eggs are set. Place a large plate over the skillet and turn the omelet onto the plate. Slide the uncooked side of the omelet back into the pan and sprinkle with cheese. Cook until golden brown.

When omelet is set, slide onto a plate and cut into wedges. Serve hot.

# CARROT SOUFFLE

serves 4

3 medium carrots
   boiling salted water
3 tablespoons butter
3 tablespoons flour
1 cup milk
½ teaspoon salt
4 eggs, separated

Preheat the oven to 375°.

Peel and finely chop the carrots. Place them in a pot of boiling salted water and cook until just tender, about 8 to 10 minutes. Drain well and mash.

In a skillet melt the butter. Add the flour and blend well, stirring constantly. Gradually stir in the milk. Continue cooking over low heat until mixture is smooth and thick. Remove from heat. Stir in the salt and cool.

In a bowl beat the egg yolks until light and lemon-colored, about 3 minutes. Add to the slightly cooled milk mixture. Add the mashed carrots. Stir well.

In a small bowl beat the egg whites until stiff but not dry. Fold egg whites into the carrot mixture, half at a time. Turn into a buttered 2-quart soufflé dish. Bake for 35 to 40 minutes or until puffed and lightly browned. Remove from oven and serve *immediately.*

# GOAT CHEESE SOUFFLE

serves 4 to 6

  2 tablespoons butter
  2 tablespoons flour
 ¾ cup half-and-half
  3 eggs, separated
1⅓ cups goat cheese, crumbled
  4 teaspoons chives, chopped
  1 teaspoon dried oregano
    salt and pepper to taste
    grated nutmeg to taste

Preheat the oven to 400°.

In a saucepan melt the butter. Add the flour and stir until well blended. Gradually stir in the half-and-half.

Cook, stirring constantly, until mixture is smooth and thick. Remove from heat.

In a small bowl beat the egg yolks. Gradually stir yolks into the half-and-half mixture. Return saucepan to low heat and stir in the goat cheese, oregano, salt, pepper, and nutmeg. Cook, stirring constantly, until mixture is smooth and creamy. Do not allow mixture to boil. Remove from heat and cool to room temperature. Adjust seasonings.

In a bowl beat the egg whites until stiff but not dry. Fold into the goat cheese mixture. Fold in the chopped chives.

Turn the mixture into a lightly buttered 1½-quart soufflé dish. Place the dish in pan of hot water and place in oven. Bake for 25 to 30 minutes or until top is browned. Serve *immediately.*

# HOLLYWOOD LEMON SOUFFLE

serves 6

  4 eggs, separated
  1 cup sugar
    grated rind of 1 large lemon
    juice of 1 large lemon
 ⅛ teaspoon salt
    sugar
    confectioner's sugar

Preheat the oven to 325°.

In a bowl beat the egg yolks until thick and lemon-colored, about 3 minutes. Slowly beat in ½ cup sugar. Add the lemon rind and lemon juice.

*(continued on next page)*

In a separate bowl beat the egg whites with salt until foamy. Slowly beat in the remaining ½ cup sugar. Beat until whites are stiff and hold a peak. Fold the egg whites gently into the yolk mixture.

Turn the mixture into a lightly buttered 1½-quart soufflé dish that has been sprinkled with sugar. Place the dish in a pan of hot water and bake for 40 minutes. Remove from oven. Dust with confectioner's sugar and serve *immediately*.

# STOCKTON ASPARAGUS SOUFFLE

serves 4 to 6

3 tablespoons butter
3 tablespoons flour
¾ teaspoon salt
½ teaspoon pepper
1 cup milk
6 eggs, separated
1 cup asparagus, cooked and sliced into 1-inch pieces
1 tablespoon onion, minced
1 pimiento, chopped

Preheat the oven to 350°.

In a saucepan melt the butter. Stir in the flour, salt, and pepper. Mix until well blended. Slowly add the milk. Cook, stirring constantly, until the mixture thickens. Remove from heat and cool.

In a small bowl beat the egg whites until stiff but not dry.

In a large bowl beat the egg yolks until thick and lemon-colored, about 3 minutes.

Stir the cooled mixture slowly into the egg yolks. Fold in the egg whites, asparagus, onion, and pimiento. Turn the mixture into a buttered 2-quart soufflé dish. Bake for 45 minutes or until a knife inserted into the center comes out clean. Remove from oven and serve *immediately*.

# OREGON APPLE SOUFFLE

serves 4 to 6

3 to 4 large tart apples, peeled, cored, and chopped
3 eggs separated
1 cup sugar
  juice of ½ lemon
1 cup bread crumbs
1 tablespoon melted butter
  whipped cream

Steam the chopped apples in 2 inches of boiling water until tender, about 20 minutes. Drain well and mash. There should be about 2 cups of pulp.

Preheat the oven to 375°.

Place the apple pulp in a mixing bowl. Add the egg yolks, sugar, and lemon juice. Beat well.

In a small bowl beat the egg whites until stiff but not dry. Fold into the apple mixture and combine thoroughly. Turn the mixture into a 1½- or 2-quart soufflé dish.

In a skillet brown the bread crumbs in 1 tablespoon butter. Sprinkle crumbs over top of apple mixture. Bake for 20 to 30 minutes. Remove from oven and serve *immediately* with whipped cream.

# MOCHA CAFE SOUFFLE

serves 6

⅔ cup sugar
⅓ cup unsweetened cocoa
¼ cup powdered instant espresso
3 tablespoons cornstarch
¾ cup milk
¼ cup butter
1 teaspoon vanilla extract
4 eggs, separated
¼ teaspoon cream of tartar

Preheat the oven to 375°.

Combine ⅓ cup sugar with the cocoa, espresso powder, and cornstarch in a saucepan. Add the milk and stir until smooth. Cook mixture over moderate heat, stirring constantly, until thick and smooth.

Remove from heat. Add the vanilla and butter. Stir until the butter melts. Blend well. Add the egg yolks, one at a time, beating well after each addition.

In a mixing bowl beat the egg whites until foamy. Add the cream of tartar and beat. Slowly sprinkle in the remaining ⅓ cup sugar. Beat until whites are stiff but not dry. Stir one-quarter of the egg whites into the chocolate mixture. Then pour the chocolate mixture over the egg whites. Fold in gently.

Fit a 1½-quart souffle dish with a 2-inch collar of aluminum foil. Turn the mixture into the dish. Bake in the lower half of the oven for 25 to 35 minutes. The shorter baking time will result in a saucy center; the longer baking time will result in a firm center. Remove from oven. Remove foil collar and serve *immediately.*

# HANGTOWN FRY

serves 4

12 oysters, shelled
flour
salt and pepper to taste
9 eggs
fine bread crumbs
3 tablespoons butter

Drain the oysters thoroughly on paper towels.

Beat 1 egg in a small bowl.

Place the bread crumbs in another small bowl.

Combine the flour, salt, and pepper in a bowl. Dip each oyster into the flour mixture, then into the egg, and then into the bread crumbs.

Heat the butter in a large skillet. Add the oysters and fry until golden brown on both sides, about 3 minutes.

Beat the remaining 8 eggs with salt and pepper. Pour over the oysters in the skillet. Cook until eggs are firm on bottom. Turn the eggs with a large spatula and continue to cook on the other side for 1 to 2 minutes. Remove from pan and serve.

Legend has it that Hangtown Fry was created during the California Gold Rush of 1849. A miner who had struck it rich swaggered into Hangtown and demanded the most expensive meal the hotel could offer. When informed that oysters and eggs were the most costly items on the menu, he told the chef to combine the two. The result is a genuine California dish. For true authenticity, small Pacific Coast Olympia oysters should be used.

# Meat and Poultry

## ORIENTAL BEEF

serves 4

1¼ to 1½ pounds boneless round sirloin,
 sirloin tip, or rump
3 tablespoons peanut oil
1 green pepper, cut into thin strips
1 sweet red pepper, cut into thin strips
2 celery stalks, sliced lengthwise
2 small onions, thinly sliced
6 fresh mushrooms, thinly sliced
1 small can water chestnuts, drained and sliced
2 tablespoons cornstarch
2 teaspoons sugar
1 teaspoon chopped fresh ginger or
 ¾ teaspoon ground
1½ cups beef broth
3 tablespoons soy sauce

Slice the beef into thin slices ¼ inch thick and about 2 inches long.

In a large skillet heat 1 tablespoon oil. Add the beef strips and fry quickly over high heat for 2 minutes. Stir constantly. Remove beef and reserve.

Add the remaining oil to the skillet and heat. Add the green pepper, red pepper, celery, onions, mushrooms, and water chestnuts. Sauté quickly, turning frequently, for 3 minutes or until vegetables are tender but still crisp. Remove skillet from heat. Return beef to skillet.

Combine the cornstarch, sugar, ginger, beef broth, and soy sauce in a saucepan. Quickly bring the mixture to a boil and boil for 3 minutes. Stir frequently.

Pour the sauce over the meat and vegetables and mix lightly. Heat the mixture thoroughly. Remove from heat and serve at once with rice.

## OREGON BEEF STEW

serves 4 to 6

3 tablespoons vegetable or olive oil
2½ pounds stewing beef, cubed
3 cups apple cider
4 leeks, sliced (white parts only)
½ cup dried apricots
½ cup dried prunes
1 teaspoon sugar
1 slice lemon
⅛ teaspoon pepper
3 tablespoons flour
3 tablespoons butter

Heat the oil in a large skillet. Add the beef cubes and brown on all sides, about 5 to 8 minutes. Add the apple cider and reduce the heat. Add the leeks and stir. Add the apricots and prunes, placing them on top of the leeks and meat. Stir in the sugar, lemon slice, and pepper.

Cover and simmer until the meat is tender, about 2 hours.

In a small bowl combine the butter and flour. Blend well and add to the stew. Continue cooking 3 to 5 minutes longer or until the stew thickens. Serve hot with baked potatoes.

# SEATTLE STEAK

serves 6

    1  3-pound chuck steak
    2  tablespoons butter, softened
 1½  teaspoons salt
  ½  teaspoon pepper
    1  large lemon, sliced
    2  medium onions, sliced
    1  tablespoon chives, minced
    1  tablespoon parsley, chopped
    2  teaspoons dried thyme

Preheat the oven to 350°.

Place the steak in a large baking dish and rub all over with butter. Season with salt and pepper. Sprinkle the chives, parsley, and thyme over the steak. Cover with lemon and onion slices. Tightly cover the dish with aluminum foil.

Bake until meat is tender, about 2 hours. Remove from oven and remove foil. Cool briefly and slice. Discard lemon slices and serve with onion slices.

# PORTLAND POT ROAST

serves 6

    1  4-pound chuck or rump roast
    2  tablespoons salt
  ½  teaspoon pepper
  ⅛  teaspoon ground ginger
    3  tablespoons vegetable oil
    2  cloves garlic, finely chopped
    3  onions, finely chopped
    2  cups water
 1½  cups dried prunes
    1  cup black olives, pitted and sliced
    1  cup fresh mushrooms, sliced

Sprinkle the meat with the salt, pepper, and ginger. Rub in well.

In a large skillet heat the oil. Add the beef and brown on all sides, about 2 to 3 minutes per side. Add the garlic, onions, and ½ cup water. Cover and simmer for 1½ hours. Turn the meat 2 or 3 times as it simmers.

Soak the dried prunes in 1½ cups water. When the meat has cooked for 1½ hours, add prunes and liquid to the skillet. Add the olives and mushrooms. Cover and simmer gently for 1 hour or until the meat is very tender.

Remove meat to a serving platter and surround with the prunes and other vegetables. Serve hot.

# WEST COAST PEPPER STEAK

serves 4

    2  pounds beef round
  ¼  cup flour
        salt and pepper to taste
  ¼  cup vegetable or olive oil
  ½  cup onion, chopped
    1  clove garlic, finely chopped
    1  cup fresh or canned tomatoes, chopped
 1½  cups water
    1  tablespoon Worcestershire sauce
    2  large green peppers, cut into strips

Trim the meat and slice into strips ½ inch thick and 2½ to 3 inches long.

Combine the flour, salt, and pepper. Dredge the meat strips in the mixture. Shake off excess.

*(continued on next page)*

In a large skillet heat the oil. Add the meat and brown on all sides over high heat, about 3 to 4 minutes.

Reduce the heat and add the onion, garlic, tomatoes, water, Worcestershire sauce, and green peppers. Cover and simmer gently for 50 to 60 minutes or until meat is tender.

Serve hot with rice or potatoes.

# ROAST PORK WITH CALIFORNIA BRANDY

serves 8 to 10

    1  8-pound loin of pork
       salt and pepper to taste
    8  baking apples, cored
    8  large white onions
 1½  cups apple cider
    2  tablespoons flour
  ¼  cup brandy

Preheat the oven to 375°.

Season the roast generously with salt and pepper. Place roast on a rack in a roasting pan and roast for 1½ hours.

Remove the roast and pour off any fat that has accumulated in the pan. Surround the roast with alternating circles of apples and white onions. Pour in 1 cup apple cider and return roast to the oven for 1 hour longer.

When roast is done remove from the rack to a platter. Surround the roast with the apples and onions. Keep warm.

Skim the fat from the top of the pan juices. Place the pan over low heat and slowly stir in the flour. Add the remaining apple cider and the brandy. Stir constantly, scraping the bottom of the pan to loosen the brown bits. Simmer the gravy for 5 to 6 minutes. Remove from heat and serve with the roast.

# LOIN OF PORK TERIYAKI

serves 4 to 6

    1  5-pound loin of pork
    1  clove garlic, slivered
  ¾  cup soy sauce
  ¾  cup sherry
 1½  tablespoons fresh ginger, chopped,
       or 1 teaspoon powdered
       rind of ¼ orange, thinly sliced
       salt to taste

Rub the roast with the garlic and insert 4 to 5 slivers into the meat. Place the roast in a shallow pan.

In a small bowl combine the soy sauce, sherry, ginger, and orange rind. Mix well and pour over pork. Marinate the pork for 4 to 5 hours, turning frequently.

Preheat the oven to 350°.

Remove the roast from the marinade and place it on a rack in a roasting pan. Roast for 2 hours and 5 minutes, or 25 minutes per pound. Baste every 20 minutes with the marinade and pan juices.

When roast is done, sprinkle lightly with salt and remove from oven. Transfer to a serving platter and cool slightly before slicing. Serve with pan juices.

## SPIRITED LEMON PORK CHOPS

serves 4

> 4 center-cut pork chops
> salt and pepper to taste
> ½ teaspoon dried oregano
> ½ teaspoon dried basil
> flour
> bread crumbs
> 2 eggs, lightly beaten
> 1 tablespoon shallots, chopped
> 2 tablespoons capers, chopped
> ¼ cup lemon juice
> ¼ cup brandy

Sprinkle the pork chops with salt and pepper. Rub in well.

In a bowl combine the oregano, basil, and bread crumbs.

Dredge the pork chops in the flour. Dip into the beaten eggs and then dredge in the seasoned bread crumbs.

In a large skillet heat the oil. Add the chops and brown well on both sides, about 3 to 4 minutes per side. Add the shallots and capers. Cook chops over medium heat for 5 to 10 minutes longer on each side, depending on the thickness of the chops. Stir in the lemon juice and continue cooking until chops are done to taste. Remove chops from skillet to a serving platter. Keep warm.

Add the brandy to the skillet and deglaze. Stir and scrape the bottom of the skillet to loosen the brown particles. Pour sauce over the chops and serve.

## HAWAIIAN PORK CHOPS

serves 4

> 4 large loin pork chops
> salt and pepper to taste
> ¾ cup brandy
> 1 to 2 tablespoons butter
> 4 slices fresh pineapple
> 1 cup seedless grapes, chopped
> 4 tablespoons honey

Sprinkle the pork chops with salt and pepper. Rub in well. Place the chops in a shallow dish and pour the brandy over them. Marinate for 1 hour in refrigerator.

Melt the butter in a skillet. Add the pork chops and sauté until golden brown on both sides, about 3 to 5 minutes per side.

Add one-half of the marinade and loosely cover the pan. Cook the pork chops over medium heat for 10 minutes. Turn chops and cook for 10 minutes longer. Add more marinade if additional liquid is needed. Remove the chops and keep warm. Add the pineapple to the skillet and sauté until well browned. Arrange the pork chops on top of the pineapple. Place an equal amount of the chopped grapes on top of each chop. Top each chop with 1 tablespoon honey. Cover and cook until honey is slightly melted and chops are heated through. Serve chops on pineapple.

# BARBECUED LAMB

serves 6 to 8

8 *lamb chops, 2 inches thick*
   *salt and pepper to taste*
3 *cloves garlic, halved*
¼ *teaspoon dried rosemary*
½ *cup red wine vinegar*
¼ *cup olive oil*

Season the lamb chops with salt and pepper. Rub with the garlic.

In a small bowl combine the rosemary, vinegar, and oil. Whisk together until well blended. Baste chops with sauce and coat well.

Place a grill 5 to 6 inches above hot coals. Grill chops 6 to 7 minutes for rare meat, 9 to 10 minutes for medium meat, and 12 or more minutes for well-done meat. Turn frequently and baste often while cooking.

# SIERRA LAMB CHOPS

serves 4

4 *shoulder lamb chops, 1 inch thick*
6 *tablespoons olive oil*
2 *tablespoons lemon juice*
1½ *teaspoons salt*
1½ *teaspoons dried oregano*
½ *teaspoon pepper*

In a shallow pan combine the olive oil, lemon juice, salt, oregano, and pepper. Add the lamb chops and coat well. Cover and marinate in refrigerator for 3 to 4 hours.

Remove chops from refrigerator and transfer to a skillet. Reserve the marinade.

Sauté the chops on both sides over moderate heat. If liquid is needed, add marinade. Cook 10 minutes per side for medium meat; cook 15 minutes per side for well-done meat. Remove from heat and serve.

# SHERRIED LAMB STEW

serves 4

2 *pounds boneless lamb, cubed*
   *salt and pepper to taste*
   *flour*
3 *tablespoons butter*
1 *large onion, thinly sliced*
½ *teaspoon dried marjoram*
1½ *cups chicken broth*
⅓ *cup dry sherry*
1 *cup turnips, peeled and diced*
2 *carrots, peeled and diced*
2 *cups fresh peas*

Trim fat from the lamb. Season with salt and pepper and dredge cubes in flour.

Heat the butter in a large saucepan. Add the lamb and cook over high heat, stirring constantly, until lightly browned, about 3 minutes per side. Add the onion, chicken broth, and sherry. Quickly bring the mixture to a boil. Reduce the heat and simmer, covered, for 30 to 40 minutes or until meat is tender. Add the turnips and carrots. Cook 5 minutes longer. Add the peas and cook 5 minutes longer or until vegetables are just tender.

Remove from heat and serve hot. This stew may be refrigerated and served the next day; it ages well.

# HERBED LAMB SHANKS

serves 4

- 4 *lamb shanks*
- 2 *cloves garlic, finely chopped*
- 2 *teaspoons olive oil*
  *salt and pepper to taste*
- 1/4 *teaspoon dried marjoram*
- 1/4 *teaspoon dried thyme*
- 1/4 *teaspoon dried rosemary*
- 2 *teaspoons flour*
- 6 *tablespoons white wine*
- 2 *tablespoons plus 2 teaspoons water*

Preheat the oven to 325°.

In a small bowl combine the garlic, olive oil, salt, and pepper. Rub the mixture into the lamb shanks. Sprinkle the shanks with the marjoram, thyme, rosemary, and flour. Coat evenly. Place the shanks in a shallow roasting pan.

In a small bowl combine the wine and water. Pour over the lamb and roast for 2 hours or until the shanks are tender. Baste with the pan drippings. If more liquid is needed, add water to the bottom of the pan. Remove and serve hot.

# VEAL SCALLOPS WITH LEMON SAUCE

serves 4

- 16 to 20 *veal scallops*
- 4 *teaspoons lemon juice*
  *flour*
- 3 *tablespoons butter*
- 1/2 to 3/4 *cup beef broth*
- 2 *tablespoons capers*
- 6 *teaspoons lemon juice*
- 1 *teaspoon freshly grated lemon peel*

Pound the veal scallops gently between two sheets of wax paper until very thin. Place the scallops in a shallow dish with 4 teaspoons lemon juice. Marinate for 1 hour.

Remove the veal and gently pat dry. Dredge in the flour to coat lightly.

Melt the butter in the skillet. Add the veal and sauté over high heat until lightly browned on both sides, about 3 minutes per side. Remove veal from skillet and keep warm.

Add the beef broth to the skillet and cook until it is reduced by half. Stir often. Add the capers, 6 teaspoons lemon juice, and lemon peel. Stir. Return the veal to the skillet. Cover and cook 2 to 4 minutes or until tender.

Remove veal from skillet and serve immediately with sauce spooned over each piece.

# VEAL KEBABS

serves 4

- 1 to 1 1/2 *pounds stewing veal, cubed*
- 1 *medium zucchini, cut into 1/2-inch slices*
- 4 *large fresh mushrooms, halved*
- 1 *sweet red pepper, cut into 8 squares*
- 1 *small eggplant, cut into 8 1/2-inch rounds*
- 1/4 *cup Triple Sec, Curaçao, or other orange liqueur*
- 1/4 *cup white wine*
- 1/4 *cup olive oil*
- 1/4 *cup lemon juice*
- 1 *teaspoon garlic, finely chopped*
  *salt and pepper to taste*

Place the veal, zucchini, mushrooms, pepper, and eggplant together in a shallow dish.

In a bowl combine the liqueur, white wine, olive oil, lemon juice, garlic, salt, and pepper. Whisk to blend well. Pour the marinade over the veal and vegetables. Cover and marinate in the refrigerator for 3 to 4 hours.

Preheat the broiler.

Arrange the veal and vegetables on 4 long skewers. Broil 6 inches from the heat. Turn and baste frequently with the marinade until well browned and cooked through, about 12 minutes. Serve on skewers.

# CHICKEN TERIYAKI

serves 4 to 6

  6 *large chicken breasts, boned and skinned*
    *rind of 1 medium orange, freshly grated*
    *juice of 1 medium orange*
  1 *cup soy sauce*
  4 *thin slices ginger root*
  2 *cloves garlic, minced*
  ¾ *cup sherry or brandy*
  2 *tablespoons light brown sugar*
  1 *scallion, chopped*
    *salt and pepper to taste*

Place the chicken breasts in a shallow dish large enough to hold them in one layer. Sprinkle the breasts with the orange rind and pour the orange juice over them.

In a small bowl combine the soy sauce, ginger root, garlic, sherry, sugar, and scallion. Whisk until well combined. Pour over the chicken breasts. Cover dish and marinate in the refrigerator for 4 to 5 hours.

Preheat the broiler.

Place the chicken breasts in a broiler pan. Reserve the marinade. Broil the breasts 3 inches from heat until tender, about 7 to 10 minutes per side. Baste often with marinade. Remove from broiler and serve hot.

# LEMON CHICKEN WITH RAISINS

serves 4

  1 *3½-pound broiling chicken, cut into serving pieces*
  ¼ *cup golden raisins*
  4 *tablespoons brandy*
  2 *tablespoons water*
  4 *tablespoons butter*
  2 *tablespoons olive oil*
  8 *small white onions, thinly sliced*
    *rind of 1 lemon*
    *juice of 3 lemons*
    *salt and pepper to taste*

Place the raisins in a bowl with the brandy and water. Soak for 50 minutes.

In a skillet, melt the butter. Saute the chicken pieces until golden but not browned, about 5 to 8 minutes. Remove the chicken and keep warm. Add the onions to the skillet and saute until translucent, about 10 to 15 minutes. Skim off any fat that has accumulated in the skillet.

Smooth the onions into an even layer. Place the chicken pieces on top of the onions and add the raisins with their liquid, the lemon juice, and the lemon rind. Cover tightly and simmer for 45 to 50 minutes or until the chicken is tender. Serve at once.

# SKILLET LEMON CHICKEN

serves 4

1  3-pound frying chicken, *quartered*
½  *cup butter*
2  *tablespoons lemon juice*
1  *teaspoon salt*
1  *clove garlic, crushed*
¼  *teaspoon pepper*
1  *cup fresh mushrooms, sliced*
1  *tablespoon capers*

In a skillet combine the butter, lemon juice, salt, garlic, pepper, mushrooms, and capers. Quickly bring the mixture to a boil. Add the chicken pieces to the skillet. Bring mixture back to a boil. Cover and simmer for 30 minutes or until chicken is tender. Turn pieces frequently.

Serve chicken pieces topped with sauce.

# CHICKEN WITH LEMON-LIME SAUCE

serves 4 to 6

6  *large chicken breasts, boned*
    *salt and pepper to taste*
2  *egg whites, lightly beaten*
1½  *cups almonds, finely chopped*
Lemon-lime sauce:
2  *tablespoons butter*
2  *tablespoons flour*
1  *cup chicken broth*
¼  *teaspoon salt*
¼  *teaspoon pepper*
2  *egg yolks*
2  *eggs*
1  *teaspoon freshly grated lemon peel*
2  *tablespoons lime juice*

Preheat the oven to 350°.

Sprinkle the chicken with the salt and pepper. Dip chicken in the beaten egg whites and then roll in the chopped almonds. Arrange breasts in one layer in a buttered baking dish. Bake for 20 to 25 minutes or until tender.

To make the lemon-lime sauce, melt the butter in a saucepan. Add the flour and stir until well blended. Add the chicken broth, salt, and pepper. Cook, stirring constantly, until the mixture comes to a boil. Remove from heat.

In a small bowl beat the egg yolks and eggs together. Quickly stir the hot broth mixture into the eggs. Return the saucepan to very low heat and cook until the sauce thickens. Stir constantly. Remove from heat and stir in the lemon peel and lime juice. Serve chicken and sauce together.

# GRILLED CHICKEN HALVES

serves 8

4 2- to 2½-pound broiling chickens
Basting sauce:
¾ cup olive oil
¼ cup melted butter
¼ cup lemon juice
2 tablespoons tomato sauce
1 tablespoon French-style mustard
1 tablespoon salt
2 teaspoons onion, finely chopped
½ teaspoon pepper
2 cloves garlic, halved
½ teaspoon Worcestershire sauce
¼ teaspoon Tabasco sauce

In a bowl combine the olive oil, melted butter, lemon juice, tomato sauce, brown sugar, mustard, salt, onion, pepper, garlic, Worcestershire sauce, and Tabasco sauce. Whisk until well blended. Transfer the sauce to a bottle or jar and let stand for 2 hours before using. Shake well before using.

Split the chickens. Brush generously with the basting sauce and refrigerate for 2 to 3 hours.

Place the chicken halves, skin-side up, on a grill above hot coals. Cook 20 to 25 minutes. Brush with sauce and turn. Cook 20 minutes longer or until chicken is tender. Remove from grill and serve.

# CHICKEN LIVERS IN WINE

serves 4

1 pound fresh chicken livers
marsala or port wine
½ cup scallions, chopped (including green parts)
6 to 9 tablespoons butter
flour
⅓ cup marsala or port wine
1 tablespoon lemon juice
½ teaspoon dried sage
¼ teaspoon salt
⅛ teaspoon pepper

Place the livers in a bowl and add enough marsala or port to cover. Marinate for 1 hour.

Heat the butter in a skillet. Add the chopped scallions and sauté until the white parts are transparent, about 3 to 5 minutes.

Remove the livers from the wine and gently pat dry. Dredge very lightly in the flour. Add the livers to the scallions and sauté for 3 minutes or until livers begin to stiffen. Stir in ⅓ cup marsala or port, lemon juice, salt, and pepper. Continue cooking over medium heat for 6 to 8 minutes, stirring occasionally.

Remove livers from skillet and serve with sauce.

# SAN FRANCISCO GLAZED DUCK

serves 4

> 1 5-pound duck
> ½ lemon
>    salt and pepper to taste
>    Lemon-Carrot Sauce

Preheat the oven to 350°.

Rub the skin of the duck with the lemon half. Rub the inside of the duck with salt and pepper. Close the cavity with poultry skewers or toothpicks.

Place the duck on a rack in a roasting pan. Roast for 1½ hours. Remove from oven and cut into quarters. Reassemble on a serving platter into the shape of a whole duck. Spoon Lemon-Carrot Sauce over duck (see below).

# LEMON-CARROT SAUCE

for 1 5-pound duck

> ½ medium onion, finely chopped
> 1 carrot, peeled and grated
> 2 tablespoons butter
> 1 tablespoon cornstarch
> 1 cup chicken broth
> 1½ tablespoons lemon juice
> 5 tablespoons sugar
>    salt and pepper to taste
> 1½ tablespoons parsley, chopped

In a saucepan melt the butter. Add the onions and carrots and sauté until limp, about 5 to 7 minutes. Do not brown.

In a small bowl, blend the cornstarch with ¼ cup of the chicken broth. Add to the vegetable mixture. Add the remaining broth, lemon juice, and sugar. Season to taste with salt and pepper. Cook over medium heat, stirring constantly, for 5 minutes or until sauce is clear and slightly thickened. Stir in the parsley and remove from heat.

Pour ⅓ cup of the sauce over the duck. Return duck to the oven and cook for 10 minutes or until heated through. Remove from oven and serve duck with the remaining sauce.

# HONEYED DUCK

serves 4

> 1 5-pound duck
> 1 orange, peeled and quartered
>    juice of 1 orange
> ½ cup butter
> ½ cup honey
>    rind of 1 lemon, freshly grated
> 1 teaspoon dried basil
> 1 teaspoon dried thyme
> 1 teaspoon dried oregano
> 1 teaspoon ground ginger

Preheat the oven to 350°.

Rub the inside of the duck with ½ teaspoon each of the basil, thyme, oregano, and ground ginger. Place the quartered orange inside the duck. Place the duck on a large piece of heavy aluminum foil.

Melt the butter in a saucepan. Add the remaining basil, thyme, oregano, and ground ginger. Add the honey, orange juice, and lemon rind. Heat and stir until well blended.

Pour the sauce over the duck and close the foil tightly. Place duck in oven and cook for 1½ hours.

Open the foil and fold it back. Baste the duck and cook, uncovered, for 20 to 30 minutes longer or until browned. Baste occasionally. Remove the duck from the foil and cut into serving pieces. Serve with the pan juices.

# BROILED CALIFORNIA DUCK

serves 4

1  *5-pound duck*
2  *tablespoons melted butter*
3  *tablespoons Triple Sec, Cointreau,*
   *or any orange liqueur*
   *salt and pepper to taste*
   *paprika to taste*
2  *cups potatoes, peeled and cubed*
2  *cups turnips, peeled and cubed*
¼  *cup Triple Sec, Cointreau, or any orange liqueur*

Preheat the oven to 450°.

Trim the duck of any visible fat.

Combine the melted butter, salt, pepper, paprika, and liqueur. Mix well. Brush the duck inside and out with the mixture.

Place the duck on a rack in a roasting pan. Roast for 1 hour, basting frequently.

Lower the temperature to 350°. Add the potatoes and turnips to the roasting pan. Cook, basting duck and vegetables frequently, until duck is done, about 1 hour longer.

When the duck is done, remove it to an ovenproof platter. Place the vegetables in a serving bowl.

Gently warm ¼ cup of the liqueur. Pour the liqueur over the duck and carefully flame it. Spoon the liqueur over the duck until the flame dies. Cut the duck into serving pieces and serve with the vegetables.

# ·Fish and Seafood·

## HAWAIIAN PLANKED RED SNAPPER

serves 4 to 6

1 4- to 5-pound whole red snapper, cleaned
coarse salt
meat of 1 fresh coconut, broken into small pieces
1 cup water
2 tablespoons sherry
1 orange, peeled and sectioned
1 fresh pineapple, cut into chunks
1 papaya, sliced

Season the fish well, inside and out, with coarse salt. Place the fish in a shallow buttered baking dish.

In an electric blender or food processor, combine the coconut meat and water. Blend at high speed for 30 seconds. Strain through a sieve into a bowl. Press with the back of a spoon to extract all the liquid. Let the liquid stand for 1 hour or until the coconut cream has risen to the top. Skim off the cream and pour over the fish. (Canned coconut milk may be used instead, but the results are not as good.)

Preheat the oven to 350°.

Bake the fish for 20 minutes. Pour the sherry into the pan and bake for 25 minutes longer or until fish flakes easily.

Heat a hardwood plank by letting it stand under hot running water. Remove the fish to the plank and serve surrounded by the orange, pineapple, and papaya pieces.

This dish should properly be made with the *opakapaka* fish, which is found in Hawaiian waters. It is traditionally an important feature of a luau. Red snapper is a very close substitute.

## COLUMBIA RIVER BAKED SALMON

serves 6 to 8

1 4- to 6-pound salmon, cleaned
¼ cup flour
8 slices bread, wet and crumbled
¼ cup melted butter
1 small onion, minced
3 tablespoons parsley, chopped
½ pound slab bacon, cut into 8 pieces

Preheat the oven to 300°.

Dredge the fish evenly in the flour.

In a small bowl combine the crumbled bread, butter, onions, and parsley. Mix well. Stuff the cavity of the fish with the mixture. Fasten the cavity closed with toothpicks or gently sew closed.

Place 4 pieces of the bacon in a large shallow baking dish. Place the fish on top. Place the remaining pieces of bacon on top of the fish at 2-inch intervals.

Bake for 1 to 1½ hours, or 15 minutes per pound. Remove from oven, remove toothpicks or thread, carve, and serve.

## POACHED SALMON WITH RUM VINAIGRETTE

serves 6 to 8

   1  *6-pound salmon, cleaned*
  ½  *cup light rum*
13¾  *ounces chicken broth*
   1  *onion, sliced*
   2  *bay leaves*
   1  *cup celery leaves, chopped*
   1  *lemon, thinly sliced*
   1  *cucumber, thinly sliced*

Vinaigrette:
  1½  *cups olive oil*
  ⅓  *cup white wine vinegar*
  ⅓  *cup gold rum*
   1  *teaspoon sugar*
   3  *tablespoons salt*
  ⅓  *teaspoon pepper*
   1  *teaspoon paprika*
  ¼  *cup chopped fresh* cilantro *(coriander)*
   4  *hard-cooked eggs, finely chopped*

Preheat the oven to 375°.

Place a large doubled sheet of heavy aluminum foil on a cookie sheet. Turn up the edges. Place the salmon on the sheet and add the rum, chicken broth, onion, bay leaves, celery leaves, and lemon. Place another piece of foil over the salmon and crimp the edges of the top and bottom sheets together. Bake for 40 minutes.

Remove from oven and cool, covered.

In a blender, combine the oil, vinegar, gold rum, sugar, salt, pepper, paprika, and *cilantro.* Blend until thick. Pour into a bowl and fold in the eggs. Chill.

Remove the foil from the salmon. Pour off all the pan juices and discard. Carefully strip the skin from both sides of the salmon and scrape off all dark meat. Chill, covered.

Serve the salmon garnished with the cucumber slices. Stir the vinaigrette and spoon over each serving.

## ALASKA BARBECUED SALMON

serves 6 to 8

   1  *5- to 6-pound salmon, cleaned*
      *salt and pepper to taste*
   2  *tablespoons butter, softened and cut into pieces*
  ½  *medium onion, thinly sliced*
  ½  *lemon, sliced*
   2  *sprigs parsley*
      *oil*
      *lemon wedges*

Sprinkle the salmon inside and out with the salt and pepper. Dot with the butter. Arrange overlapping slices of onion, lemon, and parsley in the cavity. Brush the fish with oil.

Wrap the salmon in heavy aluminum foil; seal edges with double folds. Place package on grill over medium-hot coals. Carefully turn the package every 10 minutes. Test for doneness after 45 minutes. Fish is done when it flakes easily when tested with a fork at the thickest part.

To serve, transfer the salmon to a serving platter and fold back the foil. Cut between bone and meat with a spatula; lift off each serving. Serve with lemon wedges.

## SEA BASS WITH CHESTNUT STUFFING

serves 4

1 3-pound sea bass
  salt and pepper to taste
½ pound chestnuts
  boiling water
1 tablespoon bread crumbs
1 teaspoon parsley, chopped
½ teaspoon dried thyme
1 tablespoon freshly grated lemon rind
  juice of 1 lemon
1 egg yolk, slightly beaten
1 tablespoon olive oil

Preheat the oven to 375°.

Clean the bass and remove the central bone. Dry thoroughly and rub inside and out with salt and pepper.

Cut a slit in each chestnut shell and cook in boiling water for 15 to 20 minutes or until tender. Shell immediately.

Place the chestnut meats in an electric blender or food processor and blend until puréed.

Mix the chestnut purée with the bread crumbs, parsley, thyme, lemon rind, lemon juice, egg yolk, salt, and pepper. Stuff the cavity of the fish with the mixture. Close the cavity with skewers or sew closed. Brush fish with the olive oil and bake for 30 minutes.

Remove from oven. Remove skewers or thread and serve.

## SEATTLE FRIED TROUT

serves 4

4 10-ounce trout, cleaned
2 teaspoons salt
  pepper to taste
1 cup flour
1 cup yellow corn meal
2 eggs
1 cup olive oil
½ cup butter, cut into pieces
¼ cup lime juice
2 tablespoons chives, finely chopped

Clean the trout, leaving the heads and tails intact. Wash and pat dry. Season inside and out with salt and pepper.

Place the flour and corn meal on separate plates. Beat the eggs in a shallow bowl.

Dredge each trout in the flour, then dip it in the egg and roll it in the corn meal, coating evenly.

Heat the olive oil in a heavy skillet over moderate heat. When oil is very hot, fry the trout, 2 at a time, for 4 to 5 minutes on each side or until golden brown. Remove trout from skillet and drain briefly.

In a separate saucepan melt the butter over low heat. Do not brown. Remove from heat and stir in the lime juice and chives. Season to taste and pour over trout. Serve at once.

## SANTA MONICA POACHED SOLE

serves 4

4 4-ounce fillets of sole or flounder
1 tablespoon butter, cut into pieces
¼ cup shallots, finely chopped
¼ teaspoon dried rosemary
½ teaspoon salt
⅛ teaspoon pepper
½ cup dry white wine
1 cup water
½ cup heavy cream
2 egg yolks

Preheat the oven to 350°.

Generously butter a shallow baking dish large enough to hold the fillets in 1 layer. Sprinkle the shallots over the bottom of the pan.

Season the fillets on both sides with the rosemary, salt, and pepper. Arrange the fillets in the baking dish. Pour in the wine and water and dot the fillets with butter.

Cover the dish with buttered wax paper. Bake for 10 minutes or until fillets flake easily. Remove from oven and transfer fillets to a serving platter. Keep warm.

Strain the pan juices through a sieve into a saucepan. Press with the back of a spoon to extract all the liquid. Quickly bring the liquid to a boil. Cook, uncovered, until the liquid is reduced to approximately 1 cup. Stir in the cream and cook over high heat, stirring constantly, until the mixture begins to thicken. Reduce the heat to very low.

In a small bowl beat the egg yolks. Pour ½ cup of the cream mixture into the egg yolks and whisk to blend. Slowly pour the yolk mixture back into the remaining cream mixture. Whisk constantly. Cook over very low heat for 2 to 3 minutes or until the sauce thickens. Be very careful not to let the sauce approach the boiling point or it may curdle. Remove sauce from heat. Season to taste and pour over fish fillets. Serve immediately.

## BROILED SWORDFISH WITH SOY SAUCE BUTTER

serves 4

1½ pounds swordfish steaks
    salt and pepper to taste
4 tablespoons butter, softened
1½ teaspoons soy sauce
1 lemon, thinly sliced

Preheat the broiler.

Wash and dry the swordfish steaks. Season on both sides with salt and pepper.

Arrange the steaks in 1 layer in a well-buttered shallow baking pan.

In a small bowl combine the butter and soy sauce. Spread this mixture over the steaks.

Broil the steaks 3 to 5 inches from the heat for 8 to 10 minutes. Turn once. Remove steaks from broiler. Transfer to a serving platter and garnish with lemon slices.

# FLOUNDER WITH GARLIC AND TOMATOES

serves 4

4 ½-pound flounder fillets
3 medium ripe tomatoes
3 tablespoons olive oil
1 tablespoon butter
2 teaspoons garlic, finely chopped
1½ teaspoons salt
¼ teaspoon pepper
2 tablespoons parsley, finely chopped

Drop the tomatoes into a pot of boiling water and boil briskly for 10 to 12 seconds. Drain the tomatoes and rinse with cold water. Peel off the skins using a small sharp knife. Cut out the stems. Halve the tomatoes and remove the seeds. Chop the tomatoes coarsely.

Place the butter and oil in a large skillet and heat until the butter melts. Add the fish and sauté for about 2 minutes per side. Transfer the fish to a serving plate.

Pour off all but 1 tablespoon fat from the skillet. Reduce the heat. Add the garlic and sauté for 2 to 3 minutes or until soft. Stir in the tomatoes and raise the heat. Cook, stirring often, until the tomatoes are thick and almost all the liquid has evaporated. Add the salt, pepper, and parsley. Stir well.

Return the fish to the skillet. Cover the skillet and reduce the heat. Cook just long enough to heat the fish through, about 3 minutes. Remove the fish to a serving platter. Pour the sauce over the fish and serve immediately.

# YERBA BUENA BAKED SHAD

serves 4

2 1-pound shad fillets
¼ cup soy sauce
3 tablespoons sherry
2 teaspoons sugar
3 ¼-inch slices ginger root, crushed
3 scallions, sliced
½ cup dried Chinese black mushrooms
½ cup canned sliced bamboo shoots

In a shallow baking dish combine the soy sauce, sherry, sugar, ginger, and scallions. Mix well. Add the shad fillets and turn to coat evenly. Cover dish and marinate 4 to 5 hours or overnight.

Blanch the bamboo shoots in boiling water for 1 minute. Drain well.

In a small bowl soak the dried mushrooms in boiling water to cover until they are soft, about 20 minutes. Drain the mushrooms. Discard the stems and slice the caps.

Remove the shad from the refrigerator. Remove the ginger from the marinade. Bake the fish in the marinade for 10 minutes.

Scatter the mushrooms and bamboo shoots over the shad. Bake 5 minutes longer or until fish flakes easily. Remove from oven, transfer to serving platter, and serve.

# ORIENTAL FRESH TUNA

1 pound fresh tuna steaks
salt
soy sauce
½ cup slivered almonds
½ cup leek, chopped (white part only)
⅔ cup sliced canned bamboo shoots
2 ¼-inch slices ginger root
6 dried black Chinese mushrooms
8 tablespoons dry white wine or sherry
4 tablespoons soy sauce
2 tablespoons olive oil
2 tablespoons green pepper, julienned
1 teaspoon cornstarch
½ teaspoon ground cardamom

Soak the mushrooms in boiling water for 20 minutes to soften. Drain well.

Cut the tuna steaks into strips 2 inches long and ½ inch wide. Sprinkle with soy sauce and salt.

Combine 2 tablespoons cold water with the cornstarch. Stir to mix well.

In a deep skillet or wok heat 1 tablespoon olive oil. Add the tuna and sauté, stirring quickly, for 2 to 3 minutes. Remove the fish and juices to a plate. Add 1 tablespoon olive oil, the almonds, ginger root, and ground cardamom to the skillet. Sauté, stirring quickly, for 2 minutes. Add the leek, mushrooms, bamboo shoots, and green pepper. Sauté, stirring quickly, for 2 minutes. Stir in the white wine and 4 tablespoons soy sauce. Steam, covered, for 1 to 2 minutes. Add the reserved fish and juices. Stir well.

Add the cornstarch mixture to the skillet and stir well. Cook until fish is thoroughly heated. Remove from heat and serve immediately.

# DUNGENESS CRAB CASSEROLE

serves 4

12 tablespoons melted butter, cooled
¼ cup heavy cream
1½ teaspoons dry mustard
⅛ teaspoon cayenne pepper
2 cups freshly cooked Dungeness crabmeat
1 cup celery, finely chopped
1 cup onions, finely chopped
2 tablespoons parsley, finely chopped
1½ cups coarse cracker crumbs

Preheat the oven to 350°. Generously butter a 1½-quart casserole or baking dish.

Crush unsalted soda crackers to make the cracker crumbs.

In a large bowl combine the cooled butter, cream, mustard, cayenne, and salt. Stir until mustard is dissolved. Add the crabmeat, celery, onions, and parsley. Add the cracker crumbs and mix well.

Carefully spoon the mixture into the prepared dish. Bake for 30 minutes or until top is golden brown. Remove and serve directly from dish.

Dungeness crabs are quite large. They are found along the Pacific Coast from Alaska to Mexico.

Any crabmeat, fresh or frozen, may be substituted for the Dungeness crab. Pick over the meat carefully to remove all cartilage and shell.

# SHRIMP WITH ZUCCHINI

serves 4

1 pound shrimp, peeled and deveined
3 tablespoons olive oil
1 large onion, chopped
2 cloves garlic, finely chopped
1 green pepper, chopped
2 cups fresh tomatoes, chopped
2 small zucchini, sliced
½ teaspoon salt
½ teaspoon pepper

Heat the oil in a skillet. Add the onion, garlic, and green pepper. Cook over moderate heat for 3 minutes, stirring occasionally. Add the tomatoes, zucchini, salt, and pepper. Cover and simmer for 5 minutes.

Add the shrimp and simmer for another 5 minutes or until the shrimp turn pink. Remove from heat and serve at once.

# BAJA SHRIMP

serves 4

1¼ pounds shrimp, peeled and deveined
12 small dried hot red peppers
1 cup cider vinegar
1 cup water
1 teaspoon salt
½ teaspoon dried oregano
1 medium onion, sliced
½ cup olive oil
boiling water

Split the peppers lengthwise and remove the seeds and vein. Place the peppers on a piece of aluminum foil and place under the broiler just for 1 or 2 seconds.

Combine the cider vinegar and the water. Soak the peppers in the mixture for 2 hours.

Place the peppers and their liquid in the container of an electric blender or food processor. Add the salt, oregano, onion, and oil. Blend the mixture for 2 minutes or until well mixed.

Cook the shrimp in boiling water for about 5 minutes. Drain and place in a large bowl. Add the blended pepper mixture to the shrimp and marinate in the refrigerator overnight.

Remove shrimp from the marinade and serve cold with hot rice.

# BROILED GARLIC SHRIMP

serves 4 to 6

2 pounds shrimp
4 cloves garlic, crushed
½ onion, finely chopped
¼ cup chopped parsley
⅔ cup butter
salt and pepper to taste

Preheat the broiler.

Shell the shrimp, leaving the tails on. Butterfly the shrimp down the back with a sharp knife. Rinse and flatten the shrimp; pat dry.

In a saucepan combine the garlic, onion, parsley, and butter. Cook over low heat until the butter melts. Add salt and pepper to taste.

*(continued on next page)*

Dip the shrimp into the butter mixture and arrange them in 1 layer in a shallow oven-proof dish or broiler pan. Broil near the heat for 7 minutes or until sizzling.

Remove from broiler and serve from the dish with the remaining sauce poured over the shrimp.

# PACIFIC COAST MARINATED MUSSELS

serves 4 to 6

60 mussels
 1 cup water
 1 onion
1½ teaspoons dried thyme
 1 bay leaf
10 peppercorns
 1 tablespoon onion, minced
 ¾ cup dry white wine
1½ cups mussel liquid
1½ tablespoons flour
 3 tablespoons butter
 2 teaspoons lemon juice
 1 tablespoon butter
 3 teaspoons parsley, chopped

Scrub and debeard the mussels. Place them in a saucepan with the water, onion, thyme, bay leaf, and peppercorns. Cover tightly and cook for 2 minutes over high heat. Stir and cook for 2 minutes; stir again and cook 2 minutes longer. Remove the mussels, draining as much liquid as possible from them back into the saucepan. Keep mussels in a warm place.

In a saucepan, cook the minced onion in the white wine until the wine is reduced by half. Add 1½ cups of the mussel liquid.

In a small bowl make a paste of the flour and 3 tablespoons butter. Add the paste to the liquid, stirring until smooth. Add the lemon juice, 1 tablespoon butter, and parsley. Add the mussels and cook for 2 minutes. Place in a large serving bowl and serve.

# SAUTEED SEA SCALLOPS

serves 4

1½ pounds fresh sea scallops
 1 teaspoon salt
   water
 1 cup butter
 2 tablespoons brandy

Place the scallops in a saucepan with the salt and enough cold water to cover. Bring the water to a simmer and gently cook the scallops for 2 to 3 minutes or until they are opaque. Drain well.

Melt the butter in a skillet over high heat. Add the scallops and toss gently until the butter turns brown.

In a saucepan heat the brandy until sizzling. Carefully ignite it and pour over the scallops. When the flame dies, serve the scallops.

# ABALONE STEAK

serves 4

4 abalone steaks
2 eggs
½ teaspoon salt
¼ teaspoon pepper
1½ cups bread crumbs
6 tablespoons butter
1 lemon, thinly sliced

Lay the abalone steaks flat on a hard surface. With a kitchen mallet or the flat side of a cleaver, pound the steaks until they are about ⅓-inch thick.

In a small bowl beat the eggs. Add the salt and pepper and stir well. Dip each abalone steak into the eggs and then roll it in the bread crumbs.

In a large skillet, heat 4 tablespoons butter over moderate heat. Add the abalone and sauté until lightly browned on one side, about 2 to 3 minutes. Turn and brown on the other side. Do not overcook or steaks will be very tough.

Remove the steaks to a serving platter. Melt the remaining butter in the skillet and pour over the steaks. Serve with lemon slices.

The abalone is a single-shelled mollusk found along the California coast. It clings to the rocks with a large strong muscle— this is what makes the abalone steaks. However, the muscle must be tenderized by pounding before cooking; otherwise it is too tough to eat. Fresh abalone is preferable but hard to come by outside of California. Frozen abalone is acceptable. It must still be tenderized.

# CIOPPINO

serves 6

1½ pounds sea bass
1 pound shrimp, peeled and deveined
1 live lobster
1 quart clams
½ cup olive oil
1 large onion, coarsely chopped
2 cloves garlic, chopped
1 green pepper, coarsely chopped
4 ripe tomatoes, peeled and chopped
½ cup canned tomato purée
2 cups red wine
½ cup parsley, chopped
1 teaspoon salt
¼ teaspoon pepper

Cut the sea bass into serving pieces. Insert a knife into the lobster where the tail and body meet. Sever the spinal cord and cut the lobster into pieces. Scrub the clams.

Place the fish, shrimp, and lobster in layers into a large kettle.

In a saucepan heat the oil. Add the onion, garlic, and green pepper. Cook for 5 minutes. Add the tomatoes, tomato purée, wine, ¼ cup parsley, salt, and pepper. Cover and cook over low heat for 15 minutes.

Pour the sauce over the layers of fish, shrimp, and lobster. Cover and simmer gently for 30 minutes or until the bass flakes easily when tested with a fork. Add the clams and continue cooking until the clams open, about 5 minutes.

Transfer to a large serving dish and sprinkle with the remaining ¼ cup parsley. Serve hot.

# ⇒ Vegetables ⇐

## CARDAMOM PEAS

serves 4

    3   cups fresh peas
    ½   cup water
    1   teaspoon salt
    ½   teaspoon pepper
    ½   teaspoon dried marjoram
    ½   teaspoon ground cardamom
    2   tablespoons parsley, chopped

In a saucepan bring the water to a boil. Add the peas and cover. Cook for 2 to 3 minutes or until peas are tender. Drain off all but 1 tablespoon of the cooking liquid.

Toss the peas with the cooking liquid, salt, pepper, marjoram, and cardamom. Season to taste and stir in the parsley. Serve hot.

## SAUTEED CUCUMBERS

serves 4 to 6

    2   medium cucumbers
    ¼   cup butter
        flour
        salt and pepper to taste

Peel the cucumbers and cut into ¼-inch slices. Pat dry with paper towels to remove excess moisture.

Sprinkle the slices with salt and pepper. Dredge the slices in flour.

In a skillet melt the butter. Add the cucumber slices and sauté until golden brown on both sides, about 3 minutes per side. Remove from skillet, drain briefly, and serve.

## CALIFORNIA CARROTS

serves 4

    ¼   cup sugar
    1½  teaspoons cornstarch
    2   tablespoons lemon juice
    2   tablespoons water
    1   tablespoon soy sauce
    1   pound carrots
    3   tablespoons olive oil
    ½   green pepper
    ½   cup walnut halves

In a small saucepan combine the sugar, cornstarch, lemon juice, water, and soy sauce. Bring the mixture to a boil, stirring, and cook about 1 minute or until thick and clear. Set aside.

Trim and peel the carrots. Cut them into 2-inch pieces. Place the carrots in a saucepan and add the oil. Stir well. Cover tightly and cook over low heat for 20 minutes.

Cut the green pepper into thin, 2-inch strips.

Add the green pepper to the carrots. Add the sauce and cook for 5 minutes over low heat. Stir in the walnuts and cook 5 minutes longer. Place mixture in a serving dish and serve at once.

# HAWAIIAN GINGER CARROTS

serves 4

6 *medium carrots, peeled and cut into ½-inch slices*
2 *teaspoons fresh lemon juice*
¾ *teaspoon salt*
2 *¼-inch slices fresh ginger root, chopped, or 1*
  *teaspoon ground ginger*
  *pepper to taste*
2 *tablespoons butter, cut into pieces*

Preheat the oven to 400°.

Butter a 1-quart casserole or baking dish. Place the carrots in the casserole.

In a small bowl mix the lemon juice, salt, ginger, and pepper. Pour the sauce over the carrots and dot with butter pieces. Cover and bake for 1 hour or until carrots are tender.

Remove from oven and serve at once from baking dish.

# CARROTS WITH HERBS AND GRAPES

serves 4 to 6

1½ *pounds carrots*
 ½ *teaspoon salt*
 1 *teaspoon dried basil*
   *boiling water*
 ½ *cup butter*
 1 *small clove garlic, chopped*
 ½ *teaspoon dried thyme*
 1 *cup seedless grapes*
 1 *tablespoon lemon juice*
 ⅛ *teaspoon salt*
   *pepper to taste*

Wash, trim, and peel the carrots. Cut them into narrow strips 3 inches long. Place strips in a saucepan with the ½ teaspoon salt, basil, and enough boiling water to cover. Cook, covered, for 12 to 15 minutes or until carrots are just tender but still crisp.

Melt the butter in a saucepan. Add the garlic and thyme. Reserve.

When carrots are done, remove saucepan from heat. Add the grapes, stir, and cover. Let stand for 2 minutes. Drain well.

Stir the lemon juice into the garlic butter. Pour the mixture over the hot carrots. Season with salt and pepper to taste. Mix gently and serve.

# ASPARAGUS IN PESTO SAUCE

serves 6 to 8

3 *pounds fresh asparagus, trimmed*
1 *cup olive oil*
1 *cup firmly packed fresh basil leaves*
½ *cup chopped walnuts*
2 *cloves garlic*
1 *teaspoon salt*
¼ *cup light rum*
  *juice of 1 lemon*
½ *cup freshly grated Parmesan cheese*

Cook the asparagus in boiling salted water to cover until just tender, about 10 minutes. Drain and cover with cold water; drain well again. Chill the asparagus.

Place the olive oil, basil leaves, walnuts, garlic, salt, rum, lemon juice, and cheese in the container of an electric blender or food processor and blend until thick. Pour the mixture into a bowl and let it stand for 1 hour to allow flavors to develop.

Place the chilled asparagus on a serving platter. Beat the pesto sauce to mix it and spoon it over the asparagus.

# TURNIPS WITH CORIANDER

serves 6

1 pound turnips, peeled and cut into pieces
¾ tomato, peeled, seeded, and chopped
2 cups fresh peas, or 1 10-ounce package frozen
3 tablespoons butter
2 tablespoons fresh coriander, chopped,
    or 1 teaspoon dried

In a steaming basket set over simmering water, steam the turnips, covered, for 5 to 6 minutes or until tender.

In a large skillet melt the butter. Add the tomato and sauté over medium heat for 2 minutes. Stir often.

Blanch the peas in boiling water for 2 to 3 minutes. Remove and drain well.

Add the turnips, peas, coriander, salt, and pepper to the skillet with the tomatoes. Cook the mixture, stirring, until it is heated through. Transfer vegetables to a serving dish and serve hot.

# NAPA VALLEY LEEKS

serves 4 to 6

12 large leeks
1¼ cups chicken broth
 1 cup dry white wine
 4 tablespoons butter
 ¼ cup flour
    salt and pepper to taste
 1 cup grated Swiss or Parmesan cheese

Trim the leeks, removing all but 2 inches of the green leaves. Rinse thoroughly to remove all grit.

In a shallow saucepan combine the chicken broth and wine. Quickly bring the mixture to a boil. Reduce the heat and add the leeks. Cover and simmer over low heat for 5 to 7 minutes, or until the leeks are just tender. Drain the leeks and reserve the liquid. There should be about 2 cups of liquid; if not, add more wine.

Preheat the broiler.

Place the leeks into a buttered shallow baking dish in 1 or 2 layers.

Heat the butter in a saucepan. Stir in the flour and blend. Cook for 2 minutes. Gradually stir in the reserved leek liquid and cook, stirring constantly, until mixture is smooth and thickened. Stir in the salt, pepper, and ¾ cup cheese. Cook until the cheese is melted. Spoon the sauce over the leeks and sprinkle with the remaining cheese. Place under the broiler and cook until bubbly, about 5 minutes.

# SAUTEED LEEKS

serves 4 to 6

12 *large leeks*
 4 *tablespoons butter*
¼ *teaspoon dried thyme*
½ *teaspoon salt*
⅛ *teaspoon pepper*
¼ *cup brandy*
⅓ *cup beef broth*
 2 *tablespoons lemon juice*

Trim the leeks and cut away the green leaves. Rinse thoroughly to remove all grit.

Heat the butter in a large skillet and add the leeks. Sauté for 2 minutes. Add the thyme, salt, pepper, brandy, broth, and lemon juice. Cook over high heat for 10 minutes.

Reduce the heat and simmer until the leeks are tender, about 5 to 10 minutes longer. Remove from heat and serve hot.

# ZUCCHINI WITH PESTO

serves 4 to 6

½ *cup fresh basil leaves*
 2 *cloves garlic, finely chopped*
 2 *tablespoons pine nuts, chopped*
 2 *tablespoons freshly grated Parmesan cheese*
 5 *to 6 tablespoons olive oil*
 3 *medium zucchini*
   *salt and pepper to taste*

Place the basil, garlic, nuts, cheese, and 4 tablespoons olive oil into the container of an electric blender or food processor. Blend until smooth. Pour mixture into a bowl.

Trim the zucchini and cut them into narrow, 2-inch strips.

In a large skillet heat 1 to 2 tablespoons olive oil. When oil is hot, add the zucchini and sauté, stirring rapidly, for 2 to 3 minutes. Lower the heat and add the basil mixture. Cook until the pesto is heated through. Season with salt and pepper and serve.

To make pesto the traditional Italian way, crush the basil leaves using a mortar and pestle. Slowly grind in the other ingredients until a smooth paste is formed. Use the very freshest possible basil. Pesto keeps well in the refrigerator. It is a pleasant addition to any freshly steamed or sautéed vegetable and a colorful and delicious sauce for pasta.

# CALABACITA

serves 4 to 6

 3 *tablespoons butter*
 1 *onion, chopped*
 1 *clove garlic, chopped*
 2 *pounds zucchini, cut into ½-inch slices*
 1 *cup fresh corn, cut from the cob*
 1 *sweet red pepper, thinly sliced*
   *salt and pepper to taste*

In a deep 12-inch skillet, heat the butter. When hot, add the onion, garlic, zucchini, corn, and red pepper. Cook, stirring constantly, over medium-high heat for 5 minutes or until vegetables are tender but still crisp. Season with salt and pepper and serve at once.

# SAN JOSE SUMMER SQUASH

serves 4 to 6

3 small zucchini
3 small yellow summer squash
2 scallions
2 tablespoons butter
1 tablespoon olive oil
  salt and pepper to taste

Wash and trim the zucchini and summer squash. Cut them into ¼-inch rounds.

Chop the scallions.

Heat the butter and oil together in a large skillet. Add the zucchini and summer squash. Sauté, stirring occasionally, for 2 to 3 minutes. Add the scallions and cook 2 to 3 minutes longer. Add more butter if needed. Remove skillet from heat when vegetables are still slightly crisp. Season with salt and pepper and serve hot.

# WASHINGTON SWEET AND SOUR SQUASH

serves 4

¼ pound dried apples
  boiling water
4 tablespoons butter
½ pound small zucchini, cut into ½-inch slices
½ pound yellow summer squash, cut into ½-inch slices
½ teaspoon dried basil
½ teaspoon salt
¼ cup cider vinegar
2 tablespoons light brown sugar

Put the dried apples in a bowl with enough boiling water to cover. Soak for 30 to 45 minutes. Drain well and dry the apples on paper towels.

Preheat the oven to 350°.

Melt the butter in a large skillet. Add the apples and squash. Cook, stirring frequently, over moderate heat until lightly browned. Add the basil and salt. Remove the mixture from the skillet and place in a buttered 1-quart casserole or baking dish.

Add the vinegar and sugar to the skillet. Cook, stirring constantly, over high heat for 3 to 4 minutes. When the mixture begins to thicken, remove skillet from heat and pour mixture over the squash and apples. Toss mixture well until all pieces are coated. Bake, uncovered, for 20 to 25 minutes or until squash is tender. Remove from oven and serve directly from dish.

# GREEN BEANS WITH DILL SAUCE

serves 6 to 8

2 pounds fresh green beans, trimmed and left whole
  boiling water
¼ cup butter
¼ cup flour
1½ cups chicken broth
¼ cup lemon juice
¼ cup light rum
3 tablespoons fresh dill, chopped, or ¾ teaspoon dried
  salt to taste

Cook the green beans in boiling salted water to cover until tender but still crisp, about 15 minutes.

While beans are cooking, heat the butter in a saucepan. Stir in the flour and blend well. Gradually stir in the chicken broth, lemon juice, and rum. Add the dill and cook, stirring constantly, over medium heat until the sauce bubbles and thickens. Season to taste with salt.

Drain the green beans and place them on a serving platter. Cover the beans with the hot sauce. Serve at once.

# GREEN BEANS AND CARROTS WITH HOT ONION DRESSING

serves 4

12 ounces fresh green beans, trimmed and cut into
    2-inch pieces
 2 large carrots, julienned
 1 cup boiling salted water
 1 medium onion, coarsely chopped
 2 tablespoons vegetable oil
 2 tablespoons red wine vinegar
 1 tablespoon fresh dill, chopped, or ¼ teaspoon dried
 ¼ teaspoon pepper

Add the green beans and carrots to the boiling water. Reduce the heat. Cover and simmer for 10 to 15 minutes or until vegetables are tender but still crisp.

While the vegetables cook, heat the oil in a saucepan. Add the onion and cook until tender, about 5 to 7 minutes. Add the vinegar, dill, and pepper. Stir well.

Remove the green beans and carrots from the heat and drain. Transfer to a serving bowl. Pour the hot dressing over the vegetables. Toss and serve at once.

# BAKED TOMATOES

serves 4

 4 fresh tomatoes, peeled, seeded, and coarsely
    chopped
 2 cups bread crumbs
 3 tablespoons butter, cut up into pieces
 ¼ cup onion, minced
 1 teaspoon sugar
 1 teaspoon salt
 ½ teaspoon pepper
 ⅛ teaspoon cayenne pepper

Preheat the oven to 350°.

Drain the tomatoes of as much liquid as possible. Gently combine the tomatoes with the bread crumbs. Turn the mixture into a buttered 1-quart baking dish. Dot with the butter. Scatter the minced onion over the top and season with sugar, salt, pepper, and cayenne.

Bake, uncovered, for 30 minutes or until the top is nicely browned. Remove from oven and serve directly from the dish.

# MARINATED FRIED MUSHROOMS

serves 4

 ½ pound fresh mushrooms, trimmed and sliced
 ¼ cup lemon juice
 ¼ cup sherry
 ¼ cup vegetable oil
    salt and pepper to taste
 ½ teaspoon dried tarragon
 2 tablespoons butter

*(continued on next page)*

Place the sliced mushrooms in a shallow bowl or dish.

In a separate bowl, whisk together the lemon juice, sherry, and oil until well blended. Pour over the mushrooms. Season with salt, pepper, and tarragon. Stir the mixture to coat all the slices evenly. Cover and marinate for 2 hours.

Melt the butter in a skillet. Remove the mushroom slices from the marinade and drain. Add the mushrooms to the skillet and fry until brown and crisp, about 5 to 10 minutes. Transfer to a serving bowl and serve at once.

# CELERY VICTOR

serves 6

    3 bunches celery
      chicken broth
    3 sprigs parsley
    1 bay leaf
    1 teaspoon dried thyme
    1 medium onion, sliced
    1 carrot, cut into pieces
 1½ cups olive oil
    ½ cup white wine vinegar
      salt and pepper to taste
    6 anchovy fillets, drained
    6 strips pimiento

Rinse the celery and trim off the tough outer stalks. Cut off the tops and bottoms, leaving stalks about 7 inches long. Cut each stalk in half lengthwise.

Place the parsley, bay leaf, and thyme in a double-thick square of cheesecloth. Tie square closed with string.

In a large saucepan arrange the celery in a single layer. Pour in just enough of the chicken broth to cover the celery. Add the cheesecloth bag, the onion, and the carrot. Quickly bring the mixture to a boil. Lower the heat and simmer for 10 minutes until the celery is tender but still firm. Drain well and remove the onion and carrot pieces.

Cool the celery. Using the hands, gently squeeze the celery to press out excess liquid.

Arrange the celery in 1 layer in a serving dish.

In a small bowl whisk together the oil, vinegar, salt, and pepper. Pour the mixture over the celery and marinate in the refrigerator for 2 to 3 hours. When ready to serve, garnish each serving with an anchovy fillet and strip of pimiento.

Victor Hirtzler was chef of the famed St. Francis Hotel in San Francisco. This dish, at one time extremely fashionable, is his creation.

# CALIFORNIA ARTICHOKE HALVES

serves 6

    6 large artichokes
      water
      juice of 3 lemons
    1 tablespoon flour
    1 cup onion, chopped
    1 cup olive oil
    ½ cup water
      salt and pepper to taste

Remove the stems from the artichokes. Tear off the bottom leaves. With a scissors trim off the brown thorny tips of the remaining leaves. Cut off the tops of each artichoke and cut the artichokes in half. Soak the artichokes in 4 cups of water mixed with the juice of 2 lemons.

Heat the olive oil in a skillet. Add the onion, sprinkle with flour, and sauté until lightly browned, about 5 to 10 minutes. Add the salt, pepper, and juice of 1 lemon.

Arrange the artichoke halves, cut-side up, in a large skillet. Pour the onion mixture over. Add ½ cup water. Cover the skillet and simmer over low heat until the artichokes are tender, about 20 to 40 minutes. Remove the artichokes from the skillet and serve hot or cold.

# CALIFORNIA VEGETABLE STEW

serves 6

1 medium eggplant, peeled and cubed
2 large onions, thinly sliced
2 cloves garlic, minced
4 large ripe tomatoes, peeled and chopped
2 large sweet red peppers, thinly sliced
2 small zucchini, sliced
2 small yellow summer squash, sliced
1 cup fresh okra, sliced
2 cups fresh corn kernels
½ cup olive oil
   salt and pepper to taste
3 tablespoons fresh basil, chopped, or 1 tablespoon dried

In a deep heavy pot, heat the olive oil. Add the onions, garlic, peppers, and eggplant. Cook over low heat for 30 minutes or until vegetables are soft. Do not brown. Add the tomatoes, zucchini, yellow squash, okra, and corn. Season with salt and pepper. Cover and simmer for 15 minutes over low heat.

Add the basil and simmer, uncovered, for 15 to 25 minutes longer or until the excess liquid has evaporated. Remove from heat and serve.

# Noodles, Grains, and Beans

## SHRIMP-FILLED PASTA SHELLS

serves 6

2 pounds shrimp, peeled and deveined
3 egg whites
1 cup heavy cream
   juice of 1 lemon
⅓ cup light rum
1½ teaspoons salt
4 scallions, minced
36 large pasta shells, cooked and drained
1½ pounds mozzarella cheese, shredded
   chopped chives

Place the raw shrimp and the egg whites into the container of an electric blender or food processor and blend until a smooth paste is formed.

Empty the mixture into a bowl and add the cream, lemon juice, rum, and salt. Stir until the mixture is smooth. Fold in the scallions. Chill, covered, for 2 hours.

Preheat the oven to 350°.

Remove the shrimp mixture from the refrigerator. Fill the pasta shells with the mixture. Place the shells side by side in a buttered shallow baking dish. Top with the mozzarella cheese.

Bake for 20 to 25 minutes or until cheese is melted and golden. Sprinkle with chopped chives and serve hot.

## CALIFORNIA BEANS AND BRANDY

serves 6 to 8

2 cups dried pinto beans
   water
   boiling water
2 cloves garlic, chopped
1 onion
1 bay leaf
1 teaspoon dried thyme
6 tablespoons butter
1 small onion, finely chopped
2 cups canned plum tomatoes
2 teaspoons salt
⅓ cup brandy or madeira

Place the beans in a large pot. Add enough cold water to cover and soak beans overnight.

Drain the beans and return them to the pot. Add the garlic, onion, bay leaf, and thyme. Cover with boiling water and cook over low heat, covered, until beans are tender, about 1 hour or more.

Drain the beans, reserving 1 cup of the liquid.

Heat the butter in a skillet. Add the onion and sauté until soft, about 5 minutes. Add the tomatoes, salt, brandy, and reserved bean liquid. Bring mixture to a boil. Reduce the heat and simmer for 30 minutes.

Preheat the oven to 325°.

Add the beans to the skillet and mix well. Turn mixture into a 3½- or 4-quart casserole or baking dish. Bake, uncovered, until mixture begins to bubble. Remove from oven and serve directly from the baking dish.

# SAN DIEGO PINTO BEANS

serves 8

  2 cups dried pinto beans
  3 quarts water
  1 1-pound can tomatoes
  1 large onion, coarsely chopped
  ¾ cup sliced celery
1½ teaspoons salt
  ¾ teaspoon cinnamon
  6 tablespoons sugar
  3 tablespoons vinegar

Place the beans in a large pot with the water. Bring to a boil. Reduce the heat and simmer, covered, for 4 hours or until tender. Drain well, reserving the cooking liquid.

Preheat the oven to 350°.

In a mixing bowl combine the beans, tomatoes, onion, bacon, celery, salt, cinnamon, sugar, vinegar, and reserved cooking liquid. Mix until well blended.

Turn the mixture into a 4-quart casserole or baking dish. Cover and bake for 2½ to 3 hours. If mixture gets dry while baking, add water. Serve hot.

# TANGY KIDNEY BEAN BAKE

serves 4

  2 1-pound cans kidney beans
  ½ teaspoon salt
  ½ cup chili sauce
  ¼ cup pickle relish
  1 medium onion, thinly sliced
  1 tablespoon butter, cut into pieces

Preheat the oven to 375°.

Drain 1 can of beans well. Do not drain the second can. Place the drained and undrained beans into a large mixing bowl. Add the salt, chili sauce, relish, and onion. Mix well.

Turn the mixture into a 1½-quart casserole or baking dish. Dot with butter. Cover and bake for 35 minutes. Remove from oven and serve directly from baking dish.

# NAPA VALLEY HAM AND BEANS

serves 6 to 8

  6 cups cooked kidney beans
1½ cups onions, finely chopped
  6 tablespoons butter
  1 teaspoon dried savory
  1 teaspoon dried thyme
  3 cups cooked ham, diced
  2 cups red wine
  2 tablespoons tomato paste
    salt and pepper to taste
  ½ cup scallions, finely chopped

*(continued on next page)*

Drain the beans well.

Heat the butter in a skillet and add the onions. Sauté until onions wilt, about 3 minutes. Add the savory, thyme, and ham. Stir to mix well. Stir in the wine and tomato paste. Simmer over low heat for 25 minutes or until all ingredients are well blended. Season with salt and pepper to taste. Add the beans to the skillet and stir to combine. Heat until beans are very hot.

Serve from a large bowl garnished with chopped scallions.

# WHITE BEANS VINAIGRETTE

serves 4

2 cups dried white beans
1 tablespoon onion, chopped
1 clove garlic, chopped
2 tablespoons green pepper, finely chopped
Vinaigrette dressing:
½ cup olive oil
1 teaspoon French-style mustard
1 tablespoon wine vinegar
½ teaspoon salt
½ teaspoon pepper

Place the beans in a pot and cover with cold water to a depth of 1 inch. Bring to a boil and cook for 2 minutes. Remove pot from heat. Cover and let stand for 1 hour. Return to heat and simmer until beans are tender, about 1 hour or more. Drain well and cool.

In a bowl combine the mustard, vinegar, salt, and pepper. Whisk in the olive oil slowly. Continue to whisk until mixture is well blended.

Place the cooled beans in a serving bowl. Add the onion, green pepper, garlic, and vinaigrette. Toss thoroughly and serve warm or cold.

# BEANS AND CHEESE

serves 4

½ pound dried kidney beans
1 tablespoon butter
1 small onion, finely chopped
½ pound Monterey Jack cheese, coarsely grated
2 tomatoes, coarsely chopped
1 dried red chili pepper, grated
½ pimiento, finely chopped
¼ cup dry white wine
½ teaspoon salt

Place the beans in a pot and add enough cold water to cover to a depth of 1 inch. Bring beans to a boil and cook for 2 minutes. Cover and let stand for 1 hour.

Return pot to heat and simmer beans until tender, about 1 hour or more. Drain well.

Melt the butter in a large skillet. Add the onion and cheese. Stir until the cheese is melted. Add the beans, tomatoes, chili pepper, pimiento, wine, and salt. Cook over low heat until the mixture is smooth and creamy. Remove from heat and serve hot.

# GARBANZOS WITH GARLIC

serves 4 to 6

3 cups cooked garbanzos (chick peas)
4 cloves garlic, crushed
½ cup butter
2 tablespoons olive oil
  salt and pepper

Heat the oil and butter in a skillet. Add the garlic and sauté over low heat for 3 to 5 minutes. Remove half the garlic from the skillet and discard. Add the chick peas and continue cooking over low heat. Shake the skillet and stir occasionally. Cook until beans are lightly browned, about 10 to 15 minutes. Season with salt and pepper and place in a serving dish. Serve hot or cooled.

# HAWAIIAN RICE

serves 4

¾ cup chopped onion
4 tablespoons butter
1¼ cups long-grained rice
½ teaspoon curry powder
½ cup golden raisins
1¼ teaspoons salt
2½ cups water
½ cup shredded coconut

Preheat the oven to 400°.

In a skillet melt the butter. Add the onion and sauté until soft, about 5 minutes. Remove skillet from heat.

Place the rice, curry powder, raisins, salt, and water into a buttered 1½-quart casserole or baking dish. Add the onions and butter and stir until well combined. Cover dish and bake for 5 minutes. Lower the temperature to 350° and bake 40 minutes longer.

Remove from oven and cool slightly. Sprinkle coconut over top and serve directly from the baking dish.

# LEMON RICE

serves 4 to 6

4 cups cooked hot rice
¾ cup freshly grated Parmesan cheese
4 eggs
3 tablespoons lemon juice
2 tablespoons butter, softened
1 teaspoon dried thyme
½ cup pine nuts

In a bowl beat together the egg, cheese, lemon juice, and thyme.

Place the rice in a saucepan. Add the softened butter and then the egg and cheese mixture. Gently stir until well combined. Cover and cook over very low heat until heated through, about 3 to 4 minutes.

Remove from heat and stir in the pine nuts. Place mixture in a serving bowl and serve hot.

# BAKED RICE AND ONIONS

serves 4

*½ cup long-grain rice*
*2 quarts boiling water*
*1 teaspoon salt*
*¼ cup butter*
*4 cups onions, thinly sliced*
*½ teaspoon salt*
*2 tablespoons freshly grated Parmesan cheese*

Preheat the oven to 325°.

Place the rice in a large pot with the boiling water and 1 teaspoon salt. Boil, uncovered, for 5 minutes. Remove from heat and drain.

Place the butter in a 2-quart casserole or baking dish. Heat the dish in the oven until the butter melts. Remove the dish from the oven and add the onions. Stir well. Add ½ teaspoon salt and the rice. Stir well.

Cover the dish and bake for 1 hour. Remove from oven and sprinkle with grated cheese. Serve at once from the baking dish.

# BAKED RICE WITH OLIVES

serves 4

*1½ cups long-grain rice*
*2 cloves garlic, chopped*
*3 tablespoons olive oil*
*2 tablespoons butter*
*40 black olives, pitted and coarsely chopped*
*1½ teaspoons salt*
*1 teaspoon pepper*
*2 teaspoons chili powder*
*1½ teaspoons basil*
*5 cups tomato juice*
*freshly grated Parmesan cheese*

Preheat the oven to 350°.

Heat the oil and butter together in a skillet. Add the rice and sauté until just lightly golden.

Place the rice in a buttered 2-quart casserole or baking dish. Add the olives, salt, pepper, chili powder, and basil. Toss lightly but well.

Heat the tomato juice in a saucepan until just boiling. Pour over the rice mixture. Cover dish and bake for 1 hour or until the liquid has been absorbed by the rice and the rice is tender.

Remove from oven. Sprinkle with the grated cheese and serve directly from the baking dish.

# SAGE RICE

serves 4

2 cups chicken broth
1½ cups long-grain rice
1 cup dry white wine
2 teaspoons dried sage, crumbled
   salt and pepper
3 tablespoons butter
½ cup pine nuts

In a saucepan combine the chicken broth, rice, wine, and sage. Bring to a boil and reduce the heat. Season with salt and pepper.

Cover and simmer for 15 minutes or until rice is tender.

Melt the butter in a small skillet. Add the pine nuts and cook for 2 minutes or until nuts are lightly golden. Stir constantly.

Stir the pine nuts and butter into the rice. Transfer to a serving dish and serve hot.

## ·Breads·

# PEACH AND WALNUT BREAD

yields 1 loaf

¼ cup butter
½ cup sugar
1 egg
2½ cups flour
3 teaspoons baking powder
1 teaspoon salt
1 cup milk
¾ cup chopped walnuts
1 cup dried peaches, chopped

Preheat the oven to 375°.

Combine the flour with the baking powder and salt in a large bowl or on a large sheet of wax paper.

In a mixing bowl cream together the butter, sugar, and egg. Add the flour mixture to the creamed mixture alternately with the milk. Stir in the walnuts and peaches.

Turn the batter into a buttered 9 × 5 × 3-inch loaf pan. Bake for 50 to 55 minutes or until a cake tester inserted in the center of the loaf comes out clean.

Remove from oven to a cooling rack. Cool in the pan for 10 minutes, then turn out onto the rack and cool completely.

The tangy flavor of San Francisco sourdough bread is a reminder of Gold Rush times, when prospectors carried starter pots of sourdough with them to the gold fields, which were a long way from places to buy yeast. Make your own sourdough starter using the recipe below, or purchase ready-made starter at a grocery or health-food store.

## SOURDOUGH STARTER

yields approximately 1½ cups

1 cup flour
1 cup water
1 tablespoon sugar

In a large bowl or crock mix together the flour, water, and sugar. Cover and let mixture stand in a warm place for 2 to 3 days or until fermented.

Natural yeasts in the atmosphere will make the mixture ferment. Once the starter is made, it will keep for about 3 days at room temperature and longer if refrigerated. To replenish the mixture as it is used up, simply make a new batch using the recipe above and mix in the remainder of the previous batch. Strains of yeast have been perpetuated for years using this method.

# SAN FRANCISCO SOURDOUGH BREAD

yields 1 large round loaf

1 cup Sourdough Starter
1 package active dry yeast
1½ cups warm water (110° to 115°)
6 cups flour
2 teaspoons salt
2 teaspoons sugar
½ teaspoon baking soda
water

Sprinkle the yeast into the warm water and let stand for 2 minutes. Stir to dissolve.

Transfer the yeast to a large mixing bowl. Stir in the Sourdough Starter, 4 cups flour, salt, and sugar. Stir rapidly for 3 minutes. Transfer to a large oiled bowl, cover with a clean towel, and let rise in a warm place until doubled in bulk, about 2 hours.

Combine the baking soda with 1 cup flour and add it to the dough. Stir well.

Turn the dough onto a lightly floured surface and knead in the remaining 1 cup flour. More may be needed. Knead until the dough is smooth and not sticky. Shape the dough into 1 large round loaf and place it on a buttered baking sheet. Cover dough and let rise a second time until almost doubled in bulk, about 1 hour.

Preheat the oven to 400°.

Brush the top of the loaf with water and slash the top diagonally with a sharp knife. Place a shallow pan of hot water in the bottom of the oven. Bake the bread for 45 to 50 minutes or until golden. Remove from oven and cool before slicing.

# SOURDOUGH ROLLS

yields 12 rolls

 1 *package active dry yeast*
1¼ *cups warm water (110° to 115°)*
 1 *tablespoon sugar*
 1 *cup Sourdough Starter*
3½ *to 4 cups flour*

Place ¼ cup warm water in a bowl and sprinkle in the yeast and sugar. Let stand for 2 minutes and then stir to dissolve. Move the bowl to a warm, draft-free area and let stand 5 minutes longer.

Place the Sourdough Starter in a large mixing bowl. Add the yeast mixture. Add the remaining water and 1½ cups flour. Stir well to combine all ingredients. Cover with a clean towel and let rise in a warm place until doubled in bulk, about 2 hours.

Stir the mixture and remove 1 cup. Place the removed mixture in a tightly sealed jar and save to use as sourdough starter for future recipes.

Gradually add 2 to 2½ cups flour to the mixture remaining in the bowl. Beat hard after each addition. Add only enough flour to make a dough firm enough to be gathered into a ball.

Turn the dough out onto a heavily floured surface. Knead until the dough becomes smooth and elastic, about 10 minutes. Sprinkle more flour on the surface as needed. Shape the dough into a ball and place in a lightly buttered bowl. Cover with a clean towel and let rise in a warm place until doubled in bulk, about 1 hour.

Preheat the oven to 375°. Generously butter a baking sheet.

Punch the dough down. Using a sharp knife, cut the dough into 12 equal pieces. Shape the pieces into balls and flatten slightly. Place the balls 2 inches apart on the baking sheet. Bake for 20 to 25 minutes or until golden brown. Serve warm.

# ORANGE GROVE RYE BREAD

yields 2 small loaves

  2 packages active dry yeast
1½ cups warm water (110° to 115°)
  ½ cup dark honey
  2 tablespoons vegetable oil
  2 tablespoons freshly grated orange peel
  1 tablespoon salt
  1 teaspoon ground cardamom
2½ cups rye flour
2½ cups whole wheat flour
    yellow corn meal
    softened butter

Place the warm water into a bowl and sprinkle in the yeast. Let stand for 2 minutes and then stir to dissolve.

Pour the yeast mixture into a large bowl and add the honey, oil, orange peel, salt, and cardamom. Mix well. Add 1 cup of the rye flour and 1 cup of the whole wheat flour. Stir until smooth, about 2 to 3 minutes. Stir in the remaining flour. Combine thoroughly.

Turn the dough out onto a lightly floured surface. Knead until the dough is smooth and elastic, about 15 to 20 minutes. Form the dough into a ball and place in a lightly buttered bowl. Cover with a clean towel and let rise until doubled in bulk, about 1½ hours.

Punch down the dough. Divide it in half and form the halves into small ovals.

Butter a baking sheet and sprinkle with corn meal. Place the loaves on the sheet.

Make 3 slashes across the top of each loaf with a sharp knife. Cover with a clean towel and let rise again in a warm place until almost doubled in bulk, about 45 minutes.

Preheat the oven to 375°.

Bake the loaves for 45 minutes or until golden. Remove from oven and brush with softened butter. Cool completely before slicing.

# SWEET WALNUT BREAD

yields 1 loaf

  2 cups flour
  2 teaspoons baking powder
  ½ cup sugar
  ½ teaspoon salt
  1 cup chopped walnuts
  1 cup light cream
  1 egg, slightly beaten

Preheat the oven to 325°.

Combine the flour, baking powder, sugar, and salt in a large bowl. Add the walnuts and mix well.

In a small bowl blend the cream and egg. Stir into the flour mixture. Turn the batter into a buttered and floured 9 × 5 × 3-inch loaf pan. Let bread rest for 20 minutes.

Bake for 1 hour or until a cake tester inserted into the middle of the loaf comes out clean.

Remove from oven to a cooling rack. Cool for 10 minutes in the pan, then turn out onto the rack and cool completely.

# WILLAMETTE VALLEY APPLE BREAD

yields 1 loaf

2 cups flour
2 teaspoons baking powder
1 teaspoon salt
½ teaspoon cinnamon
¼ teaspoon grated nutmeg
½ cup butter
1¼ cups sugar
2 eggs
1½ cups apple, peeled and finely grated
½ cup chopped pecans

Preheat the oven to 350°.

In a bowl or on a large piece of wax paper combine the flour, baking powder, salt, cinnamon, and nutmeg.

In a mixing bowl cream together the butter and sugar until light and fluffy. Add the eggs, 1 at a time, beating well after each addition. Stir in the dry ingredients and the apple, one-half at a time. Fold in the pecans.

Turn the batter into a generously buttered and floured 9 × 5 × 3-inch loaf pan. Bake for 1 hour or until a cake tester inserted into the center of the bread comes out clean.

Remove from oven to a cooling rack. Cool in the pan for 10 minutes, then turn out onto the rack. Cool completely before slicing.

# APRICOT LOAF

yields 1 loaf

3 cups flour
1 tablespoon plus ½ teaspoon baking powder
1 teaspoon salt
1 cup sugar
2 tablespoons butter
1 egg, beaten
¾ cup milk
¼ cup orange juice
1 tablespoon plus 1 teaspoon freshly grated orange rind
1 cup dried apricots, chopped
¾ cup chopped walnuts

Preheat the oven to 350°.

In a mixing bowl combine the flour, baking powder, salt, and orange rind. Mix well and set aside.

In a medium mixing bowl cream together the butter and sugar. Add the egg and mix well.

Combine the milk and orange juice.

Add the flour mixture alternately with the milk mixture to the creamed butter and sugar. Stir in the apricot and walnuts.

Turn the batter into a buttered 9 × 5 × 3-inch loaf pan. Let the bread rest for 20 minutes.

Bake for 60 to 70 minutes or until a cake tester inserted into the center of the bread comes out clean.

Remove from the oven to a cooling rack. Cool in the pan for 10 minutes. Turn bread out onto the rack and cool completely.

# WEST COAST BREAD

yields 1 loaf

1½ cups apple, peeled and chopped
⅓ cup frozen orange juice concentrate
⅓ cup butter
1 cup sugar
1 egg
2 cups flour
1 teaspoon baking powder
¾ cup raisins
¾ cup chopped pecans

Preheat the oven to 350°.

Mix the chopped apple and orange juice concentrate together in a small bowl. Set aside.

In a mixing bowl cream together the butter and sugar until light and fluffy. Add the egg and beat well. Stir in the apple and orange concentrate mixture.

In a small bowl combine the flour, baking powder, and baking soda. Beat in the creamed mixture. Add the raisins and pecans. Stir well.

Turn the batter into a buttered 10-inch tube pan and bake for 45 minutes or until golden brown.

Remove from the oven to a cooling rack. Cool in the pan for 10 minutes. Turn bread out onto the cooling rack and cool completely.

# HAWAIIAN BANANA BREAD

yields 1 loaf

2 cups flour
1 teaspoon baking soda
½ teaspoon salt
½ cup butter
1 cup sugar
2 eggs
1 to 2½ very ripe bananas, mashed
⅓ cup milk
1 teaspoon lemon juice or ½ teaspoon vanilla extract
½ cup chopped nuts

Preheat the oven to 350°.

Combine the flour, baking soda, and salt in a bowl or on a large piece of wax paper.

Cream the butter in a mixing bowl. Gradually add the sugar and mix until well blended. Add the eggs and bananas. Mix until well blended.

Combine the milk and lemon juice in a large bowl. Alternately mix the flour mixture and the milk mixture into the banana mixture. Add a little at a time, beginning and ending with the dry ingredients. Blend well after each addition. Stir in the nuts.

Turn the batter into a heavily buttered 9 × 5 × 3-inch loaf pan. Bake for 1 hour or until bread is golden and springs back when touched.

Remove from the oven to a cooling rack. Cool in the pan for 10 minutes. Turn bread out onto the cooling rack and cool completely.

# PORTLAND PRUNE BREAD

yields 1 loaf

1 cup flour
½ cup whole wheat flour
½ teaspoon baking soda
½ teaspoon baking powder
½ teaspoon salt
½ cup sugar
1 egg, slightly beaten
2 tablespoons melted butter
½ cup milk
½ cup cooked prunes, chopped
½ cup prune juice

Preheat the oven to 375°.

In a bowl or on a large piece of wax paper combine the flour, whole wheat flour, baking soda, baking powder, salt, and sugar.

Using an electric mixer, combine the egg, butter, milk, prunes, and prune juice in a large mixing bowl. Mix until well blended. Add the flour mixture and beat at medium speed until well combined.

Turn the batter into a buttered 9 × 5 × 3-inch loaf pan. Bake for 40 to 60 minutes or until a cake tester inserted into the center of the bread comes out clean.

Remove from the oven to a cooling rack. Cool in the pan for 10 minutes. Turn out onto the rack and cool completely.

# CALIFORNIA DATE NUT BREAD

yields 2 loaves

2 cups boiling water
1 cup sugar
1 cup dates, pitted and chopped
1 teaspoon salt
2 tablespoons butter
2 teaspoons baking soda
1 egg, beaten
2 teaspoons vanilla extract
2 teaspoons baking powder
3 cups flour
1 cup chopped walnuts

Preheat the oven to 350°.

In a mixing bowl combine the sugar, chopped dates, salt, butter, and baking soda. Pour the boiling water over the mixture. Stir well and set aside to cool.

When mixture is cool add the egg, vanilla extract, baking powder, flour, and chopped walnuts. Mix well.

Turn the batter into 2 buttered and floured 8 × 4 × 3-inch loaf pans. Bake for 45 minutes or until a cake tester inserted into the center of the bread comes out clean.

Remove from the oven to cooling racks. Cool in the pan for 10 minutes, then turn out onto the racks and cool completely.

# ALASKAN BLUEBERRY MUFFINS

yields 20 muffins

2½ cups ripe blueberries
2 cups flour
2 teaspoons baking powder
½ teaspoon salt
½ cup butter
1 cup sugar
2 eggs
½ cup milk

Preheat the oven to 350°.

Rinse the blueberries and remove any stems and blemished berries. Dry berries completely on paper towels.

Mash ½ cup of the blueberries in small bowl until smooth. Set aside.

Place the remaining berries in a bowl with 2 tablespoons flour. Toss to coat berries and set aside.

Combine the remaining flour with the baking powder and salt in a bowl or on a large piece of wax paper.

In a mixing bowl cream the butter and sugar together until light and fluffy. Add the eggs, 1 at a time. Beat well after each addition.

Add 1 cup of the flour mixture to the creamed mixture. Mix well. Beat in half the milk. Beat in the remaining flour and the rest of the milk. Continue to beat until the batter is smooth. Add the mashed berries and beat again. Fold the whole berries into the batter. Mix gently.

Spoon the batter into 20 well-buttered muffin cups, filling each about three-quarters full.

Bake for 20 to 25 minutes or until a cake tester inserted into the center of a muffin comes out clean.

Remove from the oven. Turn muffins out of tins and serve warm.

# ORANGE BISCUITS

yields 16 biscuits

2 cups flour
5 teaspoons baking powder
1 teaspoon salt
2 tablespoons butter
½ cup milk or more
  juice of 1 large orange
  freshly grated rind of 1 orange
16 small sugar cubes

Preheat the oven to 375°.

In a large bowl combine the flour, baking powder, and salt. Cut in the butter with a pastry blender or two knives until the mixture resembles a coarse meal. Add enough milk to make a soft dough. Mix well.

Turn the dough out onto a lightly floured surface. Roll dough out ¼-inch thick and cut out 16 rounds with a lightly floured biscuit cutter.

Place the biscuits into 16 buttered muffin cups. Sprinkle the grated orange rind over the biscuits.

Place the orange juice in a bowl. Dip the sugar cubes into the juice and quickly press 1 cube into the center of each biscuit.

Bake for 20 minutes or until golden. Remove from oven, turn out of tins, and serve at once.

# CALIFORNIA JOHNNYCAKE

serves 4 to 6

2 tablespoons butter, melted and cooled
2 eggs
2 cups buttermilk
2 tablespoons honey
½ cup flour
1 teaspoon baking soda
1 teaspoon salt
2 cups yellow corn meal

Preheat the oven to 425°.

Whisk the egg whites in a bowl until light and foamy. Add the buttermilk and honey. Beat well. Add the flour, baking soda, and salt. Beat until the batter is smooth. Beat in ½ cup of the corn meal at a time. Stir in the cooled butter. Pour the batter into a generously buttered 9 × 9 × 2-inch baking pan.

Bake for 20 minutes or until the cake begins to come away from the sides of the baking pan and the top is golden brown.

Remove from oven and serve directly from the baking pan.

# SEATTLE PUFF PANCAKES

serves 4

3 eggs
½ cup flour
½ cup milk
2 tablespoons melted butter
¼ teaspoon salt
    freshly grated rind of ½ lemon
    confectioner's sugar

Preheat the oven to 400°.

Beat the eggs in a mixing bowl. Add the flour, 2 tablespoons at a time, beating well after each addition. Beat only until smooth. Beat in the milk, butter, salt, and lemon rind.

Turn the batter into 2 heavily buttered 9-inch pie pans. Divide the batter evenly.

Bake for 10 minutes. Reduce the oven temperature to 350° and bake 5 minutes longer.

Remove from the oven and sprinkle with confectioner's sugar. Serve immediately.

# ·Desserts·

## LEMON MERINGUE PIE

yields 1 9-inch pie

   1 cup sugar
   2 tablespoons cornstarch
  1/4 teaspoon salt
 1 1/2 cups hot water
 1 1/2 cups bread crumbs
   3 eggs, separated
   1 tablespoon butter
    freshly grated peel of 1 lemon
    juice of 2 medium lemons
   1 pastry for 9-inch pie shell
   6 tablespoons water
  1/4 teaspoon salt

Preheat the oven to 400°.

Roll out the pastry on a lightly floured surface. Fit into a 9-inch pie pan and flute the edges. Prick the pastry all over with a fork and bake for 15 to 20 minutes or until golden brown. Remove from oven and cool.

Beat the egg yolks in a bowl.

Mix the sugar, cornstarch, and salt together in the top of a double boiler. Add the hot water and first stir, then beat, the mixture until it is smooth. Add the bread crumbs. Cook over boiling water, stirring constantly, until mixture is thick and smooth.

Stir 2 tablespoons of the bread crumb mixture into the beaten egg yolks. Add the egg yolk mixture back to the crumb mixture in the double boiler. Cook for 2 to 3 minutes. Remove from the heat and add the butter, lemon rind, and lemon juice. Cool slightly.

To make the meringue, in a small bowl beat the egg whites with 1/4 teaspoon salt until foamy. Gradually beat in 6 tablespoons sugar. Beat until whites are stiff but not dry.

Pour the cooled filling into the baked pie shell. Pile the meringue lightly on top of the filling. Cover the filling and the edges of the pie completely with the meringue.

Bake for 5 minutes or until lightly browned. Remove from oven and cool completely before serving.

## SAN JOAQUIN BRANDY CHOCOLATE PIE

yields 1 9-inch pie

   1 cup semisweet chocolate bits
   5 eggs, separated
  1/4 cup brandy
  1/2 teaspoon vanilla extract
  1/8 teaspoon salt
  1/8 teaspoon cream of tartar
  1/2 cup sugar
   1 cup heavy cream
  3/4 cup chopped walnuts
   1 9-inch Graham Cracker Pie Shell
    walnut halves

Preheat the oven to 375°.

Melt the chocolate bits in the top of a double boiler over hot but not boiling water. Beat in the egg yolks, 1 at a time, alternating with the brandy. Beat well until smooth. Stir in the vanilla extract and remove from heat. Let cool.

In a small bowl beat the egg whites with the salt and cream of tartar until stiff but not dry. Gradually beat in the sugar, 1 tablespoon at a time.

Fold a small amount of the meringue into the chocolate mixture, then fold the chocolate mixture back into the meringue.

Whip the cream until stiff and fold half of it into the chocolate and meringue mixture. Add the chopped walnuts and blend.

Pile the chocolate and meringue mixture into the Graham Cracker Pie Shell. Refrigerate until firm, at least 4 to 5 hours. Decorate with remaining whipped cream and walnut halves before serving.

# CALIFORNIA FIG PIE

yields 1 pie

    2 tablespoons unflavored gelatin
    ¼ cup water
    2 eggs, separated
    6 tablespoons sugar
    ⅛ teaspoon salt
    ¾ cup milk
    1 tablespoon freshly grated orange peel
    2 tablespoons Triple Sec, Cointreau,
       or any orange liqueur
    2 cups fresh figs, unpeeled and diced
    ½ cup heavy cream, whipped
    1 9-inch Graham Cracker Pie Shell

Add the gelatin to the water. Stir to blend.

In a small bowl beat the egg yolks with 4 tablespoons sugar and the salt.

Scald the milk in a saucepan. Add 2 tablespoons of the scalded milk to the egg yolks. Blend well, then add the egg mixture into the scalded milk. Blend well. Cook, stirring constantly, over very low heat until the mixture thickens. Add the gelatin and stir until it dissolves.

Remove the saucepan from the heat and stir in the orange rind and orange liqueur. Set aside to cool until the custard begins to jell.

In a small bowl beat the egg whites with the remaining sugar until stiff but not dry.

Fold the figs, whipped cream, and egg whites into the cooled custard. Turn the mixture into the Graham Cracker Pie Shell (see below) and chill until set, at least 3 to 4 hours.

# GRAHAM CRACKER PIE SHELL

yields 1 9-inch pie shell

    1½ cups graham cracker crumbs
    ¼ cup sugar
    ¼ cup melted butter

Mix the crumbs, sugar, and melted butter together well. Press the mixture into a 9-inch pie pan. Cover the entire pan and pat down. Bake at 375° for 8 minutes. Remove from oven and cool completely before filling.

# BROILED GRAPEFRUIT PIE

yields 1 9-inch pie

½ cup flour
1 cup sugar
½ teaspoon salt
2 eggs, beaten
1¼ cups milk
½ cup unsweetened grapefruit juice
1 teaspoon vanilla extract
1 cup fresh grapefruit sections
½ cup brown sugar
1 pastry for 9-inch pie shell

Preheat the oven to 400°.

Roll the pastry out onto a lightly floured surface. Fit into a 9-inch pie pan and flute the edges. Prick the pastry all over with a fork and bake for 15 to 20 minutes or until golden. Remove from oven and cool.

Preheat the broiler.

In a large bowl combine the flour, sugar, and salt. Add the eggs and milk. Mix well. With a rubber spatula transfer the mixture to the top of a double boiler. Cook, stirring constantly, over hot but not boiling water until the mixture is thick and smooth. Add the grapefruit juice and cook 10 minutes longer. Stir in the vanilla and remove from the heat.

Pour the mixture into the pie shell. Arrange the grapefruit sections on top of the custard. Sprinkle grapefruit sections with brown sugar.

Broil the pie 6 inches from heat until the brown sugar is caramelized and the grapefruit is lightly browned. Remove from the broiler and cool completely before serving.

# FRESH FRUIT TART

yields 1 9-inch tart

1 cup flour
1 tablespoon sugar
⅛ teaspoon salt
½ cup butter, softened
3 ounces cream cheese, softened
½ cup apricot preserves
1 tablespoon amaretto or almond liqueur
4 to 6 fresh medium nectarines
⅓ cup sliced almonds

Sift the flour together with the sugar and salt into a large bowl. Cut in the butter with a pastry blender or 2 knives until the mixture resembles a coarse meal. Add the cream cheese and mix to form a soft dough. Shape the dough into a ball, wrap in wax paper, and chill for 2 hours.

Preheat the oven to 400°.

Place the almonds in a metal baking pan and toast in the oven for 5 minutes or until golden. Remove from oven and cool.

Roll the pastry out onto a lightly floured surface with a floured rolling pin. Invert it into a 9-inch metal tart pan, preferably one with a removable bottom. Prick the crust with a fork and line it with aluminum foil. Weight the foil down with a handful of rice. Bake the crust for 20 minutes. Remove and discard rice and foil; continue baking the crust for 8 to 10 minutes longer or until lightly browned. Remove from oven and cool completely.

Brush the bottom of the cooled shell lightly with apricot preserves. Place the remaining preserves and the amaretto liqueur into a saucepan. Heat until the preserves melt. Set aside to use for glaze.

Peel, pit, and slice the nectarines. Arrange the slices in slightly overlapping concentric circles in the shell. Brush slices with the melted glaze. Sprinkle with the toasted almonds. Refrigerate for 3 to 4 hours or until set.

# EVERGREEN STATE APPLE PIE

yields 1 9-inch pie

2½ cups canned sour red cherries, pitted and drained
2 cups unsweetened applesauce
2½ tablespoons quick-cooking tapioca
½ cup light brown sugar, firmly packed
½ teaspoon cinnamon
⅛ teaspoon salt
2 tablespoons butter, cut into pieces
1 pastry for 2-crust 9-inch pie

Preheat the oven to 425°.

Roll half the pastry out onto a lightly floured surface. Fit into 9-inch pie pan.

In a bowl combine the cherries, applesauce, tapioca, sugar, cinnamon, and salt. Mix well.

Pour the filling into the pie shell and dot with the butter.

Roll out the remaining pastry and cut it into strips using a pastry wheel or sharp knife. Form a lattice over the pie. Trim, fold ends under, and flute.

Bake for 35 minutes or until brown. Remove from oven and cool slightly before serving.

# PECAN COFFEE CAKE

yields 1 9-inch cake

1 cup butter
2 cups sugar
2 eggs
1 cup sour cream
2 teaspoons vanilla extract
2 cups flour
1 teaspoon baking powder
¼ teaspoon salt

Filling:

2 cups chopped pecans
2 tablespoons sugar
2 teaspoons cinnamon

Preheat the oven to 350°.

Place the pecans in a shallow metal baking pan. Toast in the oven for 5 minutes or until lightly browned. Remove from the oven and cool slightly.

In a small bowl combine the pecans, 2 tablespoons sugar, and 2 teaspoons cinnamon. Mix well and set aside.

In a large mixing bowl cream the butter and sugar together until light and fluffy. Add the eggs, 1 at a time, beating well after each addition. Stir in the sour cream and the vanilla.

Combine the flour, baking powder, and salt. Add to the butter mixture and fold in gently.

Spread one-third of the batter into a well-buttered 9-inch tube or bundt pan. Sprinkle batter with half the filling. Spread one-third more of the batter into the pan. Sprinkle with remaining filling. Spread with remaining batter.

*(continued on next page)*

Bake for 1 to 1¼ hours or until a cake tester inserted into the center comes out clean.

Remove from oven to a cooling rack. Cool in the pan for 5 minutes. Turn out onto the rack and cool for 30 minutes. Serve cake warm or let it cool completely.

# CHOCOLATE YOGURT CHEESECAKE

serves 8

  1 cup chocolate wafer crumbs (about 16 wafers)
 ¼ cup melted butter
16 ounces cream cheese, softened
  1 cup sugar
  3 eggs, at room temperature
1½ teaspoons vanilla extract
  6 ounces semisweet chocolate, melted and cooled
  1 cup plain yogurt
Glaze:
  3 ounces semisweet chocolate
  2 tablespoons butter
  1 tablespoon corn syrup
 ½ teaspoon vanilla extract

Preheat the oven to 300°.

In a small bowl combine the wafer crumbs with the melted butter until well blended. Press crumbs firmly into the bottom of a heavily buttered 8-inch springform cake pan. Refrigerate until ready to use.

In a large mixing bowl combine the cream cheese and the sugar. Beat until smooth. Beat in the eggs and vanilla. Stir in the cooled chocolate and the yogurt. Mix until well blended. Turn the batter into the prepared crust.

Place a pan of hot water on the oven floor. Place the cheesecake in the middle of the oven and bake for 50 to 60 minutes or until the cake pulls away slightly from the sides of the pan. Turn off the oven. Let the cake sit in the oven with the door slightly ajar for 1 hour.

Remove cake from oven. Separate the cake from the sides of the pan with a thin knife; remove the sides. Transfer the cake to a serving plate.

To make the glaze, combine the 3 ounces chocolate, butter, corn syrup, and vanilla in a small saucepan. Cook over low heat until the butter melts and the mixture is smooth. Remove from the heat and cool slightly.

With a knife spread the glaze only on the top of the cake. Swirl with the back of a spoon. Chill 5 to 6 hours or overnight before serving.

# CHOCOLATE TRIPLE LAYER CAKE

serves 8

 ¾ cup Dutch cocoa
1¾ cups sugar
  3 eggs, separated
 ½ cup milk
  1 whole egg
 ½ cup butter
  2 cups flour
  1 teaspoon baking soda
  1 teaspoon baking powder
 ½ teaspoon salt
  1 cup sour cream
  1 teaspoon vanilla extract
    Chocolate Frosting

Preheat the oven to 350°.

Combine the cocoa, ¼ cup sugar, 1 egg yolk, and milk in a saucepan. Cook over low heat, stirring constantly, until thick. Remove from heat and cool.

In a bowl or on a sheet of wax paper combine the flour, baking soda, baking powder, and salt.

In a large mixing bowl cream the butter until soft. Slowly beat in the remaining sugar. Continue beating until well blended. Add the remaining 2 egg yolks and the whole egg. Mix thoroughly. Add the flour mixture alternately with the sour cream, mixing well after each addition. Stir in the vanilla and the cooled cocoa mixture.

In a small bowl beat the egg whites until stiff but not dry. Gently fold the egg whites into the batter.

Butter 3 8-inch layer-cake pans. Line the pans with wax paper and butter again. Turn the batter into the 3 pans, distributing evenly.

Bake for 30 to 35 minutes or until cake springs back when touched lightly.

Remove from oven and cool 2 minutes in the pans, then turn layers out onto cooling racks. Peel off the wax paper and cool completely. Frost with Chocolate Frosting (see below).

# CHOCOLATE FROSTING

yields enough frosting for 1 3-layer cake

  6 *ounces unsweetened chocolate*
  3 *cups confectioner's sugar*
  6 *egg yolks*
  ½ *cup butter, softened*
  5 *tablespoons hot water*

In a saucepan melt the chocolate. Add 1½ cups confectioner's sugar and the hot water. Beat until well blended. Add the remaining sugar and beat well. Slowly beat in the egg yolks, 1 at a time. Continue beating until smooth and well blended. Beat in the softened butter. Beat only until frosting is smooth and well blended.

To frost the cake, place 1 layer top-side down on a serving plate. Surround the layer with strips of wax paper to keep the plate clean. Place about one-quarter of the frosting on top of the layer and spread evenly. Place the second layer on top, top-side down. Spread about one-quarter of the icing on top. Place the last layer on top, top-side up. Frost the sides together and then frost the top. Swirl frosting with a knife or the back of a spoon. Let cake sit for a few hours before serving.

# BLUEBERRY BUTTER CAKE

serves 6

  1 *cup butter, softened*
  2½ *cups flour*
  1¼ *cups sugar*
  4 *eggs*
  2½ *teaspoons baking powder*
  ¼ *teaspoon salt*
  1½ *teaspoons vanilla extract*
  1½ *cups fresh blueberries*
  1 *cup heavy cream, chilled*

Preheat the oven to 375°.

*(continued on next page)*

Using an electric mixer, cream the butter and sugar together in a large mixing bowl until light and fluffy. Beat in the eggs, 1 at a time.

In a bowl or on a sheet of wax paper, combine 1 cup flour with the baking powder and salt. Beat the flour mixture into the creamed mixture, a little at a time. Beat in the vanilla extract.

Place the blueberries in a small bowl and toss with the remaining 1/4 cup flour. Coat berries evenly. Gently fold the berries into the batter.

Turn the batter into a generously buttered and floured 8-inch springform cake pan. Bake for 1 hour or until a cake tester inserted into the center comes out clean.

Remove from oven. Remove the sides of the pan. Cool cake for 15 minutes.

Beat the chilled cream in a chilled mixing bowl. Sweeten with a little confectioner's sugar if desired. Beat the cream until it is thick enough to form peaks. Serve the cream with the warm cake.

# FIG AND NUT SQUARES

yields 48 small squares

3/4 cup flour
1 teaspoon baking powder
1/4 teaspoon grated nutmeg
1/4 teaspoon cinnamon
1/4 teaspoon salt
3 eggs
1 cup sugar
1 teaspoon vanilla extract
2 cups dried figs, finely chopped
1 cup finely chopped walnuts
  confectioner's sugar

Preheat the oven to 325°.

In a bowl or on a large sheet of wax paper combine the flour, baking powder, nutmeg, cinnamon, and salt.

In the large bowl of an electric mixer beat the eggs until smooth. Add the sugar and the flour mixture, half at a time. Beat well after each addition. Add the vanilla, figs, and nuts; stir well to combine.

Turn the batter into a generously buttered and floured 13 × 9 × 2-inch baking pan. Smooth the top with a knife or spatula.

Bake for 25 minutes or until lightly brown and firm to the touch.

Remove from oven to a cooling rack and cool in the pan. Cut the cake into 1 1/2-inch squares. Dust lightly with confectioner's sugar and serve.

# HAZELNUT COOKIES

yields approximately 24 cookies

1 1/2 cups hazelnuts
1 cup sugar
3 egg whites
2 tablespoons cornstarch

Preheat the oven to 350°.

Spread the hazelnuts on a cookie sheet and place in oven for 20 minutes or until lightly roasted. Remove the nuts from the oven and place them on a clean, damp towel. Rub the nuts with another damp towel to remove the skins. Put the nuts in the container of an electric blender or food processor and pulverize until nuts are a finely ground powder.

Place the powdered hazelnuts in a large bowl. Add the sugar. With the back of spoon, mix the nuts and sugar together. When they are well mixed, add the egg whites, 1 at a time. Beat well. Continue to beat until the dough is smooth and thick enough to hold its shape.

Reduce the oven temperature to 300°. Heavily butter 2 baking or cookie sheets and sprinkle them with cornstarch. Drop the dough by tablespoons onto the sheets, about 1 inch apart. Bake for 30 minutes or until the cookies are golden and firm to the touch.

Remove the sheets from the oven. Using a metal spatula, transfer the cookies to a cooling rack. Cool completely. Cookies will keep well for 2 weeks in a tightly closed container.

# CHOCOLATE WALNUT PUFFS

yields approximately 36 puffs

> 1 cup semisweet chocolate bits
> 2 egg whites
> ⅛ teaspoon salt
> ½ cup sugar
> ½ teaspoon vanilla extract
> ½ teaspoon distilled white vinegar
> ¾ cup chopped walnuts

Preheat the oven to 350°.

Melt the chocolate in the top of a double boiler over hot but not boiling water. Remove from heat.

In a mixing bowl, beat the egg whites with the salt until they are foamy. Gradually add the sugar and beat until stiff but not dry. Beat in the vanilla and the vinegar. Fold in the melted chocolate and the walnuts.

Drop the batter by teaspoons onto a buttered cookie sheet. Bake for 10 minutes.

Remove sheet from oven. With a wide metal spatula transfer the puffs to cooling racks. Cool completely. Store in an airtight container.

# APRICOT CREAM

serves 4 to 6

> 2 cups dried apricots
> 1 cup water
> 1 cup orange juice
> ½ cup superfine sugar
> 1 tablespoon lemon juice
> 1½ cups heavy cream

Combine the apricots, water, and orange juice in a saucepan. Cook, uncovered, until the apricots are soft, about 5 to 8 minutes. Add the sugar and continue cooking, stirring constantly, until sugar dissolves.

Remove from heat. Place the apricots in the container of an electric blender or food processor and purée. Stir in the lemon juice and cool.

In a chilled mixing bowl beat the cream until very stiff. Fold it into the apricot mixture.

Turn the mixture into a serving bowl and chill 3 to 4 hours before serving.

# LEMON MOUSSE

serves 6 to 8

  1  teaspoon unflavored gelatin
  ⅓  cup lemon juice
  6  egg yolks
  ¾  cup sugar
     freshly grated rind of 1 lemon
1½  cups heavy cream

In a small bowl, soften the gelatin in the lemon juice.

In a mixing bowl, beat the egg yolks and sugar until thick and light, about 3 to 4 minutes. Add the lemon rind and stir. Transfer the mixture to a saucepan.

Cook, stirring constantly, over medium heat until the mixture is very thick, about 5 minutes. Remove from the heat and stir in the gelatin and lemon juice mixture. Continue stirring until the gelatin is dissolved.

Turn the mixture into a bowl placed in a larger bowl of ice water. Cool completely.

Beat the heavy cream in a mixing bowl until soft peaks form. Fold the cream into the lemon mixture. Transfer the mousse to a serving bowl. Serve at once or chill.

# PINEAPPLE SNOW

serves 4 to 6

  1  fresh pineapple
  4  egg whites
  2  cups heavy cream
  ½  cup confectioner's sugar
  1  tablespoon sherry

Place the heavy cream in a bowl placed in a larger bowl filled with cracked ice. Refrigerate until needed.

Trim, peel, and grate the pineapple. Reserve all the juice and pulp.

In a bowl, beat the egg whites until foamy. Add the sugar, a little bit at a time, and continue beating. Gently stir in the sherry. Stir in the very cold cream. Beat in the pineapple pulp and juice and continue beating. Add only as much pineapple as the mixture will hold without becoming too soft.

Transfer to a serving bowl and chill 3 to 4 hours before serving.

# BANANA SORBET

yields approximately 2 ½ to 3 quarts

12  bananas
  1  pound sugar
  4  cups water
     juice of 2 oranges

Peel and mash the bananas.

Combine the sugar and water in a large saucepan. Bring the mixture to a boil and boil for 5 minutes. Remove from heat and cool. Stir in the bananas and the orange juice. Push the mixture through a sieve, pressing with the back of a spoon.

Pour the mixture into a chilled electric ice-cream maker and churn, following the manufacturer's instructions, until mixture is firm, about 15 minutes. Serve immediately or freeze.

This sorbet will keep well in the freezer for up to 1 week. Remove from the freezer 10 to 15 minutes before serving.

# Accents

## CALIFORNIA RELISH

yields approximately 3 cups

1 tablespoon French-style mustard
1 cup sugar
⅓ cup cider vinegar
⅔ cup water
2 cinnamon sticks
1 large piece fresh ginger root
4 medium apples, peeled, cored, and cut into eighths
½ cup seedless raisins
¼ cup chopped walnuts

Combine the mustard and sugar in a saucepan. Add the vinegar, water, cinnamon sticks, and ginger root. Bring the mixture to a boil. Reduce the heat and simmer for 10 minutes.

Cut each eighth of an apple into 4 equal pieces.

Remove the cinnamon sticks and ginger root from the hot mixture. Add the apples, raisins, and nuts. Bring mixture to a boil. Reduce the heat and simmer for 10 minutes.

Remove mixture from heat and cool. Store in the refrigerator in a tightly covered bowl or jar.

## TANGY LEMON RELISH

yields approximately 2⅓ cups

6 thin-skinned lemons
  boiling water
1½ cups sugar
1 teaspoon dried sage

Cut the rind from 2 lemons. Slice into very fine strips and cover with boiling water. Soak for 1 minute. Drain and set rind aside. Reserve the water.

Cut the rind and white membrane from the remaining 4 lemons. Cut the lemons into very thin slices. Remove all seeds from the slices and place them in a bowl.

In a saucepan combine the sugar and sage. Stir in 1 cup of the reserved lemon rind liquid and bring mixture to a boil. Boil for 4 minutes or until thick. Add the lemon rind slices and stir. Pour the mixture over the lemon slices in the bowl. Cover tightly and chill.

## ZUCCHINI RELISH

yields 4 pints

2½ cups zucchini, thinly sliced
2½ cups onions, thinly sliced
2 cups cider vinegar
1 cup sugar
4 tablespoons salt
1½ teaspoons celery seed
½ teaspoon ground turmeric

Combine the vinegar, sugar, salt, celery seed, and turmeric in a saucepan. Cook over moderate heat, stirring constantly, until the sugar dissolves and the mixture comes to a boil.

Remove from heat. Add the zucchini and onion. Cover and let stand for 1 hour.

*(continued on next page)*

Return the saucepan to the heat and quickly bring the mixture to a boil. Reduce the heat and simmer gently, uncovered, for 3 minutes. Remove from heat.

Using a slotted spoon, carefully spoon the mixture into hot sterilized jars. Add the hot liquid, filling to within ½ inch of the top. Let the liquid settle, then add more. Seal, cool, and store.

# PINEAPPLE AND RAISIN CHUTNEY

yields 4 pints

1 fresh pineapple
8 ounces dark raisins
7 ounces golden raisins
2 tablespoons ginger root, finely chopped
2 tablespoons garlic, finely chopped
3 cups sweet red pepper, finely chopped
1½ cups distilled white vinegar
1½ cups light brown sugar, firmly packed
1 tablespoon salt
1 cup chopped macadamia nuts

Peel and core the pineapple. Cut it into small pieces. There should be about 4 cups.

Combine the pineapple pieces, dark raisins, golden raisins, ginger root, garlic, sweet red pepper, vinegar, brown sugar, and salt in a large saucepan. Cook over medium-low heat until the pineapple is tender, about 40 to 50 minutes. Stir in the nuts and continue cooking until the chutney reaches the desired consistency.

Carefully spoon the chutney into hot sterilized jars. Seal, cool, and store.

# FORTY-NINERS' FRUIT

yields approximately 5 cups

3 cups dried apples, coarsely chopped
1 cup canned pumpkin
½ cup dark brown sugar, firmly packed
¼ cup roasted sunflower seeds
¼ cup seedless raisins
¼ teaspoon coriander seeds
1 teaspoon salt
1 quart water

In a heavy pot or casserole, combine the dried apples, pumpkin, brown sugar, sunflower seeds, raisins, coriander, salt, and water. Mix well. Quickly bring the mixture to a boil. Reduce the heat and cover. Simmer for 1½ hours or until the apples are tender. Check occasionally to see if more liquid is needed; if so, add water 3 tablespoons at a time.

Remove from heat. Spoon the mixture into a bowl and cool. Serve immediately or cover tightly and refrigerate.

# SIX-CITRUS MARMALADE

yields approximately 15 pints

1 medium grapefruit
1 lemon
2 oranges
2 limes
5 kumquats
2 tangerines
1½ quarts water
6 cups sugar

Cut all the fruits in half. Discard all seeds and pits. Slice the fruits very thinly. Place slices in a large pot and cover with the water. Soak overnight.

Cook the fruit over moderate heat, covered, for 40 minutes or until peels are tender. Add the sugar and bring to a boil. Cook, covered, until the mixture reaches the jelling stage, 220° on a candy thermometer.

Remove from the heat and cool. Carefully spoon the marmalade into hot sterilized jars. Seal, cool, and store.

## ORANGE PLUM JAM

yields 4 pints

24 *large plums*
 1 *large orange*
½ *pound seedless raisins*
½ *cup cold water*
½ *cup honey*

Cut the rind from the orange. Discard all the white membrane. Cut the rind into very small pieces. Dice and seed the orange pulp.

In a saucepan combine the orange rind, orange pulp, raisins, water, and honey.

Halve and pit the plums. Cut the halves into quarters. Add plums to the saucepan.

Cook fruit over moderate heat for 1 hour or until thick. Stir frequently.

Remove from heat and skim the top. Pour the jam into hot sterilized jars and cool slightly. Seal, cool, and store.

## RASPBERRY CURRANT JAM

yields 2 pints

 3 *cups currants*
   *water*
 2 *cups raspberries, crushed*
 3 *cups sugar*

Place the currants in a saucepan and cover with water. Cook until currants are soft, about 5 to 7 minutes. Drain well. Press the currants through a fine sieve. There should be 2 cups of pulp.

In a saucepan combine the currant pulp, raspberries, and sugar. Slowly bring the mixture to a boil. Stir occasionally until the sugar dissolves. Cook rapidly for 30 minutes or until the mixture reaches the jelling stage. Stir constantly as the mixture begins to thicken.

Carefully spoon the jam into hot sterilized jars. Seal, cool, and store.

## AVOCADO SPREAD

yields approximately 2 cups

 2 *large ripe avocados*
 2 *tablespoons lemon juice*
 2 *large firm ripe tomatoes*
   *boiling water*
 1 *canned green chili pepper, drained, seeded, and chopped*
 3 *tablespoons red wine vinegar*
 1 *tablespoon vegetable oil*
   *salt*

*(continued on next page)*

Pour boiling water over the tomatoes. With a sharp knife, remove the skins. Seed the tomatoes and cut them into small cubes.

Halve the avocados and remove the pits and any brown fibers around the pits. Carefully peel the avocados, using the fingers or a paring knife. Cut the avocados into small cubes and place cubes in a bowl. Add the lemon juice and toss gently to coat the avocado. Add the tomatoes, chili, vinegar, and oil. Toss together until well mixed. Season with salt and let stand for 30 to 45 minutes before serving as a spread with tortillas or crackers.

This dish is sometimes called poor man's butter, perhaps from the buttery taste of a ripe avocado and the relative cheapness of both avocados and tomatoes in fertile Southern California. It makes an excellent filling for tacos.

# LEMON BARBECUE SAUCE

yields 1½ cups

½ cup onion, minced

2 tablespoons vegetable oil

2 tablespoons butter

2 tablespoons light brown sugar

½ teaspoon cayenne pepper

½ cup lemon juice

2 tablespoons cider vinegar

1 tablespoons horseradish

1 cup water

In a skillet heat the oil and butter. Add the onion and garlic and sauté until the onion is transparent, about 3 to 5 minutes. Stir in the sugar, salt, cayenne, and mustard. Mix well. Add the lemon juice, vinegar, horseradish, and water. Simmer over low heat for 10 to 15 minutes.

Remove from heat and cool. Use as a barbecue sauce for chicken, pork, beef, or lamb.

# MEAT MARINADE

yields approximately ½ cup

¼ cup soy sauce

¼ cup dry sherry

1 tablespoon sugar

1 teaspoon dry mustard

¼ teaspoon ground ginger

1 large clove garlic, crushed

In a large bowl combine the soy sauce, sherry, sugar, mustard, ginger, and garlic. Mix well.

Dip the meat in the marinade and place in a bowl. Pour the marinade over the meat and cover. Let stand at room temperature or in the refrigerator for at least 1 hour.

Remove meat from the marinade and cook as recipe directs. Reserve the marinade for basting meat.

# HOW TO PREPARE
## ➵ AND SEAL STANDARD JARS ❧
### AND JELLY GLASSES

Make sure that the jars, lids, and rings are clean. Place the jars, upside down, in 4 to 5 inches of boiling water. Boil over low heat for 8 minutes. Turn off the heat and let the jars remain in the water while you finish preparing the food. Add the lids and rings to the hot water. It is imperative that the jars and lids be hot when they are filled or packed with food.

When the food is ready, place the hot sterilized jars on a heat-proof surface, such as a wooden board or rack. Let the rings and lids remain in the hot water. Fill the jars to within ½ inch of the top. Run a knife down along the insides of the jars to release all air bubbles. Wipe the edges of the jars clean. Place the hot lids on the jars and screw tightly closed. Allow the jars to remain in a draft-free area and cool overnight.

In the morning, check the seals by turning the jars upside down or pressing the center of the inner lids. If there is no leakage or if the inner lids do not move, then the jars are sealed properly. Store the jars in a cool place.

For additional information on home jarring and canning, you may wish to consult: U.S. Department of Agriculture, *Complete Guide to Home Canning, Preserving and Freezing*; U.S. Department of Agriculture, *Home Canning of Fruits and Vegetables*; and *Better Homes and Gardens* Book Editors, *Better Homes and Gardens Home Canning and Freezing*. Your librarian can help you order the Department of Agriculture titles.

# Recipe Index

Abalone Steak, 283
Acorn Squash with Rum Butter Glaze, 45
Alabama Stuffed Pompano, 125
Alaska Barbecued Salmon, 276
Alaskan Blueberry Muffins, 304
All-Purpose Dumplings, 225
Almond-Avocado Butter, 251
Anadama Bread, 58
Apple Coleslaw, 182
Apple Dumplings, 234–235
Apple Fritters, 66
Apple-Nut Bread, 137
Apple Pandowdy, 69–70
Apple Slices and Bacon, 12
Apple Spice Cake, 231
Apple-Tomato Relish, 238
Apricot Cream, 313
Apricot Loaf, 301
Arkansas Fried Catfish, 119–120
Asparagus in Pesto Sauce, 285
Avocado Spread, 317–318

Baja Cream of Almond Soup, 248–249
Baja Shrimp, 281
Baked Apple Omelet, 185
Baked Bluefish, 40
Baked Bread-and-Cheese, 19
Baked Cabbage, 213
Baked Halibut, 45
Baked Lamb Chops, 193
Baked Pike in Dill Sauce, 204
Baked Redfish, 124
Baked Rice and Onions, 296
Baked Rice with Olives, 296
Baked Tomatoes, 289
Banana Sorbet, 314
Barbecued Lamb, 268
Barbecued Spareribs, 100
Basque Barbecued Lamb, 113–114
Batter-Fried Liver, 188
Batter Shrimp, 37
Bay State Pumpkin Pie, 67
Beans and Cheese, 294
Beefy Okra Soup, 82
Benne Biscuits, 87

Blackberry Flummery, 236
Blackberry Pie, 226
Blackberry Vinegar, 242
Blackberry Cake, 146–147
Black Walnut Bread, 221–222
Black Walnut Soup, 175
Block Island Codfish Chowder, 7
Block Island Scallop Stew, 36
Blueberry Butter Cake, 311
Blueberry Pie, 68–69
Blueberry Relish, 240
Boiled Leg of Lamb with Caper Sauce, 27
Boiled Lobster, 34–35
Boiled Midwestern Crayfish, 207
Boiled Pinto Beans, 135
Boston Baked Beans, 52
Boston Brown Bread, 57
Boston Fried Scallops, 35
Braised Pork with Leeks, 25
Braised Short Ribs, 26
Braised Short Ribs (Midwest), 196
Braised Tongue with Raisin Sauce, 188
Braised Turnips, 48
Brandied Sweet Potatoes, 128
Brandied Whole Peaches, 149
Broiled Blowfish, 42
Broiled California Duck, 274
Broiled Crawfish, 118
Broiled Garlic Shrimp, 281
Broiled Grapefruit Pie, 308
Broiled Lobster, 34
Broiled Mackerel, 121
Broiled Salmon Steaks with Lemon Butter, 43
Broiled Swordfish with Soy Sauce Butter, 278
Broiled Trout, 123
Broiled Weakfish, 40
Brown Beef Stew, 198
Bruna Böner, 217
Brunswick Stew, 108
Buckeye Maple Cake, 232
Buck Stew, 187
Buckwheat Pancakes, 222
Buttermilk Biscuits, 136
Butternut Squash Pie, 226
Butter-Stuffed Trout, 203

Caesar Salad, 254
Calabacita, 287
Calas, 133
Caldillo, 104
California Artichoke Halves, 290–291
California Beans and Brandy, 292–293
California Carrots, 284
California Chicken Salad, 258
California Date Nut Bread, 303
California Fig Pie, 307
California Johnnycake, 305
California Relish, 315
California Vegetable Stew, 291
California Walnut Spread, 251–252
Candied Cranberries, 73
Candied Virginia Sweet Potatoes, 128
Cape Cod Oatmeal Cookies, 61–62
Cardamom Peas, 284
Carolina Clam Fritters, 118–119
Carolina Mint Relish, 152
Carolina Rice Pilau, 132
Carrot Soufflé, 260–261
Carrots with Herbs and Grapes, 285
Catfish Fry, 119
Celery Victor, 290
Charleston Torte, 143
Cheese Straws, 88
Cheesy Rice, 215
Cherry Soup, 178
Chestnut Soup, 174
Chicken-Corn Soup with Rivels, 6
Chicken Livers in Wine, 272
Chicken Liver Spread, 250–251
Chicken Pot Pie, 32
Chicken Teriyaki, 270
Chicken with Lemon-Lime Sauce, 271
Chilali, 96
Chili Relish, 150
Chilled Avocado Soup, 247
Chilled Blueberry Soup, 177
Chilled Poached Salmon Steaks, 44
Chocolate Frosting, 311
Chocolate Triple Layer Cake, 310–311
Chocolate Walnut Puffs, 313
Chocolate Yogurt Cheesecake, 310
Chow-Chow, 74–75
Cider Flounder, 41
Cioppino, 283
Citrus Conserve, 152
Clam Omelet, 18
Cod Broiled in Lemon Butter, 44

Cold Curry Soup, 85
Cold Kidney Bean Mix, 89
Collard Greens, 128
Colonial Spice-and-Vinegar Pie, 65
Colorful Cabbage Salad, 182
Columbia River Baked Salmon, 275
Confectioner's Icing, 229–230
Connecticut Spinach, 51
Corn and Okra Mix, 126
Corn and Pepper Salad, 238
Corn Bread, 141
Corn Muffins, 55
Corn Omelet, 20
Cornsticks, 140
Country Fried Potatoes, 209
Crabapple Jelly, 76
Crabmeat Salad with Hot Caper Dressing, 257
Crab-Stuffed Haddock, 42
Cranberry-Nut Loaf, 54
Cranberry-Pineapple Relish, 73
Cranberry Snow, 70
Cranberry-Stuffed Mackerel, 42
Creamed Cabbage, 213–214
Cream of Artichoke Soup, 247–248
Cream of Turnip Soup, 177
Creamy Carrot Soup, 173
Creamy Cole Slaw, 15
Creamy Potato Salad, 181
Creamy Rabbit Stew, 189
Creole Boiled Shrimp, 117
Creole Canapés, 88
Creole Grillades, 102
Creole Honey Bread, 137
Creole Omelet, 93
Creole Roast Pork, 99
Creole Salpicon, 83
Creole-Style Breaded Ox Tails, 115
Creole-Style Stewed Okra, 127
Creole Veal Stew, 101
Crullers, 234
Crustless Black Walnut Pie, 235
Cucumber Slices, 238

Dakota Eggs, 183
Danish Stuffed Cherry Tomatoes, 179
Deep-Fried Codfish Balls, 12
Deep-Fried Eggs, 94
Deep-Fried Hominy Balls, 87
Deep-Fried Porgy, 121
Delaware Spoon Bread, 59
Dill Sauce, 204

Dirty Rice, 131
Dixie Brown Sugar Pie, 145
Double-Deck Pork Tostadas, 100
Dried Beef and Gravy, 104
Dried Beef with Eggs, 259
Drop Biscuits, 223–224
Dungeness Crab Casserole, 280
Dungeness Crabmeat Bisque, 250
Dutch Apple Butter, 72–73
Dutch Apple Soup, 8
Dutch Baked Chicken, 32
Dutch Baked Corn, 47
Dutch Cheese Spread, 11
Dutch Corn Pancakes, 56
Dutch Cucumber Salad, 13
Dutch Dandelion Salad, 14
Dutch Dandelion and Lettuce Salad, 14
Dutch Egg Pfannkuchen, 19
Dutch Ginger Pears, 72
Dutch Liver Oysters, 33
Dutch Navy Bean Soup, 7
Dutch Oven-Barbecued Chicken, 31
Dutch Potato Croquettes, 47
Dutch Wine Soup, 6–7

Early American Apple Pie, 70
Eastern Shore Corn Fritters, 46
Eastern-Style Sweet Potato Casserole, 49–50
Eggplant Caviar, 88
Eggs and Cream, 184
Endive Salad, 16
Ensalada de Verdolaga, 253
Evergreen State Apple Pie, 309

Fennel Salad, 256
Fig and Nut Squares, 312
Fire Island Broiled Soft-Shell Crabs, 37
Fisherman's Wharf Halibut Broth, 249
Fiskekroketer, 178–179
Flan, 148
Florida Egg Bake, 94–95
Florida Seafood Salad, 90
Flounder with Garlic and Tomatoes, 279
Forty-Niners' Fruit, 316
Fresh Fruit Tart, 308–309
Fresh Tuna Salad, 258
Fried Corn, 126
Fried Grits, 134
Fried Mushrooms, 48
Fried Okra, 126
Fried Okra Soup, 82–83

Fried Soft-Shell Crabs, 38
Frijoles Refritos, 135
Fruit Bread, 56
Fruit Frosting, 147
Fruit of the Sea Chowder, 9
Frukt Soppa, 177
Fudge Frosting, 61

Gallina Rellena, 109
Garbanzos with Garlic, 295
Georgia Jelly Omelet, 95
Georgia Pecan Cake, 142
Ginger Rhubarb Jam, 242
Gingersnaps, 63
Ginger Squash Soufflé, 186
Glazed Loin of Pork, 191
Glazed Onions, 51
Glazed Parsnips, 49
Glazed Turnips, 130
Goat Cheese Soufflé, 261
Golden Jam, 75
Goose Stuffed with Apples, 31
Graham Cracker Pie Shell, 307
Great Lake Baked Chicken, 201
Great Lake Smelts, 205
Great Plains Carrot Pie, 228–229
Green Beans and Carrots with Hot Onion
    Dressing, 289
Green Beans with Dill Sauce, 288–289
Green Chili and Corn Soufflé, 96
Green Chili Sauce, 151
Green Mountains Onions and Eggs, 20
Green Peas and New Potatoes, 48
Grilled Bass with Herbs, 120
Grilled Chicken Halves, 272
Grits and Cheese Casserole, 134
Guacamole, 89
Gulf Coast Shrimp, 116
Gulf Crab Bisque, 84
Gulf Crab Soufflés, 86
Gumbo Filé, 105

Hangtown Fry, 263
Hard Sauce, 68
Harvard Beets, 50
Hasenpfeffer, 189
Hawaiian Banana Bread, 302
Hawaiian Ginger Carrots, 285
Hawaiian Planked Red Snapper, 275
Hawaiian Pork Chops, 267
Hawaiian Rice, 295

Hawaiian Shrimp Balls, 251
Hazelnut Cookies, 312–313
Heartland Vegetable Soup, 173
Herbed Bean Salad, 92
Herbed Lamb Shanks, 269
Hermits, 63
Hoecakes, 141
Holiday Fruitcake, 71
Hollywood Lemon Soufflé, 261
Hominy, 133
Hominy Grits, 133–134
Honey Custard, 236
Honeyed Duck, 273
Hoosier Baked Tomatoes, 211
Hoosier Chicken Pie, 200
Hoosier Fried Tomatoes, 211
Hoosier Pork Chops, 190
Hoppin' John, 129
Hot Potato Salad, 15
Hot Potato Salad with Lemon Dressing, 255
Hubbard Squash Pie, 46
Huckleberry Bread, 221
Huckleberry Pie, 145
Huevos Fritos, 94
Huevos Rancheros, 94
Hush Puppies, 138
Hutzel Brod, 56

Idaho Potato Omelet, 183
India Relish, 239
Indiana Cataloupe Balls, 237
Indian Bread, 59
Indian Pudding, 66
Inlagd Rödbetor, 181–182
Iowa Corn Chowder, 174
Iowa Apple Fritters, 235

Jambalaya, 107
Jam Cake, 147
Joe Froggers, 62

Kale with Onions, 214
Kansas City Pickled Beef, 197
Kansas Corn Oysters, 210
Kentucky Bourbon Balls, 148
Kentucky Bourbon Cake, 146
Kentucky Burgoo, 106
Kentucky Scramble, 95–96
Key Lime Pie, 144
Key West Lime Chicken, 111
Kidney Bean Bake, 52
Korean Salad, 256

L.A. Gazpacho, 248
Lake Erie Coho Salmon, 208
Laksloda, 208
Lamb Stew, 193
Lancaster Corn Meal Mush, 56–57
Lefse, 220
Leg of Lamb in Caper Sauce, 114
Lemon Barbecue Sauce, 318
Lemon-Carrot Sauce, 273
Lemon Chicken with Raisins, 270–271
Lemon-Lime Red Snapper, 124
Lemon Meringue Pie, 306
Lemon Mousse, 314
Lemon Rice, 295
Limpa, 220
Lobster Newburg, 34
Loin of Pork Teriyaki, 266
Long Island Braised Duckling, 29
Long Island Rice Casserole, 53
Long Island Stuffed Clams, 11
Louisiana Cheese Biscuits, 138
Louisiana Crab Stew, 119
Louisiana Frogs' Legs, 105
Louisiana Liver and Bacon, 115
Louisiana Rum Omelet, 93

Macaroni and Cheese Bake, 51
Macaroni Salad, 180
Maine Doughnuts, 64
Maine Watercress Salad with Mushrooms, 13
Mallard Duck and Turnip Stew, 109–110
Manhattan Clam Chowder, 10
Manhattan-Style Mustard Shad Roe, 43
Maple Icing, 233
Maple Nut Frosting, 60
Maple Omelet, 17
Marinated Artichoke Hearts, 253
Marinated Broiled Shrimp, 117
Marinated Fried Mushrooms, 289–290
Marinated Vegetable Salad, 16
Maryland Crab Cakes, 38
Maryland Fried Chicken, 33
Mashed Potato Soup, 176
Meat Marinade, 318
Mexican Rice, 131
Michigan Booyaw, 190
Michigan Frogs' Legs, 202
Michigan Yellow Pea Soup, 175
Midwestern Buttermilk Raisin Cake, 230
Minnesota Apple Pancakes, 223
Minnesota Roast Duck, 198–199
Minnesota Wild Rice and Mushrooms, 215

Mississippi "Shushed" Eggs, 97
Missouri Apple Nut Pudding, 237
Missouri Baked Corn, 210
Mixed Chutney, 150
Mocha Café Soufflé, 263
Molasses Spice Muffins, 224
Montauk Point Broiled Bluefish
  with Spicy Sauce, 39
Mulligatawny Soup, 84
Mushroom-Olive Salad, 16
Mustard Greens with New Potatoes, 130

Napa Valley Leeks, 287
New Bedford Pot Roast, 21
New Bedford Sailor's Omelet, 21
New England Boiled Dinner, 23
New England Cheese and Chives Soufflé, 19
New England Clam Chowder, 9
New England Fiddleheads, 47
New England Griddlecakes, 55
New England Ham and Apple Pie, 24–25
New England Hashed Brown Potatoes, 48
New England Honey Bread, 58
New England Lamb Stew, 28
New England Pot Roast, 22
New England Salt Pork Dinner
  with Milk Gravy, 23
New England Scalloped Tomatoes, 49
New Hampshire Cream of Tomato Soup, 10
New Mexico Baked Eggs, 97
New Mexico Corn Bake, 125
New Mexico Picadillo, 102
New Orleans Carrot Soup, 83
New Orleans Herb Omelet, 95
New Orleans Pompano en Papillote, 121
New Orleans Steamed Oysters, 117–118
New Orleans Stewed Hen, 110
New York Sautéed Scallops, 35
North Carolina Sweet Potato Biscuits, 138
North Dakota Barley Soup, 176
Norwegian Fish Stew, 207
Norwegian Spritz Cookies, 233
Nut Brownies, 63–64

Ohio Braised Celery, 214
Ohio Flank Steak, 196
Ohio Lemon Pie, 227
Ohio Pork Casserole, 191
Old-Fashioned Blackberry Jam, 152
Old-Fashioned Muffins, 224
Old-Fashioned Nut Cookies, 232–233
Old-Fashioned Oatmeal Bread, 218–219

Old-Fashioned Raisin Bread, 59
Old-Fashioned Rhode Island Johnnycakes, 57
Old-Fashioned Strawberry Jam, 76
Omelet Schnitzel, 184
Orange and Cranberry Relish, 73
Orange Biscuits, 304
Orange Grove Pork Chops, 101
Orange Grove Rye Bread, 300
Orange Plum Jam, 317
Oregon Apple Soufflé, 262
Oregon Beef Stew, 264
Oriental Beef, 264
Oriental Fresh Tuna, 280
Osgood Pie, 145–146
Oven-Fried Catfish, 207
Oven-Fried Chicken, 111
Oyster Fry, 36

Pacific Coast Marinated Mussels, 282
Pacific Mussel Soup, 250
Pan-Fried Smelts, 205
Pan-Fried Tomatoes, 49
Pan-Fried Trout, 202
Papaya Seafood Salad, 91
Parker House Rolls, 54
Pasta Salad with Broccoli, Tomatoes, and Olives,
  256–257
Peach and Walnut Bread, 297
Peach Chutney, 150
Peach Pie, 227
Pear and Pepper Relish, 240
Pear Salad, 257
Pecan Butter Balls, 148
Pecan Coffee Cake, 309
Pecan Meringues,
Pecan Pie, 144
Peconic Pickled Mussels, 12
Pecos River Pecan Bread, 136–137
Pennsylvania Baked Ham with Spiced Oranges, 25
Pennsylvania Dutch Cream Corn Soup, 6
Pennsylvania Lamb and Apples, 28
Pennsylvania Pepper Pot Soup with Dumplings, 5
Pepper Cabbage Relish, 75
Perfect Broiled Chicken, 32–33
Persimmon Pudding, 236
Pheasant and Apple Casserole, 201
Philadelphia Cinnamon Buns, 65
Philadelphia Snapper Soup, 8
Pickled Beet and Onion Salad, 181–182
Pickled Figs, 149
Pickled Peaches, 149
Pickled Salmon, 252

Pickled Shrimp, 85
Pineapple and Raisin Chutney, 316
Pineapple Snow, 314
Piperade, 184
Plain Pastry, 72
Planked Connecticut Shad, 43
Planked Michigan Whitefish, 206
Poached Eggs in Cream, 17
Poached Eggs with Chicken Livers, 183
Poached Salmon with Rum Vinaigrette, 276
Poached Trout with Scallions, 203–204
Pompano à lá Maitre d'Hôtel, 120
Popovers, 55
Pork and Cabbage Stew, 192
Portland Leek and Potato Soup, 248
Portland Pot Roast, 265
Portland Prune Bread, 303
Potage Crécy, 83
Potato and Bacon Salad, 181
Pound Cake, 142
Providence Seafood-Egg Bake, 17
Pumpernickel, 219
Pumpkin Pie, 67
Purslane Salad, 253

Quail in Wine, 112
Quail with Mushrooms and Onions, 30
Quail Stuffed with Grapes, 29
Quick Oatmeal Muffins, 225

Rabbit Fricassee, 189
Ranch-Style Eggs, 94
Raspberry Currant Jam, 317
Red Flannel Hash, 26–27
Red and Green Pepper Hash, 74
Red Rice, 132–133
Red River Glazed Squash, 212
Red Snapper Texas Gulf-Style, 123
Red Snapper with Chili Pepper, 123
Refried Beans, 135
Rhode Island Cabbage Soup, 10
Rhode Island Shrimp and Corn Soufflé, 18
Rhubarb Custard Pie, 228
Rhubarb Pie, 66–67
Rice Bread, 141
Rice Fritters, 132
Rice Pudding, 71
Rice with Mussels, 53
Roasted Pork with Turnips, 98
Roast Fresh Shoulder of Pork with Apple
　Stuffing, 24

Roast Goose, 30
Roast Leg of Lamb, 27
Roast Leg of Lamb with Sweet Potatoes, 113
Roast Pork with California Brandy, 266
Roast Quail, 112
Roast Stuffed Turkey, 109
Roast Turkey with Sausage and Sage Dressing,
　28–29
Roast Wild Duck, 199
Robbin's Island Baked Oysters, 12
Rutabaga-Potato Soup, 176
Rutabaga Soufflé, 185
Rutabaga with Bacon, 212

Sacramento Salad, 254
Saffron Bread, 140
Sage Rice, 297
San Diego Omelet, 259
San Diego Pinto Beans, 293
San Francisco Chicken Wings, 252
San Francisco Glazed Duck, 273
San Francisco Lentil Salad, 255
San Francisco Sourdough Bread, 298
San Joaquin Brandy Chocolate Pie, 306
San Jose Summer Squash, 288
Santa Monica Poached Sole, 278
Saucy Creole Fish, 122
Sautéed Cucumbers, 284
Sautéed Leeks, 287
Sautéed Parsnips, 214
Sautéed Pickerel, 204–205
Sautéed Sea Scallops, 282
Savory Rabbit, 190
Scalloped Oysters, 37
Scandinavian Apple Beans, 216
Scandinavian Herring Salad, 180
Scandinavian Raisin Ring, 229
Scandinavian Walnut Honey Cake, 231
Scrapple, 23–24
Sea Bass with Chestnut Stuffing, 277
Seafood Puffs, 86
Seattle Fried Trout, 277
Seattle Puff Pancakes, 305
Seattle Steak, 265
Senate Bean Soup, 8–9
She-Crab Soup, 81
Sherried Lamb Stew, 268
Sherried Smithfield Ham, 99
Shoofly Pie, 69
Shreveport Shrimp, 86
Shrimp and Bean Salad, 90

Shrimp and Rice Soup, 82
Shrimp Creole, 116–117
Shrimp-Filled Pasta Shells, 292
Shrimp Fritters, 85
Shrimp Gumbo, 116
Shrimp with Zucchini, 281
Sierra Lamb Chops, 268
Simmered Radishes, 212
Six-Citrus Marmalade, 316–317
Skillet Lemon Chicken, 271
Smothered Parsnips, 127
Snickerdoodles, 62
Soft-Shell Crabs à lá Creole, 118
Sopa de Arroz, 82
Sopapillas, 139
Sour Cream Biscuits, 223
Sourdough Rolls, 299
Sourdough Starter, 298
South Dakota Apple Crumb Pie, 227–228
Southern Fried Chicken, 110–111
Southern Rice, 131
Southern Rum Pie, 143
Southern Smoked Fish, 124
Southern-Style Baked Ham, 98
Southern-Style Green Tomato Relish, 151
Southern-Style Popovers, 136
Southern-Style Potato Salad, 91
Southern-Style Tartar Sauce, 151
Southwestern Beef Stew, 104
Southwestern Cabbage Salad, 90
Southwestern Sweet Potato Pie, 129
South Yarmouth Swordfish, 41
Spanish Omelet, 260
Spiced Apple Bread, 222
Spicy Blackberry Jam, 241
Spicy Chick Pea Salad, 92
Spicy Pickled Vegetables, 74
Spicy Plum Jam, 75
Spiked Crabmeat Soup, 249
Spinach Frittata, 260
Spinach Salad, 254–255
Spinach Soufflé, 186
Spirited Lemon Pork Chops, 267
Split Peas and Noodles, 217
Spoon Bread, 138
Springhouse Watercress Omelet, 20
Standing Rib Roast, 198
St. Louis Sauerbraten, 197
Stockton Asparagus Soufflé, 262
Strawberry-Rhubarb Jam, 76
Streusel, 230

Stuffed Acron Squash, 46
Stuffed Lamb Shanks, 194
Stuffed Pork Shoulder, 192
Stuffed Striped Bass with Raisin Sauce, 39
Succotash, 50
Summer Squash Casserole, 127
Summer Squash Casserole (South), 213
Summer Squash Relish, 239
Sunken Meadow Fried Mussels, 38
Swedish Beans, 217
Swedish Fish Croquettes, 178–179
Swedish Fruit Soup, 177
Swedish Meatballs, 194
Swedish Potato and Smoked Salmon
    Casserole, 208
Swedish Potato Breads, 220
Swedish Rye Bread, 220–221
Swedish-Style Rutabagas, 212
Sweet and Sour Apple Relish, 239
Sweet Potato and Apple Bake, 209
Sweet Walnut Bread, 300
Swordfish and Apples, 41

Tamale Pie, 104–105
Tangy Dutch Cabbage Salad, 14
Tangy Kidney Bean Bake, 293
Tangy Lemon Relish, 315
Tartar Sauce, 76
Tennessee Sweetbreads, 114–115
Texas Chili Con Carne, 103
Texas Green Bean Salad, 89
Texas Vegetable Salad, 91
Three-Meat Stew with Buttermilk
    Dumplings, 195
Tile Fish Simmered in Wine, 44
Toll House Cookies, 64
Tomato Ginger Marmalade, 240
Turkey Barbecue, 108–109
Turnip Casserole, 211
Turnip Greens and Ham Hock, 130
Turnips with Coriander, 286

Upstate Braised Pork Chops with Sauerkraut, 26

Veal Kebabs, 269
Veal Scallops with Lemon Sauce, 269
Veal Stew with Dumplings, 195
Vermont Cheese Puffs, 11
Vermont Cider Pudding with Hard Sauce, 68
Vermont Maple Syrup Cake, 60
Virginia Ham Omelet, 96–97

Waldorf Salad, 15
Walnut-Chocolate Drops, 233
Walnut Sweet Potatoes, 209
Washington Sweet and Sour Squash, 288
Water Island Scrambled Oysters, 18
Wellesley Fudge Cake, 60–61
Welshkorn Pfannkuchen, 56
West Coast Bread, 302
West Coast Cucumber Bisque, 247
West Coast Pepper Steak, 265–266
Western Omelet, 259
White Beans Vinaigrette, 294
Whitefish with Walnut Sauce, 206
Wild Duck in Wine, 199
Wild Rice Casserole, 215
Willamette Valley Apple Bread, 301
Williamsburg Cream of Peanut Soup, 81
Wilted Lettuce, 179
Wisconsin Blue Cheese Salad, 182
Wisconsin Cheddar Cheese Soup, 174
Wisconsin Cheddar Cheese Squares, 178
Wisconsin Cheese Rabbit, 187
Wisconsin Hickory Nut Bread, 218
Wyoming Bean Salad, 180

Yankee Pot Roast, 22
Yankee Vegetable Soup, 5
Yerba Buena Baked Shad, 279

Zucchini Relish, 315–316
Zucchini with Pesto, 287